# DOUBLE DECEPTION

# DOUBLE DECEPTION

## STALIN, HITLER, AND THE INVASION OF RUSSIA

James Barros and Richard Gregor

NORTHERN ILLINOIS UNIVERSITY PRESS

DeKalb 1995

Published by the Northern Illinois University Press, DeKalb,
Illinois 60115

Manufactured in the United States using acid-free paper

Design by Julia Fauci ⊛ ♾

Library of Congress Cataloging-in-Publication Data

Barros, James.

Double deception : Stalin, Hitler, and the Invasion of Russia / James Barros and Richard Gregor.

p. cm.

Includes bibliographical references and index.

ISBN 0–87580–191–9 (alk. paper)

1. World War, 1939–1945—Soviet Union—Diplomatic history. 2. World War, 1939–1945—Campaigns—Soviet Union. 3. Soviet Union—History—German occupation, 1941–1944. I. Gregor, Richard. II. Title.

D749.5.R8 1994

940.53′2247—dc20 94–11771

CIP

*In memory of*

RCMP Superintendent **Terence M. Guernsey** (1912–1992),
innovative practitioner and
avid student of the "Great Game,"

*and*

**Raymond G. Rocca** (1917–1993),
Deputy Chief, Counterintelligence Staff, CIA, intelligence officer and
scholar whose breadth of knowledge
was only exceeded by its depth.

# Contents

# Preface

The outbreak of the second World War and the stunning defeat of the British, French, and others in the spring of 1940 produced a setting in which no state was sure of its survival. Of the remaining independent and neutral European states, Soviet Russia, under the grinding dictatorship of Joseph Stalin, assumed weighty import. Whether it would continue to abide by its treaty obligations toward the Germans or maintain its ostensibly neutral stance until hostilities had ceased or enter the struggle in support of one side or the other were topics of serious discussion in foreign ministries around the world.

By the late spring of 1941, another topic began to attract the attention of foreign ministries, chiefs of staff, and intelligence services. Did the continuous but unsettling rumors that increasing German troop concentrations along the German-Russian border and other moves by Berlin presage an attack against Soviet Russia? There was no saber rattling, however. Calm appeared to prevail in Moscow. Up to the moment of the attack on Sunday, June 22, nothing appeared out of the ordinary. Why so?

In view of the longtime political, military, and intelligence experiences of Moscow's leaders, one would think that some reaction would have been in the offing. These were the same leaders whose intelligence services during the interwar period had undermined the anti-Communist White Russian refugee community in western Europe that they perceived as capable of overthrowing the Communist regime. They had scoured for enemies real or imagined among the Left opposition, for example, the Trotskyites, and among the police, the party, the military, and the society at large. Their intelligence services had burglarized and penetrated with agents many an embassy in Moscow and had bribed, blackmailed, and ideologically suborned personnel in the intelligence services, foreign ministries, military establishments, and sensitive government departments of other states. Indeed, until the German invasion of June 22, 1941, the performance of the Russian intelligence services was deemed second to none. The apparently collective aphasic behavior in Moscow in the spring of 1941 has never been fully explained. Why did Moscow's leaders fail to comprehend that one of the greatest "surprise" attacks in military history was imminent? To answer this question is the purpose of our investigation.

# Acknowledgments

Examination of the disparate sources that comprise this study was made possible by the financial generosity of the Lynde and Harry Bradley Foundation of Milwaukee, Wisconsin, and the Earhart Foundation of Ann Arbor, Michigan, as well as the Humanities and Social Sciences Committee of the University of Toronto. Our gratitude toward all of them is immeasurable.

We are likewise grateful to the personnel of the Public Record Office in London and the National Archives in Washington, D.C., including the personnel of the institutions cited in the table of abbreviations, who rendered yeoman service in assisting us in our archival endeavors. Special thanks are due to Jane Lynch of the Interlibrary Loan Services Office of Robarts Library of the University of Toronto, who corralled for us many a far-off tome, often on short notice.

We would like to express our appreciation to the Clerk of the Records, House of Lords Record Office, for permission to cite and quote from the Diary of Lord Balfour of Inchrye, the Bruce Lockhart Diary, and the Beaverbrook Papers; to the Masters, Fellows, and Scholars of Churchill College, Cambridge, for permission to refer to the Victor Mallet Memoir; to the Master and Fellows of Balliol College, Oxford, for permission to consult the Monkton Papers at the Bodleian Library; to the Hoover Institution Archives for permission to consult the Hugh Gibson Collection; and to the Borthwick Institute of Historical Research, University of York, for permission to consult the Halifax Diary. We would also like to acknowledge the generous assistance of Georg Korter, formerly of the German Consulate in Harbin.

Finally, our thanks to Andrew Barros for his last-minute additions to the manuscript and to Anne Barros for her role in seeing the manuscript through the publication process.

It is understood that we alone are responsible for the views and opinions expressed in this work, which in no way reflect those of the people or institutions that supported us in this endeavor.

J.B.
R.G.

# DOUBLE DECEPTION

# 1

# Perceptions and Deceptions

## The Setting

The murderous German artillery barrage in the early morning hours of June 22 initiating the invasion of Soviet Russia has been likened to the explosion of the first atomic bomb on Hiroshima. The antecedents of the unexpected attack and its ferocity can be traced to the German-Russian nonaggression pact of August 23, 1939. "England, despite its weakness, would wage war craftily and stubbornly," Joseph Stalin had observed to the Germans when the pact was signed. And France "had an army worthy of consideration," he thought.[1] The second observation proved incorrect and was to cause him many anxious moments.[2]

The nonaggression pact of August 23, 1939 momentarily obviated the fear of a two front war for both sides: for Berlin, against the Anglo-French and the Russians, and for Moscow, against the Germans and the Japanese. This fear was an omnipresent consideration in Stalin's mind.[3] For the Russians, it also projected the strong probability of a long and exhausting conflict between the Germans and the Anglo-French, not dissimilar to what had occurred in 1914–1918; it was a situation to be welcomed and fraught with possibilities since its fruition would lead to enormous political, military, and economic advantages for Soviet Russia.[4] Eduard Beneš, the president of the Czech government-in-exile, believed as a result of his conversation with Ivan Maisky (né Liakhovetsky), the Russian ambassador in London described as a "little gnome," that Soviet Russia would attempt to avoid the struggle as long as possible. If this avoidance could be achieved, then when the war neared its end and the two sides were exhausted, Soviet Russia "could intervene decisively and bring about an automatic solution of European problems by means of social revolution."[5]

Politically the empiricist view in Moscow was that the arrangements with Berlin did not exclude the possibility of German aggression. What the pact offered was time to strengthen Soviet Russia's defenses and stave off the materialization of an anti-Soviet coalition.[6] On the other hand, in attempting to fathom the foreign policy process during the Stalinist period, one authority has concluded after extensive empirical investigation that its ideological aspect "was genuine and deeply ingrained."[7] The difficult task for any investigator is weighing ideological considerations and placing these considerations in their proper political setting. Certainly for Stalin, the *Vozhd* or Great Leader, armed conflict between the bourgeois states of Western Europe was manna from heaven and to be encouraged.[8]

Indeed, Moscow's long-held view was that, despite its revolutionary rhetoric, the Nazi party, like other political parties of varying persuasions in Weimar Germany before Hitler's advent to power, served the same gorgon, the bourgeoisie.[9] The Nazi party was the "tool of monopoly capitalism" and of the German army. What Stalin could not discern was that the Nazi party was a phenomenon enormously different from anything that had previously appeared on the German political stage.[10] Consequently, the nonaggression pact, in line with Stalin's desire and no doubt much to his relief, neatly allowed Hitler to focus his attention in a direction other than Soviet Russia. Whatever ideological considerations Stalin wrestled with during the negotiations before the signature of the nonaggression pact no doubt fell victim to his paramount consideration, namely, the survival of the Soviet state.

Following the German invasion on June 22, 1941, Stalin told the British that he had agreed to the nonaggression pact because of the fundamental hostility to Soviet Russia of Prime Minister Neville Chamberlain's conservative government. War was coming, Stalin held, and his country had to know where it stood. If no agreement could be hammered out with Great Britain, he could not afford to be left isolated and fall victim to the war's winner. He had no choice but to accept the nonaggression pact with Nazi Germany. However, Stalin explained, he had insisted that he would never fight alongside Germany against Great Britain. When Germany made it clear that it would invade Poland, Soviet Russia had protested, he falsely claimed. Moscow could not countenance a forward movement by the Germans up to the Soviet Russian frontier. When invited by Hitler to occupy Eastern Poland, he accepted. Not to have done so, Stalin ruminated, would have led to the German occupation of positions needed by the Russians.[11]

Variations of this apologia offered by Stalin in October 1941 had been voiced well before the German attack in June by some of his obsequious apparatchiks, for example, Konstantin Umansky, the ambassador in Washington,[12] and Mikhail Korj, the first secretary of the London embassy. The latter specifically complained of the makeup of the British mission to Moscow during the abortive Anglo-French-Russian military discussions of August 1939 and of the absence on the British side of someone of stature and power. Korj characterized the sluggish arrival of the mission by cargo steamer as "hardly impressive or flattering to its prospective hosts."[13] At the time of the discussions, however, the Russians had raised no such objections. The possibility that Korj was a member of the intelligence services is highlighted by his earnest loquacity during the discussions, the secluded area in an otherwise crowded room chosen for the conversation, the distant glances of Ambassador Ivan Maisky, and the forty minutes Korj took to voice his opinions. One must keep in mind the sphinx-like silence of most Russian diplomats during this period.

Stalin's comments and those of his minions were self-serving. Even if Chamberlain had been positively disposed toward the Communist government in Soviet Russia, he would have been in no position to satisfy Russian wishes regarding Eastern Europe. Leaving aside British treaty commitments to the Poles, neither the British government nor the French government thought itself capable of pressuring either Poland or Rumania to allow Russian troops to enter their territory in order to confront German forces should these countries be attacked. The long and the short of it was that Hitler did not suffer from the same political, military, legal, and moral restraints that faced his Anglo-French rivals. He could promise the Russians a great deal, including territorial compensation for their neutrality in any forthcoming struggle, and he did so.[14]

This promise is reflected by the terms of the secret protocol appended to the 1939 nonaggression pact, signed by the respective foreign ministers, the taciturn Vyacheslav Molotov (né Skriabin) and the pompous Joachim von Ribbentrop. In later years, Molotov would obstinately insist that the nonaggression pact contained no secret clauses, but this was patently untrue.[15] Under the pact's secret protocol, it was agreed that, in the "event of a territorial and political transformation," Lithuania would become a German sphere of interest and Lithuania's claim to the Vilna area in Poland would be recognized. Russia's spheres of interest would be Estonia, Finland, and Latvia. Most important, the fourth partition of Poland was spelled out. In addition, Germany recognized Russia's interest in Rumania's Bessarabia, and declared its "complete *désintéressement*" in southeast Europe.[16]

Moscow only needed to occupy Bessarabia, Eastern Poland, Estonia, Finland, and Latvia to assure its control over these regions. The nonaggression pact reflected greater German concessions to the Russians than Russian concessions to the Germans. This imbalance can be partially traced to the misinformation about British policy during this period that was apparently "fed" to Berlin by Moscow and that stemmed from secret materials culled by its agent, John Herbert King of the British Foreign Office's Communications Department.[17]

The pact, however, opened the way for Germany's attack on Poland a week later and triggered the outbreak of the second World War. Likewise, it allowed the Russians to attack the Finns in late November 1939. Despite

Germany's sympathy for Finland, its options were limited by the nonaggression pact. Accordingly, Berlin's worldwide diplomatic missions, as well as its press and radio, were instructed to support the Russian aggression and to express no sympathy for the victim.[18]

The Nazi conquest in April–June 1940 of Belgium, Denmark, France, Luxemburg, The Netherlands, and Norway, as well as Stalin's moves in the Baltic and Rumania, propelled Hitler in late July 1940 to order military planning for the invasion of Soviet Russia. This was no snap decision, for as early as October 18, 1939, six weeks after the outbreak of the second World War and seven weeks after the signing of the Russian-German nonaggression pact, he had alluded to using occupied Polish territory as an "assembly area for future German [military] operations."[19]

Hitler's stunning and rapid victories, especially against France, had undercut Stalin's assumptions that victory in the West for either side would be a long time coming and that Moscow would never have to face alone a strong and victorious Nazi Germany.[20] According to his biographer, General Dmitri Volkogonov, Britain's continued resistance made it possible for Stalin to hew to the consistent line that Hitler would never turn against Russia until he had vanquished the British and that Hitler would never repeat the error of the first World War and entrap Germany in a two-front war.[21]

The new reality produced by the swift German victories was reflected in the London comments of Ambassador Maisky, who admitted that Germany's military successes had been a huge surprise to his government, which did not desire a German victory. Maisky was seconded by the director of the *Tass* news agency in London, the Balliol-trained Andrew Rothstein, who earned himself a "place in the hierarchy of the small but rigidly organized British Communist Party." On this matter, Andrew Rothstein divulged to a Foreign Office official, Moscow did not relish sharing a common frontier with a Germany that was both powerful and victorious.[22]

Faced with limited options, Moscow decided to expand the Russian frontier as far west as possible and to execute the nonaggression pact's secret protocol. On the very day the French asked for an armistice, June 17, 1940, Berlin was informed of Moscow's occupation of the Baltic states of Estonia, Latvia, and Lithuania. Under the 1939 secret protocol, Moscow could justify the occupation and absorption of Estonia and Latvia. Its occupation of Lithuania, initially given to Germany, was allowable under a subsequent revision of the protocol on September 28, 1939, which stipulated that Lithuania fell within the Russian "sphere of influence"; the trade-off was that the Polish province of Lublin and large parts of the province of Warsaw were assigned to Germany.[23] Concurrently, the Germans were asked to close their diplomatic and consular missions in these three states, in view of their incorporation as part of the territory of Soviet Russia.

After the French-German armistice at Compiègne, Stalin struck once more, this time against Rumania. Molotov took up the matter with the German ambassador, Count Friedrich Werner von der Schulenburg, a man of sartorial splendor described as a "diplomat of the old school . . . a gentleman and a moderate."[24] He informed him that Russia would use force should Rumania not agree to the Russian occupation of Bessarabia. Again under the secret protocol of 1939, Moscow could justify its action, but it raised the ante by also extending a claim to Bukovina, which had been part of Austria-Hungary, never of Czarist Russia, and moreover was not covered by the secret protocol. With German forces concentrated in Western Europe and Hitler busy consolidating his gains and looking across the channel to invade Great Britain, Stalin had acted with ruthlessness and dispatch.

Nevertheless, Molotov was cautious. Goading a powerful and victorious Germany had its risks. Sensitive to Rumania's importance to Germany's war effort, he limited Moscow's claim to northern Bukovina and assured Count Schulenburg that the Soviet Union recognized that the Third Reich had a "primary interest in Rumanian petroleum." Moscow's performance, however, in absorbing Bessarabia and northern Bukovina had necessitated that Berlin restrain Bucharest's voracious neighbors from partaking in the feast. Under German pressure Rumania surrendered half of Transylvania to Hungary and the Southern Dobrudja to Bulgaria. What remained of the Rumanian state, under the so-called Vienna Award, was guaranteed by Germany and Italy. Molotov was not amused by the German guarantee, which he claimed violated Article 3 of the 1939 nonaggression pact, providing for joint consultation about matters of interest to both states. Russia, he held, had interests in the matter in view of its geographic proximity to the involved states. Germany, he maintained, had presented his country with a *fait accompli*. Ribbentrop retorted that since Moscow had been satiated by the absorption of Bessarabia and northern Bukovina, no common interest had been involved in the Rumanian territorial guarantee. Thus Berlin was not obligated to consult with Moscow under the nonaggression pact.[25]

Aside from geopolitical considerations, Hitler's decision to invade Soviet Russia was also based on ideological and racial hostility. The enormous ideological antipathy between Hitler's Nazi Germany and Stalin's Soviet Russia was succinctly and visually summed up in David Low's famous cartoon "Rendezvous," which appeared in the *London Evening Standard*. A delighted Hitler and Stalin, bowing from the hips and tipping their hats to each other, stand over a bludgeoned and prostrate Poland. Hitler to Stalin: "The scum of the earth, I believe." Stalin to Hitler: "The bloody assassin of the workers, I presume?"[26]

From the inception of the Nazi movement, specifically in the frenzied pages of *Mein Kampf*, Hitler had made no bones about racial hostility. The antecedents of this racial hostility were manifested in the occult world of prewar Europe, a world with which Hitler was not totally unfamiliar.[27] In Hitler's pseudo-anthropological world, the division into culture-creating, culture-bearing, and culture-destroying groups clearly placed the Aryan, read here Germans, into the first category. Their cultural decline, according to

Hitler, could be traced to "race-mixture" and to "blood mixing," which led to a lowering of the Aryan's "racial level." The Gypsies and the Jews, along with the Slavic people of eastern Europe, manifestly fell under the rubric of culture-destroying groups.[28] This was a view, as one would expect, that engendered marked hostility within the Russian leadership.[29] Accordingly, Hitler warned the German military that during the invasion of Russia the intelligentsia developed by Stalin had to be "exterminated"; "force" was to be "used in its most brutal form." The Russian campaign would "be very different from the war in the West." Because of this difference, military commanders would have to "make the sacrifices of overcoming their personal scruples."[30] Not all Germans shared Hitler's view. For example, Ambassador Ulrich von Hassell, who had been forced out of the German diplomatic service by the Nazi regime, and who was implicated and would be executed for his role in the attempted assassination of Hitler in July 1944, was appalled by his genocidal policy.[31] Described as "a gentleman of the old school to his finger tips,"[32] Von Hassell exemplified a Germany that no longer steered the ship of state. Nazi behavior after 1933 proved that.

The German-Russian diplomatic skirmishes, especially those concerning Rumania, and the moment and manner used by Moscow to implement its policy desires annoyed Hitler and the German leadership no end.[33] Using the influence it gained through its acquisition of Bessarabia and northern Bukovina and access to the Danube, Moscow then successfully pressured Berlin for representation on the river's new regime, which was created to exclude the British and French through a dissolution of the European and International Danube Commissions established in 1856 and 1919, respectively.[34] The competition between Berlin and Moscow across the Balkans and in other areas such as Finland was punctured on September 27, 1940, by the Tripartite Pact, signed by Germany, Italy, and Japan. Aimed at the United States and designed to isolate Great Britain, the pact, later adhered to by Bulgaria, Croatia, Hungary, Rumania, and Slovakia, was based on mutual assistance and on spheres of influence in which Europe was assigned to Germany and Italy, and Asia and the Far East to Japan. The pact specifically excluded its terms of reference from affecting the political status existing between the signatories and Soviet Russia.[35]

Since Germany's attack on Russia could only begin in the spring of 1941 at the earliest, Hitler had time to string the Russians along and was apparently not adverse to enticing them into concentrating their attention on expanding in a direction that did not clash with immediate German interests. Hitler apparently wanted to divert the Russians southward, preferably toward the Indian Ocean. The added advantage was that expansion in this direction would place Soviet Russia in a collision course with Great Britain.[36] Therefore an invitation to discuss future relations between the two states was conveyed to Stalin, and on November 12 Molotov arrived in Berlin.

Stalin's attitude at this juncture was succinctly voiced by Andrei Zhdanov.

A member of the Politburo of the Party's Central Committee, chief of the Leningrad party organization, and close to the *Vozhd,* Zhdanov observed during this period that the Germans and the British were so involved with each other militarily that Russia had the opportunity to do what it wanted. Although he did not say it, he still believed that a German attack was improbable. Zhdanov pointed to the First World War to show that Germany was incapable of fighting on two fronts and recalled Bismarck's famous comment that Germany should never sever its contacts with Russia.[37]

The attitude that Moscow had choices, that its desires had to be considered and satiated, was reflected in the two days of wide-ranging discussions that Molotov had with Hitler and Ribbentrop, who pressed him to accept the option of expanding southward. Specifically, the Tripartite Pact would be expanded to include Russia, and in a secret protocol, its "territorial aspirations" centered toward the Indian Ocean would be recognized. English resistance, Molotov was assured, had virtually collapsed.[38]

The German ploy to turn Soviet Russia's attention toward the Indian Ocean was undisguised, and Molotov demurred. He questioned German moves in Finland. Why not provide a Russian guarantee to Bulgaria, Molotov queried, similar to the German one to Rumania? Hitler objected. Molotov did not accept the German offer but held that what interested his country at the present moment was Europe, the Turkish Straits, as well as Rumania and Hungary. Likewise, he wanted to know about German intentions regarding Greece, Poland, and Yugoslavia, and raised the question of Sweden's neutrality, as well as the question of passage from the Baltic.[39] Regarding the reiterated German assertion that Great Britain was finished, Molotov did not remain silent. "If England is defeated, then why are we sitting in this air raid shelter? And whose bombs are falling so close that we can hear their explosions even here?" he asked Ribbentrop as they marked time in the Wilhelmstrasse's underground bunker[40] during a British bombing raid timed to coincide with the negotiations.[41]

Therefore the initial seepage of information orchestrated from the Russian embassy that Molotov was in an "excellent mood" and much impressed by his talks with Hitler and Ribbentrop was so much sop to both the Nazis and an anxious world.[42] Probably closer to the truth was the subsequent impression of a German penetration agent, seemingly serving the NKVD, that the Russians within the embassy believed that Germany was attempting to "encircle" Soviet Russia.[43] The Russians' negative view of the whole visit is shown by Molotov's postwar observation that the German purpose in arranging the meeting was to discover whether Russia could be fooled into joining the struggle against Great Britain.[44] Since that clearly was not the intent of the visit, the German offer to include Russia in the Tripartite Pact was not intended seriously, while the limitations imposed by logistics and time would derail any territorial aspirations Moscow might have toward the Indian Ocean. Any "long term agreement with the Kremlin," one German authority has claimed, "ran counter to all of the Fuehrer's deepest prejudices, and could not be harmonized with Hitler's repeated expressions of intent since July 1940." The German proposals were probably "designed as a smoke screen" behind which the invasion of Russia could be prepared.[45]

The German proposals, however, provoked a counteroffer from Stalin about two weeks later. This offer repeated the gist of Molotov's Berlin proposals: the withdrawal of German troops from Finland, the conclusion of a mutual assistance pact with Bulgaria, the establishment through a long-term lease of a Russian military and naval base within the Turkish Straits, the recognition of the area south of Batum and Baku in the direction of the Persian Gulf as the center of Russian aspirations, and Japan's renunciation of her coal and oil concessions in Northern Sakhalin. Molotov again raised the counteroffer in January 1941.[46] Berlin, however, did not respond.[47]

If the purpose of inviting Molotov to Berlin had been to turn Moscow's attention away from Europe and toward the Indian Ocean, then it had clearly not succeeded. Molotov's comments during the Berlin discussions and the counteroffer showed clearly that Stalin had not been persuaded to disinterest himself in Europe. He wanted to control Finland, Bulgaria, the Turkish Straits, and for all practical purposes, the oil fields in Iran and the Arab states that supplied Europe with the major part of its oil requirements. All of these demands and conditions, of course, were unacceptable to Berlin.

Understandably, Hitler was not amused by the counteroffer, and whatever inhibitions he might have had about his initial July decision to invade Soviet Russia now disappeared. He brushed aside the misgivings of the German military who feared any attack on Russia before Great Britain was brought to its knees.[48] "Russia's inclination to interfere in Balkan Affairs," he argued, made it "necessary to eliminate at all cost the last enemy remaining on the continent" before he could come to any agreement with Great Britain.[49] To one of the doubters, Grand-Admiral Erich Raeder, he later observed that Stalin was "a cold-blooded blackmailer" who would, "if expedient, repudiate any written treaty at any time."[50]

Hitler's decision, therefore, in late July to invade Soviet Russia was formally confirmed on December 18, 1940, with the issuance of Directive 21, entitled "Operation Barbarossa." The directive spelled out in some detail the main lines of the military thrust into Soviet Russia, defined the roles of Finland and Rumania, and set May 15, 1941, as the date when all preparations had to be completed. That the intended attack go undiscovered was of "decisive importance." Tight security was to be maintained to prevent leakage of the plan, and military orders based on the directive had to indicate clearly that they were "*precautionary measures* for the possibility that Russia should change her present attitude toward us." The number of officers assigned to do the preparatory work was to be kept to the minimum; others, briefed as late as possible and only to the extent needed to execute their task. Otherwise, the discovery of Barbarossa's preparations, its execution not even set, entailed the "danger that most serious political and military disadvantages may arise."[51] The stage was prepared, and there would be no turning back.

## The *Vozhd*

How intelligence matters were handled in Stalin's regime is best exemplified by events in the spring and early summer of 1940, as the German armies sliced their way through Europe. In Moscow, Stalin's crony and fellow Georgian, Lavrentii Beria, the director of the NKVD,[52] tendered the Politburo an intelligence report evaluating the order of battle of Germany's European forces. Code-named the 'Yugoslav scheme,' because allegedly the source or sources were from Yugoslavia, the report contended that the visible absence of any pattern in the order of battle was a "clear sign" that the German armies were only resting.[53] Objections, however, were raised within the army that this was planted "misinformation." It was held that the report was based on unreliable and unskilled observers, that a quarter of the German forces went unnoticed, and that the order of battle was really one preparing for an attack. Moreover, the Yugoslav scheme was a "childish explanation" for German battle order since the German General Staff, even if it was planning an invasion of the British Isles, would at the minimum take the necessary defensive measures to cover the eastern flank.[54]

To thrash out the disagreement that had arisen, which was really an indirect assault on the 1939 nonaggression pact and the arrangements with Nazi Germany, Stalin convened a special meeting of the Politburo on July 3, 1940, to defend Beria's Yugoslav scheme. After the scheme's supporters had spoken in its defense, Air Force General Ivan Proskurov, the chief of the GRU,[55] took the floor. He mounted a rigorous and plausible attack on the scheme that "impressed the Politburo" and supposedly even impressed Stalin. The *Vozhd* himself appeared to waver, although along with Beria he had initially made some "nasty comments" during Proskurov's assault on the scheme. Whatever second thoughts the *Vozhd* might have had, however, quickly dissolved, for on the following day, July 4, it is claimed that Proskurov was arrested and promptly shot without trial.[56]

This was not the case, but unfortunately for Proskurov the *Vozhd* had a long memory and, even more important, a longer reach. In April 1941 when Marshal Semyon Timoshenko, the minister of defense, and General Georgii Zhukov, the chief of staff, reported that a lack of air force discipline was causing increasing airplane losses and recommended the removal, as well as the court-martial, of several senior air force officers, Stalin agreed, provided Proskurov also be added to the list.[57] Despite his heroism as a fighter pilot during the Spanish Civil War,[58] he was arrested and executed on October 28, 1941.[59]

Proskurov's stance had clearly not been to Stalin's liking, and he had to be punished. Stalin distrusted his GRU chiefs.[60] In addition to the GRU's apparent lackluster performance during the Russian-Finnish war, which in large measure could be traced to the decimation of its ranks during the purges,[61] Proskurov had seemingly sealed his fate by indirectly assaulting the arrangements with Nazi Germany that were the sheet anchor of Stalin and Molotov's foreign policy. The irony of it all was that Proskurov was a man ahead of his time. Objectively, Beria's intelligence report that the German order of battle showed no hostile intent against Soviet Russia was correct. Hitler, as we have seen, did not come to his decision to invade Russia until late July, weeks after Beria's report had been filed and Proskurov supposedly executed. Indeed, it was not until the end of July that the number of German troops facing the Russians was increased from five to fifteen divisions.[62]

General Filipp Golikov was appointed to succeed Proskurov. Unlike many of his predecessors and successors who were shot, Golikov served as chief of the GRU until 1941 and survived. He had joined the Red Army as a volunteer in 1918, serving as a machine gunner. He was then involved in suppressing anti-Communist peasant uprisings while on the staff of the special punitive brigades. Formal military training followed, and Golikov was assigned increasingly more important commands. His promotions were accelerated in the late 1930s by the vacancies created in the Red Army's senior positions by Stalin's purges. In September 1939, following the nonaggression pact and the agreement with Germany to partition Poland, he led the Sixth Army in the occupation of eastern Poland. After he left the GRU and involvement in several important missions abroad, he served at the front. He was then appointed Stalin's deputy for Red Army cadres. Concurrently, he assumed operational control in the struggle against those Russians who opposed Stalin's regime and had joined the German invaders. In the postwar period, he directed the enforced repatriation and execution of countless thousands who were forcibly returned to Russia. Golikov likewise directed postwar purges of the army. He then fell out of favor and was removed from his command and imprisoned for two years. In 1950 he was again in Stalin's good graces and reinstated; and by 1956 he was chief of the military academy. Finally he was made chief political commissar of the armed forces in 1958, a marshal in 1961, and summarily removed from his commissar's office in the spring of 1962. He died in 1980, two weeks short of his 81st birthday.[63]

In view of Golikov's track record, it would not be unfair to say that he had an instinct for survival. Unlike Proskurov, Golikov was "a 'political' general," more at home "in administrative and quasi-diplomatic assignments than in the field."[64] Golikov was a protege of newly appointed Defense Comissar Timoshenko and had no background in intelligence work. He was a "typical military apparatchik,"[65] who knew on which side his bread was buttered and acted accordingly. Proskurov's fate reflected, as nothing else could, the need to mesh one's thoughts and actions with the *Vozhd*'s perceptions of the unfolding world scene. If Stalin had asserted that the world was flat, Golikov would have assured him that it was as flat as a billiard table.

It has been claimed that Golikov misinformed Stalin on intelligence matters.[66] It is more likely that, to please or ingratiate himself with Stalin, he told him what he wanted to hear, for example, that the possibility could not be excluded that the British were concocting spurious reports that the Germans were poised to attack.[67] Golikov faithfully believed in and clutched tightly to his chest the three *Us*: *ugadat* (sniff out), *ugodit* (suck up), and *utselet* (survive), which might be figuratively translated as "find out what the boss wants, and give it to him regardless."[68] As Marshal Andrei Grechko pointed out in postwar testimony, the top military and intelligence leaders raised no objections to Stalin's intuitive excursions into the political-military scene and showed neither consistency nor the ability to influence him. Rather, they often supported and reinforced Stalin's views.[69] This attitude of survival might help explain why Nikita Khrushchev often saw Golikov "in Stalin's presence."[70] Being wired directly to the *Vozhd* often prolonged one's life expectancy.

The successful attempt to circumvent the Yugoslav scheme is a case in point. Because Stalin supported the Yugoslav scheme, the instructions given were that it be disseminated "as the basis for evaluating the composition and grouping"[71] of the German forces. The endeavor of Vasili Novobranets to ignore the Yugoslav scheme when preparing a draft of the regular intelligence summary on the ground that the scheme was misinformation moved Golikov to insist that the Yugoslav scheme be the basis of any intelligence summary. He cautioned the transgressing officer to obey orders and to be careful since Stalin himself believed in the Yugoslav scheme.

But Novobranets persisted and ignored the Yugoslav scheme as the basis for evaluating the composition and grouping of the German forces. Instead, in a clever and dangerous ploy, his Intelligence Summary Number 8, drawn up in the late spring of 1941 and stating that a German attack group was "in a take-off position," was circulated to all military commands in a manner that prevented its recall. When informed by Novobranets of what he had done, Golikov was beside himself. Novobranets was immediately replaced. Only the German attack saved him from being shot.[72]

Golikov's truckling to Stalin was compounded by the manner in which GRU intelligence information flowed through the chain of command. According to General Zhukov, Golikov was "directly responsible" to Stalin and reported to no one else, not even to Zhukov, or to Marshal Timoshenko.[73] For example, Zhukov was never made privy to the invaluable information being conveyed from Tokyo by the German journalist, Richard Sorge, one of the GRU's most accomplished agents,[74] although Zhukov's exclusion might have been justified by the "need to know" principle. Suffice it to note that a trusted courier delivered Golikov's intelligence data directly to Stalin and Molotov.[75] Since Stalin rarely consulted with the Politburo and when he did it was in a niggardly manner,[76] one can suggest that he probably retained most of whatever intelligence data was given to him.

This retention had the practical effect of denying senior military officers access to high-level intelligence data, and even to knowledge of its existence, placing Stalin in a virtually unassailable position regarding substantive intelligence information.[77] No doubt in large part this was the intent of Stalin's arrangement. Because he recognized that knowledge can be power, Stalin's virtual monopoly of intelligence data gave him an advantage, one might even say a form of power, over those he wished to control physically and psychically, who in this instance were his associates on the Politburo, and especially the Russian military.

The flow of NKVD intelligence to Stalin was equally unstructured. Beria, a former Chekist and the head of the NKVD, was a Stalin stalwart and the "author" of a disingenuous hagiographic biography of Stalin's early years and activities as a member of the Communist party in Transcaucasia. Beria's climb up the slippery rungs of the bureaucratic and party ladders was achieved over the bodies of many colleagues and competitors and due solely to Stalin's self-serving largess and paranoia—qualities that Beria played upon to great effect. Depraved, driven by the ambition for power, and as demonically evil as his chief, Beria was the faithful executioner who ingratiated himself with and flattered the *Vozhd*. He used the NKVD to serve Stalin's every whim, especially in isolating, unmasking, and liquidating his enemies, real or imagined.[78] Like Golikov, Beria would never have questioned Stalin and Molotov's support of the 1939 nonaggression pact, and in all likelihood, he would have tailored his intelligence data accordingly. The symbiotic nature of the relationship between Stalin and Beria probably allowed an even more informal chain of command between Stalin and the NKVD regarding intelligence information than that enjoyed by the GRU under Golikov. Nevertheless, the apex in the movement of intelligence data, whether GRU or NKVD, was still Stalin.

This chain of command, whether with the GRU or the NKVD, reflected Stalin's desire to partake in intelligence activities and be his own intelligence chief. As noted previously, this chain gave him greater power since it isolated his subordinates, who, by his machinations, were ill-informed, and obviated the need to consult or argue with them. Stalin's biographer informs us that the *Vozhd* was fascinated by documentation and tended to place inordinate value on any information that was handwritten or published.[79] However, Stalin apparently "did not receive 'raw intelligence' from the GRU but had it presented or edited by the intelligence staff."[80]

These intelligence reports appear to have included summaries of important documentation purloined from other governments or information supplied by exceptional sources. Stalin admonished the intelligence services to avoid hypotheses, to acquire valuable sources, and to ascertain the most closely guarded secrets of other governments. Intelligence service hypotheses, Stalin held, were to be eschewed, since they could lead to disaster. He opposed the submission of periodic intelligence reports to him since they would be speckled, he insisted, with assumptions and subjective comments. In his periodic meetings with the intelligence chiefs, Stalin would almost always pepper the conversation with the warning that he was not interested in their thoughts on the matter at hand, only in the facts and in the source that supplied those facts.[81]

This approach was clearly exhibited during the crucial period of May–June 1941. Andrei Vyshinsky, who had won his spurs from Stalin by conducting the infamous Moscow Purge Trials, was restricted merely to summarizing, not analyzing, the intelligence data flowing into the Kremlin for the *Vozhd*, Molotov, and Beria.[82] The comments of the NKVD resident in the Berlin embassy partially reflected this attitude. As he pointed out to one of his agents, the agent's work would prove far "more valuable if he brought him documents and plans concerning the intentions of the Germans. He had to provide such evidence without fail."[83] Stalin's attitude on the matter of intelligence was perhaps best mirrored in his comment to General Zhukov that intelligence data could not be believed in every instance.[84] The role played by Stalin's private secretariat/secret chancellery, which was presided over by the ubiquitous and loyal Stalinist Aleksandr Poskrebyshev, in sifting and analyzing the data conveyed to Stalin by the intelligence services cannot be adequately assessed, but Poskrebyshev's role could not have been anodyne.[85]

## Through A Glass, Darkly

Stalin's stance toward Hitler and the 1939 nonaggression pact caused additional complications. The German attack, Stalin admitted to the Americans in July and to the British in October 1941, had been a "surprise."[86] Privately he confessed that he himself had "believed that Hitler would not strike."[87] As Maxim Litvinov (né Vallak), the former foreign minister appointed as ambassador to Washington after the German attack, publicly divulged in mid-December 1941, Moscow had received warnings of Hitler's intention to attack, but had dismissed them. It had done so, Litvinov explained, not because Moscow believed in Hitler's virtue, or in his being incapable of violating his treaty obligations and the solemn promises he had made, but because Moscow, read here Stalin, considered that it would have been "madness" on Hitler's part to begin a war against a powerful Soviet Russia in the East before terminating his struggle with Great Britain in the West.[88]

Stalin was convinced, according to the Armenian Anastas Mikoyan, the minister of foreign trade, that any future German attack could not occur before mid–1942.[89] He held to this line of analysis with a bloody-mindedness that brooked no contradiction, despite the accumulating creditable evidence reaching Moscow that showed otherwise. Furthermore, Stalin's policy stance that Hitler would not attack made sense, for obviously the whole purpose of the 1939 nonaggression pact, or so Hitler made it appear, was to remove the danger of a two-front war that had been the bugaboo of German military, strategic, and political thinking since the end of the First World War.[90]

Moreover, the accelerating campaign to reequip and reorganize the Red Army must have strengthened Stalin's belief that it was a military force that was fast closing the gap between itself and the Wehrmacht.[91] Regarding the production of new equipment and the fitting out of troops, this belief might have been correct. However, the Red Army was hindered by mediocre performance and training and by the lag in adopting modern tactics based on speed, maneuvers, and bringing together armor, motorized infantry, and close air support. But doubtlessly, in Stalin's mind, the Red Army presented the Wehrmacht with a creditable deterrent. The notion that any German attack would provoke a vigorous riposte and that Moscow feared no such attack was a recurring theme, as we shall see, in Russian reactions to any possible high risk German policy.[92]

Indeed, Litvinov's comments are not unsupported. "Stalin believed Ribbentrop's signature on the nonaggression pact," the Foreign Ministry's strategically placed and well-informed Valentin Berezhkov assures us, and although it "may seem astonishing . . . he reckoned for some reason that Hitler would not decide to start a war" against Soviet Russia.[93] No less a personality than Andrei Gromyko tells us "to note that Stalin was convinced that Hitler would honour the treaty and that therefore the USSR would not be drawn into the war by a German attack." Once Stalin was committed to "an idea, he would cling to it," Gromyko insists. No matter how many warnings Stalin received about an impending German attack, none "could shift his *idée fixe*."[94] It was not until after Stalin's death that the Russian authorities were willing to admit that "Stalin overestimated the significance" of the nonaggression pact.[95] Until the German attack, however, woe came to any Russian general who openly manifested his aversion to Germany. It was unhealthy to bad-mouth the Germans as long as Stalin maintained his stance that Hitler would honor the pact. Officers who failed to restrain themselves could be accused of being *"provocateurs."* The unlucky ones were arrested, and others were threatened with arrest.[96]

Stalin was willing to go far and do much to fend off the Germans and also any complaints, real or imagined, that Hitler raised. This willingness is reflected in his 1943 ruminations to the Americans when, without his specifically saying so, it was apparent from his comments that Stalin believed that Hitler "through his stupidity in attacking the Soviet Union had thrown away all the fruits of his previous victories."[97] This was quite true, but what Stalin failed to see or to admit is that not all players in the international arena act in a rational fashion,[98] to wit, in a manner that objectively serves to advance the state's national interests. Hitler's invasion of Soviet Russia in June 1941 is a case in point. Stalin was committed to the 1939 nonaggression pact because it appeared to serve so well the interests of both sides: their mutual desire to avoid a two-front war, Germany's desire to retain Russia as an important supplier of vital raw materials,[99] and Soviet Russia's desire to avoid involvement in the struggle and keep Germany at bay. "The Soviet Government,"

Stalin assured the Germans when the nonaggression pact was signed, "takes the new Pact very seriously." He "could guarantee on his word of honor that the Soviet Union would not betray its partner."[100] How much weight one could place on Stalin's word of honor is a moot point, but there is no doubt that in Stalin's view Hitler's unilateral annihilation of the pact was unexpected and uncalled for. He held to this view until the bitter end. He was so petrified of a war with Germany that even when the final hour came, Khrushchev has written, Stalin "convinced himself that Hitler would keep his word and wouldn't really attack us."[101] Stalin's mind-set "desensitized" him to all genuine warnings of an impending German attack. He viewed all such warnings, as we shall see, as provocation or disinformation, especially when conveyed by sources that he suspected wanted to generate German-Russian tension, for example, the British.[102]

Accordingly in 1941, as winter gave way to spring and the evidence mounted that invasion might take place, Stalin's inventive mind conjured up all manner of explanations and rationales to refute the incoming information submitted by his own diplomats and the intelligence services. Understandably, he assumed the same stance whether the information was submitted by the Americans, the British, the Czechs, or others. The list of complaints and suspicions against the British in particular ran the gamut: their attitude during the Spanish Civil War; their efforts since the inception of the hostilities to reduce American trade with Soviet Russia; and especially, "British intervention in Russia (of which Churchill was the principal sponsor) in 1918/1919."[103] Churchill's role in the interventionist effort was front and center in Stalin's mind, and he did not hesitate to bring up this role during Churchill's visit to Moscow in October 1944. This provoked Churchill to observe that when he joined the British cabinet the intervention had already commenced, although he himself had had no wish to kill Stalin.

Moscow's complaints about British actions and about Churchill's earlier role were made about seven weeks before the German attack. In a telling admission, Konstantin Umansky, the tight-lipped Russian ambassador in Washington, said that Moscow looked scornfully upon any information coming from London, especially from a government presided over by Churchill. Umansky held to the expected view radiating from Moscow that Germany would not dare attack his country,[104] and he admitted his surprise when it did so.[105]

The mutuality of interest served by the 1939 nonaggression pact, as perceived by Stalin, and Hitler's eradication of the pact provoked the *Vozhd* to comment about an obviously good deal that had soured. Soviet Russia and Nazi Germany together, he nostalgically noted, would have been unbeatable. This postwar admission made by Stalin to his daughter Svetlana[106] should be juxtaposed against his wartime comment to Prime Minister Winston Churchill that he had thought he might gain six more months of preparation before the Germans attacked.[107] That Stalin wanted to keep Germany at bay is not open to question, but how he planned to do this and the price he was willing to pay he never discussed. The courier who brought Golikov's intelligence data to Stalin has rightly asserted that, when the *Vozhd* assumed from Molotov the political office of prime minister in May 1941, he did so not to prepare for Russia's defense but to reach an understanding with Hitler.[108]

Stalin no doubt believed, as we shall see, that Hitler could be fended off with additional concessions that would allow Germany to conduct unimpeded its war against Great Britain.[109] The Red Army's deplorable performance in Finland, which in large part could be traced to the decimation of its officer corps during the purges, and the Nazi army's lightning victories in France and elsewhere convinced Stalin, as nothing else could, that though Russia was getting stronger with each passing day, she was still relatively weak militarily and in no position to take on Germany single-handedly.[110] On the issue of fending off the Germans and the lengths to which he would be willing to go to achieve this, the *Vozhd* was a dissembler. As we shall see, Vojtech Mastny's suggestion that in the days just before the German attack Stalin was prepared to offer Hitler wide-ranging concessions reducing Russia "to the status of Germany's junior partner" is worthy of merit[111] and invites investigation.

## Sleight of Hand

Stalin's perceptions were in turn influenced by the deception operations mounted against Soviet Russia by Hitler and the German military before the invasion of June 1941. Indeed, the need for deception operations had been recognized well before Hitler issued the directive for Operation Barbarossa on December 18, 1940.[112] Deception has been defined as a "purposeful attempt by the deceiver to manipulate the perception of the target's decisionmakers in order to gain a competitive advantage."[113] In its modern setting, military deception *(maskirovka)* can be expanded to include, aside from the "standard measures of military secrecy and concealment," "subversion and disinformation, the creation of images, the use of 'diplomatic noise,' and the interruption of decision-making capabilities—in short, a form of ambush."[114] The memorandum circulated in early September 1940 by General Alfred Jodl of the Oberkommando der Wehrmacht (High Command of the Armed Forces) is the earliest extant order reflecting the German deception endeavor. As we have seen, by late July the Germans had increased their divisions along the Russian frontier from five to fifteen and continued to increase troop concentrations as summer gave way to autumn. This eastward movement of men and equipment could not go unobserved and unreported; accordingly, an appropriate "cover" story had to be devised to deceive the Russians. The increasing troop concentrations, Jodl pointed out, "must not create the impression in Russia" that Germany "was preparing an offensive in the East."[115] At the same time, this strong troop concentration would cause Moscow to conclude that whenever Berlin wished it could protect its interests in the area, including the Balkans, with powerful forces against any Russian moves.

To assist the German intelligence service as well as to answer any questions posed by Russian intelligence certain precautionary steps were to be taken. For example, as much as possible, German troop strength along the frontier was to be "veiled." To do so, it was suggested that publicity might be circulated about the "frequent change" of units in the area, citing troop movements to training bases and troop regroupings. On the surface, it was to appear that the center of German troop concentration was in and around Austria and that concentrations in the north were not as important. The amelioration of the transport systems was to be explained as within the "normal limits" needed to improve the recently occupied eastern areas and as intended primarily for economic reasons. Finally, the High Command of the Armed Forces would decide what, if any, "correct details" would be furnished for counterespionage purposes.[116]

By the end of October, the concentration of German forces in the East had jumped from fifteen to thirty-three divisions and included five armored, two motorized, and one cavalry division. Moreover, the logistical infrastructure was being rapidly constituted with the establishment of training centers, airfields, supply depots, and communication facilities. German forces in northern Norway had also been increased.[117] A German explanation to the Russians of these troop movements and the resultant activities could no longer be delayed.

Accordingly, in November 1940 the German military attaché in Moscow, General Ernst Köstring, who was the doyen of the military attachés, was instructed to inform the Russian General Staff that because military operations had ceased in Western Europe, Germany intended to replace its older troops in Eastern Europe with younger ones. Thus, the older men could be employed in war production. In addition, Köstring was to tell the Russians that "training and supply conditions were better in the East and there was no danger" of British air attack. They were to be assured that there was "no reason for them to be alarmed by these measures."[118]

The mounting German troop concentrations in Poland moved Stalin in early 1941 to write to Hitler and point out that Moscow was both aware of and surprised by them and had the impression that Hitler intended to attack. In his very confidential reply, Hitler admitted the correctness of Stalin's information, but he was confident that his rejoinder would not circulate beyond the *Vozhd*'s immediate circle. He insisted that the German troop concentrations were not targeted against Soviet Russia. Indeed, Hitler assured Stalin that he was committed to abiding by the 1939 nonaggression pact, an assurance that no doubt was sweet music to the *Vozhd*'s ears and confirmed his belief that the pact continued to anchor German-Russian relations. As Germany's leader, Hitler gave his word that the troop concentrations in Poland served an entirely different purpose. He then gave Stalin a variant of what

General Köstring had been instructed to tell the Russian General Staff, namely, that both western and central Germany were open to British air attack. He had therefore transferred sizeable troop contingents eastward in order to regroup and rearm them secretly in Poland. Zhukov thought that Stalin believed Hitler.[119]

Subsequent evidence supports Zhukov's view. One can suggest that Stalin believed the Führer because he was subconsciously receptive to any comments or evidence that appeared to support and give meaning to the 1939 pact. In fact, Stalin was willing to rationalize the German troop concentrations. He argued that it was "natural" for Germany to maintain these concentrations along the border in view of a possible Russian violation of the 1939 pact and in view of Moscow's maintenance of significant troop formations on its side.[120]

Additional plans for the deception measures to be mounted developed between early December 1940 and early February 1941. In particular, Hitler directed that "Operation Sea Lion" (the invasion of Great Britain) and "Operation Marita" (the invasion of Greece and Yugoslavia) would form the core of the planned deception operations against the Russians. In the case of Sea Lion, Hitler wanted to convey the impression that an attack on Great Britain would occur sometime in 1941. However, Hitler's thoughts were not elaborated on until mid-February when Field Marshal Wilhelm Keitel issued the basic order spelling out in detail the various steps to be taken.

The purpose of the deception operations, Keitel explained, was to screen the preparations for Operation Barbarossa. This basic goal was the "guiding principle for all measures aimed at keeping the enemy misinformed." The uncertainty of Germany's intentions was to be maintained during the first period of the operation, which extended to mid-April. During this period, the present impression of an upcoming invasion of Great Britain was to be strengthened. The significance of other operations, such as Marita, was to be exaggerated, as well as were the forces involved. The shifting of troops to the east was to be presented as a "concentration of reserve units" for Marita and also as a "defensive rear cover" against the Russians.[121]

In the second period, which extended from mid-April to the day that Russia was attacked, troop movements for Operation Barbarossa were to be *"seen as the greatest deception operation in the history of war,"* and were intended to be seen by the Russians as a mask for the final phases of the British invasion. The ploy would be that the troop concentration in the East was made possible because the attack against England would be executed with "relatively weak forces," thanks to new German combat techniques and British naval superiority. To assist the whole process, false intelligence information was to be passed along with routine information to German service attachés in neutral states and to the service attachés of neutral states in Berlin. The pattern of deception would be a "mosaic picture, determined by this general policy." The notion was to be conveyed that the invasion of Great Britain was being prepared. Troops in the East were to be given the impression that their deployment was a deception operation, meant as a "defensive rear cover for the forthcoming blow against England." Moreover, everything was to be done to synchronize measures connected with Barbarossa with the inception of Marita, the invasion of Greece and Yugoslavia. The Luftwaffe was to contribute to the deception's mosaic by making it appear—through the assignment of English interpreters, the use of recently printed maps of England, and so on—they were targeted against Britain. The greater the troop concentration along the Russian frontier, Keitel observed, the more difficult would be the "attempts to foster uncertainty" about Germany's plans. Likewise, the more the preparations for Barbarossa stood out, the more difficult it would be "to maintain a successful deception."[122]

As winter gave way to spring and the day of the attack approached, the deception operations were accelerated and expanded. About mid-March, a disinformation campaign was directed against the Russian military attaché in Berlin, General Vasili Tupikov, who, like all Russian military attachés, was an overseas surrogate of the GRU. Preinvasion activities against Great Britain were simulated as camouflage for Barbarossa, and troop deployments in the East were presented as a precautionary move in the event that Russia's present attitude toward Germany should change. A disinformation operation using the German naval attaché in Tokyo was directed against the Russian military attaché, and the German army was directed to construct defensive fortifications along the frontier to make it appear as only a reaction to a Russian buildup. By spreading rumors and allowing air reconnaissance, the Germans assisted Russian intelligence in discovering these fortifications. March ended with the German military commander in Holland being directed to maintain the threat that Britain was on the threshold of an invasion.

On April 22, to conceal the buildup of Field Marshal Wilhelm Leeb's forces, which were to strike in the direction of Kiev, Leeb was ordered to remain in Munich. For the next two days, "Operation Harpoon South," a deception operation in Norway, and "Operation Shark," a deception operation in the English Channel, were mounted to simulate Sea Lion. Concurrently, the German naval attaché denied the war rumors prevailing in Moscow, prompting Berlin to point out that all rumors of a German-Russian war were no doubt an attempt by London to create distrust between both states and that the German buildup along the frontier was merely a rear cover for Marita. Finally, on April 30 it was decided that Germany's allies (Finland, Hungary, and Rumania) were to be given the placebo explanation that their presence was required in the East only as a rear cover along the Russian frontier during the German buildup for the upcoming attack on Great Britain.

May 11, 1941, led to a directive on the "tactical deception measures" to be adopted to disguise the time of the German attack and on the direction to be pursued by panzer units. On the following day, Field Marshal Keitel's order of mid-February was updated, and it was stipulated that the civil and military authorities were to be issued false orders. "Operation Mercury," the invasion of Crete (the Greek mainland had been occupied), was to be hailed as a forerunner for the landing in England. At the Foreign Ministry, the Japanese and Swedish ambassadors were assured that the alleged buildup in the East was only a defensive step to counter the Russian buildup and that relations between Germany and Russia depended on Stalin's future conduct. Less than a week later, Hitler agreed that a "plausible cover story" had to be concocted "to mask the stoppage of supplies to Russia." A subsequent directive was issued to prevent by a "false pretext" the departure of merchant ships to Russia. Some days later, the defensive nature of the German buildup was stressed to the Finns, but it was emphasized that a preventive war might be launched if Moscow did not reach a "political accommodation" with Berlin—an action that would be construed in Moscow as additional pressure to make economic and political concessions to the Germans. In the German capital, the minister of propaganda, Joseph Goebbels, disingenuously informed his staff that the invasion of England was momentary and ordered a renewed propaganda campaign against the British.[123]

A week later, Goebbels wrote in the Nazi party organ, the *Volkischer Beobachter,* that the invasion of Crete foreshadowed an imminent invasion of Great Britain. This particular issue of June 13 was then confiscated by the police as soon as copies reached the foreign press corps. The whole incident, Ribbentrop was informed by his staff, had "increased the confusion among foreign circles in Berlin."[124]

The recommendation was broached to begin false German transmissions in Hungary and Rumania to create communications deceptions aimed at the Russians. The central themes of these German deceptions, the invasion of Great Britain, defense against Soviet Russia, and eastern troop concentrations as a rear cover for an attack on Greece and Yugoslavia, were buttressed whenever needed by planted rumors diffused through radio broadcasts. These specific and well-documented actions were supported by disseminating false information or by amalgamating false and correct information and feeding it to the Russian intelligence services. Deceptive hints were dropped in places frequented by foreigners, while the issuance of misleading press releases and orders to the military helped round out the deception measures.[125]

Without a doubt, many more specific actions than those cited by the Germans and others were taken to deceive and misdirect the Russians about the upcoming attack. As we shall see, in mid-May, Berlin cleverly manipulated diplomatic negotiations to feign a desire to come to a settlement of the outstanding differences between both states.

It would be safe to assume that some of these deceptive actions were based on oral commands, and in the instances in which the commands were written, the pertinent documentation has either been destroyed or has not yet surfaced. The long and the short of it is that German deception operations were extensive, integrated, imaginative, plausible, and pervasive. The question is what impact, if any, these operations had on the Russians, and specifically on Stalin.

Certainly the Russian intelligence services, as the Germans expected, were soon enmeshed in trying to comprehend the deception operations that had been mounted. It is alleged that they finally "determined" that Berlin's intentions were to attack Soviet Russia.[126] Any such information, however, whether acquired by the NKVD or the GRU, would have had to pass through Beria or Golikov to Stalin. One must keep in mind the personalities of Beria and Golikov and the roles that they envisaged for themselves and leave aside how they would have presented any creditable data unearthed by their intelligence services. All information would have been subjected to Stalin's intelligence sieve, already described. The possibility that Stalin would have imbibed and accepted any of the filtered matter would have been minimal because of his desire and what he perceived was Hitler's desire at that moment, to execute faithfully the 1939 nonaggression pact. As Khrushchev later and no doubt correctly asserted, Stalin "would usually either ignore our reports or contradict our assessment of what the Germans were up to."[127] Clearly, Stalin's mind-set on this point facilitated the ability of Hitler (the deceiver) to misdirect the *Vozhd* (the deceived) into accepting the deception operations mounted by the Germans.[128]

The acceptance of German deception operations also had a corollary, namely, that the greatest caution had to be exercised in dealing with the German High Command. According to General Zhukov, Stalin thought that the German military "favoured a preventive war and [was] ready" to confront Hitler with a *fait accompli*.[129] Indeed, Marshal Nikolai Voronov tells us Stalin believed that if war came at all it would come because of "provocations" instigated by Fascist elements within the German military, and it was these very provocations that he feared most.[130] Stalin's earliest demonstration of his fear of the German High Command surfaced in September 1939 when he expressed "certain doubts" to Ambassador Schulenburg about whether at the appropriate moment the German military would honor the agreements regarding the partition of Poland. Assured by Schulenburg that this would be the case, Stalin responded that he had not the slightest doubt about Berlin's good faith, but he expressed his concern, "based on the well-known fact that all military men are loath to give up occupied territories."[131] Indicating his mistrust, Stalin concluded that there might be Germans who thought that Soviet Russia might forge a common front with a defeated Poland against Germany. Without hesitation, the military attaché, Köstring, interjected that the German military would do exactly what Hitler ordered.

To clear the air, Ribbentrop instructed Schulenburg to inform Stalin that the agreements he had negotiated with Moscow on Hitler's authority would, of course, be executed and that Berlin regarded these agreements "as the foundation stone of the new friendly relations" between Nazi Germany and Soviet Russia.[132] By the spring of 1941, Stalin was convinced that the Abwehr, the German Army's Intelligence Bureau, which he held was controlled by the generals, was interested in concocting evidence and mounting provocations to bring about a war between Germany and Russia.[133]

How Stalin latched onto this absurd notion is as much a mystery as is his notion that any German attack would be preceded by an ultimatum. If the history of the previous eight years of Nazi rule in Germany proved anything, it proved that the High Command's exercise of political power and its privileged position had collapsed, thanks to Hitler. Starting in the spring of 1934, Hitler had first suborned and then undermined the military through its agreement to support him as President Hindenburg's successor, provided it continued to be the only legitimate military force in the country. Ernst Roehm's competing storm troopers or Brownshirts, the Sturmabteilung, had to be suppressed, and they were. The expansion of the armed forces led to a marked increase in an officer corps that was either totally committed to Nazism or sympathetic to it. The removal of generals who were out of step with Hitler's desires[134] soon led to a command structure more to the liking of the Führer and his entourage, but, most important, one incapable of presenting Berlin with *faits accomplis,* contrary to what Stalin believed. Yet in the months preceding the German invasion, as we shall see, many a salient piece of intelligence data was dismissed by the *Vozhd* on the ground that it was provocation or disinformation planted either by the Germans, the British, the Americans, or someone else. In Stalin's warped world, to sift intelligence data one had to overcome the phantoms and shadows of fairy tales rather than follow sound tradecraft and statecraft criteria.

The Russians contended with one final, self-inflicted deception: both Stalin and the Russian military expected that any struggle with the Germans would follow the "classic" route.[135] For Stalin, any German attack would "be preceded by demands which could be discussed or at least by an ultimatum."[136] In view of Hitler's contempt for the tenets of international law, how Stalin latched onto this legalistic notion is unclear. In fact, if he had looked carefully, Stalin would have noted that, in form and certainly in substance, demands or ultimata, according to the norms of international law, were not a major consideration in Hitler's statecraft as his armies hurdled across Europe.

For the Russian military, the collision at the frontier would be "followed by the concentration and irruption of the main forces." This, of course, did not occur. The German attack came unannounced and was swift and massive. Stalin, like the Russian generals, had misread the dynamics of the Wehrmacht's "military doctrine in a tactical, operational" sense, despite the pattern of German military operations in Poland, France, the Low Countries, Denmark, Norway, Yugoslavia, and Greece. Nevertheless, Stalin's misreadings of deception operations, provocation, an ultimatum, and German military doctrine dovetailed neatly with the German deception operations themselves. Stalin's perceptions about the 1939 nonaggression pact and his belief that Hitler would continue to honor it as long as he was involved with the British in the West were major blunders. This stance by Stalin led to "misinterpretation, or the manipulation, even the discarding of intelligence." Indeed, in the military framework of analysis in which the *Vozhd* had locked himself, "accurate intelligence could very plausibly be regarded as 'disinformation.' "[137]

# 2

# War and Rumors of War

## First Inklings

It did not take long for the Russian embassy in Berlin to stumble across the German General Staff's planning of the invasion of Russia. Although unaware of the substantive discussions being held in the higher echelons of the German Army, the embassy correctly reported to Moscow in the summer of 1940 that the German Transport Ministry had been approached by the military and asked to furnish details on railway capability for troop movements heading east.[1] Concurrently, it also reported indications that Germany was preparing to attack Soviet Russia. This July warning by the military attaché, General Vasili Tupikov, inexplicably came to the attention of MI6, Britain's overseas intelligence service. In addition, a letter from an embassy informant pointed out that for over a week German military formations had been headed east. This information was seemingly supported by the military call-up ordered in Gdynia (Gottenhafen) of all Baltic Germans as well as of those Poles born between 1900 and 1921 who had opted for German nationality.[2]

Then on December 29, about eleven days after the Barbarossa directive was issued, the military attaché, General Tupikov, informed Moscow that a source had ascertained from very senior military circles that Hitler had ordered the launching of preparations for a war against Soviet Russia that would begin in March 1941.[3] The information had apparently been conveyed by Tupikov's source in an anonymous letter that summarized the German attack plan.[4] The next month, January 1941, was busy. It commenced with German violations of Russian air space over military installations in the Baltic-Murmansk area. Concurrently, General Kirill Meretskov, the chief of the General Staff, assured Admiral Nikolai Kuznetsov, the minister of marine and commander in chief of the navy, that he saw no signs of any intended German aggression and that the navy would be kept informed.[5] That same month in Berlin, Lieutenant Harro Schulze-Boysen of the Air Ministry, a member of the GRU's Rote Kapelle (Red Orchestra), whose code name was probably "Starshina," reported "precise information" on Barbarossa, including the "massive bombardments" scheduled for Leningrad, Kiev, and Vyborg (Viipuri) and the "number of divisions involved" in the invasion.[6] Even the comments of the Japanese naval attaché who had returned from a trip to Berlin and who reported that a German move toward the east was in the offing and that a German-Russian collision could not be excluded appear to have generated no interest, although his report was duly conveyed to Marshal Kliment Voroshilov.[7]

On February 7, Admiral Kuznetsov conveyed to Molotov a number of reports that German military technicians were arriving in the Bulgarian Black Sea ports of Varna and Burgas to install shore batteries and anti-aircraft weapons. The Germans were also active in Rumania, and intelligence reports divulged that there were German troop concentrations in Finland. Kuznetsov claims that after some "sharp" exchanges with Stalin, he became more frightened of the *Vozhd* and less swayed by "his infallibility."[8] Additional information during this month also arrived from the Berlin embassy and was made available by a printer who supplied a German-Russian phrase book that would soon appear in a huge printing. It contained a Latin alphabet transliteration from the Cyrillic script and suggestive expressions, such as "Where is the chairman of the collective farm?" "Are you a communist?" "Hands up!" and "Surrender!"[9]

Germany's penetration of the Balkans and the increasing troop concentrations in Poland and elsewhere were cause for unease and may partially account for Admiral Kuznetsov's query to Zhdanov during this period about whether he believed German moves along the border were a prelude to war. Zhdanov retorted that Berlin was incapable of fighting a two-front war and explained away the Luftwaffe's overflights and the mounting troop concentrations along the frontier with the somewhat sophomoric and simple explanation that these moves were merely "precautionary measures on Hitler's part or a means of applying psychological pressure."[10] In view of Zhdanov's close rapport with Stalin, it would be safe to say that his comments reflected the *Vozhd*'s views.

February also saw Moscow receive information containing the essence of the Barbarossa invasion plan, with the tentative date of the invasion given as May 20, although the source of this information is unclear. Further news was transmitted by General Tupikov in Berlin on March 9, reporting information from Belgrade that the German military had decided to cancel the invasion of England and to turn to the capture of the Ukraine and Baku in April–May. Also involved in this operation would be Bulgaria, Hungary, and Rumania. Tupikov's communication on March 14 appeared to buttress the information from Belgrade. He reported the remarks of a Wehrmacht major that Germany's plans had completely changed—Germany would head east against Russia and would seize her grain and energy resources. Once this was done, according to the major, Germany would be unbeatable, and the struggle could be continued against England and the United States. Military operations against Russia, General Tupikov predicted in a subsequent message, could be expected to begin anytime between mid-May and mid-June.[11]

Moreover, during this period the Abwehr, the Intelligence Bureau of the High Command of the Armed Forces, intensified its cross-border operational and tactical spying, restricting itself to ascertaining troop dispositions and frontier installations. The dispatched agents, however, were better trained than in the past.[12] During the period of January 1 to June 10, 1941, for example, 2,080 individuals were apprehended illegally crossing the border from the German side. Concurrently thirty-six of them were killed and twenty-five wounded when they resisted arrest. The agents of German intelligence who were arrested inside Russia carried portable wireless transmitters, small arms, and hand grenades.[13] Their apprehension, and thus their failure to report anything of substance, in part explains Germany's abysmal lack of intelligence about Russia's military capabilities and war potential.[14]

Understandably, these reports about German activities raised no suspicions in Moscow. Western Poland was under German occupation, and the rotation of troops was an unavoidable military and logistical problem. There seemed to be little solid evidence to support the Russian embassy's July 1940 assertion that there were indications that Germany was preparing an attack? The reported call-up in Gdynia was militarily sound, especially in view of British determination to continue the war after the fall of France and of Hitler's desire to invade the British Isles. Indeed, one could have expanded the argument to maintain that all the German measures reported by the intelligence and other services[15] were perfectly legitimate precautionary steps in view of the hardening British resistance and of the German need to cover its eastern flank.

In retrospect, we now know that the anonymous writer of the December 29, 1940, letter addressed to the Russian military attaché, General Tupikov, had come across some of the most important points touched upon in Hitler's December 18, 1940, Barbarossa directive. But who was this writer? What was the source for the information imparted, and was the writer reliable? Moreover, the writer's contention of a German attack in March 1941, at the end of a Russian winter, before the thaw and following quagmire, could only have been viewed as preposterous. Admiral Kuznetsov's worries were unwarranted—they clashed with Stalin's mind-set as it was reflected in Zhdanov's comments that German activities were only precautionary measures meant to increase the psychological pressure on Moscow. This framework of analysis would have also structured the examination of the report that there had been discussions in Bucharest about Rumania's participation in a German war against Soviet Russia and that the German invasion plans for Great Britain had been postponed until the war with Russia was concluded.[16]

Perhaps indicative of this psychological pressure were the Abwehr's intensified spying activities that were not strategic but rather focussed on operational and tactical matters, the type of ongoing intelligence activities that all military organizations are prone to conduct and thus not to be viewed as imminently hostile. Indeed, it could have been pointed out that from the beginning of September 1940 reconnaissance overflights by the Luftwaffe had ceased,[17] although they recommenced in early October.[18] This understanding view is seen in October 1940, when a German aircraft made a forced landing in Russian territory, the pilots and passengers, although arrested and accused by the NKVD of espionage, were released and returned to Germany on orders from Moscow.[19]

Harder to dismiss would have been the information from Schulze-Boysen. Although it dovetailed with subsequent information, it would have been attributed not to coincidence but rather to planted and erroneous information. The comments of the Japanese naval attaché would also have fallen into that category. The phrase book proved nothing. The German authorities, it could have been argued, had been lax in not having printed one already, in view of the Hobbesian world they were all living in. General Tupikov's reports of February and March were not based on a "controlled" source or on purloined documentation. His projections were more intuitive than based on solid evidence—what value, then, could be placed on the ruminations of a German major or on the remarks of others, voicing perhaps their own inclinations and desires?

In the summer of 1940, after the Russian embassy in Berlin had made its initial report to the Transport Ministry on the German military's approach, information that the Germans might strike in a direction other than Great Britain was received in London by Czech military intelligence of the government-in-exile. According to this August 22 report, an officer of the Oberkommando des Heeres (Army High Command) had divulged that the army's intelligence branch responsible for Russia had been expanded. Furthermore, counterintelligence activities against Russia by the Abwehr "were to be increased as a matter of urgency," and in Rumania the Abwehr "had been reinforced by specialists on the southern Ukraine, the Crimea and the Caucasus."[20] Additional information followed in October. The German High Command was occupied with new operations, the informant reported to Czech military intelligence, although he could offer no details. What he had ascertained was that the High Command had ordered the formation by May 1, 1941, of a military force of 180 divisions to be concentrated mainly in Poland.

Subsequent information from the Czech Resistance Intelligence left no doubt as to the target state. The Vienna Military Cartographic Institute was printing maps of Russian territory, it reported to London. Moreover, a Russian-speaking German nurse who worked for the Reichsprotektor's office in Prague had received instructions to be ready in the future to proceed to

Odessa in the Crimea and to select twenty other Russian-speaking nurses to work under her. Other officials of the Reichsprotektor's office had received similar orders and were to be prepared to proceed immediately to different Russian cities. The Abwehr was preparing for a Russian campaign. Since Berlin was far removed from the Russian border, the High Command had established near Warsaw a special intelligence unit whose acronym "AAA" stood for Amt-Ausland-Abwehr—Intelligence Office Abroad. Actually, AAA was the Abwehr's intelligence headquarters in the East.

In a November 1940 follow-up, the Czech Resistance Intelligence reported that in the previous month the Prague Abwehr had established special training courses in demolition, terror, and sabotage. The trainees were emigré Russians—whom, the British and Russians knew, the Germans were "engaging and inciting"—and the courses taught had sections based on nationality. For example, there was one course given in Ukrainian and another was being prepared to be given in Georgian. Some of the trainees, however, had been indiscreet and had been arrested by the secret state police, the Gestapo (Geheime Staatspolizei), when they boasted while drunk that the Germans had appointed them as occupation officials to be posted to Kiev, Kharkov, and as far east as Moscow.

Of course, any intelligence information is only as good as its source, and the Czech source had gilt-edged credentials. Code named A-54, he was in reality Paul Thummel, who had joined the Nazi party in the 1920s, but most important, he was a serving major in the Abwehr. Stationed in Dresden and subsequently in Prague following Germany's occupation of Czechoslovakia in March 1939, he was strategically placed to acquire the accurate and enormously important information that he supplied Czech military intelligence. Thummel was a classic "walk-in," someone who seemingly of his own volition contacts the intelligence service of another state and offers to supply sensitive political, military, and other information. Before the war, when he first contacted Czech military intelligence, his motives were mercenary, but thereafter, until he was unmasked by the Gestapo in 1942, Thummel never again asked for remuneration. President Eduard Beneš of Czechoslovakia had doubts about Thummel, and the thought that he was a double agent crossed his mind. However, the overwhelming evidence points to exactly the opposite conclusion. One can speculate on Thummel's motives in turning against the Nazis. Did he do it of his own volition, or was he encouraged and protected by someone else, for example, Admiral Wilhelm Canaris of the Abwehr, who was opposed to the Nazi regime? Since his execution in 1945, no adequate explanation has surfaced.[21]

The problem with Thummel's alleged reports and those of the Czech Resistance Intelligence is the possibility that they are confused versions of Thummel's report of August 22, 1940. Supporting this view is the lack of any evidence that the reports, subsequent to Thummel's report of August 22, were ever conveyed to the British by Czech military intelligence. Even if these reports were conveyed, as in the case of Thummel's report of August 22, for various reasons their significance went unappreciated or ignored in Whitehall.

Since it can be argued that the British "paid too little attention" to Thummel's report of August 22, it is possible and probable that Czech military intelligence decided to convey subsequent reports about anti-Russian German activities directly to Moscow, where, as we shall see, unidentified Czech intelligence reports were sent.[22] This procedure is probable because by the autumn of 1940 the cooperation between Czech military intelligence and its Russian counterpart, which had been severed by the events of 1938–1939, was re-established.

Some of the information corraled by Czech military intelligence reached Moscow either via London or via Prague and was also made available to other countries if their interests were affected, for example, Switzerland[23] and Yugoslavia.[24] Indeed Beneš and Ivan Maisky, the Russian ambassador in London have admitted that, although there were no diplomatic relations between their two states, they nevertheless maintained informal and unofficial contacts.[25] This association was known to the British.[26] According to Maisky, whom the Foreign Office's Permanent Under Secretary Sir Alexander Cadogan characterized as a "crook,"[27] Beneš possessed "very valuable information about the situation in Germany and Central Europe which he willingly shared with me."[28]

Unsuccessfully, Beneš attempted in May–June 1940—at the height of the German victories in Europe—to re-establish contact with Moscow that had been broken in December 1939.[29] By the autumn of 1940, however, the Russian stance toward the government-in-exile had changed. In October, Colonel Heliodor Pika, following a dramatic escape from the Gestapo in Bucharest, where he had served as a member of Czech military intelligence, had established a new intelligence station in Istanbul. Upon his arrival in Turkey, he was contacted by the Russians, who requested "secret collaboration" between Czech and Russian military intelligence against Germany. It would be safe to suggest that the Russian agents who approached Pika in Istanbul were from the GRU. That a similar proposal for collaboration was echoed by the Russian consulate in Prague to the Czech underground is suggested by feelers put out in midsummer by the government-in-exile.

Preliminary discussions on collaboration started in December in London between Colonel František Moravec, the director of Czech military intelligence, and a representative of Russian intelligence code-named "Dorn," who wanted to discuss an exchange of military intelligence, especially of information revealing the location of German forces in Finland, Norway, Poland, and Rumania. Although the negotiations went smoothly, Moravec recommended to Beneš that the government-in-exile not act until the "military situation in the East was clarified." The exchanges dragged on until the spring of 1941 and were successfully concluded when reports to Czech military intelligence from "Germany left no doubt" that Soviet Russia would be attacked.[30]

Beneš then went through the motions. He wanted to appoint a "military agent" to the Russian capital, Beneš told the British in mid–March 1941. He thought such an appointment would benefit not only the Czechs but also the British, although Moravec had his misgivings about any such appointment. Beneš proposed that Pika be appointed. The colonel has been described as a "remarkable man," an experienced officer fluent in Russian, who had made a good impression in the Foreign Office and "was on excellent terms with the Russian military." The appointment would take place if Moscow did not restrict Pika's movements and his right to send coded messages.[31]

The British embassy in Moscow thought the Russians might agree to such arrangements and saw no objections in Beneš's approaching them with his proposal. Supposedly after discussions with the government-in-exile, the Russians agreed to accept Pika. As Beneš tells us, from October 1940 until April 1941, when Pika went to Moscow, the colonel was in "permanent contact" with the Russians. The appointment of Pika proved to be a wise one. In September 1941, following the German invasion, the Foreign Office thought his information was the "best and most objective of any" received from Russia. Prescient, Pika had had misgivings about his Moscow assignment, but like a good officer he followed his orders. It cost him his life.[32]

The Russian approach to Colonel Pika in Istanbul made sense, for during the interwar period Czech military intelligence had been built up to be one of Europe's finest and most professional intelligence services by Colonel Moravec, an outstanding intelligence officer but not one without foibles.[33] In fact, in the late 1930s, the Abwehr ranked Czech military intelligence first as a service whose activity it considered very dangerous to Nazi Germany's national interests.[34]

Because it is a cardinal principle in the tradecraft of intelligence never to divulge one's sources and methods, it would be very safe to say that the Czechs, in conveying intelligence data to Moscow, would not have identified their sources, especially Thummel. The available evidence shows that the question of whether Moscow did or did not receive the pertinent information from the Czechs of an upcoming German attack against Russia is not open to discussion. Indeed, in 1966 Marshal Semyon Timoshenko, who was minister of defense in 1940–1941, recalled that among the reports he received from the military attaché in London at that time was data from Czech military intelligence. He admitted that some of the Czech information appeared "incredible[,] almost provocative," but re-examination of this data and the passage of time had shown that "for the most part it involved truthful and amazingly accurate information."[35]

One of the pieces of information that Timoshenko might have been alluding to was a report from Thummel, conveyed a week after Hitler had issued the Barbarossa directive, that Russia would be attacked by mid–May 1941.[36] This report dovetailed, as we have seen, with the report filed about the same time by the Russian military attaché, General Tupikov, in Berlin. The dismissal of both reports would have been justified on the grounds that the matching reports were not the result of coincidence but planted information.

If Timoshenko's admission was not enough, it appears that in February 1941 at the latest, Thummel was in touch on several occasions with the Czech Kurt Beer, who also went by the name Kurt Konrad. Ostensibly Beer was employed as a press official in the Russian consulate in Prague. In reality, he was a prominent Marxist historian and, before the German occupation of Czechoslovakia, the editor of the Communist party organ, *Rude Pravo*.[37] How Beer knew about Thummel is unknown. He might have been alerted to Thummel by a Communist source within the Czech resistance or, as we shall see, by a possible Communist source within Czech military intelligence in London. Possibly Thummel himself might have approached Beer because Thummel was uneasy that the information he had supplied had produced no reaction in Moscow and feared that perhaps Czech military intelligence had never conveyed it.

No, the only question open to discussion is how Moscow perceived the information that the Czechs conveyed. The lines of communication established by Beneš through Ambassador Maisky and by Moravec through Colonel Pika, in Istanbul and later in Moscow, were not the first Czech-Russian collaboration on intelligence matters pertaining to Germany. As early as the summer of 1936, Colonel Moravec had been directed by the Czech authorities to establish contact and to coordinate activities with Russian military intelligence. Accordingly, he had led a group of his officers on a journey through Rumania to Moscow to confer with the director of the GRU, General Seman Uritsky.

During this visit, Czech authorities also called on Marshal Mikhail Tukhachevsky, the chief of the General Staff. The discussions with Uritsky, which lasted a week, led Colonel Moravec to conclude that the Russians were ignorant of military developments in Hitler's Germany. The arrangement agreed upon was that a mixed Czech-Russian military intelligence post would be constituted in Prague. The single Russian assigned to Czechoslovakia would be serviced by personnel supplied by Moravec's organization. This Russian would work under Czech surveillance and direction. His contacts would be known to the Czechs, and the information acquired by him would be shared with Prague. Lastly, each operation would have to be approved by Moravec's organization, and the intelligence post would be entirely under its control, no doubt to make sure that the Russian's activities were targeted only against Nazi Germany.

In the autumn of 1936, the arrangement was implemented when the first GRU officer arrived in Prague. Further collaboration followed when Moravec's people helped obtain Czech passports for Russian pilots and tank crews in transit through Austria, Switzerland, and southern France on their way to Spain to fight in the civil war. A second Czech-Russian intelligence conference was held in Prague in 1937, but two important Russian participants of the 1936 one were not present. In the interim, Uritsky and Tukhachevsky, among countless others, had been liquidated in the purges.[38]

Apparently during this period, Polish counterintelligence often noticed the director of the GRU, protected by a diplomatic passport, crossing Poland on his way to Czechoslovakia. This director was probably General Yan Berzin, who both preceded and succeeded Uritsky in the post. But Warsaw's request for permission to establish an intelligence station in Czechoslovakia targeted against Russia was rejected by Prague.[39] Acceding to the request might have compromised Prague's arrangements with Moscow.

The following year, 1938, thanks to information supplied by Thummel, German agents spying against Russia in Estonia, Finland, and Latvia were identified, and Moscow was soon alerted to these agents by Moravec's organization. In late July 1940, additional information from Thummel about German espionage against Russia was passed by Moravec's people in occupied Prague to Beer, whom we have already met, and through him the information passed to a member of the Russian consulate in Prague, Leonid Ivanovich Mokhov, code-named Vana. Whether Mokhov's affiliation was NKVD or GRU is unknown. When Czech Resistance Intelligence informed Moravec in London that they were collaborating with Beer, the Czech government-in-exile admonished them not to share information from Thummel with anyone else.[40] Based on intelligence tradecraft, this was a wise admonition.

The dismemberment of Czechoslovakia in the autumn of 1938 following the Munich settlement had led to a withering of the collaboration between the GRU and Czech military intelligence. Moscow's disengagement from Prague became final with the German invasion of the rump Czech state in mid–March 1939 and the signing of the Ribbentrop-Molotov nonaggression pact six months later. The establishment in March 1939 of the German protectorate over Bohemia and Moravia, however, did not lead to the dissolution of Moravec's intelligence organization. At the very moment German troops entered the rump Czech state, Moravec and a small select group of his officers departed for London by air, with British concurrence and assistance, taking with them their operating funds, archives, and other materials. Beneš considered their presence in London the government-in-exile's "most important asset."[41]

The British desire to establish some sort of working relationship with Czech military intelligence is understandable, for Moravec left behind in Czechoslovakia an extensive and well-knit underground intelligence network. This is reflected in Beneš's observation in early 1941 that during the previous year 14,000 "filed and registered messages" had passed between Prague and the government-in-exile.[42] This traffic entailed the encryption and decryption of about 38 messages each day, a heavy daily workload for Beneš's small staff. It is possible that the message traffic was less than Beneš claimed and that he "deliberately exaggerated" the volume of traffic with the "underground to improve his bargaining position with his reluctant allies."[43]

The government-in-exile's arrangement with Whitehall was that Moravec's organization and the British would exchange intelligence information acquired by their respective agents. In addition, the British would render the Czechs technical assistance, including preparing false documentation. Moravec would have personal contact with the chiefs of the British intelligence and with its security organizations, MI5, which deals with Britain's internal security, and MI6. Liaison officers from these intelligence services and from the War Office were assigned to Czech military intelligence. MI6's Claude Dansey was responsible for operations. Finally, on March 14, 1940, the arrangements were topped off by a British loan of £50,000 sterling to supplement the operating funds that Czech military intelligence had brought to London during its flight from Prague the previous year.

In the spring of 1939, Russian intelligence in London soon re-established contact with Moravec. Moscow, he was told, wished to continue the intelligence collaboration against Berlin. He responded that while he would very much like to cooperate, he had given priority to the British, who had assisted him at the crucial hour. Several weeks later, Colonel Ivan Chernyi, the Russian air attaché, called on Moravec and invited him to dinner. After consulting the British, he accepted the invitation, but the dinner proved to be merely a social occasion. Though Moravec reciprocated Chernyi's hospitality, he never heard from him again,[44] and contact with the GRU was not formally re-established, as we have seen, until Colonel Pika arrived in Istanbul in the autumn of 1940.

Moravec also established contact with the NKVD by the autumn of 1941 at the earliest, as recently released NKVD archival material shows us. His code name was "Accountant," and his association with Moscow was no doubt struck to acquire Russian support for the Czech Resistance. To this end, he supplied information to the NKVD acquired by his own organization from Abwehr channels and also from MI6.[45] Swapping information in wartime with an ally about enemy intelligence activities is standard practice in intelligence tradecraft, but making available intelligence information from an ally without permission, as in the case of the information from MI6, is definitely not standard. Moravec's vast experience in intelligence work allows him no excuse for his action except perhaps the overriding claim: "reasons of state."

Why did Moscow ignore the information about the upcoming German invasion supplied by Beneš and Moravec? One would think that the Russians would have been receptive to this information in view of Beneš's proven friendliness and his desire to maintain close relations with Moscow, as well as of the collaboration and the information offered to the GRU by Moravec and his officers. Beneš's attitude toward Moscow has even moved one former high-level British intelligence officer to label him a "Soviet stooge,"[46] which of course he was not. If anything, he was a dupe.

The explanation of Moscow's negative stance can probably be discerned in no single factor. Certainly Beneš's and Moravec's protection of Czech sources, especially of Thummel, although understandable to the Russians as sound tradecraft, must have generated shadows of doubt. To the Russians, then and now, there is no substitute for purloined documentation.[47] Sensitive to possible deception operations, having conducted them so successfully against others, Moscow would have perceived the Czech information about Germany as provocative, improbable, and without substantiating documentation, certainly unproven.

Then there were other considerations. In the period before the outbreak of the war, Beneš's presence in London depended on the grudging hospitality and largess of the British authorities. Indeed, the operations of Czech military intelligence were made possible only by the acquiescence and active cooperation of the British intelligence and security services. Moreover, Colonels Moravec and Pika, but especially the former,[48] were less than enamored by Stalin's regime. What value, Moscow must have been asked, could be placed on the veracity of anything these men said or conveyed? In view of Stalin's attitude toward the whole question and the nature of the leadership in his intelligence services, Beneš and certainly Moravec would have been perceived as being under British "control." Their information to Moscow would have been viewed as "tainted" and cleverly "planted" by the British in order, at the minimum, to sour relations between Berlin and Moscow, and possibly to provoke a conflagration between the two dictatorships. The Czechs, the argument would have been, were being used to cause bad blood, to lead Moscow to align itself with London, and thus to help pull British chestnuts out of the fire.

In addition, Beneš's track record in intelligence matters did not inspire great confidence. In 1935–1936 it is alleged that Reinhard Heydrich, the director of the Sicherheitsdienst-Ausland (Security Service Abroad), acquired information that Marshal Tukhachevsky was plotting with the German General Staff against Stalin's regime. It is open to debate whether this information was planted on Heydrich by Stalin through Nikolai Skoblin, the White Czarist general and double agent, whether Heydrich merely wished to use what he knew was false information to curb the German military and simultaneously deliver a damaging blow to the Red Army's High Command, or whether he ordered the General Staff's files rifled to secure documentation about Tukhachevsky. What is not open to debate is that, with the assistance of White Russian emigrés, documentation was forged by Heydrich's organization to validate the charges against Tukhachevsky and then was fed back to Moscow through Beneš.

In a circuitous manner over a ten-month period, contact with Stalin was then established by the Sicherheitsdienst-Ausland through Beneš. The conduit to Beneš was primarily the German agent *cum* journalist, Carl Wittig, whose career in the great game extended into the postwar period. Beneš, however, appears to have made no attempt to consult or to check with Moravec or with any other part of the Czech intelligence community, except the intelligence section of the Foreign Ministry, about the alleged Tukhachevsky conspiracy. The forged documentation was then passed on by Beneš to Moscow. Whether Stalin had provoked the whole affair was not the point. What was important was that Beneš had accepted at face value the information conveyed to him by the Sicherheitsdienst-Ausland about Tukhachevsky, then conveyed the forged documentation to Stalin, but made no move to consult either Moravec or others in the Czech intelligence community (excluding the Foreign Ministry), about the allegations made against the marshal. True enough, Beneš's friendliness to Moscow had been tested and not found wanting, but this test could have generated little faith in his powers of discernment,[49] especially if Stalin had played no role in the affair, and if he subsequently learned that Tukhachevsky's death and the deaths of many others had been needless and could be traced to Heydrich.

There is one last point: the postwar contention made by some Czechs that Communist sympathizers in Moravec's London organization maintained contact with Moscow during the war[50] might go far to explain how Beer and Thummel established contact by February 1941. If this contention were true, and in view of the information now available the possibility is not remote,[51] it would also explain why the Russians never again contacted Moravec after his dinners with Colonel Chernyi, the air attaché, until they approached Colonel Pika in Istanbul in the autumn of 1940. But any information imparted by Thummel to Beer in early 1941, which might have redressed the balance and given credence to the intelligence conveyed by Beneš, Moravec and others, was overshadowed by Stalin's perceptions of the international setting, and especially by his arrangements with Germany under the 1939 nonaggression pact. Added to German deception operations targeted against the Russians, these factors caused the communist leadership, especially Stalin, to construe incoming intelligence information about a German invasion as British-inspired and false, regardless of its source. This Russian aversion to anti-German information was buttressed by their own innate suspicions, policy stances, and ideological preferences.

## Meets in a Cinema

Despite the precautions taken to insure the secrecy of the Barbarossa directive, a major break in security soon developed. In Berlin, the American commercial attaché, Sam E. Woods, had developed an excellent source. Woods, described as a "genial extrovert whose grasp of world politics and history was not striking," appeared to those "who knew him and liked him the last man in the American Embassy likely to have come by such crucial intelligence."[52] Woods, however, was more astute in intelligence matters than his colleagues credited him to be.[53] By prearrangement, Woods would sit alongside his source in a darkened Berlin cinema, and the source would then slip the pertinent notes into Woods's pocket.[54] It is possible that Woods's source also conveyed his information to the anti-Nazi Eduard Schulte, chief executive officer of the leading mining firm, Giesche. Schulte, who warned the Polish government-in-exile and the Swiss of Barbarossa, was also the first person to warn the West of Hitler's genocidal policy against the Jews.[55]

It has been incorrectly claimed that Woods's source was the German career diplomat, Hans Heinrich Herwarth von Bittenfeld, who had been closely associated with his American counterparts, Charles "Chip" Bohlen, George Kennan, and others, when he had served as second secretary in the German embassy in Moscow in the 1930s. It is alleged that, commencing in August 1940, Herwarth von Bittenfeld "informed Woods in general terms" of Hitler's conferences with the military about the Russian invasion. During September Herwarth von Bittenfeld's "information became increasingly specific."[56] He is said to have assured Woods that the ongoing preparations for Sea Lion, the invasion of Great Britain, were a deception. Likewise, he is supposed to have made the claim that the Luftwaffe raids against Great Britain were only a blind for Hitler's plans and arrangements for a swift and massive attack against Russia. Measures to administer Russia once it was occupied had been drawn up, and ruble banknotes had been printed. It is asserted that it was only in early January and certainly no later than mid-February 1941 that Herwarth von Bittenfeld supplied, thanks to a friend in the High Command of the Armed Forces, details of what was probably the Barbarossa directive or possibly the minutes of Hitler's meeting in early January 1941 with the military leadership. These minutes included the directive's strategic operational plan of a three-pronged attack on Russia and the stipulation that all planning for the invasion was to be completed by the spring of 1941.[57]

Although Herwarth von Bittenfeld admitted to a "number of far-reaching conversations" with Woods, he denied the subsequent "legends" that developed about his "supposed links with American intelligence." He granted he had done favors for the Americans in Moscow in the 1930s and that his "reports to Woods may have been useful," but he could not flatter himself that he had "played the cloak-and-dagger role assigned" to him after the events had actually occurred.[58] Indeed, Herwarth von Bittenfeld points out that he was posted with his regiment in France or Poland during most of the period when Woods was meeting his source.[59]

Herwarth von Bittenfeld's contention that he was not Woods's source can be confirmed both tangentially and directly. For example, because Woods's source considered the United States and Great Britain his "friends,"[60] he conveyed data on December 27, 1940. These data arrived in Washington a few days later,[61] probably by coded message, well before the alleged information dealing with the German invasion was supplied by Herwarth von Bittenfeld in early 1941. In addition, Secretary of State Cordell Hull subsequently admitted that "Woods had a German friend who, though an enemy of the Nazis, was closely connected with the Reich ministries, the Reichsbank and high Party members."[62] Herwarth von Bittenfeld was certainly an anti-Nazi, but he had none of the associations or contacts that Hull credited to Woods's source. It was years later that "Chip" Bohlen would identify Woods's source[63] as an individual unknown to Herwarth von Bittenfeld, someone to whom we shall turn presently.

The problem with Woods's information, however, was that it "was so circumstantial" that Hull believed it had been planted on Woods by the Germans.[64] Hull's attitude was not far different from that of the military attaché in Berlin whose report about Woods's information reached the War Department on February 19, 1941, almost eight weeks after Woods had been contacted. In evaluating the information, Colonel B. R. Peyton noted that the numerous journalists, diplomats, and military attachés in Berlin explained how easy it was to trip over rumors. When these rumors were mixed with those planted by the Germans, things became very complicated. Peyton had been reticent to accept rumors not backed by substance as experience had taught his office that "mere rumors do not furnish much real military information, and generally are incorrect." Although he forwarded the information from Woods's source, Colonel Peyton did not give it "too much credence."[65]

The War Department required, however, that a report of this nature discuss the source and his degree of reliability. Peyton therefore explained that the information was "voluntarily given" to an embassy official—for security reasons Woods's name was not invoked—by a source who in the past had been a high official in the Weimar Republic. The source was reported to head a secret organization opposed to the "aims and methods of the Nazi Party."[66] Previous information from the source had proved to be correct, and the embassy official vouched for him. The source was committed to overthrowing the Nazis. There was no regular contact with the source, and he was not personally known to Peyton. The colonel's most important comment was saved for the end: there was the possibility that the source's information, he cautioned, "may be a 'plant.' "[67]

The substance of the report may also have contributed to Hull's attitude. In its ten single-spaced pages revealing some of the most secret political and military plans of Nazi Germany, about a page and a quarter under the subsection "The Downfall of Soviet Russia as a Military and Political Aim" was reserved for a discussion of Russia. As a disguise and for obvious security reasons, it postulated that a two-front war was to be "avoided at all costs." The step-by-step measures, especially military preparations, that Germany would take to destroy Soviet Russia were then spelled out and were to culminate in the "destruction of the Red Army, its capture and disarmament." Following the army's destruction, there was to be a "rigorous liquidation of Bolshevism, all its political and other institutions, and, in particular, the 'extermination' of its leaders by the SS," the Schutzstaffel, the elite guard of the Nazi party.[68]

In view of the actions committed by the Nazis during the course of the

Second World War, we now know that this report was no idle threat and certainly was not planted disinformation to influence America's leadership. Unfortunately, the governing elite in Washington, like Hull, were men of a different and gentler age, whose political culture and societal values made it impossible for them to fathom so monstrous an evil as the wholesale physical liquidation of thousands of one's foreign political opponents.

In line with his suspicions, Hull conveyed Woods's report to J. Edgar Hoover, the director of the Federal Bureau of Investigation (FBI), and asked for his opinion. Hoover thought the information was genuine. Since Woods had noted that a "prominent German exile" living in the United States could confirm the "standing and contacts of the source," Hull instructed Breckinridge Long, assistant secretary of state, to contact the exiled German.[69]

From the evidence available, however, the exiled German was not contacted immediately, but only after additional information and documentation were supplied by Woods's source in the following weeks. On this point, at least, Hull's memory appears to have gone astray. With Woods's important data in hand, Hull discussed the matter with President Roosevelt. The consensus was that Sumner Welles, the under secretary, should immediately broach the matter with Ambassador Umansky.[70] He did so in mid or late January 1941.[71] When Welles informed Umansky of the American information, naturally without divulging the source, Umansky "turned white." He was "silent for a moment" and then merely noted that he realized the gravity of Welles's message, that his government would be grateful for Welles's confidence, and that he would inform it immediately of their conversation.[72]

However, Umansky, who was anti-American and followed faithfully his master's predilections about the 1939 nonaggression pact and Nazi-Communist collaboration,[73] was too clever by half. He promptly conveyed, as the State Department probably ascertained via the FBI, Welles's information to Hans Thomsen, the chargé d'affaires of the German embassy in Washington.[74] It is unknown whether Thomsen in turn conveyed to Berlin this startling breach in German security about the planning of Barbarossa. The conventional wisdom that in the ongoing Umansky-Thomsen conversations Umansky gave Thomsen "only routine information"[75] about Russian-American discussions is clearly not true.

Certainly by the summer of 1940, the FBI had alerted President Roosevelt, Hull, and Welles to the meetings between Umansky and Thomsen. In mid-September Welles in turn alerted Henry Morgenthau, Jr., the secretary of the treasury. Welles did not doubt that the Germans would inform the Japanese of any information they obtained.[76] Only weeks before Welles met with Umansky the FBI reiterated to President Roosevelt that the Russian kept Thomsen "advised on all moves" he made with the American government.[77] Since Welles had not discussed with Umansky the source of his information. Woods's Berlin source was not compromised.[78] The fact was that during this period Russian-German collaboration on intelligence matters was close. As Adolf Berle, the assistant secretary of state, noted to President Roosevelt's adviser and assistant, Harry Hopkins, Umansky "regularly interchanged espionage reports with the Germans" before the attack on June 22.[79] Hoover likewise pointed out that Umansky and Thomsen conferred as late as Thursday, June 19, or Friday, June 20.[80] Umansky's activities and his hostility to his host country go far to explain his ineffectiveness and proved him to be more of a liability than an asset in Washington, as Moscow, in time, was to learn.[81]

By the second week of February 1941, almost a month after the Welles-Umansky conversation, Woods forwarded to Washington additional information from his Berlin source.[82] The document, supposedly submitted to Hitler in early January, was a two-part report about future economic and financial questions. Its most important disclosure was of the German intention to attack Russia as soon as England was conquered—a deceptive comment included in the report, no doubt to throw anyone off the invasion scent. Nevertheless, Assistant Secretary of State Breckinridge Long thought the report might be "used to incite Russia against Germany." The important point was to have the report verified, something only one man in the United States could do "because of his former connections"; he would be asked to come to Washington to examine the report.[83]

On the morning of March 1, however, before any meeting could be arranged, Hull contacted Laurence Steinhardt, the ambassador in Moscow. He was described by one of his ambassadorial counterparts as " 'the best consul who ever came to Moscow.' "[84] Unlike the views of his immediate predecessor, Joseph E. Davies, Steinhardt's views of Stalin and the ruling Communist elite were not based on a misplaced and naive idealism. Hull instructed Steinhardt to approach Molotov and alert him to the information that had come into Washington's possession. It appeared that the planned German attack, Hull observed, would be contingent upon England's ability, supported by America's endeavor, "to oppose not only the military strength but also the economic efforts of Germany."[85] That afternoon Welles again raised the issue of the German invasion with Umansky.[86] Understandably, Hull's desire to have Steinhardt approach Molotov was no doubt triggered by Moscow's long silence and by the suspicion that the anti-American Umansky may have appended his January message to Moscow with editorial comments denigrating the American information and Welles's warning.

Steinhardt, who was not enamored of the host government, correctly pointed out that Moscow's "cynical reaction" to Hull's proposed step "would lead it to regard the gesture as neither sincere nor independent." His call on Molotov might end up as a *Tass* agency news story and, notwithstanding any prior assurances, be imparted to the Germans. Moreover, if the Russians lacked similar information "tending to confirm our information regarding [a] German attack," and especially if subsequent events failed to confirm Welles's warning, Washington's action would be regarded as "having been merely an attempt to drive a wedge between the Soviet Union and Germany, at British instigation." Conversely, the confirmation by Washington's warning of information already in Moscow's possession might lead to one or more consequences. It might accelerate a Russian-Japanese political settlement, far beyond any settlement previously contemplated by Moscow. It might propel Moscow to examine a deal with Berlin at Ankara's expense. It might move Moscow to consider occupying Finland in view of the large German troop concentrations in Norway. It might be invoked to justify new demands by Moscow on Washington for additional concessions and assistance. Lastly, it might speed up Moscow's assistance to Berlin in an attempt to fend off or postpone any German invasion. Hull appreciated Steinhardt's hardheaded arguments and assured him that the State Department deferred to his judgment in matters of this nature.[87] The approach to Steinhardt had led nowhere, but it might well explain Mrs. Steinhardt's acute desire to learn from Ambassador Schulenburg whether it was true that a German-Russian conflict was in the offing. Schulenburg, uninformed of the momentous decision taken by Hitler to invade Russia, honestly assured her that this was not the case.[88]

In Washington, Assistant Secretary of State Long set the wheels in motion to invite to the nation's capital the one person in the United States mentioned by Woods as capable of vouching for the source and of verifying the documents that had been conveyed. The gentleman in question was no less a figure than Heinrich Brüning, who was teaching at Harvard University and who, unlike his successors, Franz von Papen and General Kurt von Schleicher, was the last Chancellor of the Weimar Republic committed to democratic government. In February, much to Brüning's surprise, he was invited to give a talk at the Brookings Institution. On March 6, before the lecture, a dinner was held at which Long was present. When he asked whether they could have a private conversation on the following day, Brüning agreed.

When they met, Long showed Brüning a bundle of documents and asked him for his opinion. Brüning recognized them as similar to reports that he had received previously through Woods from the economist and financial expert, Erwin Respondek. Brüning claimed that they reflected the skeptical view General Friedrich Fromm and his staff held of the armament industry. Brüning vouched for Respondek. He had known him a long time and described him as "good and highly reliable," although he thought Respondek tended to be pessimistic. Years later Brüning observed that the documentation mentioned by Hull in his memoirs was not discussed.[89]

Hull admitted that the initial information from Woods's source was somewhat circumstantial, based, as it was, on various conversations, and this was confirmed by Colonel Peyton's first report, which reached the War Department on February 19. This admission explains why the initial material sent by Woods was not submitted to Brüning.[90] Without question, Erwin Respondek was Woods's source. Brüning's comments are confirmed by Bohlen's postwar admission.[91] Moreover, as Hull observed, the source was anti-Nazi and had close contacts with different ministries, the Reichsbank, and senior Nazi party members. Respondek fits the profile, especially in his association with General Fromm. Respondek had been a member of the Reichstag (1932–1933), representing the Deutsche Zentrumspartei (German Center party) just before Hitler's assumption of power. He had served in the Finance Ministry (1917–1925) and at different periods had held important economic and financial positions inside the government and in the private sector.[92]

Even before the Brüning-Long encounter and in the days that followed, additional documents were furnished by Respondek through Woods; by March 13, Washington had three documents about Germany's oil and raw material needs, as well as finance and labor questions.[93] The new documentation was brought to President Roosevelt's attention, and steps were taken to refer the materials to the British.[94] The hint was soon dropped to Ambassador, Lord Halifax. He reported on March 7 to London that a "prominent" State Department official, experienced in German-Russian relations, had opined that recent exaggerations by Berlin and "certain other indications" had given this official the impression that the German motive "might be to build up a case vis-a-vis their own public opinion that Great Britain was already virtually finished in order that Germany might proceed to attack [the] Soviet Union without causing undue alarm in Germany." A perceptive member of the Foreign Office underlined the words about a possible German invasion of Russia.[95]

About the third week of March, a fourth document arrived from Respondek through Woods. Unlike the previous materials, the first half was "probably not a copy of a document but a relation of information of a military character as to present naval, land and air warfare plans," while the second half was a resumé of Germany's "psychological condition and state of morale." It proved to be a "very important communication." It envisaged a war against Russia. Because it referred to poison gas and a new floating mine, it appeared as if it might have been planted in Washington's hands. The document aroused the suspicion that it was conveyed with the intention of deterring American activities. At the same time, some of the statements in the document could be checked and proved reasonable. To be sure of the document's authenticity, the FBI was given all four documents so that the paper, typewriter, and other materials used in creating the fourth one could be compared forensically to those of the previous three. The examination proved, Long noted in his diary, that the four documents "came from the same hand, though the hand is unknown here." Since he had not had time to check the fourth document with Brüning, he arranged for another meeting. When Long gave the latest document to General Sherman Miles, who was in command of G-2, Military Intelligence, Miles opined that it "was the most important document that had been received by the Army from the State Department in his recollection."[96]

The documentation was then given to Lord Halifax and forwarded to the Foreign Office on March 21, but whether Woods's initial report of late December 1940 was also included is unclear.[97] If the report was given, it was undoubtedly in "sanitized" form to protect the source of the information. Concurrently, on the afternoon of March 20, Welles had his third and last conversation with Umansky on the question. The ambassador asked if Welles had further information confirming Washington's belief that Germany was planning to invade Russia. Welles responded that he had received confirmatory data. Nothing more was said.[98]

The data that Welles alluded to were from multiple sources. First, of course, there were the four documents unknown to Umansky supplied by Respondek through Woods, and the fourth document in particular, which envisaged a war with Soviet Russia. Moreover, in an operation code-named "Magic," cryptologists of the Army's Signal Intelligence Service had unraveled Japan's highest level, top secret diplomatic code "Purple," and on March 14, about a week before the interview with Umansky, they decrypted a message from the Japanese embassy in Moscow directed to Foreign Minister Yosuke Matsuoka. Translated on the 19th, the message pointed out that German-Russian relations had "changed considerably very recently" because of events in the Balkans.[99] To Welles, this Japanese observation from Moscow meshed neatly with the information initially sent by Woods in December 1940 and with the four documents conveyed by Respondek through Woods, as well as with the information Kimon Diamantopoulos, the Greek minister, supplied to Welles the day before Welles's interview with Umansky.

In his memorandum, Diamantopoulos divulged that Athens had learned from its diplomatic mission in Moscow that the Swedish minister in Berlin had had indications that Germany would invade Russia. What was "worthy of attention," the memorandum observed, was that Stockholm had received similar information from its legations in Bucharest and Helsinki.[100] Somewhat similar information had been conveyed to the Foreign Office a week before by the Greek minister in London.[101] The gist of the Swedish minister's information in Berlin was divulged to Ambassador Steinhardt in Moscow by his Swedish counterpart and reached Washington on March 25.[102] Unknown to Welles, the Greek Foreign Ministry had ascertained that an apparent source of the Swedish minister in Berlin was General Erhard Milch, the Luftwaffe's inspector general.[103] Another Swedish source was the anti-Nazi Mayor of Leipzig, Carl Goerdeler, who no doubt got his information from the army's former chief of staff, General Ludwig Beck, with whom he was closely associated. Beck, like Goerdeler, lost his life in the unsuccessful attempt to assassinate Hitler in July 1944. When Gunnar Hagglof, who dealt with German matters in the Swedish Foreign Ministry, whispered to the Russian minister in Stockholm, Alexandra Kollontai, that what he had recently seen in Berlin indicated that Germany was preparing itself for an invasion of Russia, Kollontai admonished him with tears in her eyes. He had no right to say this to her, she remarked, and she had no right to listen to him. Obviously, as Hagglof points out, Moscow or the *Vozhd* himself had issued strict instructions that rumors of a German invasion should be disregarded or repudiated.[104] Hagglof repeated the probability of a German attack to the Americans in Stockholm.[105]

During this period the British minister in Budapest, Sir Owen O'Malley, reported that the naval attaché had been informed by Admiral Miklós Horthy, the regent, that based on his information sizeable German troop formations were now on Russia's frontier and contemplated the "invasion of the Soviet Union and the Baltic States."[106] His ambassadorial counterpart in Stockholm, Sir Victor Mallet, observed that it was "thought most probable" that the report of a German invasion of Russia was merely another "phase of the war of nerves" and that Berlin would not, at this stage, provoke a two-front war.[107] Stalin, as we have seen, thought the same thing. Sir Alexander Cadogan, the Foreign Office's permanent under secretary, shared this view. Nothing received by the Foreign Office convinced him otherwise. Mallet's report, for example, was "just anonymous talk" most likely disseminated by the Germans, he penned, while Halifax's report of March 7 was founded on the intuition of an important State Department official and was not a "very sure guide.". Days later, he observed that London would only be "playing" Berlin's game by passing on to the Russians any German threats. In fact, the "Germans probably 'plant' them in Moscow direct, anyhow," he concluded.[108]

On April 3, Assistant Secretary of State Long and Brüning met for a second time to examine the documents that Respondek had conveyed through Woods.[109] Brüning explained the provenance of the first three documents and vouched for their authenticity. Brüning thought the fourth document, which envisaged a war against Russia, was the "genuine and honest expressions of opinion of a man who has had many years of experience in analyzing information which he himself compiled, and which were prepared for presentation" to Woods who received them.[110] He later noted to Long that comparing the military and political views in the fourth report "would [make it] seem that the author hears a lot of discussion going on in the highest places." Brüning warned Long, as though he needed any warning, that he, Brüning, "would be very sorry if the author [Respondek], who is one of the most passionate opponents of the Nazis, should be caught by the Gestapo."[111]

## Disbelief

During May, June, and July, additional documentation was conveyed by Respondek through Woods. It dealt with Germany's food situation, crop conditions, and raw materials, and especially with the opening of German offensive operations and the "strategic plans for the campaign against Soviet

Russia . . . worked out by the Chief of Staff of the German Army, General [Franz] Halder."[112] As in the past, the information was brought to President Roosevelt's attention[113] and also conveyed to Lord Halifax and transmitted to the Foreign Office on June 17, only days before the German attack.[114] Additional material followed on June 26.[115] Throughout this period stretching from January to June, despite three discussions between Welles and Umansky, Moscow made no move either to acknowledge receipt of the initial information or to pose questions about it. In view of Golikov's candid postwar admission that well before Welles approached Umansky warnings had come from the GRU about a German attack,[116] one would think that at the minimum Moscow would have asked questions. Accordingly, neither the more detailed data about the scheduled German attack that Respondek conveyed in the spring of 1941 nor the data yielded by the Magic intercepts and the decryptions of Japan's Purple code that led American intelligence to predict a German attack[117] were ever made available to the Russians. Since the Americans knew that Umansky was sharing information with Thomsen, it is hardly surprising that they did not supply additional evidence to the Russians. All of this can be clearly traced to Moscow's suspicions and rejection of Washington's revelations, suspicions and rejection prophesied by Ambassador Steinhardt. In the political and military atmosphere that gripped the Russian capital and especially its intelligence establishment, information of the nature supplied by Welles could have been viewed by Stalin only in the same light as all other information, as a British-inspired provocation to be filed and removed to the archives.[118] In this instance, the simpleminded Americans, like the Czechs before them, were used as the conduit to convey the data. Certainly, it would have been argued that since the inception of the European hostilities the Americans had played the British game by restricting the export of important materials needed by Russia—a point made by Umansky, as we have seen, only weeks before the German attack.[119] Were the Americans not also playing the British game in this instance?

Moreover, neither the provenance of the information nor purloined documentation was offered to substantiate the American allegations against Germany. Recent public moves made by the Germans showed no pronounced anti-Russian animus. The contentious issue of the German-Russian demarcation line in Lithuania was settled on January 10, and an economic agreement between the two nations was concluded on that same day.[120] Even the movement of German troops east was no secret.[121] It apparently was made known to Moscow by Vichy through the Russian embassy[122] and also by the French resistance through the Russian intelligence services, probably the GRU.[123] Certainly we now know that on February 21 a GRU network in Switzerland using information supplied by a Swiss officer, had reported the German troop concentrations, although they were inaccurately numbered at 150 divisions. The officer's opinion was that Germany would "attack at the end of May."[124] The credibility of the latter comment was no doubt undermined by the less than cordial relations between Switzerland and Russia since neither government enjoyed diplomatic representation in the other. Likewise, knowledge of German troop movements was supplied by the Polish resistance to British intelligence, with whom it had "strong links,"[125] and allegedly repeated by London to Moscow.[126] This Franco-Polish information was in the hands of British intelligence certainly between late January and early February 1941.[127] Since the initial source, the Polish resistance, would not have been identified, the Russians would have approached with the greatest reserve any British-supplied information on this matter. They would certainly have rejected any Polish information, but similar data from the French and the GRU "supported" the observations of the Russian embassy in Berlin[128] and were probably sufficient to convince the Russians of its credibility. Indeed, the GRU's Richard Sorge in Tokyo inaccurately reported on March 1 that 20 German divisions had been transferred from France to the Russian borders, augmenting the 80 divisions already there.[129] Despite these reports, especially Sorge's, these troop movements posed no immediate threat. During this period, German forces along the Russian frontier had not increased markedly beyond the 33 divisions that had been stationed there since late October 1940. They began to increase slowly only from mid-January to early April, going from 34 to 46 divisions,[130] a sizeable force, but not one sufficient to mount a creditable attack.

This view that the Germans posed no threat to the Russians was shared by the British. Instructed to "prepare a brief strategical appreciation" from the German point of view, the Future Operations Enemy Planning Section of the Chiefs of Staff responded on January 8 that, based on the present military situation perceived from a German slant, it could not recommend an invasion of Russia. Amusingly, the planning section signed the memorandum as coming from Field Marshal Wilhelm Keitel, chief of the Armed Forces High Command.[131] Over a week later, after examining German military dispositions in East Prussia, Finland, Norway, Poland, Rumania, and Slovakia, the War Office branch on military intelligence for Germany, MI14, concluded that the "*military* evidence does not at present support the view that Germany intends to attack Russia." The salient factor supporting this view was that German "troop dispositions and other military preparations" in the vicinity of the Russian frontiers could not at present be "described as anything but normal."[132] Early February saw no change in attitude, and a war between Germany and Russia was thought "unlikely for the present."[133] If there was any disconcerting sign during this period, it was that the three or four German divisions stationed in northern Norway were considered more than necessary merely to garrison the area but adequate to protect it against Russian or British action, especially the latter, which the Germans were said to expect.[134] The War Office "on military grounds," Fitzroy Maclean of the Foreign Office's Northern Department scribbled in mid-January, had reached the "same conclusion as we have reached on political grounds, namely that there is at present no reason to anticipate an early German attack on the Soviet Union."[135] Stalin was not alone in the belief that a German attack, despite Welles's warning, was not in the cards, at least for the moment.

Moscow's stance of disbelief about the American information and Welles's warning was reflected in the comments of senior Russian diplomatic personnel who, although they obviously knew nothing about the Welles-Umansky conversations, were well informed about the thrust of Moscow's attitude and goals. Confident for the moment that relations with Germany were "correct," that Berlin posed no immediate threat, and that mutual advantage drew the two governments together, Moscow was not hesitant to explore a possible trade-off arrangement with Berlin. Through this arrangement, Moscow would consent to German "penetration" of Bulgaria if Berlin would agree to a "modification" of Russian-Finnish relations that presumably involved a change of government in Helsinki.[136] This trial balloon by the first secretary of the Russian legation in Sofia led nowhere.[137] In Stockholm, Minister Kollontai emphasized that her country had no intention of becoming involved in the war, now or in the future. The nexus, she held, in German-Russian relations was Germany's need for Russia's products—a thought not too far from Stalin's mind. For example, by keeping Germany partially dependent on Russian oil, Moscow "might be able to impose restraint" on Germany's ambitions regarding Bulgaria. She admitted, perhaps disingenuously, that often she was not "fully aware" of the government's "high policy" but that she had no reason to think that Moscow had "disinterested" itself in Balkan matters. Nor did Kollontai believe that Germany was "planning aggression against" her country, an action that she judged "would be an act of stupidity." Consequently, she was not alarmed by the rumors prevalent in Sweden about German troop movements heading east toward Russia's frontiers. In making these comments, Fitzroy Maclean noted, Kollontai seemed to "have been somewhat less misleading than usual."[138] If Kollontai's personal views represented Moscow's, the American minister correctly observed from Stockholm, then Stalin placated Hitler only when it suited him and was not averse to exerting pressure on the Germans when he felt it "advisable by stopping supplies from Russia."[139]

Accordingly, Churchill's comment to the War Cabinet in late February that Moscow's position was unenviable and that the "Russian attitude was one of making concessions to Germany in order to gain time"[140] did not exactly parallel Moscow's view of the situation during this period. Moscow's ability to expand, constrict, or prevent the flow of supplies from Russia was perceived as a pressure to which the Germans would respond. In fact, Moscow had not the slightest hesitation in increasing freight rates manyfold. The "average increase" was somewhere near 400% with a corresponding yearly windfall to the Russian treasury of $350,000,000.[141] Some of these "very heavy increases" in freight rates were as much as 800% over prewar levels.[142] Although the Germans do not appear to have raised objections to these draconian freight rates, the Japanese did. The rate increases created a point of friction between Japan and the Soviet Union, but they also put the Japanese on notice that Trans-Siberian freight rates and transit facilities were political pressure points that could be squeezed by Moscow to force the Japanese to concede on other matters.[143]

Certainly the *Vozhd*'s perspicacity about whether the political gap between Moscow and Berlin was narrowing or widening determined his largess on oil shipments, which were a good barometer of German-Russian relations. In 1940, for example, when, one could argue, relations were "correct," Russia shipped 696,600 tons of oil to Germany.[144] The settlement of the demarcation line in Lithuania and the concurrent economic agreement led to Russian oil deliveries to Germany of 42,267 tons in January 1941, but due to competition and increasing tensions in the Balkans and a corresponding widening of the political gap between Germany and the Soviet Union, oil deliveries declined to an estimated 36,742 tons in February with a further drop to about 20,000 tons in March. The decline in oil shipments was based on a deliberate policy decision by Moscow to withhold supplies[145] preceding the German invasion of Yugoslavia in early April.

The sharp cutback of oil supplies in March dovetailed with information given to the British ambassador in Madrid, Sir Samuel Hoare. According to a "good B source," Hoare informed the Foreign Office, Kollontai had informed the Swedes in February that her country had no designs on Finland or elsewhere and that Moscow had focussed its attention on preventing a German takeover of Bulgaria and Yugoslavia. Although Kollontai admitted that Russia would take no military action to prevent Germany's occupation of these states, she "hinted that they would hamper [the] German war effort by economic obstruction"—which Hoare presumed would be the denial of raw materials. "I doubt it," someone in the Foreign Office marginally scribbled on Hoare's report.[146] Yet the sharp drop of oil shipments in March shows us that Kollontai's remarks were not personal ruminations but were based either on unofficial knowledge of Moscow's thinking or on specific instructions from Moscow. Clearly, Russia's value to Germany as a source of raw materials and as a geographical link with states that remained neutral in the war but could supply different raw materials loomed large in Stalin's thinking and in the thinking of his entourage. No warning from Welles of a coming German attack could shake them from their self-induced euphoria.

Perhaps the person who best reflected Stalin's attitude, that Welles's warning was not credible, was the Russian ambassador in Berlin, Vladimir Dekanozov, aptly described as a man of "small stature with an intelligent face and very spirited."[147] The British ambassador in Moscow, Sir Stafford Cripps, suggested that he was of mixed Georgian-Armenian parentage.[148] Molotov, on the other hand, held that he apparently was Armenian but pretended to be Georgian.[149] The diminutive Dekanozov certainly claimed to be Georgian like Stalin and Beria,[150] but the *Vozhd* denied it.[151] Dekanozov supposedly was a Kartlian by birth; the Kartlians are one of Georgia's ethnic groups.[152]

However, according to Liudas Dovydenas, the Lithuanian writer who knew him, Dekanozov's father was Russian, surnamed Protopopoff, and his mother was Jewish from a German-assimilated family.[153] This information supports J. Edgar Hoover, who claimed, based on an "ordinarily reliable" overseas source (probably British intelligence), that Dekanozov was born in Estonia and that his real name was Ivan Vasilyevitzch Protopopov.[154]

Dekanozov's "blond and pale" coloring and "light blue eyes"[155] created an appearance not usually associated with a Georgian but with someone more Nordic in antecedents, perhaps someone from the Baltic region, as Dovydenas and Hoover tell us. Dekanozov cleverly feigned that he knew no German,[156] which was not the case;[157] German was a language familiar, especially during this period, to people from the Baltic region. Pretending not to speak German was a clever ploy, but it did little to establish an intimate relationship, for example, with Ernst von Weizsäcker, the state secretary of the Foreign Ministry.[158] Indeed, Dovydenas holds that Dekanozov was not a Georgian and made the claim only to ingratiate himself with both Stalin and Beria.[159] For obscure reasons, the *Vozhd* had accepted this "legend" about Dekanozov and his bogus background in order to help disguise his true origins.[160] Dekanozov, it appears, had a penchant for legends.[161]

He allegedly grew up on Baku and when the revolution came was a medical student at Saratov University in Russia. Returning to Baku in 1918, he joined first the Red Army and then in 1921 the Azerbaijan Cheka. It was here he became Beria's secretary and henchman. Like Beria, he certainly was a hanging judge in the Caucasus. He also helped to integrate the independent states of Armenia, Azerbaijan, and Georgia into Soviet Russia. He was the point man in Lithuania in 1940, doing the same thing for the Baltic Republics. As part of Beria's coterie, he had been the head of the Foreign Intelligence Department of the NKVD's GUGB,[162] and from May 1939, as we have seen, he served under Molotov as deputy minister in the Foreign Ministry.[163] He was foulmouthed and imperious in dealing with underlings[164] and sexually exploitive,[165] but history and his sins[166] caught up with him when in 1953, along with his "close friend"[167] Beria and others, he was shot by those who had inherited Stalin's mantle of power.[168]

Cripps's predecessor had viewed Dekanozov's appointment to the Foreign Ministry as "further apparent evidence of the 'Georgianisation' of public offices" and surmised that Dekanozov would function as the ministry's chief of personnel "or in other words chief representative of the OGPU,"[169] a surmise with which the American embassy readily concurred.[170] Following his appointment, Dekanozov served on a five-man inquisitional commission including Beria and Molotov that purged the Foreign Ministry. Although he appeared uneasy and kept silent, perhaps awed by the political worthies that served on the commission with him, Dekanozov, unlike the other members of the commission, wore his NKVD uniform, which doubtlessly unnerved those who were summoned for interrogation.[171]

According to Hoover, Dekanozov had "strongly advocated" the 1939 nonaggression pact. He did so on the grounds that whenever Russia and Germany confronted each other as enemies, they "both suffered," but if allied, they "would be invincible."[172] As we have seen, according to his daughter Svetlana, Stalin had a similar view.[173] Whether Dekanozov's views on German-Russian relations were his own or conveniently adopted to mesh with those of the *Vozhd* is unclear. Nevertheless, Dekanozov's views did mesh with Stalin's, which certainly helped place him within the *Vozhd*'s charmed inner circle—Dekanozov served as minister of internal affairs in Georgia, a post that could not have been held by anyone not enjoying Stalin's "special confidence."[174] Likewise, he was appointed a member of the Communist party's Central Committee,[175] undoubtedly to enhance his prestige in Berlin,[176] but he would never have been appointed without a nod from the *Vozhd*.

Dekanozov's appointment as ambassador to Berlin was approved even by the anti-Nazi Ulrich von Hassell.[177] The appointment probably indicated Stalin's desire to have a more vigorous representative in Berlin, one who could more authoritatively reflect the Kremlin's views.[178] Its significance was indirectly impressed on the Germans by the NKVD's Ivan Filippov, whose "cover" was *Tass* correspondent in Berlin. Dekanozov's appointment, he ruminated, was to be seen not only as an "important event" but also one given to an "important personality."[179] Cripps found the appointment "a most unusual step" and credited it to a combination of Stalin's desire to "minimise possible danger to Russia" in discussions with the Germans, as well as his desire "to have someone in direct touch with and trusted by himself" to carry through such discussions. The Northern Department's Fitzroy Maclean, who had served in Moscow and knew Russian, concurred. Moreover, he believed that Dekanozov's appointment seemed "to point to a positive rather than a negative attitude on the part of the Soviet Union" toward Nazi Germany.[180]

Viewed against this background, Dekanozov's reported remark, that his country "had no fear or anxiety as regards any of her western frontiers," is understandable. Cripps, described as a person of "inhuman austerity," observed to Foreign Secretary Anthony Eden that Dekanozov's comment that Russia had no apprehensions regarding its western borders was perhaps not the exaggeration it appeared to be. No doubt Moscow feared that if Germany was "not sufficiently enfeebled" by her present enemies she would turn on Russia. Nevertheless, Cripps believed that for the present relations between the two nations were such that Moscow had "no fear of such [an] attack." Indeed, the ambassador's reported remark was a "pretty accurate expression of the present viewpoint" of the Russian government. Dekanozov's mission, Cripps held, was a "political and not an economic one"—his task was to "minimize all frictions which might lead to the danger of conflict." He was "one of the few personalities of primary importance," Cripps correctly noted, "both as being a close friend of Stalin's and as being prepared to talk with some degree of openness."[181]

Cripps's views had support in the Foreign Office and were buttressed by Dekanozov's remarks to his Turkish counterpart in Berlin, remarks that appeared to show a benign attitude toward possible German designs in Bulgaria and Turkey. The Foreign Office's denigration of Dekanozov's comments as no more significant than most comments made by Russian diplomatic representatives abroad was challenged by the Northern Department's Fitzroy Maclean. Until recently, Dekanozov was Molotov's deputy in the Foreign Ministry, Maclean scribbled, and theoretically still held this appointment and thus was in a different position from most Russian representatives abroad. In addition, he had the "reputation of being close" to Stalin.[182] What Maclean failed to mention, perhaps because he was unaware of it, was that Dekanozov "was a strong opponent of Trotsky,"[183] a stance that would have endeared him to Beria, not to mention to Stalin himself. Dekanozov will attract our attention again, for his role in these events is not unimportant.

Although Umansky was anti-American and may have appended editorial comments to his message denigrating Welles's information, he was also an experienced Stalinist apparatchik and knew the rules of the game. Following the German attack, Umansky observed to Welles that he had communicated his January warning to Moscow.[184] By raising the question of the warning with Welles at their March 20 meeting, Umansky clearly showed that Washington's allegations continued to interest him, or perhaps the doers and movers in Moscow, or both. Washington's opportunity to tweak the Russians about their disregard of Welles's warning presented itself in June 1942 when Molotov arrived in Washington to discuss American aid and other matters. Playing the mischievous sprite, Hull remarked to Molotov, in an allusion to Woods, that only the day before he had received in his office the "highly trusted person" who had procured for him the information that Germany would invade Russia in either May or June. In an "amused tone," Hull then observed that, when the war was over and both of them were seated "around the family table planning for world restoration on sound healthy lines," he might then take it upon himself to inquire just when Moscow decided that Berlin "would attack later," as indeed it did. Molotov quickly retorted that Moscow had decided in April or May that an attack would come, and of course, most Russians "did not believe it until after the war was actually on."[185] This was a startling and revealing admission, and although it appears through 20/20 hindsight, it is one that we will re-examine. Hull never got a straight answer about why Welles's warning was ignored; but then again he never got a thank-you for the warning either.

# 3

# Echoes

## Ponschab

The early days of 1941 witnessed the expansion of Germany's military presence in the Balkans, which had begun with the penetration of Rumania in the autumn of the previous year.[1] In both Berlin and Moscow, the Russians voiced their protests. Specifically, they objected to German actions in Bulgaria on the grounds that Bulgaria and the Turkish Straits were considered a Russian "security zone" and that Moscow therefore could "not remain indifferent in the face of events which menaced the security interests of the USSR." Consequently, in early March the Russian government thought it a duty to give warning that the "appearance of any foreign armed forces" in Bulgaria or in the Straits was a violation of Russian security interests.[2] Understandably, Moscow strongly objected to Bulgaria's adherence to the Tripartite Pact and to the large influx of German troops into the country, which was justified by Berlin as a riposte to prevent British entrenchment in Greece.[3]

This situation, as intolerable as it was for Moscow, obviously could not be allowed to sour relations between the two dictatorships. Accordingly, in order to influence Berlin's Balkan and other policies and to convey indirectly its assurances and concerns for what was developing in Bulgaria and in other areas, but in a manner to convince and not to annoy the Germans, Moscow engaged in a subtle and imaginative deception *cum* disinformation operation of its own design.

The method chosen was to allow Berlin to acquire what were seemingly circular messages sent by Moscow to its Far Eastern diplomatic missions. Moscow in turn buttressed these messages by repeating to these missions alleged reports emanating from Russian embassies and their chiefs of mission in Berlin, London, Washington, and other capitals. Supposed dispatches from Moscow and other spurious communications rounded out the deception *cum* disinformation campaign. The thrust of these messages, as we shall see, was clearly hostile to the British and to the Americans and sometimes, if Moscow was intent on conveying a circuitous threat, to the Germans themselves. The whole exercise was an attempt to assuage and reassure Berlin that Moscow's actions were in tandem with the 1939 arrangements and were no threat, direct or indirect, to their melded interests.

The sum of these false communications, however, was a veritable cornucopia of messages, statements, and policy stances, both political and military, of foreign officials, diplomats, military leaders, and others. Conceivably woven into this mass of false information were slivers of gilt-edged intelligence data culled by the Russian intelligence services from their operations abroad. The rich mix of messages served a double purpose: it thwarted the German attempt to delve into their authenticity while simultaneously promoting the credibility of the material. The composition and complexity of the messages preclude their being the work of one person. Rather, they were probably the work of a small NKVD committee under the constant supervision of a senior officer, perhaps Beria himself. The suggestion of the existence of such a committee is not unwarranted. Indeed, this type of Soviet activity and organization was a longstanding operational tradition, alleged accounts of which appear in Western literature as early as the mid 1920s.[4]

One author has written that the messages appeared to be "designed for interception"[5] because they were sent in a code capable of being decrypted. The interception and decryption, if such they were, possibly were accomplished by the Japanese in Harbin, Manchuria, who then conveyed the decrypted messages to the German consul, August Ponschab.[6] Although the Japanese and Polish intelligence services collaborated during this period and, as in the 1920s, this collaboration probably included unraveling Russian codes, there is not a shred of evidence that the Japanese, either on their own or jointly with the Poles, intercepted or decrypted these particular messages. It is of course conceivable that the Japanese may have intercepted and decrypted the messages, but because Ponschab's disguised memoirs written under a pen name are silent on this question,[7] that the Japanese ever did so is extremely doubtful.

Neither is there any evidence that Ponschab, or his minuscule staff, had the necessary facilities, training, or expertise in the arcane fields of codes and decryption to unravel the Russian messages within several days.[8] Nor is there any evidence, based on a postwar American examination made by the Office of Strategic Service in China, that the German intelligence services in Manchuria or Japanese-occupied China ran any intercept or decryption operations targeted against Russia.[9]

The truth of the matter is that, although coded Russian messages had been intercepted and decrypted by the Anglo-Americans in the 1920s[10] and the Americans in the late 1940s,[11] these particular "Ponschab intercepts" would have been very unusual for the early wartime period that witnessed very secure Russian codes and communication procedures.[12]

Indeed, the able and experienced Anglo-American-French board of editors of the multivolume series dealing with the documents on German foreign policy during the 1918–1945 period signaled their suspicions about the alleged decrypted Ponschab intercepts by labeling them as the "purported texts of intercepted Soviet Russian diplomatic communications."[13] Moreover, the twenty-four extant messages that began on March 6 and ran to June 12 conveniently do not appear to have been continued by Moscow after the German invasion.[14] Apparently no one has ever attempted to unravel this lengthy operation and to place the messages within their proper setting. The spotlighting of this operation found in the pages that follow might encourage others to tackle or be more sensitive to this well-honed tradecraft of the Russian intelligence services.

A more plausible explanation of what occurred in 1941 is that the Germans were "running" someone on the Russian side, probably from within the Russian consulate general in Harbin. The Germans believed that this person was giving genuine information about messages transmitted by Moscow and meant for its Far East missions. Another explanation could be that the information was being brought to the Germans by a cutout, someone who was either acting for the Russians or someone who sincerely believed that he was providing material whose provenance was not open to question and so convinced the Germans.

A syntactical and grammatical analysis of the messages raises doubts as to whether they were decrypted intercepts. In his message of May 18, 1941, for example, Ponschab specifically informs Berlin that the information he is conveying is based on memory *(Wiedergabe nach dem Gedächtnis)*,[15] implying that the information was originally related orally. From the other messages that Ponschab transmitted to Berlin, messages replete with extensive detail beyond normal human memory retention, one is led to conclude that the information transmitted was conveyed to Ponschab in written form. The fact that the May 18 message was oral and the others were probably written might in turn explain why Berlin uncharacteristically raised no questions about how the messages were decrypted. Obviously, if the messages originated from a Russian source run directly by the Germans, or if the messages were acquired by the Germans from someone they considered to be a reliable cutout acting for the Russian source, then decryption would have played no role in securing the messages.

The pertinent questions, then, are who was supplying this Russian material to Ponschab, who played the cutout role suggested, and how this material was acquired from the Russians. In the rogues' gallery of characters who resided in Harbin in 1941, the now identified candidate for the role of supplier was the Baltic German journalist Ivar Lissner (né Hirschfeld), a crypto-Jew who on the surface was a dedicated Nazi and anti-Communist. Ponschab's administrative assistant, Georg Korter, informs us, after viewing photocopies of the twenty-four extant messages, that it was Lissner who supplied the Russian material to the German consulate general in Harbin.[16]

Based on a record of questionable admissions made by Lissner to the Japanese under torture, a record filled with truths, half-truths, obfuscations, and outright lies, information about Lissner that filters through can be accepted as reasonably accurate but must nevertheless be approached with caution. Apparently, Lissner had been recruited into the Abwehr with the understanding that his parents be allowed to leave Germany. Admiral Canaris had agreed. Thanks to the largess of the Abwehr, Lissner then ensconced himself in Harbin in the early weeks of 1940. He soon established contacts with White Russian opponents of the Soviet regime, especially with the leader of the Russian Fascists in Harbin, the thirty-four-year-old Konstantin Rodzaievsky, described as a "consumate but naive demogague . . . hypnotized . . . with his own oratory," who was also "an ideological fascist, a rabid anti-Semite, [and] an anti-Bolshevik crusader."[17] Supposedly, Rodzaevsky and his ilk ran agents inside Siberia, including several officers in the Red Army's Far East Command. It is through this White Russian connection that Lissner in all likelihood acquired the documentation that he then conveyed to Ponschab.

Whether Lissner's White Russian contacts were infiltrated by the NKVD or working at Moscow's behest is unknown. If, as we have seen, a White Russian general like Skoblin[18] could be suborned and recruited, certainly it would have been reasonably simple for the Russians to dupe someone like Rodzaevsky or one of his surrogates with spurious data. In the polyglot world of 1940s Harbin, anything was possible: for example, by 1942 Rodzaevsky was suspected by the Japanese of being a Soviet agent. Suffice it to say that Moscow could ill afford to have someone like Rodzaevsky testify at the postwar Tokyo War Crimes Trial. His execution provoked the defense to protest strongly the "deliberate removal of a witness whose testimony was known to be material" to the war crimes tribunal.[19]

Following the German attack in June 1941, or perhaps even before, Lissner engaged his Soviet counterparts in the dangerous game of Spielmaterial—he made available accurate and significant information, including secret information of less than the highest order, in exchange for information pertaining to the Japanese and other matters. The Japanese became suspicious of Lissner's contacts with the Russians and they arrested him in June 1943. He was left to his fate, for Berlin could ill afford to admit to Tokyo that one of its own agents was involved in spying against its ally through a state with which Germany was at war and which was also hostile to Japan.[20]

One plausible scenario for the so-called Ponschab intercepts is that they began in Moscow, were communicated probably to the Russian consulate in Harbin, then conveyed to Lissner through his White Russian contacts, and through Lissner to Ponschab and on to Berlin. If anyone was being "run" in Harbin in 1941, it was Lissner and Ponschab, thanks to the imaginative intelligence tradecraft of the NKVD.

Although Ernst von Weizsäcker, the German Foreign Ministry's state secretary, apparently was convinced that these Ponschab messages were significant, for he placed them in his personal file on Russia,[21] their impact on the

Germans, as we shall see, was nil. The first message about the material was conveyed by Ponschab on February 24, 1941, and numbered no. 5.[22] Unfortunately, message no. 5 appears not to have survived the war, and valiant efforts by the archives division of the German Foreign Ministry did not lead to its discovery. One can suggest that this first message spelled out how Ponschab was securing the material he was forwarding to the Wilhelmstrasse. It also perhaps alluded to Lissner's role and to the source, information that might have explained why the material was being routed through Harbin and being received by Ponschab in German, which obviated its decryption and translation from the Russian. Since this message of February 24, 1941, set the stage for those messages that followed, its disappearance from the German Foreign Ministry archives can well be appreciated.

However, unlike the German deception operations occurring before the invasion, this Russian one through Ponschab and Lissner found an unreceptive target. Ponschab's information notwithstanding, Hitler had decided to invade Soviet Russia, and no clever ploy by Stalin could dissuade him from this decision and persuade him to adhere faithfully to the 1939 nonaggression pact. Accordingly, the messages from Ponschab were ignored; this would explain why they are devoid of Weizsäcker's or anyone else's marginalia and why they appear not to have been subjected to individual or collective analysis. The value of the messages, however, is the insight they give us into the twists, turns, and thrusts of Russian policy during this period.

The Russians, however, are not without hubris. In 1953, following Beria's death, an NKVD commission visited Korter at the camp where he was being held near Sverdlovsk. In an hour-long interrogation spiced with threats of violence, the commission wanted to know who the German informant had been in the Russian consulate general in Harbin. This consulate's staff of seventy, more personnel than was employed by all the other foreign consulates in Harbin, lived in a secure compound; contact with this staff would have been difficult. Since the Germans had had no such informant the interrogation went nowhere. The commission was annoyed and remarked to Korter that he would have several years to think it over. Though Ponschab was released in 1953, Korter was not repatriated until Chancellor Konrad Adenauer visited Moscow in 1955.[23] The commission had obviously been on a "damage control" expedition. The deception *cum* disinformation campaign that the NKVD had seemingly mounted through Ponschab and Lissner, a type of campaign that had so often proved lucrative in the past, had failed. Obviously, or so the NKVD thought, the campaign could have failed only because of German penetration of the NKVD's operations in the consulate general in Harbin.

The first material that Ponschab conveyed to Berlin on March 6 was a circular message sent by Moscow, purportedly relating reports for the Russian embassies in Ankara and Washington. The material recounted the recent visit to the Turkish capital made by British Foreign Secretary Anthony Eden and chief of the Imperial General Staff, Field Marshal Sir John Dill, as well as a conversation in the American capital between Under Secretary Welles and Ambassador Umansky. According to the Ankara report, the Turks had declared that the Russian attitude toward them was "still undecided." At least for the moment, Turkey was unable to fulfill its treaty obligations toward England. Should Germany invade Greece, however, Turkey could assist Greece, provided there were sufficient British troops in Greece and provided Russia promised not to invade Turkey. Eden supposedly responded that there were 250,000 British troops in Greece, and should resistance in northern Greece prove unsuccessful, southern Greece could be held. The Turks, according to the Russian embassy in Ankara, declared that this arrangement was unsatisfactory; therefore, they would close the Straits to warships and also decline the transit of German troops across Turkish territory. In Washington, the conversation supposedly centered on Welles's protests to Umansky about the activities of the Comintern in America and Asia, which were perceived as threatening to American interests, and also on the countermeasures that the Americans would adopt.[24]

We now know, of course, from Churchill's and Eden's postwar memoirs, that the details related in the circular message about the purported conversation between Eden and Dill in Ankara are spurious. Indeed, British and other allied forces in Greece never exceeded 62,000, contrary to the figure of 250,000 allegedly given by Eden.[25] The details of the Washington report were likewise spurious. During this period, although Welles had numerous conversations with Umansky, there appears to be no State Department documentation relating to protests by Welles about Comintern activities in America or Asia, to the perceived threats to the United States, or to American countermeasures. The only event even remotely related to such a subject was Umansky's attempt to effect the release of Mikhail Gorin, the former head of Intourist in Los Angeles, who had been tried and convicted of espionage.[26]

What was the purpose of this circular message? How were the Russians attempting to deceive and disinform the Germans and thus influence their thinking? The spurious recounting of the Ankara conversation was clearly an attempt to signal to Berlin that any campaign in Greece might be less than a shoo-in. The sizeable British forces that were supposedly in Greece, although they might be dislodged from northern Greece, would be able to hold their own in the south of the country behind a water barrier analogous to the English Channel. The Germans would then be involved in a long and exhausting Greek campaign that would sap their resources and divert their forces and their attention from the principal territorial target, England. Moreover, if Greece were attacked, any guarantee by Moscow to Ankara might allow the Turks to enter the war on the British side, thus expanding the Balkan thrust in a manner not anticipated, overextending the Germans militarily and logistically, and creating political and other uncertainties the Germans would prefer to avoid at this point in the war. At the minimum, a

Greek campaign would lead to the closing of the Straits to warships and also to Turkey's denial (unlike Sweden's understanding attitude) of transit to German troops. On the other hand, the spurious Washington report appeared to show that there was American-Russian tension and that Moscow was still committed to the 1939 arrangement. The gist of the circular message was patent: concentrate German resources and endeavors in the West against England, avoid the Balkan cauldron, and be assured that Moscow was still a loyal and benevolent neutral, as reflected in its deft discouragement of Ambassador Cripps's informal attempt to have Eden call on the Kremlin's leadership after his visit to Ankara.[27]

Next, the implicit Russian commitment to the 1939 arrangement was made explicit in a new decrypted intercept furnished by Ponschab to Berlin on March 9. In this circular message, supposedly intended for Russia's Far Eastern diplomatic missions, Moscow, to cover itself, now dangled before Berlin its own perceptions of what was developing in the Balkans. Russia, the diplomatic missions were informed, had decided not to interfere with Germany's intended action against Greece. Since Russia's lack of geographical proximity to Greece precluded direct intervention, Moscow was not making a major concession in this decision. This noninterference stance was thought necessary, the message continued, to pressure the British colonies, to endanger the Suez Canal, and to harass British forces in Africa who needed supplies. Because the Balkan peoples' increasing desire was to avoid war, Moscow had to warn their governments, which actively supported the Germans, against the danger that this stance entailed for the peace of the region. In particular, Yugoslavia and Turkey had to be pressured not to intervene but to remain neutral—Bulgaria went unmentioned, for German troops had already occupied the country.

The Russian stance toward Yugoslavia and Turkey dovetailed with Hitler's desire, and the pressure on Turkey would have appealed doubly to him since, based on Ponschab's previous message, it appeared that Ankara just might join the British, provided Moscow gave it a guarantee of support. Concurrently, Moscow noted it would struggle to win the sympathy of the Greeks who would have to repulse the German invasion. The point emphasized, however, was that Russia did not intend to risk the 1939 nonaggression pact, which was "necessary for the achievement of the most urgent goal, namely the destruction of the English Empire."[28] Moscow had neatly registered the points it wanted to make in Berlin.

Stalin's desire to accommodate Hitler, despite any misgivings about what was developing in the Balkans, manifested itself in Stalin's reaction when Admiral Kuznetsov gave instructions in early March that overflights by German aircraft, which were clearly photographing military and naval installations, should be attacked without warning. The instructions were executed in mid-March when Luftwaffe reconnaissance flights violated Russian airspace in the Baltic and Black Seas. Kuznetsov was immediately ordered to the

Kremlin. When he entered Stalin's office and saw Beria was also present, he immediately knew what to expect. When he attempted to respond to the question of why he had issued the instructions, Stalin cut him short. He was reprimanded and ordered to cancel the instructions immediately. The new instructions restricted any riposte: the intruder was to be intercepted and forced to land. During subsequent overflights, although warning shots were fired, the Germans refused to land. The German embassy in Moscow soon lodged a protest that a civilian aircraft involved in "meteorological" work had been attacked.[29]

Stalin's commitment, therefore, to a continuing accommodation with Germany and his seeming lack of concern about any immediate threat go far to explain General Golikov's March 20 report to Stalin, which summed up the intelligence scene. Although by this point, as we have seen, the GRU had acquired suggestive information, especially from the military attaché in Berlin, General Tupikov, that a German blow was coming, Golikov concluded that any attack would most probably commence only after Berlin was victorious in the West. This was a plausible conclusion. His last comments, however, were the most important. Documentation or rumors about an inevitable attack against Russia during the coming spring, he held, "must be assessed as disinformation coming from English or maybe even German intelligence."[30]

One could plausibly argue that during this early period the deception operations that Berlin had mounted had convinced Golikov that all German actions and particularly the troop concentrations along the frontier were targeted against parties other than Russia—the troops were supposedly targeted against England or the Balkan States. In addition, Golikov faced no risk in telling Stalin exactly what he wanted to hear,[31] a report that could also be cogently defended, for in the Byzantine world of the *Vozhd*'s Kremlin such concessionary action led to continued good health.[32]

In retrospect one can criticize Golikov's conclusions, but it is only fair to point out that British perceptions during this period were not much different from Golikov's. In the British Foreign Office, as we have seen, Sir Alexander Cadogan, the permanent under secretary, held to the view that Germany would not at present provoke a two-front war.[33] When the Greek minister in London opined that "menacing concentrations" of forces by both Germany and Russia "were more likely to be a prelude to further bargaining and a new compact" between the Germans and the Russians "than to indicate an intention to enter upon hostilities," R. A. Butler, the Parliamentary under secretary for foreign affairs, pointed out that the Greek government's "judgment, on the whole, tended to confirm" the minister's view. Nevertheless, Butler continued, should an invasion of Great Britain fail, the possibility of a German attack against Soviet Russia "was not to be underestimated."[34]

Although the British military noted the German buildup in Bulgaria against Greece, the continuing reports that suggested Germany intended to attack Soviet Russia during the summer were determined to be unconvincing.[35] Concurrently, MI14 had no doubt that Germany's ongoing activity in Finland was either an attempt to contain Russian troops or to distract Moscow's attention from the Balkans.[36] In fact, in an appreciation of the situation at the end of March, the director of military intelligence observed that there were "no grounds" to conclude that an attack on Soviet Russia was impending.[37] This observation was accepted in early April by the British military who had "little reason to believe" the circulating reports that Germany would soon invade Russia. Berlin's object, they surmised, was "undoubtedly to exert military pressure" on Moscow to prevent its interference in Germany's "plans in South-East Europe, and also to influence Russia's diplomatic decisions."[38]

There was, however, one skeptic, the Foreign Office's Victor Cavendish-Bentinck, chairman of the Chiefs of Staff Joint Intelligence Committee. At about this time, like the Russians,[39] he became aware of German airport construction in Poland. He was uneasy over Polish reports that the Germans were improving airfields in Poland and supporting anti-Communist Caucasian organizations. As Cavendish-Bentinck later noted, it seemed to him "patent that the Germans were not using the labour, concrete and steel required for this purpose just for the fun, and that it was a preparation to attack Russia" because these airfields were being established for use by "long range and heavily loaded bombers" and not for Lufthansa. These data moved him to suggest that the intelligence committee's advisory subcommittee, the Joint Intelligence Staff, "should be directed to prepare a report on the possibility of a German attack on the Soviet Union." The report was dutifully prepared and was strengthened by additional information aside from that already mentioned. On this question, however, Cavendish-Bentinck was a lone voice crying in the wilderness. The officer who was secretary of the Joint Intelligence Committee thought that the advisory subcommittee "had gone mad in predicting that the Germans intended to attack the Russians in the near future" and was incredulous when Cavendish-Bentinck admitted that he had recommended the preparation of the report.[40]

## Lucy

Golikov's approach and comments to Stalin go far to explain the negative reception allegedly given by the GRU to the revealing information conveyed by Englishman Alexander Foote. Foote was a wireless operator for an extensive network established in Switzerland and run by the Hungarian geographer, longtime Communist and GRU agent, Sándor Radó, code named "Dora." Foote's purported message of March 15 was based on information from a source code-named "Lucy"; the message dealt with German troop concentrations in Rumania close to the Ukraine, troop movements in Bulgaria, and the plans for the invasion of Soviet Russia. Moscow's retort to this message, it is claimed, was a sharp rebuke. How could Radó imagine that such data would be acceptable from a source whom the GRU knew only through a code name and who in turn, as a condition for his cooperation, stipulated absolute secrecy about his own sources of information? If they were true, Lucy's disclosures would be stupendous. Lucy's information, however, was so detailed that it could have been planted by the Germans themselves. Accordingly, Moscow decided, Lucy could not be trusted and was "probably an *agent provocateur*."[41]

No doubt, as claimed, the GRU's reaction to Lucy's information was negative. However, Lucy, who in reality was the German anti-Nazi refugee Rudolf Rössler, did not establish contact with the Radó network until the autumn of 1942.[42] Although there has been much speculation and obfuscation about Rössler and his sources, he was in all likelihood a cutout between Swiss intelligence and the Radó group. Indeed, as the Central Intelligence Agency has pointed out, it "seems probable that the German sources gave their information to the Swiss General Staff, which in turn passed to Roessler that information which the Swiss wanted to relay to the Soviets."[43] Whether the Swiss military acted with or without the permission of the civil authorities is unclear. Nevertheless, they did engage in this elaborate ploy and have never admitted doing so for overriding reasons of state, specifically that this action was "at odds with that strict neutrality which Switzerland has proclaimed for centuries as buckler and breastplate." Switzerland, the Central Intelligence Agency goes on to observe, "was not just part of the World War II scenery; it had a small piece of the action."[44]

A German victory in Europe would have been the death knell for Switzerland as a free and independent state. Bern correctly perceived that Switzerland's natural allies were England and France. Accordingly, whatever information Switzerland had about the Germans should be shared with the Anglo-French, but in a manner that would not jeopardize Swiss neutrality. Initially, a senior Swiss officer liaised with the western intelligence services. Rössler was then recruited by Swiss intelligence and in the autumn of 1939 began to convey data to Captain Karel Sedlacek of Czech military intelligence. When the intelligence data arrived in London, Colonel Moravec would make it available to the appreciative British. Rössler also established contact with MI6 in Bern. The procedure of using Rössler as a cutout with the Czechs and the British rather than using the direct liaison first established with the Anglo-French was a much safer way for the Swiss to cover their unneutral conduct.

The ties between Berlin and Moscow precluded similar arrangements with the Russians. This preclusion explains why virtually no information about Barbarossa from Swiss-controlled intelligence sources ever surfaced prior to the attack. A clash between the two great dictatorships and their mutual exhaustion were in Swiss interests. Only in the autumn of 1942, as the Germans raced toward Stalingrad and all that the fall of that city portended, was Rössler, as we have seen, put into direct contact with the Radó network. At the worst, a Russian victory over Germany would be only part of a greater struggle, and Switzerland could be confident that in any postwar European arrangements Russia's coalition partners would insist on the *status quo ante:* the continuance of a free, independent, republican, and neutral Switzerland.[45]

Rössler probably had no German sources of his own; only a national intelligence service, like the Swiss, could have supplied so quickly the wide-ranging, voluminous, and remarkably accurate information conveyed by Rössler to Radó. "This was something," we are assured, "which a private individual could neither improvise nor organise." The Swiss intelligence service, it is stressed, had "extended its ties deep into Germany," and its "espionage net . . . was spread wide and fine." Its activities were doubtlessly buttressed by the legation's service attachés and the excellent contacts, official and unofficial in all walks of life, that Bern has always enjoyed in Germany. Moreover, the information gathering of Swiss intelligence and of the Swiss legation in Berlin was enhanced by information from the thirteen Swiss consular missions scattered throughout Nazi Germany, including offices in Prague and Vienna. Since wartime German messages were intercepted and decrypted and telephone conversations tapped and overheard by others, one cannot dismiss the possibility and the strong probability that the Swiss achieved similar successes.[46]

## The Balkan Cauldron

As we have seen, Germany's mounting arrangements for a military thrust into the Balkans had moved Kollontai to inform the Swedes that Moscow might be able to restrain German ambitions regarding Bulgaria.[47] Moscow had conceded that Greece was unsavable, a concession reflected in the alleged decrypted intercept forwarded by Ponschab on March 9 to Berlin.[48] Nevertheless, on the morning of March 1, German troops entered Bulgaria unopposed, and concurrently Sofia accepted the Tripartite Pact.[49] Understandably, Moscow was not amused and strenuously protested to Berlin.[50] London's riposte, four days later, was to sever diplomatic relations with Sofia.[51] Germany's thrust into Bulgaria proved far simpler than the situation that next developed in Yugoslavia.

Berlin soon pressured Belgrade to follow Sofia's example and accept the Tripartite Pact. On March 4, Prince Regent Paul of Yugoslavia met Hitler at Berchtesgaden. Hitler pressed for Belgrade's accession to the pact and as a *quid pro quo* offered Yugoslavia access to the Aegean through Salonika. The Prince Regent reserved his decision due to his wife's Greek descent, his pro-British sympathies, and his anti-Italian attitude.[52] Although German documentation[53] and the private papers of Prince Regent Paul[54] show nothing beyond these mutual comments, the prince's subsequent but clear recollection made after his ouster as regent was that "Hitler had spoken strongly against Russia, stating that he would have to take military action against that country to secure the raw materials he now needed." Hitler added that he would choose the time and make the necessary arrangements.[55] The Yugoslav minister in Moscow, Milan Gavrilović, subsequently confirmed that, during the conversation between Hitler and the Prince Regent, Hitler stated that "as soon as the Balkan campaign was finished he would proceed against the Soviet Union."[56] Since Gavrilović was in Moscow throughout this period, his knowledge of the conversation could only have been indirect: through others in Belgrade or through the British ambassador in Moscow, Cripps.

Hitler's purported comment to Prince Paul soon came to the attention of the American minister in Belgrade, Arthur Bliss Lane, who reported on March 30 that he had been "informed by a reliable source" that during the course of the conversation Hitler emphasized that Yugoslavia had to adhere to the Tripartite Pact in its "own interests"; in June or July Hitler was going to invade Russia.[57] Actually, the story that Hitler had revealed his plans for invasion to Prince Regent Paul was making the rounds in Belgrade well before Lane reported it to Washington.[58] Lane quickly informed his British counterpart of the conversation,[59] and in Washington Under Secretary Welles informed Ambassador Halifax.[60] After the war, the Yugoslav minister in Washington, Konstantin Fotić, recounted the episode,[61] but in all probability he likewise was informed of Hitler's alleged comment by Welles.

In view of the tight security that Hitler had decreed for Barbarossa, his admission to Prince Regent Paul seems bizarre. Of course, Hitler did not have the most stable of personalities, and it is possible that his comment was an attempt to sweeten the bitter pill that the Prince Regent and Yugoslavia were being asked to swallow. If Prince Regent Paul had not initially alerted the British or anyone else[62] to Hitler's comment, his "hatred"[63] of Soviet Russia probably made him share the Swiss view that any clash between the two great dictatorships was to be encouraged. Indeed, it is this hatred of Soviet Russia, as well as "direct promises of anti-Soviet action by Hitler and his minister in Belgrade," that explains why Prince Regent Paul and the Yugoslavs silently rejected Russian overtures during this period "to enter into an arrangement with them for mutual defence."[64] Moscow's desire for collaboration had initially manifested itself in the late autumn of the previous year, but it never came to fruition. Uninvited, Moscow offered to supply "all the war material" that Belgrade desired "at whatever price" they cared to fix.[65]

Accordingly, Hitler's alleged comment may have been uttered. On the other hand, it may not have been uttered; it may have been only a "cover" story devised by the Yugoslavs, including the Prince Regent, to protect the sources and the enormously important intelligence information arriving, as we shall see, from the military attaché in Berlin. If the story was not a cover, and Hitler's comments to the Prince Regent were genuine, then Belgrade was placed in the unique position of having received directly from disparate sources extremely reliable information about German intentions toward Soviet Russia. These sources were Hitler himself, the military attaché who based his information on the excellent high-level sources he had cultivated in Berlin, and as we shall see, Gavrilović in Moscow.

In the Foreign Office, the head of the Northern Department, Laurence Collier, "knowing Prince Paul's anti-communist obsessions," thought it "quite probable" that Hitler had made such a comment. Collier, however, thought that, from London's point of view, informing Russia about Hitler's comment would "only have a good effect . . . if [the Russians] interpret it as meaning that they will be attacked *in any case,* and regardless of any concessions which they may make to Hitler." It was a prophetic comment. Moreover, informing them "might not affect their present policy of subservience, if it could be interpreted as meaning that the attack" would not begin until the British had been defeated. Indeed, Moscow's stance might be that Hitler would be unable to accomplish this defeat, and accordingly, the Russians were in no danger. Cadogan, the permanent under secretary, was inclined not to convey the information until London was sure that Moscow felt "strong enough to react in the right way to it."[66] On the very day Prince Regent Paul was speeding to Berchtesgaden, March 4, Lane learned at the Foreign Ministry that his Yugoslav counterpart in Moscow, Gavrilović, had received word from a "neutral chief of mission in Berlin"—probably the Swedish minister—that the Nazi party leadership and the army were agreed that Germany "must now attack" Soviet Russia. Hitler's recent letter to President Ismet Inonu of Turkey about Bulgaria's adhesion to the Tripartite Pact and the movement of German troops into that country, Lane's informant opined, was an attempt to ensure Turkey's neutrality and to obtain its influence to prevent any junction of British and Russian forces. Moreover, the Yugoslav informant held that recent moves by Berlin in the Balkans were for the purpose of keeping London and Moscow apart.[67]

Informed of Lane's report, the Turkish ambassador in Washington admitted that, though he had heard similar rumors, he had no concrete information on the matter. Personally he was inclined to the view, shared as we have seen by the British, that as long as the Russians were prepared to kowtow to the Germans and to yield to Hitler's every demand, the need for Berlin to attack Soviet Russia was obscure. The ambassador appeared to "believe that the concessions and sacrifices which Stalin [was] prepared to make to Hitler in order to avoid being attacked [were] practically without limit." Stalin realized that any clash with Germany in Russia's present weakened state "would mean the total collapse of the Communist regime and the consequent disappearance of Stalin's hopes of moving in on the European scene after all parties to the present conflict [were] completely exhausted and demoralized."[68]

For some Yugoslavs during this period, the stance that Belgrade should adopt against the German pressure to accept the Tripartite Pact was greatly affected by Gavrilović's information from Moscow, furnished by his Swedish counterpart, that Germany would certainly attack Russia by June 22. Whether this information was in Gavrilović's initial report, which was discussed with Lane on March 4, or in a subsequent communication is unclear.

It is sufficient to note that Gavrilović's information and certainly the various intelligence reports, especially reports from Slovakia and Poland detailing the German preparations for an attack, moved those attending the Crown Council meeting on March 6, following the Prince Regent's talk with Hitler, "to adopt any possible diplomatic maneuvers to spare Yugoslavia the horrors of war, if only until Hitler's main forces came to grips with Stalin's."[69] Additional intelligence data about Germany's policy in Yugoslavia supplied around this time to Beneš and Moravec by agent A-54, the Abwehr's Major Paul Thummel, probably buttressed this stance.[70]

Five days later, Prime Minister Dragiša Cvetković asked Milos Tupanjanin, deputy leader of the Serbian Agrarian party (Gavrilović was the leader), whether a Yugoslav military alliance with Soviet Russia made sense in view of the intelligence information flowing into Belgrade. Tupanjanin, who it is claimed was "very active on behalf of the British intelligence service"—the head of the Foreign Office's Southern Department admitted that he was "in receipt of a subsidy from us"—expressed his doubts. He correctly pointed out that it was only in June of the previous year that the two states had exchanged diplomatic representatives. When pressed by Cvetković, Tupanjanin said that if a military alliance were possible, it was a fine idea, since it would place Soviet Russia in opposition to Nazi Germany. Informed of this exchange in Belgrade, Gavrilović in Moscow was keen to have the negotiations commence. Cvetković then admitted that a "special confidential emissary"—unidentified—had been dispatched to Moscow "some weeks ago," an admission that the British minister could confirm through another source. Moreover, according to Cvetković, the Yugoslav military with whom he had been in communication appeared to favor the alliance idea. Likewise partial to the alliance, according to Tupanjanin, was Foreign Minister Aleksander Cincar-Marković. Cvetković informed Tupanjanin and the British Minister that he thought he had seen signs of change in Moscow's outlook. Belgrade had information that the Germans were moving troops to the Russian frontier from Central Europe and France, those troops moved from France perhaps drawn from those earmarked for the British invasion. Russian troop concentrations behind the Yugoslavian frontier, he observed, would be helpful.[71]

That a special military envoy was indeed in Moscow—undoubtedly Air Force Colonel Bozin Simić[72]—was soon confirmed by Cripps, who observed to the Foreign Office that the envoy had "had two long conversations" with the Russian military, who were keen for "a military arrangement with Yugoslavia" and were urging that Gavrilović should be instructed to "broach the question" with the Russian leadership.[73] Within days of Cripps's message, the Yugoslav military attaché in Berlin, Colonel Vladimir Vauhnik, a Slovene, informed the General Staff and one of Prince Paul's aides-de-camp that Germany would attack Soviet Russia. Whether they provided information wittingly or unwittingly, the colonel's sources about the German attitude toward Russia and Yugoslavia included the Luftwaffe's Reichsmarshal Hermann Göring, Admiral Wilhelm Canaris of the Abwehr, Major General Hans

Oster, his principal assistant, other well-placed and informed Germans, the Slovak military attaché in Berlin (who divulged that he had been asked for two infantry divisions for an attack on Russia), and Vauhnik's fellow Slovenes working in Germany. The second half of May had been mentioned as the planned time of the attack. When the General Staff did not react to Vauhnik's message, either because it was not believed or because of security reasons, he repeated the warning to Foreign Minister Cincar-Marković, through the minister in Berlin, Ivo Andrić. Vauhnik also approached the Russian military attaché, General Tupikov, and his assistant and alerted them to the upcoming German attack. No doubt sensitized to the *Vozhd*'s attitude toward information of this nature, Vauhnik's Russian counterparts, who, as we have seen, already had the information, vigorously denied that any such attack was possible and refused to believe the warning. Likewise, Colonel Vauhnik informed British intelligence through the Swedes and subsequently informed the American military attaché, Colonel B. R. Peyton, and his assistant, Major J. R. Lovell. Until the eve of Germany's attack on Yugoslavia, Vauhnik continued his accurate reporting, warning Belgrade of Germany's intended military and political moves.[74]

Unfortunately for the colonel, his message to Cincar-Marković proved to be his undoing, for the experts of the Forschungsamt (Research Office) of Göring's Air Ministry were partially able to decrypt the Yugoslav Foreign Ministry's codes. It is doubtlessly through this office that Vauhnik's "amazingly comprehensive and exact" messages soon came to Berlin's attention. Vauhnik was arrested as soon as Germany attacked Yugoslavia, and although some of his less important informants were discovered by his surveillants, his subsequent interrogation did not compromise his more important witting and unwitting sources.[75]

In the period between Colonel Vauhnik's initial messages of mid-March and those of early April, messages warning of a German attack on Russia and then of an attack on Yugoslavia, Belgrade was racked by momentous events. Vauhnik's and Gavrilović's messages and Hitler's alleged comment to Prince Regent Paul no doubt gave Belgrade the hope, at least until Germany and Russia clashed, that negotiations with Berlin predicated on Fabian tactics would be the wisest policy to follow. If worse came to worse, Belgrade would emasculate its acceptance of the Tripartite Pact by claiming reservations. Belgrade's desire to procrastinate, however, in order to receive assurances on various points in its serpentine negotiations with the Germans, conflicted with Berlin's desire to reach a quick settlement. Obviously, Yugoslavia's acceptance of the Tripartite Pact would have enormously simplified Germany's strategic and tactical requirements in its projected Greek campaign and elsewhere. Accordingly, Belgrade's ability to procrastinate was limited. Its initial ploy was to qualify its adherence to the Tripartite Pact by posing reservations on a number of important points: that Yugoslavia's sovereignty and territorial integrity would be respected; that Yugoslavia would not be asked for military assistance nor for passage or transit of troops through the country; and that Yugoslavia's interest in free access to the Aegean through the port of Salonika would be taken into account in Europe's reorganization. The Yugoslavs' negotiations for these reservations were not unsuccessful, but pressed by the Germans, Yugoslavia finally succumbed and, on March 25, accepted the Tripartite Pact.[76]

The unacceptability both to the public and to the Yugoslav military of what had transpired soon manifested itself. Gavrilović immediately resigned.[77] In the early morning hours of March 27, the government of Prince Regent Paul was overthrown by air force officers who had been encouraged by British intelligence and the legation's service attachés.[78] King Peter II ascended the throne, and Air Force General Dušan Simović was designated prime minister. Moscow's silent satisfaction with what had occurred in Yugoslavia, satisfaction that portended its future moves, was reflected in the sloganeering of the Communists late on the morning of the coup d'état. Their cries included *"Pakt sa Rusijom"* (a Pact with Russia) and "Belgrade-Moscow."[79] In *Pravda* it was implied that, although a congratulatory message about the coup had not been sent to Belgrade by the Kremlin, it could have been sent. This was about as far as Russia's fear of Germany would allow it to go in openly expressing sympathy toward Yugoslavia.[80]

Although the new government did not officially or formally denounce Yugoslavia's adherence to the Tripartite Pact, in spirit the agreement was dead.[81] Naturally, Yugoslavia's ordeal necessitated a corresponding adjustment of Russia's attitude toward Turkey. The new tack was brought to Steinhardt's attention as early as March 9 when an informant noted that Moscow was "motivated less by fear of a German attack on Turkey and its consequences than by the fear that Turkey might join the Tripartite Pact."[82]

Moscow's new stance toward Ankara was made public on March 25, the very day that Yugoslavia accepted the pact. In a joint Russian-Turkish statement, Moscow assured Ankara that should Turkey be forced to repel an aggressor, "it could then, in accordance with the nonaggression pact existing between Turkey and the USSR, count on the complete understanding and neutrality of the USSR."[83]

Several days later Belgrade was informed by the Czech government-in-exile that, according to Czech intelligence sources, Germany would attack during the first week of April.[84] Concurrently, the Russians attempted to shore up Yugoslavia politically and militarily. On March 31, the Yugoslav military attaché in Moscow admitted to the German naval attaché that, although the Russians had approached him and had offered to furnish Yugoslavia with "war material," he claimed that he had rejected the offer.[85] Following Yugoslavia's occupation, the Germans alleged that this arms offer was made by General Zhukov, as proved by archival evidence they had uncovered in Belgrade.[86] Then in line with the Russian military's apparent desire to conclude a military arrangement with Yugoslavia,[87] and following British-inspired probes by Gavrilović before the coup[88] and one made by the Simović government after the coup,[89] Molotov personally contacted the Yugoslavs. He asked that a delegation be dispatched at "the earliest possible moment saying that it was a matter of hours and not days." Moscow, the Russian chargé d'affaires in Belgrade divulged, favored "concluding a military and political pact with Yugoslavia."[90] Accordingly, Colonels Simić and Dragutin Savić, also of the air force, were dispatched to Moscow with the necessary instructions and authorizations for Gavrilović to conclude the negotiations and sign the proposed pact.

Substantive discussions started on April 2 with Andrei Vyshinsky, the deputy foreign minister, whose claim to fame at this point was his performance as the prosecuting attorney at the so-called Moscow show trials some years before in which many of the old Bolsheviks were tried, convicted, and executed on spurious charges. Vyshinsky held that Moscow's policy was reflected in the *Pravda* article of the previous day, which satirically denied that the paper had congratulated the Yugoslavs for having shown themselves worthy of their past glory. When Gavrilović, accompanied by Colonels Simić and Savić, again met Vyshinsky on the following day, the Russian denied any knowledge of the proposed military and political pact but promised to contact Molotov. When the discussions recommenced the next day, April 4, Vyshinsky explained to Gavrilović that his country was in no position to sign a military and political pact since doing so would disrupt Moscow's friendly relations with Berlin. As a substitute, he offered a treaty of friendship and nonaggression.[91]

What Vyshinsky offered was unexpected and unwanted by the Yugoslavs and not in tandem with the comments of the chargé d'affaires in Belgrade. Nevertheless, Article 2 had possibilities. It stipulated that if either party was attacked by another state, the other signatory would not assist the attacker. Gavrilović viewed the proposed pact as the initial step toward a military alliance. Moreover, Vyshinsky had emphasized Russia's readiness to supply war materials and asked for Yugoslavia's requirements so that the delivery of the necessary materials could be expedited. The necessary information, including a list of items in order of priority, was immediately supplied to him. Moscow, Gavrilović was informed, was also thinking of instructing Dekanozov in Berlin, in line with the draft pact, to inform the Germans that it wanted to see no threats or alterations to Yugoslavia's independence and territorial integrity. Then the Russians had second thoughts. They wanted to change the wording of Article 2 to stipulate that, if either signatory was attacked, the other signatory would continue a policy of neutrality and friendship. Gavrilović held that the intended change to Article 2 would go far to weaken the proposed pact. Vyshinsky retorted that the alteration was unavoidable; otherwise, Berlin might think that Moscow was planning to cut off supplies. War would erupt between Russia and Germany, and Russia was not prepared for such a struggle. The Yugoslavs were adamant. When Gavrilović proposed they postpone the signing ceremony until he had consulted Belgrade, Vyshinsky warned that what was possible now might not be possible the next day. He reiterated that Belgrade could count on Moscow's material assistance. The discrepancy between what the Russian chargé d'affaires proposed in Belgrade and what was being offered to the Yugoslavs in Moscow could not be resolved.[92]

Gavrilović's suggested replacing the neutrality clause with a stipulation that should Yugoslavia be attacked by a third state friendly relations would continue with Russia; he also suggested that Colonels Simić and Savić sign the treaty even though they lacked the competency to do so. Gavrilović's ploy was to make Berlin believe that the treaty was something more than an ordinary friendship treaty since it differed from the accepted form by carrying the signatures of the two colonels. Vyshinsky held that he would have to consult with his superiors.

Vyshinsky's repeated failure to convince Gavrilović to sign the treaty led to his suggestion that Gavrilović telephone Prime Minister Simović in Belgrade. After confirming that he was indeed speaking to Simović, Gavrilović made it clear that he refused to sign the proposed pact even though Simović ordered him to do so. Less than subtle, Vyshinsky pointed out to the immovable Gavrilović that Simović had ordered him to sign the pact, a clear admission that the Russians had been listening in on the conversation. No doubt everyone else along the lines between Moscow and Belgrade, especially the Germans at Budapest, had also been listening.

Then at about 10:30 P.M. on April 5, Vyshinsky again contacted Gavrilović and cordially invited him to the Kremlin. Gavrilović accepted the invitation but made it clear that he would not sign the treaty unless Article 2 was changed. When Gavrilović arrived at the Kremlin, Molotov proposed that Article 2 be altered as Gavrilović desired, to wit, he proposed the addition of a stipulation that if either party were attacked the other party would continue to be friendly. Gavrilović thanked Molotov. No, Molotov obsequiously demurred, the thanks all belonged to Stalin. Gavrilović then thanked Stalin, who opined that Gavrilović had been right. Had Article 2 stipulated neutrality, Stalin observed, it would have meant that if Yugoslavia were attacked Russia would have divorced itself from Belgrade's fate. He had tried to explain that to Vyshinsky, Gavrilović remarked, but he was oblivious to the argument. It was my fault, Vyshinsky groveled, as he bowed before the *Vozhd* and crossed his arms on his breast.[93] The whole performance revealed, as nothing else could, the decision-making process in Stalin's Russia.

Understandably, London viewed the pact as a "favourable development."[94] Gavrilović was likewise encouraged by the Kremlin ceremony and by what he had seemingly accomplished, and he reported to Belgrade that he "nursed the hope" that "Mother Russia" might come down on Yugoslavia's side should Germany attack. King Peter II, however, did not share his minister's optimism.[95] Indeed Gavrilović, who has been described as a "saint if ever there was one in politics, unselfish and loyal,"[96] should have been more cautious in what he reported to Belgrade, for last minute obstacles developed in legalizing the treaty's status. Both sides waited in the Kremlin while the necessary changes were made to the text of Article 2 of the treaty.

It was not until 1:30 A.M. April 6 that Molotov, Gavrilović, and Colonels Simić and Savić signed the treaty. At 5:15 German bombers pulverized Belgrade in a series of raids that were to level the city. The German invasion had commenced. The Russians then insisted that the treaty be dated April 5, which gave them a "loophole" to avoid the German contention that they had signed a treaty on April 6 with a state at war with the Third Reich.[97] Moscow had not known that the attack would commence on April 6, but it certainly knew that an attack was imminent.[98]

In the midst of the negotiations, Moscow again activated its deception *cum* disinformation operation through Ponschab, the German consul in Harbin, in order to remind Berlin of Moscow's value and importance to the German war effort and thus help fend off any protests Berlin might register about the upcoming pact. Devoid of authentic information, the new purported Russian intercepts that Ponschab conveyed to Berlin spoke of the Russian intention, because of railway problems far to the east, to develop an alternate route by establishing a shipping service from the Black Sea to East Asia. The service would be established as soon as the eastern Mediterranean was re-opened to merchant vessels after the expected suspension of military operations along the Red Sea coast and the Italian-held Dodecanese Islands that skirt Turkey's southern littoral. The new shipping route, Moscow held, would be profitable both politically and economically.

Moscow inferred, of course, that the development of such a route would be of great value to Berlin. Because of the British blockade, ships flying Russia's "neutral" flag would be able to supply Germany greater amounts of the needed raw materials and food stuffs more quickly by railroad transshipment from the Black Sea ports than they could by the means then at hand.

The supposed report from the Russian embassy in Chunking, China, was of equal interest to the Germans. It spoke of the rumored increase of the British air force in Malaya. Moreover, according to a Chinese source described as "reliable," Australian troops deployed in Africa and Iraq had been replaced by Indian ones, but in order to maintain the discipline of the latter, many British officers had been sent from England along with tank weapons and paratroopers.[99] The ploy was simple enough. The siphoning-off of invaluable resources, especially air force units, to defend the outposts of empire obviously weakened British defenses at home, and although it was not intimated in the intercept, Germany's attack on its only viable and also weakened opponent was far more imperative than spending time and valuable resources attacking an inconsequential Yugoslavia.

When informed of the ongoing Yugoslav-Russian negotiations, Ambassador Schulenburg remonstrated that the projected treaty was contrary to the 1939 nonaggression pact, but Molotov declined to reconsider Moscow's stance.[100] Although *Pravda* and *Izvestiia* were late in getting out their April

6 editions, predictably they warmly supported the pact as an instrument of peace and gave it front-page prominence topped off with a pictorial display of the leading actors, including Gavrilović.[101] Steinhardt pointed out that, despite *Pravda*'s editorial interpreting the pact as an attempt to thwart the spread of war and to continue the peace, it was clear that Moscow's real purpose was to "insure Yugoslav resistance to German aggression." Because of the manner in which the pact was concluded, Steinhardt had no doubt that it violated the "spirit if not the letter" of the 1939 nonaggression pact.[102]

When Gavrilović called on Molotov on the night of April 6 to discuss the delivery of war material, particularly anti-tank guns and aircraft—promised by the Russians in the early morning discussions of that same day and to be expedited through the Straits by Gavrilović—he discovered that there "would be considerable delay in such deliveries as the Soviet Union might agree to make and that there [were] serious transport problems." Ominously, Stalin was absent during this interview.[103]

The Foreign Office, however, doubted that the war material would be delivered. Whether the promise crystallized remained to be seen, the head of the Northern Department wrote, but it certainly appeared "as if the Soviet Government were 'burning their boats,' as regards their relations with Germany."[104] Nevertheless, despite this skepticism over the delivery of the war material, the London cabinet viewed the pact as a "favourable development."[105]

When Schulenburg approached Molotov again on the afternoon of April 7 in order to convey the reasons for Germany's invasion of Yugoslavia, Molotov repeated more than once what was by then the official line, namely, that it was very "deplorable" that the war's extension had proved inevitable. On the other hand, Molotov failed to mention the negotiation of the pact, and on instructions from Berlin, neither did Schulenburg.[106] That same day, the ferocity of the German attack and the apparent collapse of Yugoslav resistance moved *Pravda* to reproduce on its back page, in an unobtrusive font type, a *Tass* news agency story from Berlin relaying the news that Germany had begun military operations against Greece and Yugoslavia, but simultaneously suppressing the fact that Belgrade had been heavily bombed. Nor was the new pact with Yugoslavia mentioned. Officially, there was no Russian reaction to Yugoslavia's invasion. Moscow's only official demarche was to inform Budapest that it could not approve of Hungary's parallel attack on Yugoslavia.[107]

In the days that followed, although foreign reactions to the pact appeared in the Russian press, they were reported "without comment."[108] Any favorable reaction to the pact, for example, the claim that it "afforded new convincing proof of the powerful attraction of the peaceful policy of the Soviet Union,"[109] was ascribed to the foreign press. Press reports about the fighting assumed a pro-Greek and pro-Yugoslav "tone," minimizing the importance of German successes and publishing Greek war communiqués above those of the Germans.[110] Whereas in the past the press had published leading editorials accepting the German rationalizations for the invasion of Belgium, The Netherlands, and Norway, similar editorials did not appear about the invasions of Greece and Yugoslavia.[111] Even as late as April 16, with Yugoslavia defeated and the Greek and British forces crumpling under the German and Italian attack, *Komsomolskaia Pravda* could minimize the Axis successes in the Balkans.[112]

Moscow's backtracking, however, had commenced on April 8 as Greece and Yugoslavia reeled under the hammer blows of the Wehrmacht. In Berlin during an interview at the Wilhelmstrasse, Dekanozov said nothing of substance about the outbreak of hostilities or about the pact with Yugoslavia.[113] Publicly, *Dienst aus Deutschland,* the official Berlin mouthpiece, summed up by noting that "authorised German circles" had pointed out that the "political relations" between the two states were crystal clear and that "all problems of mutual interest" were dealt with through bilateral discussions. Indeed, Soviet Russia had had "no cause [to] express any official views on the German [military] operations in the Balkans."[114]

Dekanozov's conversation in Berlin was immediately followed on April 9 by the reactivation of Ponschab in far-off Harbin as the conduit for disinformation to Berlin. His information covered purported reports to Moscow's Far East missions, as well as reports from the American and Russian ambassadors in Ankara. Although the Simović government had desired peace with Germany on terms acceptable to the Serbian nationalists, Moscow's Far East missions were supposedly informed on April 3 that Germany would use the present struggle to annihilate Yugoslavia. Nevertheless, Moscow would "not intervene in the Balkan conflict."[115] It took this step despite its sympathy with Belgrade. At the present moment, however, it could not sympathize with London's attempt to form a united front of Yugoslavia, Greece, and Turkey, for this would strengthen British power in the Straits. Moscow had ascertained, it claimed, that the State Department had conveyed the same message to the American ambassador in Tokyo.

Russia's desire to avoid the Balkan cauldron was then seemingly repeated to its Far East missions on April 6, the day of the German invasion of Yugoslavia. The new pact with Yugoslavia, Moscow pointed out, would support "national movements" in the Balkans. Concurrently, it would not "worsen relations" with Germany, nor would it "support the English plan for a united front in the Balkans." The pact showed that Russia's intentions did not signal "hostility toward Germany." Should Germany commence hostilities against Greece and Yugoslavia, Russia would "maintain normal commercial relations with Germany, in particular oil" shipments by railroad, but the Danube, crucial to their trade relations, would be closed. Because of the paramount importance of oil to the German war machine, this provided just the kind of assurance that Berlin would like to hear, Moscow no doubt theorized.[116]

Further disinformation was then made available through an alleged report from the Russian ambassador in Ankara. During this period, Moscow was obviously keen on isolating Turkey from the struggle. If Turkey could maintain its neutral status, it could act as a buffer and thus protect Russia's southern flank. Therefore, to place Turkey in the best light possible, at least as far as Berlin was concerned, the ambassador's alleged report observed that should hostilities erupt between Germany and Yugoslavia, Greece would take no action against Turkey, provided the British did not commence military operations against Germany with more than fifty divisions. The Russians knew that, for the present, because of technical reasons, the British were in no position to land that many divisions in the Balkans. If faced with this situation, Turkey would maintain "friendly neutrality" with Greece and Yugoslavia but would not allow the passage of British ships through the Straits into the Black Sea.

The additional nonsense that Moscow fed to Berlin through Ponschab on April 9 was the claimed advice of the American ambassador in Ankara that Washington should "strengthen the resistance power" of those states opposed to Nazi Germany. The American stance, the ambassador argued, should be more aggressive; American bases should be established in the Middle East and flights extended deeper into Africa. Eden was not cooperative, however, regarding the American use of Aden as a base.[117] Feeding the anti-American attitude in Berlin was in Moscow's interest; if the Russians cultivated the impression that American penetration of the Middle East had irritated Eden, they might reap benefits in the future.

The last scene in this disinformation ploy executed through Ponschab was played two days later on April 11. The Russians again touched upon the supposed American desire to establish a presence in the Middle East. According to an alleged report from the Russian embassy in Washington, the Americans particularly needed to replace British shipping in the Middle East with their own, a need that the British were forced to accommodate because of their inability to deliver goods to the area. Senatorial opposition to establishing a base in Suez, it was asserted, was caused by the fear of German aerial attack. This fear and the Iraqi objection to an American presence in Basra led to a reconsideration of a base in Aden.

Finally, there was the alleged report from the Russian ambassador in Tokyo. Japan, he supposedly expounded, had exploited the deteriorating Balkan situation that had forced all the colonial powers to concentrate their forces in the Middle East. Japan increased the difficulties of the colonial powers by starting its own expansionist drive in Southeast Asia, thus pressuring the French government at Vichy to occupy Indochina and causing the British to ask for an increase in the number of Australian and New Zealand forces. British forces in Libya had to remain to protect East Africa. At the same time, the report continued, Australian and British troops protecting the Suez Canal would be dispatched immediately to Greece or Turkey.[118] Again as in the past, Moscow had ever so gently nudged Berlin to reconsider its policy in the

Balkans, a policy that diverted its attention from directly attacking its principal target, Great Britain, whose colonial empire's needs were draining men and money from the home island's immediate defense.

The initial Russian reaction to the signing of the treaty with Yugoslavia in the early morning hours of April 6 had been far different. In a conversation that lasted until 7:00 that morning, Gavrilović "gained the impression" from Stalin's comments that Moscow's "principal object" at the moment "was to weaken Germany as much as possible." He promised Gavrilović "substantial quantities of supplies" to be conveyed by Yugoslavian ships presently docked in Black Sea ports.[119] Gavrilović subsequently noted that, although he had been promised "armament, munitions, and planes" and although there had been adequate time to discuss with the Russians the "quantities and means of shipment," Moscow did nothing to implement the arrangement. He claimed that Moscow had contemplated watching events unfold before commencing its deliveries, and had his country "been able to offer effective resistance deliveries probably would have been made."[120] Nevertheless, it appears that when Yugoslavia was attacked Moscow did make "some effort to send war material through the Straits" and did receive some "Yugoslav officers for training," but when it became obvious that Yugoslavia and Greece would be overrun, Moscow's tactics changed.[121]

The Russian leadership, Gavrilović observed, believed that Yugoslavia's resistance would entangle the Germans in the Balkans through June; because it would then be too late in the year for Germany to commence an invasion of Soviet Russia, the entanglement would give Moscow a respite so it could complete its military preparations.[122] In view of the Yugoslav military establishment's deplorable state, its poor deployment and organization, and its demoralization, as well as of the country's weak geopolitical position, one is perplexed by Stalin and his supporters' notion that the Yugoslavs might be able to hold off until June the formidable German forces.

Past and contemporary events, incoming intelligence from the agent "Starshina" (most likely Lieutenant Schulze-Boysen of the Air Ministry in Berlin), and Stalin's own prejudices probably accounted for the popular belief in this notion. Certainly, the Serbs had fought gallantly and well against superior numbers and better equipped forces during the First World War. The previous year, the Greeks had likewise stopped and rolled back the invading Italians, and in the mountains of Epirus straddling the Greek-Albanian frontier they had savaged the Italian forces and kept them at bay for six months. Although the Italian military was not the German military, and the Yugoslavian terrain was slightly different from that in Epirus, these factors appear to have been ignored. Might not the Yugoslavs, the optimistic question must have been asked, repeat the Greek performance?

The information from Starshina was that air force sources felt that German military operations in Yugoslavia would take from three to four weeks. This would in turn postpone any attack on Soviet Russia, though Starshina was unsure whether the campaign in Yugoslavia would actually result in any postponement of the attack.[123] Then, in its issue of April 6, *Pravda* extolled the pact and emphasized the defensive possibilities offered by the Yugoslavian terrain.[124]

The "Yugoslavs were good fighters," the secretary-general of the Foreign Ministry, Arkady Sobolev, assured Steinhardt several days before the German attack, and "he expected them to defend themselves unless internal dissension prevented an organized defense."[125] He was supported by a senior NKVD official in the Berlin embassy who opined that the problems Germany would encounter in Yugoslavia would be far-reaching, and therefore, there was little likelihood of a "Blitzsieg"[126]—a lightning victory. These comments mirrored Stalin's personal thoughts about the Yugoslavs. They "were mountain folk and he himself was from the mountains," he ruminated, according to Gustav Hilger, the counselor of the German embassy in Moscow. "The German," Stalin observed, "would find them a far tougher proposition" than the French.[127]

Much to Stalin's disappointment, this did not prove to be the case in the spring of 1941. Several days after the capitulation of the Yugoslav forces, Steinhardt revealed to Washington information supplied to him by a "German source," whose identity was known to the State Department. His source believed that Stalin had "been tremendously impressed by the collapse of Yugoslavia as, being a Georgian and a mountaineer, he respects force and had assumed that the Yugoslavs with their mountainous country could resist the German mechanized equipment" for a considerable period of time.[128] Steinhardt's source could only have been Gustav Hilger.

Although they were overwhelmed in the spring of 1941, in the years that followed, the Yugoslavs and the guerrilla movements they spawned were to show their mettle and prove Stalin right. He was, however, irritated by his miscalculation and failure in Yugoslavia in the spring of 1941. His commitment to Yugoslavia under the pact and his off-the-record comments to Gavrilović, which were based on the hope that successful Yugoslav resistance and subsequent Russian aid would bog down the Germans in Yugoslavia's mountain fastness and thus postpone until the next year any intended German invasion of Russia, proved to be a serious tactical error. Hitler, as we now know, was furious over what had transpired.[129]

The Yugoslav misadventure gnawed at Stalin. If there was a culprit in all of this, it had to be someone else, for by definition the *Vozhd* was infallible. And who was this person? Clearly Milan Gavrilović. What did he think of Gavrilović? Stalin asked Milovan Djilas, one of Marshal Tito's right-hand men. Djilas thought him "shrewd." Stalin disagreed. There were politicians, he observed as though talking to himself, who thought shrewdness was the paramount consideration in politics, but the former Yugoslav minister had impressed him "as a stupid" person.[130] Although Stalin did not say it, his displeasure was that Gavrilović had gotten the better of him by his insistence that Article 2 of the pact eschew any mention of neutrality, and Stalin had finally agreed to it.

Stalin probably held one more subconscious grudge against Gavrilović: Stalin remembered the man's warning that the Germans would attack. Encouraged by his British counterpart Cripps,[131] on April 6 Gavrilović recounted to Stalin Hitler's alleged comment to Prince Regent Paul during their meeting at Berchtesgaden on March 4 that he would attack Soviet Russia by June or July. When he asked the *Vozhd* whether he was aware of the rumors that Germany intended to attack in May, Stalin had grimly responded, "Let them try it." When Gavrilović rejoined that some held that Moscow would not be able to defend itself against Germany for more than six weeks or certainly not more than six months, Stalin had again responded, "Let them try it."[132] Gavrilović had proved to be the source of a heavy subconscious burden for Stalin; not only had Gavrilović out-negotiated him but he had compounded this act by his Cassandra-like warning of the future that the *Vozhd* had failed to heed.

Gavrilović, however, was not the only Yugoslav to discuss with Stalin the possibility of a German attack. On the very night the pact was signed, the Yugoslav military attaché had raised with Stalin the specter of such an attack and had asked why Russia was furnishing oil to Germany. Stalin's disingenuous response was that no oil was being shipped to the Germans. As to a possible German attack, Russian forces were ready for a riposte, and if Berlin launched an attack it would be struck "straight on the forehead."[133] When Gavrilović had occasion to repeat to Molotov the Berchtesgaden conversation between Prince Regent Paul and Hitler, Molotov laconically observed, "We are ready."[134]

Indeed, the official line on this matter had been diffused through the bureaucracy. It was best reflected in the comments of Arkady Sobolev, who, loyal to the *Vozhd*, was to become assistant secretary-general of the postwar United Nations. When Steinhardt observed on April 2 that he assumed Sobolev had heard the rumors of a possible German invasion of Soviet Russia, Sobolev retorted that not only would such a possible move be "madness" but that he saw no reason for such an action, as this was not the time for the Germans to open a second front. Despite Steinhardt's arguments to the contrary, Sobolev insisted that he could discover "no adequate reason" for a German invasion of his country, especially in view of concurrent Balkan conditions.[135] In London just two days before, Maisky had succinctly summed up the situation: "Germany is too cautious," he replied when asked whether he had any fear that Russia would be attacked.[136]

The stance of Stalin, Molotov, Sobolev, and Maisky was perhaps a staged act of bravado. If it was, its staging was certainly not realized by Edward Coote of the Foreign Office's Northern Department, who confidently scribbled that no one knew better than Stalin "what the result of a German attack on the Soviet Union is likely to be."[137] Stalin and those around him had blundered in the spring of 1941. They had done so not only in thinking that more could be achieved in Yugoslavia than proved to be the case but also in believing that in any confrontation with the Germans the Yugoslavs would perhaps be able to hold their own. Support of Yugoslavia, of course, offered a cheaper alternative to colliding with the Germans. Understandably, when the Russian intelligence services on April 10 brought to Stalin's and Molotov's attention what Hitler had allegedly said during his discussions with Prince Regent Paul at Berchtesgaden, there was no reaction.[138] Keeping in mind Gavrilović's previous comments to Stalin and Molotov, it was *déjà vu*.

Obviously, fending off any German attack through diplomatic or other means was preferable to war, at least through the month of June. This delay would give the Russians the minimum time needed to re-equip the armed forces and shape up the military to lead to a stronger Russia by the spring of 1942. He knew war was inevitable, Stalin claimed during Churchill's Moscow visit of August 1942, but he thought he could have postponed an attack for six more months.[139] In actuality, Zhukov tells us, "Stalin believed—correctly—that we needed at least two more years to prepare [Soviet Russia] for war."[140] Stalin's miscalculations of Yugoslavia's ability to resist the Germans and of Russia's ability to withstand a German attack would create a chit for which Germany would demand payment in June, several months later.

Finally, there is one last point. There are those who might argue that Hitler's invasion of the Balkans in the spring of 1941 and the initial encouragement that Stalin gave to the Yugoslavs to resist delayed the commencement of Barbarossa from mid-May to June 22, thus subjecting German forces to a winter campaign for which they were ill-prepared and saving the Russians in late 1941 and early 1942. This myth persisted well into the postwar years. Hitler himself instituted the myth when he warned his generals about ten days before the invasion of Yugoslavia that Barbarossa would have to be postponed for a least four weeks.[141] Actually, the delay in invading Russia had nothing to do with the campaign in Yugoslavia and Greece and much to do with German unpreparedness. The expansion of the army to supply the forces needed for the projected Russian invasion led Oberkommando der Wehrmacht to realize that the "productive capacity of German industry was simply not large enough to supply the material for the newly formed units, a fact which made it necessary to introduce certain changes in the original programme."[142]

As the planning progressed, it became clear that not all the necessary forces would be readied as scheduled. The shortage of motor vehicles was particularly pronounced. When Barbarossa began, "no less than 92—or 40%—of the army divisions had to be supplied, wholly or in part, with [captured] French material." Since losses of equipment in the invasions of Yugoslavia and Greece had been very limited, Barbarossa had been delayed by shortages entirely divorced from the Balkan campaign. It has been observed that Hitler's decision to go forward, despite the fact that his attack would have to take place in the third week of June and despite a lack of reserves, pointed "to that unlimited *hubris* which, in the end, was to lead to his downfall."[143] *Mutatis mutandis*, the same flaw, compounded by personal, cultural, societal, and historical experiences, also affected Stalin.

## Eastern Approaches

Unfortunately for Stalin, dabbling in the Balkans in the spring did not lead to the type of military confrontation between Germany and the invaded states for which he had hoped, a confrontation that would unfold through June and thus obviate any possible German invasion of Soviet Russia in 1941.[144] The delay he sought so that Moscow could improve the military preparations of the country for any eventualities in 1942 seemed to elude him.

Concurrently, another opportunity for delay presented itself. Although not as attractive as a drawn-out German entanglement in the mountains of Greece and Yugoslavia, an arrangement with Japan, for example, was a possibility that offered distinct advantages for the Russians. The Japanese foreign minister, Yosuke Matsuoka, claimed that he made the first move toward an arrangement as he passed through Moscow on March 24 on his way to Berlin. When the Russians proposed that he meet with Stalin and Molotov, Matsuoka took the initiative and offered to sign a nonaggression pact, provoking a counteroffer of a neutrality pact from Molotov. At this point, of course, the arrangement had not yet crystallized. Yugoslavia was still negotiating with Germany and had not yet committed itself to the Tripartite Pact. When Matsuoka returned to Moscow in April on his way back to Tokyo, the military collapse of Yugoslavia was complete. In the interim, he had also had discussions with Hitler and Ribbentrop. Ribbentrop had broadly hinted that all was not going well with the Russians and that although a conflict with Moscow was not probable it was possible. Moreover, Matsuoka was assured that Germany would strike at Russia if Russia attacked Japan and would also promptly support Japan if it should clash with the United States. The immediate German desire displayed in these conversations was that the Japanese attack the British, specifically Singapore.[145]

With his Balkan gamble a disaster, and although he seemed to be unaware of the German commitments to Matsuoka, Stalin found Matsuoka's March proposal equally attractive in April. The arrangement was soon struck: should either signatory be attacked, the pact stipulated, the other signatory would observe neutrality throughout the ensuing struggle. The pact was to be valid for five years, and provided it was not denounced by either party a year before its expiration, it was automatically prolonged for another five years. Lastly, the pact included a reciprocal understanding that the signatories would "respect the territorial integrity and inviolability" of each others' respective satellites: Manchuria (Manchukuo) by Russia and the Mongolian People's Republic by Japan.[146] During the negotiations, Matsuoka had rejected Stalin's demand that Japan surrender its oil and coal concessions in the northern half of Sakhalin Island, whose southern half was owned by Japan. He did promise, however, upon his return to Tokyo to attempt to have the concession eliminated. Stalin, according to Matsuoka, "was a convinced adherent of the Axis and an opponent [*Gegner*] of England and America."[147]

Both in Tokyo and at the Japanese embassy in Berlin, the conviction prevailed that Moscow's "initiative toward the Pact was inspired solely by the impression" made on it by Germany's successes in the Balkans. Parallel thoughts were expressed in the Wilhelmstrasse. That the pact "was concluded without concessions or stipulations with respect to China"—the Japanese claimed that the initiative for the pact came from the Russians—proved that Moscow, in concluding the pact, "was not pursuing any Asian objectives but merely taking out insurance against the possibility of becoming involved in the West."[148]

In London, the observant Beneš thought that the Russians could not abandon their interests in the Balkans and realized that in the end they would clash with the Germans. Accordingly, Moscow would have to be prepared. It served Russian interests, therefore, to be neutral vis-à-vis Japan. Let Tokyo clash with Washington, Beneš reasoned. Japan would thus be committed, and when Russia clashed with Germany, it would have no fears about the eastern flank.[149] The more subtle and perceptive insight was furnished by Leon Helfand, who had served as Russian chargé d'affaires in Rome and had defected the previous year. His posting in Rome gives weight to his comments that Stalin's real objective was to enmesh the Americans in the war and that Stalin believed he could achieve this objective far more easily via the Pacific. By guaranteeing Russian intentions to the Japanese, Stalin went far to encourage Tokyo to attack the British bastion at Singapore. Stalin was very eager, Helfand maintained, that the "war should be *universal* with the sole exception of the Soviet Union."[150]

Unlike Matsuoka, who had limited intelligence sources to discern Russian intentions and desires, Stalin and Molotov's own intelligence sources kept them continuously informed of Matsuoka's schemes. If one is willing to accept the adage that knowledge is power, they certainly had more of it than Matsuoka had in the negotiations leading to the pact. Their Tokyo informant was the GRU's agent Richard Sorge, who through coded wireless messages and secret courier kept Moscow well briefed of Matsuoka's machinations.[151] In turn, Sorge's unimpeachable source was the well-placed journalist and longtime Communist, Hotzumi Ozaki, a recruited member of his espionage ring, whose contacts reached into the highest levels of Japan's political and journalistic worlds.[152]

Prince Kinkazu Saionji, who was a very close associate of Ozaki,[153] kept him well informed of the discussions among the elite of Japan's political world leading to the instructions issued to Matsuoka before his departure for Europe. Cabinet circles were pessimistic that anything would emerge from

Matsuoka's trip. The best that could be hoped for, the prince told Ozaki, was that, by increasing Matsuoka's knowledge of European conditions, the trip might contribute to his making the correct foreign policy choices in the future.[154] Fortuitously, Saionji was attached to Matsuoka's delegation during this European sojourn.[155] Aptly described as having "a shrewd eye to the main chance and a sharp list to port," Saionji, after the Korean War, "abandoned his native soil for the yellow clay and the red flag of the [Chinese] People's Republic."[156] What information he might have leaked to the Russians while he was in Moscow is difficult to assess, but in view of his subsequent arrest and conviction for his involvement with Sorge's espionage ring[157] (his sentence was suspended), it is difficult to believe that he was inactive during this European trek.

Although the treaty reflected, as the Wilhelmstrasse surmised, Moscow's concern over Berlin's continuing expansion into areas in proximity to Russia's frontiers, it was, for the moment, a diplomatic coup. European developments, Vichy's ambassador in Moscow correctly observed, had forced the Russians to stay their hand and settle with the Japanese for much less than most observers in Moscow had expected.[158] Stalin, however, was too much the political animal to believe even for a moment that the treaty excluded a Japanese attack on Russia if it served Tokyo's interests. Nevertheless, the treaty clearly indicated that, for the present, a consensus had developed within Japan's governing elite to place Russian-Japanese relations on a firmer and friendlier basis. On such a basis, Tokyo's fears of Russian adventures, especially in Manchuria, would dissolve, and Moscow in turn could concentrate on the European scene by allowing an unencumbered Japan to deal with the Chinese and with the Americans and British in Asia.[159] The Russian naval attaché in Ankara put it succinctly: Russia's policy, he explained, was clear, namely, to allow universal warfare as long as his own country avoided it.[160]

In Tokyo, Sorge was delighted by what had been accomplished. He perceived the pact as a Russian diplomatic breakthrough because it had succeeded in seemingly separating Japan from Germany.[161] Stalin was ecstatic. With Molotov in tow, he unexpectedly hurried to the Trans-Siberian railway station to see Matsuoka off on his return to Tokyo. As Matsuoka was not Japan's chief of state, Stalin's descent on the railway station, reported Vichy's ambassador, was "unprecedented."[162] With the exception of Stalin, noted Steinhardt, who had not been present, both the Russians and the Japanese "were somewhat intoxicated," and their collective behavior as they waited for the train's departure could "only be described as frolicsome,"[163] although one German observer's impression of this merriment was that "Stalin was pretty drunk at the time, with his left eye half-closed and his speech slurred."[164]

Whichever description is accurate, Schulenburg, who was present, recounted how Stalin sought him out, and when he found him on the station platform, how he threw his arms around his shoulders and exclaimed that Germany and Russia "must remain friends" and that Schulenburg must do everything possible toward this end. The *Vozhd* then approached the six-foot Colonel Hans Krebs, the acting military attaché, inquired if he were German, and when Krebs assured him that he was, took Krebs's right hand into both of his and squeezed hard. Russia and Germany would remain friends—*"Budiem s vami druziam[i]"*—Stalin observed. He was sure of that, Krebs responded loudly so that his words would carry and escape no one's attention. The *Vozhd* appeared pleased and patted the colonel on the shoulder in a friendly manner. Schulenburg thought that Stalin's approach to both of them had been deliberate and thus "consciously attracted" the attention of all those on the crowded platform.[165] John Scott, the British correspondent of the *News Chronicle* who witnessed Stalin's performance on the station platform, was convinced that he really wanted to co-exist peacefully with the Germans. Should hostilities erupt, Scott prophetically noted, it would be Germany that would fire first.[166]

The German reaction to the pact was inimical but muted. Steinhardt's German source—in all likelihood, Hilger—admitted that Berlin "had not been entirely satisfied with the Russo-Japanese Pact."[167] In Prague, Moravec's people reported that the German authorities were at a loss to explain the pact to the public.[168] The pact caused "concern," American interrogators discovered after the war, since it "did not harmonize with German plans."[169] General Eugen Ott, for example, the ambassador in Tokyo, privately observed to Sorge that the pact was not good for Germany.[170] Berlin's options, however, were very limited in this situation. In view of the pact's signature, the Foreign Ministry's state secretary, Ernst von Weizsäcker, observed to Ott, "matters have turned out slightly different from what had been anticipated." The Reich's reaction, he elliptically explained, followed the "philosophical maxim of 'what is, is good.' "[171]

To help rebuild its bridges with Berlin, Moscow hurriedly accepted the demarcation line of the Russian-German border in Lithuania initially proposed by Berlin in mid-February.[172] In turn, Moscow took steps to make sure that its success with Tokyo would not be misinterpreted in Berlin, at least as far as Russian interests were concerned. So, as in the past, the dependable Ponschab was maneuvered to center stage to play his important role of conduit in Moscow's deception *cum* disinformation operation targeted at Berlin.

Contacting Berlin on April 17, Ponschab conveyed purported messages from the Russian embassies in Tokyo and Washington. According to the Tokyo report of April 15, the American ambassador, who had always maintained that an agreement between Japan and Russia was not feasible, was upset by the new pact and had declared that this latest Russian move was manifestly hostile toward the United States. He argued that Washington had to strengthen its position in the region by dispatching troops to the Philippines, Australia, and Java in the Dutch East Indies in order to restore the balance of power in the Far East that had been jarred by the recent Russo-Japanese pact. The Tokyo report stated that his British counterpart was likewise upset and had remarked that Far Eastern states would perceive the pact as a threat to the British Empire; he was very much concerned about the "unfavorable impact" that the new arrangement might have on these states. Their French associate was perplexed and lacked instructions.

The embassy message from Washington supposedly sent on April 13 appeared to buttress the Tokyo one dated several days before. It spoke of differing views in Washington about how American assistance was to be given to England and other areas. A secret British mission advocated that the assistance be concentrated on England, a view supported by the Navy Department. On the other hand, the State Department was interested in the Asian question and was supported by the Army Department, whose views on the Middle East had gained sway. The embassy noted to Moscow that the movement of war material to Australia had been "significantly increased" and that, in the days preceding the signature of the pact with Japan, it had included airplanes and antiaircraft guns.[173] The intent of the two messages clearly was to convince Berlin that, if anyone was upset by the pact with Japan, it was the Anglo-American diplomatic representatives in Tokyo. They construed the pact as a hostile act by Russia, not Japan, specifically targeted against their countries. If anything, the pact had contributed to rising tensions between the Russians and the Anglo-Americans—it had turned the attention of the State and Army Departments, who were already interested in the situation in Asia, away from England to the extent that, rather than concentrating their support on Britain, they diluted that support by furnishing military supplies to Australia.

On the following day, April 18, Ponschab dispatched two more purported messages to Berlin. One, supposedly sent on April 15, was from the Russian ambassador in London, and the other was a circular message from Moscow, sent two days earlier to its missions in the Far East. The substance of the first message was that the London government believed that the pact would strengthen Japan's activity and raise the specter of war in the colonies. American assistance was now an important consideration. Hence, the ambassador in Washington would be instructed to declare that British forces in Greece were evacuating war material from the mainland and preparing for the defense of Crete. Should American assistance not increase, British forces would be forced to reduce their commitments by withdrawing from Egypt, Palestine, and Iraq. Some of these troops would be moved to India and the Far East. Troops from the home island could not be spared until American assistance could be attained, which at present was a subject of negotiation between both states.

The thrust of the message was clear. The pact had been a godsend for Germany. It had caused the British enormous complications. To protect its colonial possessions in the Far East, Britain would have to reduce its military commitments and for all intents and purposes would withdraw its forces from the Middle East. Crete would be defended only because it could help anchor the eastern end of the Mediterranean and prevent, provided Turkey remained neutral, any German descent on the coasts of Syria, Lebanon, Palestine, and Egypt. The Germans hoped that the needed American assistance might be delayed, bottling up British forces in the home island.

The circular message was more to the point. It explained that the Russian-Japanese negotiations leading to the pact were predicated on Moscow's fundamental desire "to secure peace in the Far East." The pact did not imply any alteration in Russian policy, nor was it directed against any other state—a not too disguised allusion to Germany. Indeed, the pact did not affect Russian-Chinese relations that were spelled out in the 1937 treaty. All this, the message continued, meant that the Far East missions had to act in a manner that led to no misunderstanding that Moscow was entering into any alliance "with capitalist states."[174]

The same day, April 18, Russia's value to Germany as a supplier of raw materials was highlighted in a mutual protocol inquiring into the observance of the economic agreement of February 1940. Moscow had calculated that its deliveries through February 1941 had amounted to 310.3 million reichmarks, an amount that Berlin would strive to equal by May. Indeed, the Russian complaint was that Germany did not supply sufficient rolling stock for transporting the goods delivered at the border by the Russians. Likewise, it did not furnish sufficient rolling stock for transporting German deliveries to the Russian border. Because of steps taken within Russia, Moscow, it was explained, was "in a position to carry out big shipments to Germany" during this period, but on the German side the transport difficulties, whether by land or water, hindered deliveries. In April, for example, Russia had scheduled for delivery 200,000 tons of grains, 91,000 tons of petroleum, and 20,000 tons of manganese ore, as well as considerable amounts of phosphates, nonferrous and other metals. Indeed, Moscow was not adverse to increasing these quantities.[175]

The subsequent British estimate was that petroleum exports in April 1941 from Russia to Germany probably were about 42,000 tons, double the amount exported in March. If this was a shortfall in petroleum delivery from the 91,000 tons that the Russians mentioned, it probably can be traced to the lack of sufficient German rolling stock and also to a stoppage of oil shipments by the Russians because of the German attack on Yugoslavia. The latter information, based on an "excellent German source" was reported by the American ambassador in Rome. For the spring and summer of 1941 the British estimated that Russian oil exports to Germany would probably reach 70,000 to 80,000 tons which would equal the peak months of 1940.[176]

However, despite these overtures by Moscow attempting to assure Berlin of its economic collaboration, a relationship that was necessary, Molotov later explained, to fend off a German attack, there were disconcerting signs.[177]

Led by experienced Abwehr officers, occasionally dressed in Russian army uniforms, sizeable groups were infiltrated across the frontier. Concurrently, NKVD security units in frontier districts, for example, the Ukraine, reported what appeared to be quickening German preparations for an attack from adjacent border areas, including Hungary.[178] In addition, from March 27, the day of the revolt in Belgrade, to April 18, the day of the protocol dealing with the effects of the economic agreement of 1940, Germany had continually violated Soviet Russian airspace. In a formal note to the German chargé d'affaires, Werner von Tippelskirch, the Russians claimed that there were eighty such cases. In particular, there was an unnerving case on April 15 near Rovno. In a German plane that had landed, Soviet officials discovered a camera, rolls of exposed film, and a torn topographical map of areas of Soviet Russia that gave "evidence of the purpose of the crew of this plane." The Russian Foreign Ministry stressed the hope that Berlin would "take all the measures necessary in order to prevent future violation of the national boundaries of the USSR by German planes." Tippelskirch warned Berlin that it was "very likely that serious incidents are to be expected if German planes" continued their overflights of Russian airspace.[179] His warning was not heeded, and the overflights continued.

To hammer home to the Germans that this behavior was unnecessary, another report was conveyed through Ponschab to Berlin on April 29. Because of Far East developments, Moscow purportedly warned its Asian missions on April 25 that Soviet Russia had to be prepared for a deterioration of relations with Britain and the United States. In line with this possibility, Moscow claimed that it hoped to conclude with Iran and Afghanistan treaty arrangements targeted against England, especially against its privileged position in the region. Should this treaty prove impossible, indigenous anti-British movements would be supported, despite the attitude of the two governments. Moscow had to make it clear to both states that its policy was to assist "the anti-imperialist movement of these oppressed nations."[180]

The second message, which allegedly was from the American representative in Canberra, detailed the rising tensions in Australia between the government of Sir Robert Menzies and the Labour party. Supposedly, the government's decisions to not worsen relations with Japan nor to increase troop movements to Africa and India and to curtail American business penetration of Australia's economic life had succumbed to pressure from London to do just the reverse. Should the Australians act as desired by London, the American representative opined, Australia had to expect that it would "irritate Japan"[181]; it was risky for Canberra to denude the country of troops.

The claim was made that the Labour party was opposed to the Menzies government and insisted on the immediate recall of Australian troops from Africa and on the signing of a security treaty with the Japanese. The two recommendations of the American representative, both spurious, of course, were a unilateral declaration by Washington that it would militarily defend

Australia against attack without any economic or financial *quid pro quo,* and that Washington would support the Menzies government, which opposed the Labour party.[182]

Moscow's purported message of April 25 to its Asian missions was obviously an attempt to convince Berlin that it had nothing to fear either from the Russo-Japanese Pact or from Russia itself. If anything, the pact with Japan posed a threat to Soviet Russia's relations with Great Britain and the United States. Conceivably, any rash Anglo-American move might throw Soviet Russia into Nazi Germany's arms. If an Anglo-American threat developed, Moscow was not adverse to undermining the British position in Iran and Afghanistan, and if this did not prove possible, Russia would support anti-British movements in the region regardless of the attitude of the two states.

These actions only supported the German struggle against Britain. The alleged report of the American representative in Canberra was clever, for there were actually policy differences between the Menzies government and the Labour party over the conduct of the war. But the notion that the Labour party advocated a security arrangement with the Japanese was pure invention. Again, Moscow had attempted to prove to Berlin that the value of the pact with Japan was manifest. It had caused tensions in Australia, certainly between the Labour party and Britain. Moreover, the British-Australian phalanx had lost some of its solidarity. These unexpected gains down under, which assisted the German cause, could be clearly traced to the pact.

If Stalin failed during this period to have his position accepted in Berlin, he was not alone. Concurrently, Churchill also failed, as we shall see, in his attempt to alert Moscow that its trust and faith in the 1939 arrangements and in the perceived medley of interests with Germany were misplaced.

# 4

# Imperialist Provocation and Disinformation

## Perfidious Albion

The discussions in Moscow during March and April 1941 with Gavrilović and the Yugoslavs, followed by those with Matsuoka and the Japanese, were in tandem with the exchanges with Cripps and the British. In early February, Cripps—who had been systematically snubbed—spoke to Molotov in an attempt to broaden areas of agreement and cooperation between their respective countries and thus move toward a rapprochement in their relations. From Molotov's replies, Cripps assumed that Moscow was not receptive to "any general political or economic arrangement for the present," which Cripps credited in part to its "uncertainty as to the outcome of the immediate development of new actions by the Germans."[1]

By the first week of March, the need to bridge the chasm between the two sides became more obvious to Cripps. In a confidential talk with resident American and British correspondents, a conversation that was soon picked up by the NKVD, Cripps spoke of worsening German-Russian relations and of the inevitability of a war between them. Reliable diplomats in Berlin reported a German plan to attack Russia, probably sometime in the summer, Cripps observed, carefully avoiding identification of the source of this information, the Swedish minister. Cripps thought that German peace overtures to London offering the restoration of France, Belgium, and Holland might be accepted because in his country, as in America, there were those with influence who wanted to see Russia destroyed, and if the British situation deteriorated, these people would press London to accept Berlin's peace offer. Should that occur, Hitler would very quickly invade Russia. Added reasons for the German attack of Russia were the increasing strength of the Russian armed forces and the declining strength of the German army with each day the war lasted. The Germans, Cripps held, were convinced that the Ukraine and the Caucasus would be captured after several weeks of fighting. Cripps himself, however, believed that the Russian army was better than British circles thought and was growing in strength with each passing day.[2] The NKVD source for this conversation is unidentified, but one of the participants was the *New York Times* correspondent in Moscow, Walter Duranty. Whether or not he was the source is unknown, but at the bare minimum Duranty was an apologist for the Stalinist regime and perhaps went far beyond that.[3]

In order to try to bridge the gap between the British and the Germans, Cripps approached Vyshinsky on March 22; however, this discussion, like the previous one, led nowhere. Vyshinsky claimed that "conditions did not exist for [the] discussion of such general political questions." For example, Vyshinsky felt that Cripps had chosen an inappropriate time for the discussion of Yugoslavia, a discussion that Eden had also attempted to institute with the Russians. Regardless, Cripps was ever optimistic in his dealing with Moscow. Cripps thought that he had gleaned a desire on Moscow's part "to prepare the ground for [the] possibility of a rapprochement" with London.[4]

Several days after his conversation with Vyshinsky, Cripps outlined for the Foreign Office Berlin's upcoming political and military moves leading to a German invasion of Russia. Cripps's informant thought it possible that the German steps might "well be part of the war of nerves." On the other hand, it was probable that Berlin was taking these steps "so as to work upon Russia by promises and intimidation so as to force her finally into an alliance which [would] enable Germany to exploit Russia." An attack, however, would be launched "only if [the] pressure fails in its effect."[5]

Though he did not say it, Cripps's information was probably acquired through his Swedish counterpart in Moscow, whose source in turn was the Swedish minister in Berlin. The Swedish minister in Berlin based his information on conversations at the Wilhelmstrasse and on "a number of reliable sources." Prior information from the Swedish minister, as we have seen, had filtered back to the Americans, the Greeks, the Yugoslavs, and probably others. Cripps understood that Stockholm regarded the minister in Berlin as a "reliable source."[6] He suggested that the minister's information be indirectly related to Ambassador Maisky through the Chinese or Turkish ambassadors, for example, so that it would come to the attention of the Russian authorities. Maisky's acquiring the information in this indirect and secret manner, Cripps prophetically observed, "would be more impressive than a direct communication, [the] motive of which [the Russians] would suspect."[7] Sir Victor Mallet, the ambassador in Stockholm, did not dissent. After his discussions with well-informed Swedish officials, he was inclined to the view that there was "probably something more than organised rumour-spreading behind some of these reports of a deterioration in Russo-German relations." Swedish Foreign Ministry officials were "exceedingly well-informed" and were not apt to convey to him rumors similar to those he received on a daily basis from press representatives, he observed to the Foreign Office.[8]

Concurrently, analogous data were forthcoming from the British military attaché in Switzerland. The ultimate source of the information was his Rumanian counterpart in Berlin, who was unaware that the report he had filed had been communicated to his Rumanian opposite number in Bern. The Rumanian military attaché in Berlin had reached the conclusion, based on his information, that Germany was preparing to attack Russia if it decided that an attack on England could not succeed.[9] The British military attaché's report was supported by his chief, Minister Sir David Kelly. The consul in Geneva, Kelly signaled London, had "repeatedly heard reports in the same sense" from senior officials of the League of Nations Secretariat and others. Kelly cautioned, however, that there were "grounds for suspicion that the ultimate origin of this information is in Germany where concerted attempts are perhaps being made [to] put about stories to this effect." Even if this suspicion proved to be true, Kelly observed, the very dissemination of such rumors in "responsible quarters" would be of interest.[10]

The Czechs had also been alerted to this information. Starting in February, exactly when is unclear, Beneš in London ascertained through his intelligence sources in Czechoslovakia that Hitler intended to launch an attack against Russia. Both London and Moscow were informed of this.[11] By early March, these reports were confirmed by Colonel Moravec of military intelligence, and Beneš was then furnished details of the upcoming attack. Those predicting the attack, particularly those from Prague, ran the gamut from sources controlled by Czech military intelligence, no doubt including Major Paul Thummel of the Abwehr, to underground personnel, but also included members of the Ukrainian community, who, though they occasionally "made fantastic reports, nevertheless revealed much." Indeed, information was even offered by Prague Communists.[12]

Toward the last days of March, the long-reliable Thummel in Prague correctly reported that the attack against Russia would be three-pronged, cited the number of German divisions deployed, and identified the army units that would participate and the names of the commanding officers. Although Beneš was pleased by Thummel's information, apparently he was unwilling to approach immediately the highest British authorities with this information. Perhaps his suspicion that Thummel was a possible double agent got the better of him. Colonel Moravec, however, did not suffer from the same reticence, and he immediately communicated Thummel's information to the British.[13] Further "definitive information" came into Beneš's hands in April, and again he reported it to the Anglo-Russians.[14] Indeed, in mid-April, Moravec reported the presence of a German panzer division, a type of unit that until that point had not been spotted, poised on the Russian frontier. By April 24, the information from Prague was that German concentrations on Russia's borders were meant to frighten Moscow into collaboration with the

Axis. This news was conveyed to Moscow in the hope that it would have a contrary effect.[15] The effect the information probably did have was to undermine whatever prior warnings had been given to the Russians.

Unknown to Beneš and Moravec, British intelligence had a source that was equal, if not superior, to Thummel in accuracy, the decryption operation that came to be known as "ultra." The Germans had been confident that "it would be practically impossible for anyone to break messages sent by this code machine," the American Office of Strategic Services reported in March 1946.[16] As we have seen, with the exception of the Foreign Office's Cavendish-Bentinck, chairman of the Chiefs of Staff Joint Intelligence Committee, British intelligence had concluded in late March that the continuing reports of a German attack against Soviet Russia were unconvincing.[17] Churchill was likewise unconvinced.[18] Early April appeared to bring no change in the intelligence estimate. There was "no reason to believe," MI14, the War Office branch on military intelligence for Germany, reported, that Berlin contemplated attacking Soviet Russia. MI14 thought it interesting, however, that armored and motorized units that "were to be withdrawn from Rumania and Bulgaria after Yugoslavia signed the Tripartite Pact were moved to the Cracow area" in Poland. MI14's plausible explanation was that this German move was undoubtedly made "to exert military pressure on Russia" to prevent its interference in Germany's Balkan designs.[19] This view was reflected in the weekly intelligence roundup circulated by the War Office[20] and the Chiefs of Staff.[21]

Although German troop movements headed east and into the Balkans were well known in London, these movements did not, as Churchill has written, necessarily involve an invasion of Soviet Russia and could be explained as necessary support for German interests and desires in the Balkans. The opening by the Germans of a Russian front seemed to Churchill "too good to be true." Earlier on, however, Churchill had decided to form his "own opinion"; he "preferred to see the originals" of pertinent intelligence reports and had made arrangements that they be furnished to him. Accordingly, it was with "relief and excitement" that at the tail end of March 1941 Churchill noted from decrypted Enigma intercepts, what he euphemistically described as "one of our most trusted sources,"[22] the odd movements of five panzer divisions that had crossed Rumania on their way to Yugoslavia and Greece. These same movements had, as we have seen, also caught the attention of MI14. Initially, when it appeared that Yugoslavia would sign the Tripartite Pact, three of the five divisions had been routed to Cracow. However, the coup d'état in Belgrade deposing Prince Regent Paul reversed the direction of these three formations to Rumania. Churchill held that this movement first in one direction and then in the other "illuminated [for him] the whole European scene like a lightning flash."[23] It was an intuitive insight.

The rapid deployment to Cracow of the three panzer divisions that were needed in the Balkans could only have meant that Hitler intended to invade

Russia. Churchill informed Eden, who was in Athens, of what he had discovered and also looked for a way to warn Stalin. Churchill hoped to arouse him to the danger and to establish contact with him as he had done with President Roosevelt. The question was how far he should go in supplying Stalin with any information. Attempts to relay Enigma information to Moscow without revealing where the information came from had come to naught. After consulting Sir Stewart Menzies, the director of MI6, Churchill decided to make his "message short and cryptic." He anticipated that two factors would catch Stalin's "attention and make him ponder": the short and cryptic nature of the message and its being Churchill's first communication with Stalin since his formal message in June 1940 commending Cripps as ambassador. On April 3, Churchill's warning was dispatched to Cripps, provided that he could personally deliver it to Stalin. Eden buttressed Churchill's communication to Cripps with one of his own, emphasizing the advantages of a united front and Russian assistance to Greece, Turkey, and Yugoslavia. Moscow's aid to these states, he argued, might bog the Germans down in the Balkans and delay further the intended German attack against Russia.[24]

Cripps responded that it was out of the question in the "present circumstances" to try and deliver Churchill's message personally to Stalin, but he offered no substantive argument to justify his stance.[25] Cripps's instructions were accordingly amended: deliver Churchill's message through Molotov, London signaled.[26] By the time Cripps replied, the German onslaught against Greece and Yugoslavia had begun. Cripps felt certain, he noted to London, that with Moscow's incoming diplomatic reports and his repeated observations, as well as with those of his Greek, Turkish, and Yugoslav counterparts to Vyshinsky, the Russian authorities were fully cognizant of the considerations spelled out in Eden's message and were finally acting on them. Under these circumstances, Cripps thought it "wiser not to interfere further at the moment as all is going as well as possible in our direction."[27]

To the Foreign Office's instruction that he contact Molotov, Cripps repeated his previous warnings and held that the Russians had partially mobilized their troops and that Moscow had learned from his Yugoslav counterpart, Gavrilović, about Hitler's comments to Prince Paul. Cripps incorrectly maintained, however, that the Russians obviously believed what Hitler had said and had taken note of it. If he sought a special interview with Stalin, he argued, the *Vozhd* would automatically relate it to the German attack on Yugoslavia and assume that London was attempting to enmesh Moscow with Berlin.[28] Churchill, however, was not to be put off. He thought Cripps was duty-bound to convey the pertinent data to Stalin. The importance of the information was not negated, Churchill stressed, if it was unpalatable or the source distasteful. The opening line, "Prime Minister still thinks [that the] message should be delivered," was amended at the last minute by Eden to read, "and I hope you will find this possible"[29]—in Foreign Office parlance, an "instruction to do so."[30] The message went on to note that, although the

German threat had already reached Stalin, it was important that he reflect on the fact that the thrust of the German armored forces into Greece and Yugoslavia had "deferred that threat and given Russia a breathing space." The greater the support that could be furnished to the Greeks and the Yugoslavs, the longer Hitler's divisions would be tied up in the Balkans.[31]

Before this message was received in Moscow, Cripps on April 11 addressed to Vyshinsky a long personal missive reviewing Russia's litany of failures in attempting to stem the rising tide of German expansion in the Balkans. He strongly urged that in her own interests, if Russia did not wish "to miss the last chance of defending her own frontiers in alliance with others," she had to decide on immediately implementing a "vigorous policy of co-operation" with states in the region still opposed to the Germans and the Italians. He wrote to Vyshinsky, Cripps explained to the Foreign Office, because of the difficulty of any direct approach to Stalin, after Vyshinsky's observation to him on March 22 that London's attitude precluded political discussion. Cripps had made it clear to Vyshinsky that his letter reflected his "own personal views," but he felt confident that he had said nothing with which London would disagree. He had not the slightest doubt that his letter would be immediately shown to Stalin.[32]

Consequently, if he were now to convey to Molotov Churchill's warning that expressed the "same thesis in very much shorter and less emphatic form," Cripps feared that the warning's impact would probably be to weaken the impression made by his letter to Vyshinsky. Moscow would not understand why Churchill's "short and fragmentary" comment, which was made on facts already known to Moscow and was delivered without soliciting Russia's attitude or suggesting action by it, "should be conveyed in so formal a manner." He feared that delivery of the prime minister's message would not only be "ineffectual but a serious tactical mistake." If Eden did not share this view, Cripps would, of course, attempt to arrange a meeting with Molotov.[33]

But Eden, like the Foreign Office's mandarins, shared Cripps's view.[34] There "may be some force" in the ambassador's "arguments against the delivery of your message," Eden wrote to Churchill. If Churchill agreed, Eden proposed to tell Cripps that there was no need now to deliver the message, but if Vyshinsky responded favorably to the missive, Cripps should give him the facts contained in Churchill's warning.[35] Churchill would have none of it. "I set special importance on the delivery of this personal message from me to Stalin," he retorted to Eden. He could not fathom why delivery of the message should be resisted. Cripps, he held, was "not alive to the military significance of the facts." "Pray oblige me," he advised Eden.[36]

On the day Churchill responded, April 16, Ambassador Maisky, accompanied by a youngish embassy counselor, probably Kirill Novikov, called on Eden. Though Novikov was present throughout the interview, he made no comment, which provoked Eden to write that he "seemed to be a Kremlin watch-dog upon" Ambassador Maisky.[37] The real question is whose watch-dog? Was he acting as a monitor for Molotov, or was he acting for the

NKVD? Clearly, the counselor's presence reflected Moscow's policy of not allowing someone in Maisky's position to meet officials of the country he was accredited to unless "he was accompanied by his own adviser."[38] In addition, there was probably an unease in Moscow about Maisky—a former Menshevik fortunate enough to have escaped the bloodletting of the 1930s—and the tenor of his reporting. The presence of this watchdog is our first visible sign that Maisky's star was no longer in the ascent. Maisky was recalled to Moscow in 1943 and to his subsequent falling-out with Stalin; in contrast, Novikov's career blossomed as Maisky's withered away. Perhaps Maisky's fall from grace is partially explained by the ideologically blinkered political simpleton Beatrice Webb, whom Maisky cultivated along with others in London. Her view through the smudged glass was that Maisky was not a "fanatical Marxist," although he was "inclined to apologize for the G.P.U." as a necessary organization in wartime, but one that would disappear when Russian Communism firmly established itself.[39] If so, Maisky appeared to lack the hard cutting edge indispensable to surviving Stalin's obstacle course of unswerving political reliability.

When the conversation touched on Anglo-Russian relations, Eden observed that it was London's "conviction that Germany's military ambitions were boundless." He "was quite sure," he noted to Maisky, that Russia "was threatened." Whether the attack was to be immediate or in the near future, the "German intention was quite plain." To support his case, Eden raised the matter of Hitler's alleged comments to Prince Regent Paul and the harsh remarks Hitler made against Russia. Hitler's comments, Eden emphasized, were "only a symptom of the determination which had been made plain in many ways." He proposed to Maisky a "frank discussion" of the relations between their two countries and raised the possibility of a rapprochement. Maisky did not reject Eden's proposal and asked him to make the initial suggestions, accepting Eden's rejoinder that he was not open to the notion that there would be movement only on the British side.[40] This exchange was the first official and formal warning from London to Moscow that a German attack was in the offing.

Cripps's continued silence, however, prompted Churchill several days later, on April 18, to ask Eden whether his warning to Stalin about the German danger had been delivered. Churchill was "very much surprised that so much delay should have occurred, considering the importance" he attached to this "extremely pregnant piece of information."[41] Uncommitted to the Calvinist work ethic, Eden took the blame for the unnecessary delay, claiming it was due to a visit to Sandringham.[42] Cripps was then immediately instructed that because of the "military significance of the facts" Churchill still desired his message to be delivered. Cripps was to deliver it by whatever channel he thought suitable and to add whatever subsequent remarks Eden had transmitted to him that still applied.[43]

That same day in Moscow, Cripps, acting without instructions, addressed a long memorandum to Molotov. Because Molotov, indicating the cool state of Anglo-Russian relations, declined to see Cripps, Cripps was forced to call on Vyshinsky. Cripps's remarkable memorandum was an attempt through "inducements and threats" to entice Russia into the anti-German camp. Cripps warned Molotov that the danger facing Moscow was no mere "hypothesis" but a plan by Berlin for the coming spring that stemmed from the quick conquest of the Balkans. Ominously, the memorandum contained "insinuations of a possible separate peace if Russia did not alter its policy."[44] Vyshinsky was not moved by Cripps's warning and brusquely rejected the memorandum. The "necessary prerequisites for discussing wide political problems did not exist," he explained to Cripps. This was the same position he had assumed during their last discussion on March 22. As far as the Russian authorities were concerned, "no question of improving relations existed, as they had done nothing to worsen them."[45] This stance was then reiterated in a very short note, in which Vyshinsky likewise rejected Cripps's overtures of April 11.[46]

A week after the Cripps-Vyshinsky interview, Maisky, accompanied by Novikov, his watchdog-*cum*-adviser, went to the Foreign Office to call on R. A. Butler, the Parliamentary under secretary. Alluding to Cripps's memorandum, Maisky observed that he had cautioned Butler previously that "written communications and memoranda were anathema" to both Stalin and Molotov. The root of the problem was that Cripps was trained as a lawyer. His memorandum, a complete text of which was sent by Moscow, seemed to Maisky "to be couched in the wrong sort of terms to make any appeal at all." Moscow, Maisky explained, was uneasy about partaking in "negotiations of a general character" with London. It was Butler's impression that Moscow would want any improvement in mutual relations to be based on a "unilateral" British pronouncement. Maisky's parting observation on this issue was that "he did not anticipate" that London would receive any definite response from Moscow in answer to Cripps's memorandum.[47] Weeks later, Maisky pithily summed up the situation for Beatrice Webb: the lengthy memorandum of April 18, he divulged, had "merely irritated" the Russian government.[48]

It was not until April 19, over two weeks of protracted delays after Churchill's initial request had been made, that the obstreperous Cripps finally delivered Churchill's warning to Vyshinsky with the instruction that it be conveyed to Stalin. In view of Vyshinsky's rejection of his overtures of April 11, as well as of those of the previous day, Cripps "felt it preferable to abstain from adding any commentary" to the warning.[49] Several days later, Vyshinsky assured Cripps that Churchill's warning had been forwarded to Stalin.[50] Inexplicably, despite Churchill's obvious interest in having his warning delivered to Stalin, Churchill was not informed that Cripps had done so. In frustration, on April 30, he asked Eden when Cripps had conveyed his warning to Stalin and asked to have Cripps report.[51] As in the past, Eden offered excuses for the breakdown in communication and assured his chief that his warning had indeed been conveyed by Cripps.[52] From inside the Kremlin's walls, there was no reaction, either official or unofficial, to Churchill's message.

The question of Churchill's warning was not raised again until after the German attack of June 1941. In October, Lord Beaverbrook, along with his American counterpart, Averell Harriman, arrived in Moscow to conclude an agreement about the supplies that Great Britain and the United States would make available to Soviet Russia during the coming months. During the course of these negotiations, Stalin claimed that he could not remember whether in April he had been warned of the upcoming attack by Churchill. If anyone was culpable here, it was obvious to Churchill that it was Cripps. The form and nature of the communication, the information it contained, and the fact that it came from the head of the British government and was to be delivered directly by Cripps to the head of the Russian government "were all intended to give it special significance and arrest Stalin's attention." Churchill was astonished that Cripps had the "effrontery" to delay his warning for over two weeks and then to restrict himself merely to handing it to Vyshinsky. Churchill was willing to concede that perhaps the message never really reached Stalin or was placed only "casually" on his desk. That Cripps had thought that his own personal missive to Vyshinsky would generate a greater impression than the warning of the British prime minister only showed Cripps's "lack of sense of proportion." He had "great responsibility for his obstinate, obstructive handling of this matter," Churchill rumbled. Had Cripps executed his instructions, he optimistically concluded, "it is more than possible that some kind of relationship would have been constructed between me and Stalin."[53]

Eden was unconvinced by Churchill's arguments. In the period before the German attack, he correctly noted, Moscow had been very "reluctant to receive messages of any kind." Even if Stalin had received Churchill's warning, he now probably preferred to forget this fact. "Only thus, to some extent, can he exonerate himself," Eden insightfully observed. He pointed out that a similar attitude was adopted toward his own warning messages that had been given several weeks before the invasion and that, with Churchill's permission, he had given to Maisky. These warnings, until this moment, had neither been acknowledged nor referred to.[54]

Churchill was not in a position to raise the issue directly with Stalin until the Moscow Conference in August 1942, when he personally communicated to him the warning message that had been dispatched to Cripps. After it was read and translated, the *Vozhd* "shrugged his shoulders." He admitted having seen it, but he disingenuously insisted that he needed no warning, for he knew war would come. Churchill did not press the matter or ask what the end result would have been for everyone if Great Britain had been conquered while Stalin gave Hitler time, as well as invaluable material supplies and assistance to do so.[55]

Churchill's belief that Cripps's delay in delivering his warning message to Stalin had destroyed the message's impact and the possible development of an operational rapport between himself and the *Vozhd* showed Churchill's appalling lack of acuity. That Moscow would be unreceptive to his warning message should have been obvious to Churchill in view of Molotov's rejection of Cripps's request for an interview and Vyshinsky's rejection of Cripps's overtures of March 22, April 11, and April 18 that attempted to lay the basis for a rapprochement in Anglo-Russian relations.

Indeed, although Churchill was unaware of it, the substance of the Cripps-Vyshinsky exchange of March 22 conveniently fell into Berlin's hands and was then made available to the German embassy in Moscow.[56] Likewise, it appears that Hitler was alerted to Cripps's proposal to Vyshinsky on April 11 that Moscow vigorously cooperate with those Balkan states opposed to Germany and Italy if the Russians did not wish to miss the chance to defend their own frontiers in conjunction with others.[57] Cripps's exchange with Vyshinsky on March 22 and his proposal of April 11 were probably both decrypted by the Forschungsamt, for its experts "were able, in part at least," to decrypt Cripps's messages to the Foreign Office.[58] At the minimum, the decryption of this information in Berlin showed how loyal Moscow was to the 1939 nonaggression pact despite London's efforts to woo the Russians into the anti-German camp.

Moscow's monolithic commitment to the 1939 pact was indicated by Ambassador Umansky's remark on April 18, the day before Cripps delivered Churchill's warning to Vyshinsky. Regardless of any nagging thoughts Umansky may have had on the matter, he could with confidence describe Russian-German relations to the British in Washington as agreeably "set."[59]

Stalin's reaction to the warning reflected Moscow's cool, one might even say unfriendly, attitude toward London. The *Vozhd* received Churchill's warning "incredulously," General Zhukov informs us. His reaction dovetailed with Zhukov's observation that Stalin was prejudiced "against information coming from imperialist circles."[60] This attitude goes far to explain Stalin's decision not to pass Churchill's message on to the General Staff, since the *Vozhd*, his biographer informs us, perceived it as a British attempt to hasten a clash between Moscow and Berlin.[61]

Certainly, the author of the warning message, Churchill, fell under the rubric of imperialistic circles and accordingly was not high on the Kremlin's list of reliable sources. Since the 1917 revolution, he had been undisguisedly hostile toward the Communist regime, and this fact was duly noted in Moscow. Concerning this specific warning, after the war Molotov questioned whether it was possible to trust Churchill's information. After all, Molotov claimed, Churchill had been interested in a confrontation between Moscow and Berlin and wanted it to occur as quickly as possible.[62]

As we have seen, a little over a week after Vyshinsky had forwarded the warning message to Stalin, Umansky complained of Churchill's sponsorship of the British intervention in Russia after the revolution.[63] Had Stalin forgiven him for his prewar anti-Communist stance? Churchill asked the *Vozhd* during the Moscow Conference in 1942. Through his interpreter, Stalin retorted, " 'all that is in the past, and the past belongs to God.' "[64] In a war of survival, Stalin could afford to be generous to a devoted class enemy who, for the moment, happened to be an ally as the two nations faced and fought an implacable foe.

## Multiple Warnings

As we shall soon see, Stalin perceived Churchill's warning message as a provocation. He no doubt ranked Beneš's warning, also given in April,[65] as British-inspired and likewise placed it under the same rubric. The information acquired in Berlin in late April by the Russian diplomat Valentin Berezhkov from a serving major of the Luftwaffe no doubt suffered the same fate. According to the major, his squadron had been recalled from North Africa and was assigned to the Lodz (Litzmannstadt) area in Poland. Many air force units, he remarked, had been transferred toward the Russian frontiers. He explained his comments by saying that he wanted nothing to occur between their two countries. Understandably, Berezhkov was shocked by the major's remarks. Cautious, he voiced the usual palliatives and reported the conversation to Moscow. Since Berezhkov himself thought the whole conversation "could be some sort of provocation" and since the interview occurred during a reception at the private residence of the first secretary of the American embassy in Berlin,[66] Moscow's perception of the conversation would have been no different than Berezhkov's.

Stalin's attitude during this period is best reflected in his own scribblings on GRU reports. On April 17, the GRU learned from its representative in Prague, whose cover was that of the consulate's commercial attaché, that the German military had halted the manufacture by the Škoda works of heavy armaments for Russia. Moreover, top level German military stationed in occupied Czechoslovakia had divulged that German troop concentrations were building up on Russia's western borders. The belief was that the Germans would attack in mid-to-late June. The source of the information was well known to the GRU: he was a non-Communist Czech, the chief engineer of the Škoda works, code-named "Škvor" (earwig), who as a patriot had turned to the Russians after the German occupation of the Czech state in March 1939, but he was not a paid informant. Unknown to the GRU, somewhat similar information was received by the British, no doubt from Moravec's organization.

The acting chief of the GRU's Fourth Division, the Tatar Ismail Akhmedov, who dealt with technological espionage, immediately showed the Prague report to Golikov. Carefully, Golikov checked with Akhmedov and also the GRU records about the source. This source was found reliable, and all his previous information and evaluations confirmed his *bona fides.* A full report on the Prague message and the source was then drawn up, signed by Golikov, and sent by special messenger to Stalin, Georgii Malenkov, who served in Stalin's secretariat, and Zhukov. On the evening of April 19, the very day Cripps conveyed Churchill's warning message to Vyshinsky, Akhmedov was summoned to Golikov's office. Without fanfare, he was given the report that had been filed with Stalin only days before. Scrawled across the report in red ink were the words: *"Angleyskaia Provokatsiia Rassledovat! Stalin* [This is a British provocation. Investigate the matter! Stalin]."[67]

The *Vozhd*'s comments, however, caused some anxiety for the GRU's Colonel Dmitri Konovalov in the Berlin embassy. His cover was that of the trade delegation's inspector, and he directly controlled Škvor.[68] As Konovalov well knew, GRU officers in Stalin's Russia had been shot for matters far less serious. Stalin's reaction to Churchill's warning message had been no different from his reaction to Škvor's information. Concurrently suffering the same fate was a report of the military attaché in Vichy, General Ivan Susloparov, who, using information supplied by his American, Bulgarian, Chinese, Turkish, and Yugoslavian counterparts, alerted the GRU that an attack scheduled between May 20 and May 31 would now be postponed for about a month, owing to bad weather.[69] About the same time, General Tupikov, the military attaché in Berlin, had advised the GRU that about 180 German divisions were being assembled along Russia's western borders. As required, Tupikov dutifully reported this intelligence to Ambassador Dekanozov who "had dismissed it airily as a figment of someone's imagination."[70]

The notion of "provocation" used to dismiss Škvor's information and undoubtedly Churchill's warning, as well as the notion of "disinformation," formed the reefs upon which accurate intelligence in the hands of Stalin and his entourage inevitably foundered and sank. Dekanozov, as we know, was a member of that entourage. Stalin's decision about Churchill's message was made easier because, by the time Stalin received it, Yugoslavia had fallen to the German onslaught, and the British had been outgunned and outmaneuvered in Greece and were reeling from the blows of General Erwin Rommel in the Western Desert. Britain's inept defense of Crete in May, despite the foreknowledge the Enigma decrypts gave them of the German invasion, must have sealed in Stalin's mind what he considered to be the real purpose of Churchill's warning message, as well as those of others. To Stalin, Zhukov tells us, it was "a logical wish of the British to pit us against the Germans and draw us into a war as soon as possible for which we, in his belief, were not ready."[71] In Moscow during this period of spring and early summer 1941, the notions of provocation and disinformation in their various forms and shapes pervaded the entire perception and evaluation of incoming intelligence.

In an atmosphere in which all incoming intelligence was perceived as provocation or disinformation, there was no likelihood that any information dispatched by the often accurate Sorge in Tokyo would be believed or accepted.

The story that he warned Moscow on March 5 that the German invasion would commence in mid-June can only be viewed as a tall tale planted in *Pravda* in 1964 to burnish the reputation of the NKVD by associating it with the heroic Sorge.[72] Actually, Hitler decided on the June invasion date well after Sorge supposedly reported it.

Subsequent to March, however, Sorge did come across valuable data that should have alerted Moscow to Berlin's designs. Sorge's ruminations on this data, however, occurred during his arrest and interrogation by the Japanese. Though Sorge might have been attempting to mislead the Japanese, this does not appear to be the case. His recollections were based solely on memory, and it is possible that he telescoped persons and events and made other minor errors.

In late April, according to Sorge, the senior military attaché in the German embassy in Tokyo, Colonel Alfred Kretschmer, informed him that, although it was unclear whether hostilities would erupt, Berlin had completed its military preparations for an invasion of Russia. The colonel felt that Germany's military concentrations might induce Moscow to surrender to Berlin's unannounced demands; whether war or peace would follow really depended on Hitler and was not connected in any way to Moscow's attitude. Moreover, Kretschmer had received instructions to inform the Japanese that Russia's mobilization of its western frontiers necessitated that Germany take the proper countermeasures. To support the case, Berlin had supplied a map detailing the specifics of the alleged Russian mobilization.

Sorge's conversation with Colonel Kretschmer was then followed in May by one with Colonel Oscar Ritter von Niedermayer, a special emissary sent to Tokyo to brief the ambassador, General Ott. Colonel von Niedermayer had been stationed in Russia in the 1920s during the period of Russo-German military collaboration. Von Niedermayer's unguarded comments to Sorge that a conflagration between Germany and Russia was inevitable were no doubt lubricated by a letter of introduction to Sorge that had been given to the colonel before von Niedermayer's departure from Berlin by Herbert von Dirksen, the former ambassador. Von Niedermayer explained that Germany had to occupy the Ukraine's grain-producing areas. In addition, to offset Germany's labor shortage in industry and agriculture, it needed at least one to two million Russian prisoners. According to the colonel, Hitler thought that the propitious moment had arrived to remove the Russian threat and that so opportune an occasion might not present itself again. Information from other sources associated with the embassy topped off the information that Sorge had derived from Colonels Kretschmer and von Niedermayer.

Several weeks later, Lieutenant Colonel Friedrich von Schol, who knew Sorge, arrived in Tokyo on his way to Bangkok as military attaché. He also came to give Ambassador Ott secret oral instructions concerning the coming war with Soviet Russia. According to Sorge, Colonel von Schol contended that the invasion would commence June 20, and although it might be postponed for several days, all preparations had been completed. He divulged that a German army of approximately 170–180 divisions, supplied with tanks or mechanized, was poised at Germany's eastern frontiers. The attack would be along the entire front, the main forces directed toward Moscow, Leningrad, and into the Ukraine. Such a thrust could quickly smash and capture the Red Army. No ultimatum would be given the Russians, but a declaration of war would be made after the struggle had commenced. Within several months, the army and the government might collapse. By the winter of 1942, the Trans-Siberian railroad would be operating and contact with Japan established.[73]

Sorge's ideological dedication to the cause leaves no doubt that all this information was immediately earmarked for communication to Moscow. Certainly, we know the comments by von Schol were enciphered for transmission on May 20.[74] In addition, purported messages from Sorge on May 13, 15, 19, and 22, Moscow claims, were received relating the information imparted by Colonels Kretschmer, von Niedermayer, and von Schol, especially the information on May 13 that the German invasion would take place on June 22.[75] The question that develops, however, is whether the messages really ever left Tokyo, and if they did, what the reaction was to them in Moscow.

Sorge had three ways of communicating with Moscow. One was the delivery of microfilmed material through China by members of his ring who acted as couriers. The second was surreptitious meetings with GRU personnel who had "legal" cover because of their functional position in the Russian embassy in Tokyo. For example, should service attachés, consular officers, and other embassy staff be caught red-handed by the Japanese authorities during such contacts, they would be protected by diplomatic immunity. Lastly, there was communication with Moscow by enciphered wireless messages. Once the European war commenced, communication of microfilmed material through China was discontinued by Sorge because it was very dangerous for the ring's members to act as couriers. Contacts with the Russian embassy were then established, and materials were passed to the consul, H. Leonidovitch Vutokevich, though this was probably not his true name. When he was posted back to Moscow, his place was then taken by Viktor Sergeevitch Zaitsev, whose cover name was "Serge." No doubt his given name and surname were likewise false, but like his predecessor he served as the embassy's consul. Throughout 1941, Zaitsev picked up material from the ring ten times, though Sorge was present on only one occasion.

Sorge's only other contacts with Moscow in 1941 were enciphered wireless messages. These messages were transmitted to Moscow by his German wireless operator, Max Clausen, probably a cover name, for his real surname may have been Christiansen. A longtime Communist, he had also served with Sorge in Shanghai in the early 1930s. Although he was not well educated,

Clausen was mechanically adept and during the First World War had seen service on the western front in a radio unit of the German Signal Corps. During his stay in Shanghai, Clausen had had the "assimilated rank" of a Red Army major; if so, Sorge must have been at least a colonel. Using common materials that he bought without difficulty in Tokyo's open market, Clausen assembled the wireless transmitter that he used to convey Sorge's enciphered messages to Moscow. In all probability, the receiving station, code-named "Wiesbaden," that Clausen beamed his messages toward was in Vladivostok or perhaps Khabarovsk. Because Sorge had an enormous work load, he received special permission from GRU Moscow to instruct Clausen in the code used so that Clausen could also encipher and decipher messages. All enciphered messages to Wiesbaden, however, were transmitted by Clausen because Sorge, as he admitted, knew nothing about wireless transmission.[76]

In this chain of wireless communication between Tokyo and Moscow, the weak link appears to have been Clausen. In 1939, his diary shows that he made fifty transmissions and sent 23,139 word groups—five-letter code groups—to Wiesbaden. This was increased to sixty transmissions and 29,179 word groups in 1940. But in the crucial year of 1941, he transmitted only twenty-one times and sent 13,103 word groups. "Since Sorge himself," it has been incorrectly observed, "sent 40,000 word groups in 1941, Klausen's [sic] sabotage didn't interfere with the success of the mission." Unfortunately, this comment was a misinterpretation or mistranslation of Clausen's recollections during his interrogation by the Japanese authorities, for the figure of 40,000 was his estimation of the word groups that Sorge gave him, not what Sorge had sent, since as we have seen Sorge knew nothing about wireless transmission.[77]

The important point, however, is that, though the number of transmissions declined between 1940 and 1941, the length of the messages increased. Initially in 1939, there were 463 word groups per message. In 1940, this had increased to 486 word groups per message. By 1941, the number of word groups per message had increased over 1940 by about 28 percent to 624. The decline in the number of messages, but not in their length, was probably due to the increased danger in repeated surreptitious transmissions. That was the up side of the lengthened messages. The down side was that the longer it took Clausen to transmit a message, the more time it gave the Japanese to take a "fix" on the transmitter's location.

Clausen's explanation for the decline in 1941 transmissions is open to discussion. He maintained that a heart condition that he had developed by the spring of 1940 had slowed him down. However, he admitted that even while bedridden (April to August) he transmitted to Wiesbaden.[78] He alleged that by the autumn of 1940 he began to tire of being a spy. The tension of the job was beginning to affect him. He not only had a health problem but had also developed ideological doubts about his horizontal class loyalty across national frontiers and about the Marxist-Leninism of the Stalinist variety. Concurrently, he began to develop vertical nationalistic loyalties, based on his German antecedents. This change was apparently fueled by an antipathy toward Sorge. What really appears to have "dulled his enthusiasm for the Soviet cause," however, was the prosperity he gained and pride he felt in his successful business in German blueprint machines. The business also offered him the perfect cover of a German businessman. Initially funded by the GRU, he devoted increasing amounts of time to his business. Because of the war's vagaries and the shortage of foreign exchange, the GRU in November 1940 instructed that Sorge's ring be operated largely out of the firm's profits, profits that Clausen had worked hard to accumulate. These instructions, as nothing else could, might have made Clausen decide to let his association with the GRU suffer benign neglect.

Clausen claimed all this when he was interrogated by the Japanese authorities. It is possible that he was lying and cooperating not only to lighten whatever punishment he would receive but also to protect his anti-Communist wife, who was not enamored with his secret calling. If Clausen had caused the GRU significant damage through his alleged actions, it is difficult to believe that he would have been allowed to settle in East Germany in the immediate postwar Stalinist period or that he would have been awarded the Order of the Red Banner for heroism in 1965. No doubt it would be safe to assume that during his stay in Vladivostock and Moscow, as well as in Tokyo following his release by the Japanese, he passed muster after being debriefed by his former GRU controllers. Indeed, in Tokyo immediately after the war, he was asked by the Russians to ascertain what he could about Germans residing in the city and also "about the remnants of the Sorge ring and its contacts." He expected that when he got to Moscow he would be able to settle the question of "accrued back pay" for his services to the GRU. The Russian requests for Clausen's assistance and his own equanimity in postwar Tokyo do not give the impression that he was hounded by any fears about returning to the New Jerusalem of the working class. The Japanese abet whatever game is being played on the question of Clausen's machinations, which lack independent confirmation, for the promised volume containing Sorge's messages to Wiesbaden has never appeared, and it is the texts of these transmissions that would confirm or deny Clausen's version of events.

We certainly know that by early 1941 Clausen transmitted fewer and fewer messages to Wiesbaden though they were longer than before. It has been suggested that at the minimum one-half and at the maximum two-thirds of the material that Sorge gave Clausen was never transmitted. Clausen alleges that he was selective in what he sent. Sometimes he transmitted the best parts of the material given to him before he destroyed it. Other materials he did not even bother to read. Some important material he enciphered and sent, for he could not risk suppressing it entirely, or so he insisted when he was interrogated. When Wiesbaden complained about the decrease in transmissions, Clausen responded that this was due to bad atmospheric conditions.[79]

The easy answers Clausen gave to his interrogators just do not jibe with the tradecraft of agent wireless-telegrapher operations. GRU Moscow would have quickly noted and signaled the schedule falloff in communications and would have been the first to criticize Sorge. Moreover, Sorge does not seem to be someone who would have been remiss by failing to follow up the record of the in-and-out messages sent by his own wireless telegrapher to GRU Moscow.

Some intelligence data, as we have seen, were passed to "Serge" in the Russian embassy. Despite Clausen's alleged antics, it would be fair to say that, although transmissions to Wiesbaden suffered a sharp decline in 1941, information did get through.[80] Nevertheless, in view of the attitude pervading the Russian capital during this period, there are strong indications that it was not believed.

From what we know about the movement of intelligence data within the Stalinist regime, there can be no doubt that Sorge's material transmitted by Clausen would have landed on General Golikov's desk because both he and Sorge were GRU operatives. Golikov in turn was directly responsible to Stalin and reported to no one else, not even to Chief of Staff Zhukov or Minister of Defense Timoshenko. Indeed, as Zhukov has admitted, he was not even aware of Sorge and his ring or of the invaluable information they were supplying to Moscow.[81] No doubt Golikov's opinions in May 1941 were no different from those he held the previous March, which we have examined; namely, he considered that any German blow would most probably fall only after Berlin had achieved victory in the West. This conclusion was plausible, but Golikov's own personality and the summary dismissal of his predecessor, General Proskurov, undoubtedly had an effect in convincing him to tell Stalin exactly what he wanted to hear.[82]

Though we lack direct documentary evidence about the reaction in Moscow to Sorge's information, the reaction can be discerned through secondary published Russian materials. Keeping Golikov's prior attitudes to the fore, we can conclude that he would have perceived Sorge's information as planted either by the Germans or by the British. What value, he would have asked, could be placed on information imparted by German colonels and others culled from the German embassy in Tokyo? Indeed, on important information conveyed by Sorge, Leopold Trepper, or the Luftwaffe's Lieutenant Schulze-Boysen of the Rote Kapelle, Golikov, it is claimed, routinely minuted, " 'Double agent' or 'British source.' "[83]

It is alleged that, when Golikov received one of Sorge's last reports, Stalin believed Golikov's contention that the information was a British invention and that London was keen on drawing Moscow into the war.[84] This belief would have been fueled by Stalin's apparent hostility to Sorge,[85] whose reports flew in the face of the *Vozhd*'s perception of the unfolding political scene. So it is understandable that, when given Sorge's reports, Stalin, it is asserted, scribbled on them that they were to be placed in the archives and filed.[86] This admonition to send to the archives or merely file away incoming intelligence that was obviously distasteful also served the purpose of preventing its circulation and restricting whatever impact it might generate within the higher echelons of the party and especially within the armed forces.[87] Indeed, it is alleged that in the 1960s when Sorge's material annotated by Golikov surfaced, Golikov, then a marshal and posted to the Defense Ministry, "kept his head," and although no investigation ensued, he later lost his psychic poise and had to be retired.[88]

The alleged reaction to Sorge's warnings, the Golikov-Stalin two-step, is supported by a Moscow message that purportedly enraged Sorge since in effect it doubted the accuracy of his information.[89] As Yotoku Miyagi, one of the important members of Sorge's ring, pointed out, their reports to Moscow were ignored and were not taken into consideration in preparing for the German attack.[90]

When interrogated by the Japanese authorities, Sorge claimed that, once the Germans had invaded in June 1941, he was thanked and congratulated by Moscow.[91] This message, however, does not appear in Clausen's recollection of the wireless traffic between Tokyo and Moscow.[92] If Sorge were thanked and congratulated, the gratitude probably had more to do with the accuracy of his intelligence data than with Moscow's appreciation and use of the data in formulating foreign and military policy.

## The View from London

By early April, as has been pointed out, both the British military and Churchill were unconvinced by the continuing reports that Nazi Germany would attack Soviet Russia.[93] Nevertheless, it appears that military intelligence was uneasy about the likelihood of an attack. On April 3, it noted that the German armored divisions, estimated at fifteen, were dispersed in a manner that seemed to show that, although "no offensive operations" were envisaged during the coming weeks in the West, the range of operations by German armored divisions that might begin in the Balkans was "considerably greater" than had previously been estimated.[94]

Five days later, April 8, MI14 observed that it was in receipt of continuing "reports of Germany's intention to attack Russia in the near future." These reports, it admitted, had all surfaced before the coup d'état in Yugoslavia against Prince Paul's government. Since the coup, however, no further information of troop movements headed for Poland had reached MI14.[95] In its weekly intelligence roundup for the period April 2–9, the War Office plausibly surmised that these continuous reports of Germany's intention to attack Russia may have been circulated by Berlin "as part of a war of nerves" directed against Moscow during the unrolling of the Balkan campaign.[96]

Concurrently, the weekly resumé for the Chiefs of Staff observed that, in Norway, German troop concentrations pointed at Russia were construed as a tacit warning to Moscow that Berlin would brook "no interference" in its Balkan adventures.[97] Based on MI14 summaries and views of the world situation,[98] the weekly resumé for the Chiefs of Staff for mid-April further ruminated that, although German troop movements in the direction of the Russian border had been reported, there was "still no indication that these [would] result in the total forces there being increased." However, a report of Russian troop movements westward suggested that perhaps Moscow took these threatening German moves seriously. The difficulty, it was correctly noted, was in determining whether the widespread and persistent rumors that Germany intended to attack Russia were being sowed by Berlin "as part of a war of nerves or [had] some solid basis in fact."[99]

Finally on April 20, the conflicting information that Germany was preparing to attack Russia was brought to Cripps's attention in Moscow. Intelligence reports recorded the additional call-up of men for military duty, a call-up that involved "serious long term economic risks"; the continuing development of airfields in Poland; the mapping by aerial photography of the Russian-German border area stretching east of Warsaw and as far south as Slovakia; the printing of ruble bank notes; the training of Russian emigrés from Rumania for administrative tasks; the organization of the Ukrainian and White Russian emigré communities; the construction of shelters to the east; the increase of troops in Poland and East Prussia since late March by ten divisions to sixty-five divisions, to wit, to 2,000,000 men, an increase of 250,000 troops; and finally, the ongoing preparations for German Fifth Column activity in the Ukraine and the Caucasus.

Then Cripps had to consider the other side of the coin: these reports might be disseminated by the Germans "as part of the war of nerves." Any German invasion of Soviet Russia, it was noted, would probably lead to such chaos that Berlin would have to reorganize all occupied Russian territory. During that reorganization, Germany would be deprived for a considerable period of time of the supplies that it now received from Russia. More important, it would forfeit the transportation facilities it presently enjoyed via the Trans-Siberian railway. Although Germany had immense resources, these resources would be insufficient to let it continue the Balkan campaign, which was now on in earnest. Neither would they be sufficient to permit the present level of air attack against England, nor the continuance of the Egyptian offensive concurrent with the invasion, occupation, and reorganization of a considerable part of Soviet Russia. Germany's principal impediment would be in gaining and maintaining sufficient control of the air to cover all these operations.[100]

A quick German victory in the Balkans would, of course, offset this scenario and enable Berlin to throw most of its armored divisions against the Russians. Nevertheless, for the armored divisions to be ready to partake in any attack, they would need a month's hiatus after the termination of the Balkan fighting. An indispensable ingredient for any such attack would be air power, but the eastward movement of German aircraft had not been reported. Since the necessary preparations, however, had been completed in Poland, the squadrons could be relocated and readied for an attack very quickly. Moreover, the indications were that the German generals opposed a two-front war and favored vanquishing the British before turning on the Russians. Then there was the new Russian-German oil-supply agreement that had just been concluded. Although the Foreign Office did not ruminate on this accord,[101] the question was obvious: would the Germans conclude such an agreement when they intended to attack the other signatory in the near future? The counterargument, of course, was that the agreement just might be a deceptive move to lull the opponent before the Germans plunged in the dagger. In the last analysis, everything depended on Hitler's whim.

No sooner was all this communicated to Cripps than MI14 reported that it appeared certain that German preparations leading to an eventual attack against Russia were continuing. The rub was that there was "still absolutely no confirmation of reports that Germany" would attack during the coming summer.[102] On this same day, April 22, the director of military intelligence said that, although there were no clear signs that matters would come to a head, he saw no reason why Germany should plunge into war with Russia until Great Britain had been vanquished, and he repeated the argument that any German attack would lead to a cutoff of vital oil and food supplies. Regardless, any attack appeared highly unlikely, he opined, until August at the earliest, when the Ukrainian harvest began and the Germans would discover foodstuffs on the spot. Although he admitted that there had been ceaseless rumors of the coming attack, these he dismissed as merely a "smoke screen, and part of a war of nerves," as there were "no immediate signs of any of the essential troop moves" in Russia's direction.[103]

In the evaluation of German intentions, the difficulties faced by MI14 ("no confirmation of reports") and by military intelligence ("no immediate signs") could in part be traced to the Germans putting off the movement of their armored divisions toward the Russian border during this period. In addition, the well-established telecommunication landlines in Eastern Europe obviated the use of wireless messages and thus their interception and possible decryption. Although this advantage could not be repeated in the ongoing Balkan campaign, reference to operational matters pertaining to Russia could be forbidden in wireless communications and "leakage" prevented even if messages were intercepted and decrypted.[104]

The view of military intelligence was reiterated to the Chiefs of Staff: it was not in Germany's interest to attack Russia until it had invaded Great Britain, and if any attack did take place, it would probably be after harvest time. The Foreign Office's Cavendish-Bentinck, who chaired the Chiefs of Staff Joint Intelligence Committee, had been uneasy, as we have seen, at the continuing reports of German activity in Eastern Europe. These reports had moved him to ask the intelligence committee's advisory subcommittee, the

Joint Intelligence Staff, to investigate the possibility of a German attack against Russia. The additional new information in its report of German activity parallel to the Russian border goes far to explain Cavendish-Bentinck's disagreement with military intelligence's assessment of the situation. "The threat to Russia might well develop as soon as the Greek war was over," he opined. An indication of Germany's intentions to deliver an invasion blow would be signaled, he suggested, by the movement of its armored forces.[105]

Several days later on April 25, MI14 ruminated that in any discussion of a possible German attack on Russia, Germany's principal aim, to wit, the defeat of Great Britain, had to be kept in mind. This comment was sound in view of the Clausewitzian doctrine that the destruction of the enemy's forces in the field was indispensable to achieve total victory. The widespread rumors during the previous weeks of an upcoming German attack were dismissed by MI14 as bearing "all the familiar signs of a whispering campaign."[106] They were German-propagated, conceivably as a warning to the Russians not to intervene in the Balkan campaign.

Despite these rationalizations, MI14 had to admit that an actual German threat to Russia was posed in received intelligence data. In Finland, for example, there were small German troop movements and the organization by the Germans of intelligence activities targeted directly against Russia. Likewise, there were German troop movements in eastern Poland, including the transferrence of armored and motorized units and the simultaneous evacuation of the families of German officials posted there. Airfields were being constructed in Poland, and German instructional air force units were being replaced by active ones. In the vicinity of Warsaw, twelve such airfields had apparently been established; only two had existed before the war. Other airfields were gradually being established nearer to the Russian border. Moreover, roads leading to the Russian frontier had been constructed and others improved, while concurrently railway stations had been enlarged beyond the requirements of German-Russian trade arrangements. All this was topped off by German air reconnaissance of Russian territory.

In a number of areas, these ongoing activities, MI14 continued, might be due to friction between Berlin and Moscow. In Turkey, for example, it might be traced to Russia's possible reaction to a German attack and its occupation of the Straits. If Ankara turned to Moscow for help, Russia would have to be prevented from reacting to the Turkish appeal. Then there was the question of Finland. Germany did not want Finland to fall into the Russian orbit, especially because of the valuable nickel mines at Petsamo (Pechenga). Finnish enmity against the Russians might under certain conditions encourage German action in Finland aimed at Russia. Lastly, although the possibility of a Russian invasion of Hungary was very slim, the continuing Hungarian occupation of Ruthenia, which had begun in March 1939, might cause friction and lead Hungary to support German action against Russia. MI14, however, held that at least for the moment none of these differences between

Germany and Russia, including the availability of Russian supplies to Germany, were substantial enough to justify a German attack.

Then why were all these threats against Russia reflected in the received intelligence data? MI14 credited them to Berlin's "strategic policy," which was the "establishment of a state of permanent readiness to strike quickly in any direction." This stance had been borne out by Germany's actions initially in Poland, then in Norway, and finally in Western Europe. It had now been repeated in the present Balkan campaign, "which allowed the maximum weight of attack to be delivered at a time which the German General Staff considered most opportune." An added consideration was that such a stance kept other states in the dark about Germany's next move. Of course, Moscow might be inclined to look upon the widespread rumors of Germany's aggressive intentions as no more than a bluff. A German "show of force" was therefore unavoidable "as a preventive measure against any of the causes of friction" mentioned in Turkey, Finland, and Hungary, as well as in the question of Russian supplies to Germany.[107]

Accordingly, MI14 could find absolutely no reason why Germany should attack Russia. If a successful assault on Russia would assist Hitler to defeat Great Britain, he would without doubt attempt it, but MI14 found it difficult to fathom what advantage Hitler would gain. For the moment, a German attack on Russia could be justified in anticipation of Russian opposition to a German attack on Turkey. The problem here was the lack of firm evidence that Germany intended to attack Turkey or that Russia would actively resist such an attack if it occurred. The other possibility was that Germany would attack Russia to ensure a regular flow of supplies. This possibility, MI14 held, was most unlikely. In any German occupation of the Ukraine, the result would be chaos since all industrial and agricultural officials would scatter as would most of the workers and peasants, who under the Stalinist regime had no stake in the country. Likewise, it was doubtful that a German occupation of Russian oil fields would lead to increased supplies. Russian agriculture was dependent on oil, and the Germans would have to supply it. Moreover, it was doubtful that the transportation infrastructure would allow a greater quantity of oil to be made available to Germany than at present.

Whether Stalin felt threatened by the Germans was impossible to ascertain. Anglo-Russian relations had not improved. This lack of improvement showed that Moscow realized that Berlin's strength against London had not declined enough to justify a compromise peace settlement and understood that Hitler's primary aim was Great Britain's defeat. Moscow's attitude toward London was perhaps dictated by two possibilities: by its knowledge that Berlin's threat was not serious, or conversely by its fear of the same threat that Moscow wanted to avoid assiduously. The latter possibility in turn impelled Moscow to attempt to appease Berlin's wrath by making it clear that Moscow would have nothing to do with London.

All this led MI14 to conclude that a German attack on Russia seemed "most unlikely in the immediate future."[108] The question, however, would probably remain open, ensuring Russia's continued economic collaboration and making it clear that obstruction of Germany's desires would not be countenanced. The question would also be left open as a German effort to conceal future moves from London and, to a lesser extent, from Ankara.

In Polish military circles, the opinion was that, considering Germany's failure to invade Great Britain this year and its similar failure in the battle of the Atlantic, a German invasion of Russia was a certainty. Accordingly, MI14 suggested that the ongoing German preparations against Russia were, "on this assumption, a long-term insurance against such an eventuality, in addition to any immediate purpose they may serve."[109]

MI14's position remained unchanged in the days that immediately followed. There were "no reliable indications of imminent hostilities" between Germany and Russia, it reported on April 28. However, there seemed "little doubt" that German-Russian relations had "deteriorated" and that the imminent return from Berlin of Ambassador Schulenburg might elucidate matters a little further.[110] This opinion was repeated by the War Office in its weekly intelligence summary. At the same time, the War Office noted the arrival in Finland of German troops heading north, although it was in the dark about the intended purpose of these troop movements. The same applied to reports of considerable German troop reinforcements in Moldavia. These could be relief troops, the War Office speculated, or Germany might again be reverting to a war of nerves against Russia. Whatever the case, it was unlikely that Berlin would resort to any action against Moscow until the situation in the Mediterranean had clarified.[111] The War Office's comments were then incorporated verbatim into the Chiefs of Staff Committee's Weekly Resumé covering the period April 24 to May 1.[112]

Concurrently, Enigma decrypts supplied other suggestive information. On April 24, it was learned that a Luftwaffe ground unit was moved to Poland from the Channel area and that a signals regiment was likewise ordered to Poland to serve under a Luftwaffe unit previously stationed in France. Two days later, it was reported that the movement of German forces from the Balkans to Poland, suspended in late March, had resumed.[113] Royal Air Force intelligence observed on April 30 that the recent construction of German airfields and other installations in Poland meant that considerable Luftwaffe units could be transferred to Poland "at fairly short notice" and that stocks of bombs and aviation fuel had undoubtedly been built up.[114] Additional Enigma decrypts on May 3 revealed that a Luftwaffe unit previously involved in the Greek campaign would be quickly refitted and moved to Cracow. Further movements to the Cracow area followed two days later.[115] By May 7, air force intelligence could report that the Luftwaffe was blatantly violating Finnish air space.[116]

Unlike American intelligence in the autumn of 1941, during this period of attempting to unravel the possibility of a German attack, British intelligence did not have to contend with what has been called "noise": "competing or contradictory" information "useless for anticipating" a particular disaster.[117] The confusing noise is generated "not for want of the relevant materials, but because of a plethora of irrelevant ones." The United States paid dearly at Pearl Harbor for this at times insurmountable problem, which was enormously complicated by the opponents' deception operations.

The British problem was different from that of the Americans in that the amount of incoming noise they heard was minimal. Whitehall, however, found it impossible to believe that Hitler, contrary to his "interests" as they were perceived in London, would undertake an invasion of Soviet Russia. Such an invasion would entail economic and military sacrifices at a time when Great Britain, his principal enemy, was still undefeated. It was surpising that someone in Whitehall at this time did not discern the thread of irrationality that ran through the fabric of Nazi Germany and colored the thoughts of its primary decision maker, Hitler, who had repeatedly made hostile racial comments against the Slavic peoples of Eastern Europe and expressed his enormous enmity toward the Soviet regime. The British perception that Hitler's action would be based on his interests failed to take this aberration into account. Like it or not, the British were ensnared in what might be called, for want of a better phrase, the "rationality syndrome." Stalin, as we have seen, suffered the same malaise.[118] No doubt it had much to do with his evolution beyond the Marxist-Leninist model of leadership. Unlike those who had preceded him, he felt "scientifically" certain that everything he was told that differed with his own perceptions and beliefs was "disinformation" and "provocation" sponsored by his discerned enemies, i. e., the British. During one of history's high moments in self-deception, Stalin operated on his own Gresham's law of intelligence: bad analysis had driven out good intelligence.

# 5

# Stalin Officially at the Helm

## Overtures

The British War Office's certainty in late April of 1941 that German-Russian relations had "deteriorated" was an accurate observation. Incorrect, however, was its notion that Ambassador Schulenburg, during his return to Moscow immediately following his talks with Hitler and the Nazi leadership in Berlin, would elucidate the state of Russian-German relations.[1] It was the return to Moscow of his Russian counterpart in Berlin, Vladimir Dekanozov, that actually helped crystallize events. As early as April 21, Steinhardt thought it probable that Moscow was "prepared to yield" to Berlin's pressure. Moscow would go quite far in this "yielding" in the "hope of gaining time" and intended to "give the impression" of acquiescing to Berlin with the full knowledge that it would "take the Germans some time to know to what extent any commitments undertaken by the Soviet Government are being carried out."[2]

The deterioration in German-Russian relations was clearly traceable to Stalin's Balkan machinations and especially to the treaty of friendship concluded with Belgrade only hours before the German invasion. Sir Stafford Cripps subsequently maintained that the conclusion of this treaty "was the deciding factor which precipitated the German attack on Russia."[3] This opinion was an exaggeration since the Barbarossa directive of December 18, 1940, was not yet known and was to surface only after the war. Stalin, however, had clearly overreached himself by concluding the friendship treaty; he now strove to fend off Hitler and to save whatever he could by opening wide-ranging negotiations. As we have seen, and as Molotov admitted to Secretary of State Cordell Hull in June 1942, it was during this period that Moscow decided that Berlin would attack in the future.[4]

For Molotov, "the future" undoubtedly meant sometime in the late spring or early summer of 1942. In late July 1941 following the German invasion, Stalin admitted to presidential envoy Harry Hopkins that "he himself believed that Hitler would not strike" in 1941.[5] In fact, sometime in May, as Stalin's biographer has admitted, the *Vozhd* opined to his coterie that a clash with Germany would be unavoidable by May of 1942.[6] Certainly, the Kremlin's military planning at the end of April and the beginning of May 1941 reflected Stalin's mind-set. Envisaging that "decisive actions would be preceded by a declaration of war," this planning, as one Russian army marshal observed, was "a case of preparing for the wrong war, for 1914, not 1941."[7]

Berlin no doubt discerned Stalin's desire to beat a quick retreat. One indication was Moscow's export of 40,000 tons of oil for April, which, as we have seen, was double that of March.[8] If this went unnoticed at the time, the Germans were certainly clued in subsequently by the acquisition of an insightful report filed from Moscow on May 1 by the alert and well-informed Turkish ambassador, Ali Haydar Aktay, and relayed on the 24th to Berlin.[9] The report was probably decrypted, for like the Italians and the Russians the Germans had unraveled the simple Turkish diplomatic code. As was admitted to American interrogators after the war, one of Berlin's "best sources of information . . . on the objectives of the Russians in foreign affairs was supplied by the [decrypted] messages from the Turkish Embassy in Moscow to Ankara."[10] This report by Aktay was no exception.

The ambassador, who exchanged information on a regular basis with Cripps, Gavrilović, the Greek minister Christophe Diamantopoulos, and probably others, observed in his long and repetitive report that the danger for Russia had developed from Germany's military success in the Balkans, which had occurred far swifter than Moscow had imagined. Stalin was aware that he had blundered, but then again Stalin had a proclivity for serious foreign policy mistakes; German victories in Poland and France had been made possible by his mistakes. He had expected that the Poles and the French could resist longer than they did and believed that the mutual exhaustion of the belligerents would be to his advantage. The rapid German victories in the Balkans, however, had terrorized the *Vozhd,* who by various acts showed that he wanted "to make up to the Germans" and would tolerate "very many more things in order to satisfy Germany." Aktay thought, for example, that Stalin would aid the Germans in the Middle East. The problem that presented itself was that he might "succumb to the desire both to gratify the German Chief of State and to secure some advantage for himself." Aktay had no doubts that in victory Germany would incorporate the Ukraine, the Black Sea littoral, and the Crimean basin into the Reich's Lebensraum. Stalin, he opined, was on the verge of becoming Germany's "blind tool."[11]

On the very day that Aktay dispatched his report to Ankara, May 1, Stalin took the first step to convey his desire to Berlin to make amends and to establish a new relationship with Germany through bilateral negotiations. Stalin's conciliatory desires were exemplified in a neatly played scene on the

Kremlin wall during the May Day parade. The GRU's Ismail Akhmedov, who viewed the parade from Lenin's mausoleum, notes that Dekanozov, among those assembled on the wall, was "in the front rank, alone" except for Stalin, who was to his right. The "unusual honor shown him," Akhmedov correctly observes, "must have been for the benefit of the Germans."[12] Giving Dekanozov's front-rank presence next to Stalin on this important day in the liturgy of the Communist faith was the *Vozhd*'s clever and symbolic way of drawing everyone's attention to Dekanozov's importance and thus conveying the message to all and sundry that the ambassador had his full trust and confidence. Marshal Timoshenko's speech at the parade, which said that Russia wanted the "consolidation of friendly and good-neighborly relations" with all states seeking to establish similar relations with Moscow, was a not too subtle hint of Stalin's desire for substantive negotiations with Berlin. This display and Timoshenko's comments did not escape the attention of Schulenburg,[13] who believed that the "prominence" given to the ambassador had to be "regarded as a special mark of confidence on the part of Stalin."[14] Naturally, any negotiations that would bridge the rift that had developed between the two states coincided with Schulenburg's desires and hopes to obviate what he knew was an upcoming German attack. Additional grist for the rumor mill was the story circulating in Berlin's diplomatic circles, and brought to Ribbentrop's attention, that Dekanozov's return to Moscow foreshadowed a shift in Russian policy toward Germany.[15] Then, Ribbentrop's private plane, which had brought Schulenburg to Moscow, did not immediately return to Berlin. Did this stall indicate that Schulenburg expected to return to Berlin, or did it mean that the plane was to be put at Dekanozov's disposal? Indeed, Dekanozov had divulged that he planned to "return to Berlin in the near future."[16]

It was generally held in Moscow, according to Steinhardt, that Schulenburg had brought with him "special instructions" to discuss German-Russian relations. We know, of course, that this was not the case. Should these discussions have commenced, Steinhardt had no doubt that Moscow would go far to avoid an attack by Berlin. The Russian government, he thought, was "sufficiently crafty and unscrupulous to obtain a high price for complying with any demands" that Nazi Germany might raise, and by doing so would avoid a clash and gain something in return.[17] Ominously, however, Schulenburg made no move to visit the Kremlin or to contact Stalin.[18] Because of what he had learned in Berlin of Hitler's plans to invade Soviet Russia, his lack of initiative was understandable.

The question, of course, was exactly how far Moscow would be willing to go to satiate Berlin. The acting German military attaché in Moscow, Colonel Hans Krebs, "found the Russians very conciliatory." They would "do anything to avoid war and yield on every issue short of making territorial concessions," he suggested on May 5 to General Franz Halder, the army's Chief of Staff;[19] these comments were not dissimilar to those voiced by Ambassador Sir Stafford Cripps about two weeks before.[20]

On the same day, the mounting German military preparations, which had not gone unobserved or unreported by the Russian intelligence services,[21] were brought to the attention of Stalin and Molotov, as well as that of senior military leaders. The report's findings no doubt did much to intensify the Kremlin's conciliatory posture noted by Colonel Krebs. Of special concern must have been the report's observation that 107 German divisions were facing east. Together with Rumanian and Hungarian forces, that made approximately 130 divisions, a large proportion of which were armored and mechanized units.[22]

There were additional straws in the wind. On this very day, May 5, Steinhardt reported that according to a "reliable source" Stalin, in a recent conversation with a Russian official, had observed that he expected neither an attack by nor a war with Germany in 1941 and "anticipated 'satisfactory' negotiations" with Berlin.[23] On that same day at the Kremlin, the *Vozhd* addressed the graduates of the military academies, as well as luminaries like General Zhukov and the ubiquitous Dekanozov.[24] The speech's notional emphasis, according to Stalin's biographer, was that Hitler would never involve himself in a two-front war.[25] Stalin's address, the full text of which has never been published, lasted for forty minutes and was briefly noted in the press. Zhukov's excerpts of Stalin's ruminations do not contradict the German claim that more than twenty-five minutes of the speech was an evenhanded comparison of Germany's and Russia's military potentials.

A postwar examination from "several Russian verbal sources," a description that raises immediate questions about the accuracy or reliability of these sources, tells us that the main points of Stalin's speech were as follows: the situation was most serious and the possibility of a German attack in the immediate future was not to be dismissed; the Red Army was not up to snuff; through diplomatic channels Moscow would attempt to forestall the Germans until the autumn, by which point it would be too late in the year for any attack; if Moscow was successful in this endeavor, war with Germany would be fought the following year, when the Red Army would be better prepared; depending on the world situation in 1942, the Red Army would either await a German attack or take the initiative itself; England was not finished, and the weight of America's war potential was likely to gain in importance; with the signing of the pact with Japan, Tokyo would remain quiescent toward Soviet Russia. The *Vozhd* also reiterated that the most dangerous period was from then until late August.[26]

According to Cripps, Stalin had argued that the war, which had begun as a just attempt by Germany to throw off the "shackles" of the 1919 settlement, had been "totally changed" and was now a German attempt to control all of Europe. The makeup and achievements of Germany's armed forces caused Stalin to conclude that Russia's military potential could not match Germany's. In view of this conclusion, Moscow had to "take into account the present balance of power." The Russian military and the armaments industry,

Stalin concluded, could neither boast of their successes nor "rest on their laurels." To strengthen Russia's defense, the training and supply of the army and the development of war industry had to be pressed. Stalin's comments, related by Zhukov, that to be well prepared for war necessitated a modern army and political preparation, dovetailed with the *Deutsches Nachrichtenburo* news agency report filed through Schulenburg. According to the agency, Stalin's comments clearly left his listeners with the impression that he was "anxious to prepare his followers for a 'new compromise' with Germany."[27]

German Counselor Gustav Hilger writes that the report of Stalin's speech and its "interpretation fitted very well into the picture" he had formed of "Stalin's thoughts and intentions." During the war, Hilger had occasion to discuss informally the version of the address that was reported with captured Russian officers, who were not the most reliable of sources. Their recollections were at variance with the officially reported version. According to Hilger's discussants, in response to a toast to Russia's peace policy, Stalin spoke of "*offensive* action" and the end of "peaceful policies," as well as the spreading of socialism and the expansion of Russia territorially "by force of arms."[28] Since these remarks were spontaneous reactions to a proposed toast and separate from the body of the address, they may have reflected the *Vozhd*'s subliminal thoughts, thoughts that would later surface. For the moment, however, Stalin only wanted to deliver his address, and this he had done. No doubt to impress Berlin and in the midst of the subsequent negotiations, Schulenburg sent a report but not a verbatim text of Stalin's address about a month after the speech was given,[29] but he had already noted its significance on May 12.[30]

That the secretive Stalin used a quasi-public occasion in the Kremlin to ruminate on so sensitive a policy issue as German-Russian relations shows the lengths to which he was willing to go in an unofficial and informal expression of his desire for fruitful negotiations to end the tensions that had developed between the two states. On the other hand, if pressed, Stalin would resist. Dekanozov's presence on the Kremlin wall had been only an hors d'oeuvre. By no stretch of the imagination could Stalin have expected that his remarks on such a subject and in such a setting would go "unleaked." Indeed, this is exactly what he wanted. Had there been no leak, Stalin would have soon remedied the situation by orchestrating one. It is possible that he did so and that is how the *Deutsches Nachrichtenburo* acquired an unofficial version of Stalin's Kremlin remarks.

In Berlin on the day following Stalin's comments to the graduating officers, the rumors spread that as a result of Dekanozov's recall to Moscow for "consultations" important negotiations were in the offing.[31] The rumors were, of course, accurate, but before any negotiations could start, the Russian batting order had to be redrawn. Therefore on the very day the rumor circulated in Berlin, May 6, and much to everyone's surprise, Stalin formally assumed the official and nonparty post of prime minister.[32] The only other time that Stalin had held an official government position was in the early days of the Communist regime when he had served as minister of nationalities. As Maisky admitted in London, Stalin's assumption of the office "was a recognition of [the] international crisis."[33]

According to an employee of the Russian embassy in Washington who was allegedly being run by the Federal Bureau of Investigation, during the week before Stalin's assumption of office there had been a meeting of the Politburo in which Litvinov had "advocated a return to the policy of close collaboration with the democracies" while Molotov "favored increasingly close ties with the Axis even up to an informal entry" into the Tripartite Pact. This, of course, was sheer disinformation. Though perhaps unknown at the time, Litvinov was politically isolated under a cloud and had absolutely no access to the Politburo. Equally preposterous was the source's contention that the all-powerful Stalin was finally forced by the Politburo "to agree to put a new policy into effect whereby he would do the directing openly instead of merely as the leader of the Communist party of Russia."[34]

Though it is obvious that the information was erroneous and being fed to the Federal Bureau of Investigation, there was truth in the story that a new policy was being put into effect and that Stalin would be directing affairs openly and officially rather than behind closed doors and unofficially. In fact, the story smacks of the truth, more so than did the one circulating in Berlin and alleging that the *Vozhd* and Molotov had differences that were perhaps "spontaneous" or perhaps the "result of German intrigue with Molotov against Stalin."[35] This sounds fraudulent, reminiscent of the postwar story that Molotov was the bad guy and that if only one could get through to Stalin the whole world situation would change for the better. That Stalin and Molotov saw eye to eye on the policy stance to be adopted in approaching the Germans was indicated by Molotov's continuing service as foreign minister even though he relinquished the post of prime minister.[36] Indeed, despite his seeming demotion, the British embassy in Moscow pointed out to the Foreign Office's Northern Department that both "formally as well as in practice" there was no doubt that Molotov was, and was "intended to be, subordinate to no-one except Stalin."[37]

The official who delivered the reports of the Russian intelligence services to Stalin and Molotov has observed that clearly, because of what had transpired, there "is every reason to believe" that Stalin assumed the prime ministership "not to prepare for the country's defense, but to reach an agreement with Hitler."[38] This reasoning in turn partially explains the lack of notice given to the intelligence information relayed on May 6 by Admiral Nikolai Kuznetsov, the navy's commander in chief. According to Captain Mikhail Vorontsov, the naval attaché in Berlin, Kuznetsov reported, an officer from Hitler's staff code-named "Walter" had divulged that Germany was preparing an invasion in mid-May through Finland, the Baltic area, and Rumania, concurrent with an airborne attack and heavy air raids on Moscow and

Leningrad. Although by this point the invasion had been set for June, Kuznetsov's report was otherwise very accurate. It was totally undermined, however, by his conclusion that the information was untrue; he believed that it had been planted through the naval attaché's source, a Russian named Bozer, so that Berlin could gauge Moscow's reaction.[39] This was a plausible interpretation, but one has the sneaking suspicion that Kuznetsov, like the GRU's Golikov, knew the thinness of the ice when approaching the leadership on this particular question.[40] As we have seen, Kuznetsov had received prior admonitions about his stance and policies of military preparedness.[41] Wisely, he had bowed to expediency.

Stalin's appointment and the abrupt change in the rhythm of the Russian political world, however, did not baffle Steinhardt and Cripps. Stalin, Steinhardt argued, by his acquisition of the prime ministership had become "head of the Government in name as well as in fact and thus personally assumes formal responsibility for it."[42] Cripps concurred. The *Vozhd*'s appointment, he observed, could not substantially "increase his power which was already almost absolute." What it did, if anything, was regularize a "state of affairs which had long been anomalous." Naturally, it expedited his reception of foreign visitors, which was especially important at that moment in view of the "acute tension" that racked Russian-German relations and of an expected German diplomatic offensive in Moscow. The most "obvious interpretation" of Stalin's official position, which Cripps also believed was the correct one, was that the "pilot [had] at last taken the helm when approaching really dangerous waters."[43]

Of course, Molotov's pro-German orientation might explain away what had occurred, but Cripps believed that it "would be dangerous and unjustified to conclude that the change in itself" signified any drift of Russian policy in a direction favorable to Great Britain. Certainly, Molotov had not been shelved. In periods less tense than the present one, the traditional "Soviet method of negotiation through a mouthpiece, with the master behind the curtain," had its advantages. The change was due, Cripps thought, to the "impending major crisis" in the relations between the two dictatorships and to the "consequent need for more rapid and direct methods" of negotiation. He concluded that he would not be surprised if Stalin's appointment was merely the prelude to a summit between the two great dictators although he admitted that he possessed no evidence anticipating such a meeting.[44]

The Foreign Office's reactions to Cripps's observations were positive. Stalin's assumption of the prime ministership, Edward Coote of the Northern Department minuted, meant that he could "no longer shuffle off the responsibility for mistakes and failures on subordinates." Coote did not believe that Stalin "would have taken this very grave step unless he knew that decisions of the highest import were inevitable in the near future, and that he alone was strong enough to swing the country and the party." Stalin was faced with two options: he could surrender to Berlin or go to war with it. Coote agreed with Cripps that the exchange of Stalin for Molotov did not signal a policy shift in England's favor. Moscow was never going to do anything for London gratuitously. The question that presented itself was whether the German demands, which, it could be assumed, Berlin was about to raise, would be "too strong for Stalin to stomach." All that London should do at present, Coote wisely observed, was to "sit tight and watch events." A premature approach to Moscow "would only be interpreted as a sign of weakness."[45]

The head of the Northern Department, Sir Laurence Collier, concurred. After discussion with others, he felt that the new move in Moscow, in so far as it "indicated a decline in Molotov's influence, which had always been pro-German, . . . was a good thing" from London's perspective, regardless of Stalin's motives. Foreign Secretary Anthony Eden scribbled his marginal agreement. Stalin, Collier maintained, must have realized that the announced change in leadership would be perceived abroad as an anti-Molotov move. Presumably Stalin was "not unwilling that deductions of a sort unpalatable to the Germans should be made from it." The only thing the British could do now was to wait for events to unfold.[46]

Sir Alexander Cadogan, the permanent under secretary at the Foreign Office, took Stalin's assumption of the office as a bad omen. Would the great tyrant, he rhetorically asked, assume such a responsibility if he were going to resist the Germans and involve his country in a war? Did it not signify that Stalin had decided to cave in—an action he could conceal from the Russians at large more easily than open hostilities? The infiltration of Germany's technicians would inevitably be no secret and perhaps would not be popular, but far less popular would be a devastating confrontation that could signal the end of the Stalinist regime.[47]

Eden succinctly summed up the situation. Only future events would tell all. He believed that the *Vozhd* would "cast away anything" that did "not imperil his regime."[48] Eden's minute reflected his comments to the Cabinet the previous day; Stalin's move "showed he realised the clouds were gathering," and it would be a mistake to think that Moscow "would resist any German demands except those which would affect Stalin's position at home."[49]

This abrupt change of events, however, did not please the German minister in Helsinki, who initially considered Stalin's assumption of the prime ministership as the forerunner of a "possible change in Soviet policy adversely affecting German interests." Subsequent reliable Norwegian information related that the Germans felt that Stalin's new office would "redound to their advantage."[50] No doubt Schulenburg's reporting had much to do with this reversal in attitude. The possibilities that now presented themselves, including negotiations leading to a revision of the 1939 agreement, an avoidance of conflict, and obviation of the planned invasion that Schulenburg had uncovered during his trip to Berlin, were manna from heaven. He was "convinced," a pleased Schulenburg initially observed to Berlin, that "Stalin [would] use his new position in order to take part personally in the maintenance and development of good relations between the Soviets and Germany."[51] Nevertheless, Schulenburg hedged his bets. He wrote on this same day, May 7, to the state secretary of the Foreign Ministry, Ernst von Weizsäcker requesting that, in the case of war, the personnel of the Russian diplomatic mission and other services in Germany be "treated with as much consideration as possible." Ill treatment of the Russians in Germany would occur, as did, to a much greater extent, ill treatment of Germans in Russia.[52]

Within a week, however, Schulenburg's optimism heightened because he viewed Stalin's assumption of office as an "event of extraordinary importance." Schulenburg dismissed the notion that the change was due to domestic considerations. Rather, it could be "stated with great certainty that if Stalin decided to take over the highest government office, it was done for reasons of foreign policy." He credited Stalin's assumption of office to a reappraisal of the international situation based on the lightning German military victories in the Balkans and the realization that this situation necessitated a departure from previous Russian policy that "had led to an estrangement with Germany." In addition, there was probably a clash of conflicting opinions among the party elite and senior military officers, which convinced Stalin to assume the "helm himself from now on." Schulenburg interpreted Stalin's initial steps in foreign affairs as an attempt to "relieve the tension" between Moscow and Berlin and to "create a better atmosphere for the future." Stalin "had always advocated a friendly relationship" between the two states.[53]

Among his diplomatic colleagues, the ambassador continued, the consensus was that Stalin was "pursuing a policy of rapprochement with Germany and the Axis." Schulenburg thought it could be "assumed with certainty that Stalin [had] set himself a foreign policy goal of overwhelming importance" for the country that he hoped to attain by his personal endeavors. Schulenburg strongly believed that in an "international situation which he considers serious," Stalin had set himself the task of avoiding a Russian-German conflict.[54]

In order to begin the negotiations with Berlin, Stalin, upon his assumption of the prime ministership, as Schulenburg correctly pointed out, immediately made several moves to show his good faith and to help lessen the tension with Germany. On the evening of May 8, Stalin turned on the diplomatic missions of governments-in-exile in Moscow. First to feel the winds of change were the Belgians and the Norwegians. They were curtly informed by the Foreign Ministry that because their respective countries were no longer sovereign states and because Soviet Russia had no representation in their countries, Moscow considered that their ministers' diplomatic powers had "lost their validity."[55] The Yugoslavs were handled more civilly. Vyshinsky summoned Gavrilović to the Foreign Ministry and regretfully explained that Soviet Russia had to "sever diplomatic relations" with his country. Gavrilović and his colleagues would be shown every consideration, Vyshinsky assured him. If they desired, they could continue to reside as private individuals, but "formal" diplomatic relations had to cease. Considering that only a month before, as already described, the Russians had signed a friendship pact with Yugoslavia, extending this offer was the least that Moscow could do. Gavrilović made no substantive reply. His position was that as long as Moscow could remain neutral and gather strength, its politics would be welcomed by his country and its allies.[56]

Nevertheless, before departing from Moscow, Gavrilović expressed the view that the Russian decision to withdraw recognition from his diplomatic mission had been "demanded" by the Germans before Dekanozov returned to Moscow. The concurrent action against the Belgians and the Norwegians, he believed, was "spontaneous," in order that his country "might not be singled out."[57] The Belgians agreed that the whole exercise was really targeted at the Yugoslavs and was "designed to bring about an improvement in relations with Germany," which the recent Russian-Yugoslav friendship pact had compromised.[58] Hitler's pressure, the counselor of the Belgian legation has written, was an attempt to force Stalin to "pay for the insolent signature" of the friendship pact. Moscow had to "suffer a bitter pill for Stalin to swallow."[59] If this estimation of Russia's actions is correct, it might in part explain the more civil treatment accorded to Gavrilović and denied to the Belgians and Norwegians.

A closer approximation of what probably occurred was furnished by Kollontai, the embarrassed Russian minister in Stockholm, to her British counterpart. What had befallen the Norwegians in Moscow, she explained, could be traced to the Russian insistence that the Germans close their consular missions in the Baltic states—a minor inaccuracy since the German desire was to convert its legations to consular offices. The Russians had maintained this stance for some time, but the Germans, she claimed, had been "obdurate" on the issue. These consular missions, Kollontai observed, were centers for propaganda and intelligence work and posed a threat to Russia that had to be removed. The Germans agreed to close these Baltic missions, she explained, only on a *quid pro quo* basis; namely, the Germans would comply only if the Russians would close their consulate in Oslo and the Norwegian legation in Moscow. Apparently, the Germans had then included Belgium in the arrangements and had also insisted that the Russian consulate in Antwerp be closed. But this situation did not explain the action taken against the Yugoslav mission, her British interlocutor interjected. Kollontai agreed. She admitted that closing the Yugoslav mission was "a sop [that] had to be offered to the Germans as Soviet policy was to avoid by all possible means any serious quarrel with Germany at present. 'You know' she said 'that our policy is to keep out of the war as long as possible.' "[60]

That Moscow's decision to cease relations with the three governments "had been made unwillingly" and only after pressure from Berlin seemed to be confirmed when the Russians approached the Greek minister with similar requests for the termination of diplomatic relations. He correctly pointed out to the Russians that he represented a free and independent state whose government ruled from the island of Crete. It was only on June 3, following the fall of Crete and the establishment of a government-in-exile, that Moscow ended formal diplomatic relations with the Greeks.[61] Yet, despite these seemingly definitive actions and comments made toward the four missions, Moscow hedged. The astonished Belgian minister in Helsinki was informed by his Russian counterpart that because of what had occurred there was "no question of course of any severance" of diplomatic relations between their two countries. The Russian minister repeated Moscow's stance to the Norwegian minister.[62]

However, Ambassador Schulenburg "categorically" denied to Steinhardt that the closing of the three diplomatic missions stemmed from a suggestion or request by Berlin or himself. Closer to the target was the Italian ambassador, Augusto Rosso, who thought that Stalin's assumption of the prime ministership and the closure of the missions constituted Stalin's admission that Russian policy "had erred" during the preceding months in opposing Germany. Rosso felt that the action against the missions was only the "first of a series of steps to curry favor with Germany."[63]

Though Schulenburg could speak for himself, he certainly could not speak for Berlin. Because of his proffered policy stance toward Russia, his credibility in the German capital was not high; it is conceivable that the closure of these foreign missions in Moscow was just the kind of matter that Berlin would have preferred to execute through Dekanozov. Like the German Embassy in Moscow, the Italian Embassy denied involvement and admitted that it was astonished by what had occurred. Accordingly, it is not clear whether the termination of diplomatic relations with the three governments-in-exile and subsequently with the Greek government-in-exile was due solely to German pressure or to Stalin's own initiative. Regardless, whether Stalin acted under German pressure or on his own, the opinion in the Foreign Office was that there could "be virtually no doubt" that Stalin's move "might be due to a desire to placate the Germans." There appeared to be "no other explanation" for such a move at this particular time. The termination of diplomatic relations with these four governments was certainly a matter that obviously could have been handled long before.[64] The War Office agreed: the Russian move could "almost certainly be considered as a sop to Germany" even if Moscow's action was not expressly demanded by Berlin.[65] The observation of a resident American correspondent that what had transpired had been "voluntary appeasement" is more succinct and probably closer to the truth.[66]

Cripps agreed with such a view. Yugoslav inclusion with the Belgians and the Norwegians, he wrote, showed the lengths that Moscow was prepared to go to "placate" Berlin. The legal situations of the three states were similar, but the Russian attitude toward the German conquest of Yugoslavia had "been made sufficiently clear to render this move a confession of weakness."

None of the three diplomatic missions had experienced difficulties in dealing with Russian officialdom aside from the usual problems encountered in Moscow. In fact, the Norwegians had found the Foreign Ministry helpful. Cripps thought the move might be the beginning of a Russian diplomatic cave-in under German pressure. He believed it more probable, though, that it was an attempt by Moscow to strengthen its position in anticipation of major demands from Berlin "by voluntarily removing causes of complaint wherever this [could] be done at small cost." Nevertheless, Moscow's action appeared to indicate that it would "go a long way towards 'appeasement' and that, unless the Germans over-reach[ed] themselves, they [would] get all they require without a struggle."[67]

In London, the "curt dismissal" of Gavrilović "perturbed" Beneš. He thought a big event was in the offing and perceived two possibilities: Moscow had to prepare the population for a possible war, which implied that Stalin thought Germany intended to attack Russia, or Moscow had to persuade the population and an anti-German oriented army that it was necessary to offer Berlin additional concessions in order to maintain its policy of " 'equilibristic neutrality.' "[68]

In another signal on May 9, concurrent with the expulsion of the three diplomatic missions, *Tass* denied Japanese newspaper reports of powerful Soviet Russian troop concentrations on its western frontiers. It likewise denied that any such concentrations were contemplated or that naval units had been transferred from the Baltic to the Black and Caspian Seas. These reports were all "sheer fantasy," *Tass* insisted.[69] Three days later on May 12, Moscow extended diplomatic recognition to the anti-British, pro-Axis Iraqi government of Prime Minister Rashid Ali al Gailani,[70] who had staged a successful coup d'état five weeks earlier. One can argue whether this recognition was premature under the norms of international law; however, it was certainly a "friendly gesture" as far as the Germans were concerned, who along with the Italians were in contact with Rashid Ali's government. An added advantage was that the bestowal of the diplomatic recognition to the Iraqi government curried favor among nationalist elements in the Arab world.[71] Moscow's action and especially its appointment of a Russian minister to Baghdad did not amuse the Foreign Office,[72] whose Northern Department, which dealt with Russian affairs, was opposed to the "establishment of diplomatic relations" between Baghdad and Moscow.[73]

Concurrently, because of the close ties between Finland and Germany, Moscow took steps to ease tense Russian-Finnish relations. An agreement demarcating their joint frontier was reached, discussions were resumed on trade matters and on the Petsamo nickel mines concession in Finland, and the Petrozavodsk radio station's propaganda attacks against Helsinki ended.[74] All these moves, which had been made since Matsuoka's agreement with the Russians and Stalin's assumption of the office of prime minister "indicated a trend on the part of [Russia] toward closer cooperation with the Nazis," the papal Nuncio at Bern astutely observed.[75]

As the events unfolded and as Stalin geared up to begin his negotiations with Berlin, an untoward event intervened, raising a serious spectre in Moscow about possible parallel German-British negotiations. Any alliance between these two nations or any agreement that would release Hitler to turn eastward was to be assiduously avoided or prevented by any Russian government. As Colonel Pika, the Czech military intelligence liaison officer in Moscow subsequently pointed out, the Russians were "not so much afraid of Germany as they were afraid of an Anglo-German anti-Soviet entente."[76] Specifically, Cripps had observed in April, they feared the conclusion of a peace treaty between London and Berlin based on German withdrawal from the areas occupied in "Western Europe and a free hand for Hitler in the East."[77] The untoward event was the flight of Rudolf Hess to Scotland.

## Hess's Flight: Moscow's Perceptions

Rudolf Hess, in his flight to Scotland on May 10 as the self-appointed Mercury to help bring an end to the war between Great Britain and Germany, surprised Churchill,[78] as he did everyone else, especially the Germans.[79] The reasons Hess—Hitler's muddled deputy, longtime crony, and amanuensis, as well as the leader of the Nazi party—engaged in this dangerous and desperate bid are still not absolutely clear.[80] The suppression by the British government of pertinent documents,[81] which have been described as "well-weeded official files relating to Hess' flight,"[82] has not helped matters.

Churchill assured President Roosevelt that Hess had "denied rumours that [an] attack on Russia was being planned."[83] Hess had made this denial to the Foreign Office's Ivone Kirkpatrick. When Kirkpatrick had served in the British embassy in Berlin, he had known and thoroughly disliked Hess. Now, he had been dispatched to Scotland to interrogate him.[84] However, on June 10, a month after Hess's arrival, the lord chancellor and former foreign secretary, Lord Simon, also questioned Hess at Churchill's request. Through this meeting, which produced "little of value," Simon received "some indirect indication that an attack by Germany on her ally Russia might be coming."[85] It is difficult to believe that the "indirect indication" given by Hess was not brought to Churchill's immediate attention, although it is claimed that a part of Lord Simon's report was, at Churchill's request, either held back or destroyed.[86] Moreover, in early September, well after the German invasion, Lord Beaverbrook, Churchill's friend and a member of the War Cabinet, had a "long interview" with Hess in preparation for his mission to Moscow, where the question of Hess's flight would undoubtedly be raised. During this interview, which was far from coherent, Hess conveyed to Beaverbrook a memorandum that he had written in July following the invasion; in the memorandum "he argued that Great Britain should support Germany against Russia." Oddly, however, this issue was not formally raised during their conversation. It was this memorandum, it appears, that Beaverbrook took to Moscow. When Stalin inquired why Hess had flown to Scotland, Beaverbrook responded that he had done so " 'to persuade Britain to join

Germany in making an attack on Russia.' "[87] Stalin thought that Hess had flown to Scotland not at Hitler's request but with his knowledge. Beaverbrook agreed. Hess, Beaverbrook explained, had come to Scotland with the notion that "with a small group of aristocrats a counter-Churchill Government" could be established to end the war with Germany and that these steps would be welcomed by most Britons. With London's assistance, Berlin would then attack Moscow. Stalin "relished the amusing and detailed comments by Beaverbrook."[88]

Hess indeed harbored the hope of an Anglo-German combination targeted against Russia. Harboring such a hope is not the same, however, as informing the British that an attack on Russia was planned for a specific date. The question is, outside of his indirect indication to Lord Simon of a possible upcoming German attack, whether Hess directly informed Kirkpatrick or any other official of the specific plan.

Information supporting the suspicion that Hess might have conveyed such intelligence to the British was signaled in early November to General Sherman Miles, the chief of G-2, Military Intelligence, by the American military attaché in London, Colonel Raymond E. Lee. Up to this point, as Lee had pointed out on May 24, any information that Hess had imparted to the British was kept very secret and "treated as a matter of state of the first importance."[89] Lee's November source was a "member of Churchill's 'inner circle,' " but Lee was uncertain of the information's "validity."[90] "Hess [had] said" to the British, Lee reported, that "he flew to the Duke [of Hamilton in Scotland] to tell him that Germany was about to fight Russia." In fact, if London continued the struggle, Hess threatened that Berlin would "have to destroy England after [it] destroyed Russia." The source of this information, Lee assured Miles, was an individual "whose intimate acquaintance with the affair [was] unquestionable."[91] When Colonel Lee showed the report to Winant, the ambassador noted that it was true. The only thing that he had previously been unaware of was that Hess had come to England to inform the British of the upcoming German attack on Soviet Russia. He then incorrectly credited Hess's information as London's "principal" wellspring about the invasion.[92]

The question that remains is this: who was the source of Lee's information? Who was this member of Churchill's inner circle? According to Lee's own admission, the information reached him indirectly from Major Desmond Morton, described as a "discreet and shadowy figure," but one of the "most charming and active men in Churchill's entourage."[93] Morton was certainly in a position to have supplied information of so sensitive a nature, for he had been deviling for Churchill on intelligence matters since the summer of 1940.[94] Indeed, recently released NKVD material shows that, during the course of a luncheon on October 26, Morton had made comments very similar to those reported by Colonel Lee.[95]

If the British had learned from Hess that a German attack against Russia was imminent, why did Churchill, as we have seen, tell President Roosevelt the contrary? About ten days after Hess had parachuted into Scotland, Roosevelt was himself uneasy. " 'I wonder what is *really* behind this story?' " he remarked to State Department Under Secretary Sumner Welles.[96] The answer to his question might lie in whether Hess's admission of an upcoming attack against Russia, of which Hess was fully informed,[97] was made initially or developed subsequently, either before or after Lord Simon had questioned him on June 10. If the admission was made after Hess's arrival in Scotland and his initial interrogation by Kirkpatrick, it might explain why the Duke of Hamilton's personal report of his interview with Hess immediately after his capture and Kirkpatrick's own memorandums of the conversations with Hess on May 13, 14, and 15 were released during the Nuremberg Trials.[98] Certainly Hess's indirect indication to Lord Simon or to anyone else of a possible German attack was an additional piece of information that probably contributed, as we shall see, to the later revised British intelligence estimate that a German strike at Russia was in the offing.

Finally, the reasons for Hess's flight to Scotland are not absolutely clear. He claimed he had unsuccessfully attempted the flight on three previous occasions, the earliest being in December 1940. This successful attempt, one can suggest, might have been partially prompted by Stalin's obvious overtures for talks with the Germans. The rumors circulating in Berlin that important German-Russian negotiations were on the horizon could not have escaped Hess's notice even though he no longer enjoyed Hitler's undivided attention. Hess might have feared that Stalin would ardently pursue Germany's hand far more subtly than Hitler had persued Russia's in 1939. Such rumors might have conjured up in Hess's mind the possibility that, by a last minute political sleight of hand, Stalin would suborn Hitler and undercut his decision to attack Soviet Russia, thus focusing Germany's attention westward rather than eastward. In Hess's hierarchy of demons, none preceded Soviet Russia and Communism. As Jozef Lipski, the last prewar Polish ambassador in Berlin, pointed out, "Hess was a fanatical anti-Communist." Moreover, he had been "strongly opposed" to the 1939 nonaggression pact.[99]

Hess's attitude was compounded by racial hostility based on the Nazi's pseudo-anthropological hierarchy that proclaimed the superiority of the Aryan element over the Jews, the Gypsies, and the Slavs. In comparison, Hess's and Hitler's hostility toward England was relatively anodyne. Great Britain would be tolerated and concessions would be made to terminate the war, but the negotiations would have to occur, Hess emphasized, with an English government other than the one presided over by the present prime minister.[100] These ruminations appear to have been his own; they were so construed by the British. Hess was not in Scotland, Eden assured the American ambassador, as the German government's agent.[101]

Some other events of the weeks previous to Hess's flight raise doubts about the accuracy of Eden's comment to Ambassador Winant, made only days after Hess's arrival in Scotland. On April 28, less than two weeks before Hess's flight, the former League of Nations high commissioner for Danzig and then vice president of the Swiss Red Cross, Carl Burckhardt, divulged to Albrecht Haushofer, professor of political geography and geopolitics at the University of Berlin, that he had been approached by someone "respected in London, who was close to the leading conservative and city circles." This respected visitor, whom Burckhardt refused to identify, "though he could vouch for his earnestness," had "expressed the wish of important English circles for an examination of the possibilities for peace."[102]

Haushofer's name had been raised, Burckhardt explained, as a possible go-between. This made sense since Haushofer had at Hess's request, as we shall see, approached the British in September of 1940 regarding this very matter. Moreover, both Haushofer and his father Karl, the well-known geopolitician, were friends of Hess. The approach to Burckhardt had also made sense because, starting as early as the summer of 1940, he had acted as an intermediary between the British and the Germans. The desideratum of this leading group of so-called British conservatives, according to Burckhardt, was a waiver of interests made by London regarding the eastern and southeastern regions of Europe except Greece. This was not much of a concession since the British never had any real interests in this area. The London conservative group also wanted a restoration of the Western European state system as well as of Germany's pre-World War I colonial possessions, provided the "Italian appetite [could] be curbed."[103] As it turned out, the proposals that Hess tendered on his arrival in Scotland did not dovetail in all respects with those allegedly tendered by the London conservative group to Burckhardt.[104]

For our purpose, what is of cardinal importance is Stalin's reaction to Hess's dramatic flight. Keeping in mind Stalin's fears of any arrangement between London and Berlin ending the war and allowing Germany to turn eastward or his even worse fears of an agreement leading to an Anglo-German anti-Soviet alliance, the *Vozhd*'s deep suspicions of what had occurred are understandable.[105] Within days of Hess's arrival in Scotland, Cripps would observe that the incident had "no doubt intrigued the Russian government as it had everyone else" and "may well have aroused their fears of a peaceable deal at their expense."[106] In fact, the well-informed Gavrilović observed that Hess's flight "had caused a certain anxiety" to the Russian leaders. They interpreted his arrival in Scotland as an attempt to terminate the war between London and Berlin on the understanding that Germany would be allowed freedom of action against Russia. Officials in Moscow had correctly noted to Gavrilović, but with some exaggeration, that after Hess's arrival London had not been subjected to air attack for three weeks—unknown to Moscow the Luftwaffe squadrons were being sent east—and that Churchill had declined to issue any statement regarding Hess. Gavrilović was certain that if Germany did invade, "the Soviet leaders would be convinced that the attack had some connection with Hess's visit to England"[107]—a prophetic statement, as we shall see.

Somewhat similar and plausible observations were tendered "by an individual prominent in Soviet circles to a confidential source" controlled by the Federal Bureau of Investigation. This individual held that Hess's arrival was based on instructions from Hitler to arrange contact with those described as "Liberal Communists" or with the survivors of the anti-Communist "Cliveden set" that had been led by Lady Astor. They, in turn, could contact Churchill and thus influence their government to terminate the war and then combine with Germany to attack Russia. Because of Russia's rearmament program, its position was very clear although at the present moment Russia was "not disposed to picking a quarrel with Germany."[108] Whoever this individual was, his comments appeared to reflect knowledge of Moscow's thoughts and fears.

Moscow's suspicions could only have been reinforced by information conveyed by Sorge in Tokyo that he had learned at the German embassy that Hitler was intent on making peace with England in order to turn on Russia. Hess had been dispatched to England, he reported to the GRU, as a final recourse. Despite the 1939 nonaggression pact, Sorge judged that a German invasion of Soviet Russia "was inevitable and even imminent."[109] This Tokyo information, in turn, is reflected in the comments made to the Yugoslav military attaché, probably by General Zhukov, that Moscow distrusted London and suspected that the Hess flight to Scotland was "an effort to turn [the] war against [the] U.S.S.R."[110]

Although Sorge's other warnings, as we have seen,[111] appear to have fallen on deaf ears, this one hit a raw nerve. It did so because it buttressed what the counselor of the Yugoslav legation described as Stalin's "deep seated hatred of Britain," based in part upon its "historic frustration . . . of Soviet territorial ambitions" and in part on the contempt manifested by British politicians and diplomats toward Russian officials since the inception of the Communist regime. This view that Stalin entertained a "deep-seated antipathy towards Britain" was shared, Steinhardt pointed out, "by some of the best informed diplomats in Moscow whose personal feelings [were] pro-British."[112]

The British government's "silence" in 1941—their not informing the public about why Hess had flown to England and what information, if any, he had imparted—contributed,[113] as we have seen, to the innate suspiciousness of Stalin's mind and to his anti-British propensity. This situation, in turn, was not simplified by the "rumours circulating" in Washington, as reported by Lord Halifax, that London's silence about Hess's descent on England connoted that the British government was arranging "peace talks through him."[114]

One of the principal dispensers of this story was former President Herbert Hoover, whose activities Lord Halifax complained about to Sumner Welles on June 22, the very day of the German attack. Hoover, Halifax contended, "engaged in spreading the report in many circles in the United States that Hess had brought to Great Britain specific and concrete German peace proposals." That Hess had tendered proposals seemingly of his own design has been recounted; that these proposals were dictated by Hitler or others has never been proven. Supposedly, Hoover alleged that when the Conservative party leaders learned of these overtures, they pressured Churchill to give Hess's "proposals full consideration" by threatening to withdraw support from Churchill's government unless he "agreed to discuss these proposals." This was why, according to Hoover, Churchill had pressed Ambassador Winant to return immediately to Washington to explain the situation to President Roosevelt and obtain the president's consent to London's consideration of Hess's proposals.[115]

Hoover maintained that his information was unimpeachable since he had acquired it from Hugh Gibson, a friend and former diplomat, who, in turn, had got it from "reliable inside sources." Halifax assured Welles that this information had no factual basis and that Washington was, of course, "aware of the general nature of the statements that Hess had made upon his arrival in Scotland."[116] To these comments Welles appears to have made no response.

As Gibson's appointment book for this period clearly shows,[117] he certainly had the range of contacts that could have given him access to the inside information that Hoover claimed to have received from him. Moreover, one would find it difficult to accept the notion that a person of Gibson's experience, especially when he was speaking to a former president who was a friend and under whom he had served, would fantasize or misrepresent what might have been related to him in London, no matter how fallacious.

If Hoover's assertions, based on Gibson's information, came to the attention of Lord Halifax, one would have to assume that they also came to the attention of the Russian embassy. Hoover's niche in American political life, the embassy would have surmised, would make him privy to such information. It was probably believed and conveyed to Moscow. Tangential evidence that the Russians had received this information was supplied by Maxim Litvinov, later an ambassador in Washington, who admitted to Lord Halifax—as Gavrilović had prophesied—that when he initially heard of the German attack on June 22, he was certain that London had come to an agreement with Berlin through Hess.[118] The belief was, Litvinov recalled, that the British fleet coming in from the North Sea would join a German attack on Leningrad and the naval station at Kronstadt.[119]

Any such embassy report to Moscow would not have been received skeptically; recently released NKVD archival materials show us that Stalin's suspicions had been aroused within days following Hess's flight to Scotland. On May 14, the NKVD resident in London, Ivan Chichaiev, relayed information obtained by the recruited agent, the Cambridge-educated Kim Philby, probably code-named "Sohnchen." According to the Foreign Office's Kirkpatrick, Philby reported, Hess "had brought peace offers" although the details were unknown. This news prompted NKVD Moscow to alert its residents in Berlin, London, Rome, Stockholm, and Washington to discover all they could about Hess's arrival in England. Their responses only helped buttress Philby's report and increase Stalin's suspicions.

From Washington, the NKVD resident reported that Hess had gone to England with Hitler's complete consent to commence peace negotiations because any public peace offer by Hitler himself would have adversely affected German morale. As the NKVD in Berlin reported, Hess was lucid. He had departed for England, the head of the German Foreign Ministry's American Department had remarked, "with a definite assignment and proposal" from the German authorities. Somewhat similar information was imparted by a senior staff officer in the Wehrmacht, who maintained that Hess undertook his flight with Hitler's knowledge in order to propose peace to the British. This opinion was echoed by another NKVD-controlled source, who said that Hitler sent Hess to "conduct peace negotiations" and that, should England agree, Germany would immediately turn on Russia.[120] Amaiak Kobulov, the Berlin resident, observed that perhaps Hitler and Propaganda Minister Joseph Goebbels had a difference of opinion over the war with England. Whatever the case was, Kobulov correctly held, Moscow disbelieved all of Berlin's declarations about Hess's arrival in England.[121]

On May 18, unverified intelligence offered by Philby added to the mosaic. In a discussion with an unsuspecting friend, Tom Dupree of the Foreign Office's Press Department, Philby learned that in conversation with British military intelligence Hess had admitted that he came to England with a peace plan to terminate the hostilities and preserve the British Empire as a "stabilising force" in world politics. Moreover, Beaverbrook and Eden, Dupree asserted, had visited Hess. To Kirkpatrick, Hess had observed that England harbored a powerful anti-Churchill faction whom his arrival would greatly stimulate in the struggle to achieve peace.[122]

After querying Dupree, Philby concluded that what Dupree and the Foreign Office desired to arrange with Hess was an Anglo-German coalition against Russia. However, Philby interpreted Churchill's warning that Hess was his prisoner as a warning to those opposed to Churchill "against any intrigues" involving Hess. The time for negotiations had not yet arrived, Philby advised, but he opined that as the war developed Hess could become the focal point for "intrigues for a compromise peace" and accordingly would be useful to both the peace faction in England and Hitler.[123]

In view of this intelligence, NKVD Moscow concluded that Hess's arrival in England was neither a mad act nor Hess's personal attempt to save himself from Nazi intrigue, but an attempt by the Nazi hierarchy to strike a deal with the British. Understandably, it was a "scenario that worried Stalin."[124] As late as mid-June, the NKVD in Berlin was attempting to discover "whether peace negotiations were actually being conducted between Germany and England."[125]

Despite the NKVD's information and its conclusion, there was no firm consensus in Russian intelligence circles regarding this issue. The GRU's Colonel Akhmedov was poised for his first assignment abroad. To avert the Gestapo's suspicions, he was supplied with the appropriate "legend" and "cover story" that he was the new *Tass* man assigned to Berlin. Akhmedov was requested by General Golikov "for his own information"—read here Stalin's—to ascertain the "facts about Rudolf Hess's defection to Britain." No doubt to Stalin's dismay and Golikov's unease, the colonel uncovered little if anything to elucidate Hess's flight, except information that he was mentally unstable. Akhmedov did not believe that anyone, even Hitler, knew the reasons why Hess had left for Scotland.[126]

Nevertheless, Stalin held to the NKVD line. His position was reflected in an exchange in which Nikita Khrushchev, his Ukrainian henchman and future successor, observed to Stalin that something was afoot. Khrushchev did not accept the German story that Hess had fled. He maintained that actually Hess was "on a secret mission" on Hitler's orders to negotiate with the British about "cutting short the war" in Europe to allow Hitler to drive to the east. " 'Yes that's it. You understand correctly,' " Stalin responded. He said nothing more.[127]

Obviously, Stalin believed the Philby-NKVD reports, and Schulenburg, sensitized to the impact that Hess's flight would have on Stalin's innately suspicious mind (arousing what Cripps called the "old fears of a peaceable deal" between London and Berlin at Moscow's expense), informed the *Vozhd* that Hess was "crazy."[128] In contrast, in conversation with Steinhardt, Schulenburg held to the line that what had occurred was very regrettable, but he thought that Hess was perfectly lucid.[129] Stalin naturally did not agree with or believe in Schulenburg's analysis. Rather, he strove to discover officially what was afoot between the British and the Germans. In London, Maisky, whose perceptions of Hess's arrival dovetailed with Stalin's worst suspicions,[130] was quick to respond to his master's voice and inquired at the Foreign Office what was to be made of Hess's " 'visit' " to England. He would be told more later, he was informed, when more was known. Maisky, "with a leer" then observed: " 'So you will make him talk' "—not too subtly alluding to possible torture. He was assured that Hess would probably talk of his own volition.[131] Maisky had reasonably accurate data, no doubt based on Moscow's messages alluding to the Philby-NKVD information, about what Hess had said, and he shared it with the ever-attentive Beatrice Webb.[132]

If anything convinced Stalin that something was afoot between the British and the Germans, it was the continual well-being, thanks to the British, of Rudolf Hess. It is unknown whether the presidential envoy, Harry Hopkins, mentioned to Stalin Churchill's July offer to interview Hess, which Stalin rejected on the ground it "might give rise to embarrassing rumors of an arrangement with the Nazis."[133] Suffice it to note that Hopkins greatly admired the *Vozhd*,[134] and if he did utter any words following his arrival in Moscow from London, they would have only reinforced Stalin's rampant suspicions.

Stalin's suspicions first surfaced privately but officially when he inquired during Beaverbrook's Moscow visit in the autumn of 1941 whether London had intended to make peace with Germany. Beaverbrook asked why the question was raised, and he says that in answer Stalin retorted that he had "concluded we meant to make Peace because we kept Hess in our hands instead of shooting him." To Stalin "it was plain that Hess was the line of communication."[135] His suspicions then surfaced publicly in October 1942 in two articles on the front pages of *Pravda,* one of which appeared over Molotov's name and demanded Hess's immediate trial and severe punishment as a war criminal by a special international tribunal. *Pravda* also argued that not to treat Hess, among others, as a war criminal was tantamount to treating him as Hitler's representative in England enjoying immunity.[136]

Eden has pointed out that the Hess business "never ceased to fascinate the Russians." They found it difficult to accept that there was no "sinister" aspect to the whole episode or that the British were in no way implicated. Repeatedly in the years that followed, Eden was cross-examined about Hess by Stalin, Molotov, and Politburo member Nikolai Shvernik, who subsequently became president of the Soviet Union. Though Eden writes that he held nothing back and even offered to show them the pertinent documentation containing Hess's statements—the earliest information was conveyed in November 1942—he doubted if they ever really believed that the "incident was as unexpected and inexplicable to us as to them."[137]

One can offer another possible scenario to explain Hess's flight: to wit, contrary to what the Swiss Burckhardt told Albrecht Haushofer, there were no important English circles in London or elsewhere seeking to examine the possibilities of peace with Germany. Without question, Burckhardt had acted in good faith. The connection, however, between Albrecht Haushofer and the Duke of Hamilton had been revealed when a letter Albrecht had written at Hess's urging on September 23, 1940, had fallen into the hands of MI5. The letter sought to establish contacts in England leading to possible discussions that might help end the war.[138]

From this point on, British intelligence, using the Duke of Hamilton's name, developed a spurious correspondence with Haushofer, the purpose of which was to entice Hess to come to England to engage in peace discussions with a supposedly anti-Churchill faction largely composed of aristocrats. Information that this is what happened was reported after September 1941 by the Deuxième Bureau (military intelligence) of the Vichy General Staff in a report that was purloined by a NKVD penetration agent and sent to Moscow. Analogous information was supplied in October 1942 in London to NKVD resident Chichaiev by Moravec, the Czech who claimed that he "personally saw" the spurious correspondence with Haushofer. The German replies, according to Moravec, made it clear that Berlin's plans were tied to an attack on Moscow. The letters stressed the need to terminate the struggle between Berlin and London. In these letters, the British had the documentary evidence of German culpability in preparing an attack on Russia. NKVD analysts accepted Moravec's admission, as did Beria, "as convincing evidence of a British plot" against the Nazis, and Stalin and Molotov were so informed.[139]

Considering the available evidence, one can argue that sometime after his conversation with Burckhardt on April 28, Haushofer received a green light from the British to proceed with the dispatch of the peace negotiator. The British ploy was creditable, for in the preceding months had there not been surreptitious "efforts at launching peace initiatives" made by London? The Deuxième Bureau reported that the enticement of Hess by British intelligence was retribution for the Venlo incident of November 1939 when two MI6 officers were lured to the Dutch-German frontier and kidnapped.[140] This report may well have been true, but Hess, for reasons political and ideological, was ripe for the picking. Moreover, the explanation of Burckhardt's respected visitor that important English circles wanted to examine peace possibilities was no more than a "cover story" created to tempt Hess to England and capture.

The whole ploy, one can argue, had all the ingredients of the so-called "Trust" operation run by the NKVD in the early 1920s; in this operation a small but well-organized and influential group was on the verge of overthrowing the Communist regime, and contacts with anti-Soviet groups in the West were indispensable to its success. The "Trust" had led to the capture and execution of the British agent, Sidney Reilly. Therefore, Hugh Gibson's comments to Herbert Hoover, one can suggest, were like the comments to Burckhardt, nothing more than parts of a cleverly planted cover story.

Data tending to support this thesis exist. It is alleged, for example, that Ian Fleming, who served in naval intelligence during the war and created the fictional British superspy James Bond, proposed that a defunct pre-war pro-German organization be recycled and made to appear as if it still retained an influential membership capable of undoing Churchill's government and negotiating a peaceful settlement with Germany. In order to keep the Germans militarily at bay and in view of his pro-British leanings and anti-Russian phobias, Hess was the person targeted by this operation. Apparently, because of Hess's beliefs in astrology and the occult, Fleming cleverly planted "bogus horoscopes" on him, but how they were "worded, or the advice they gave to Hess, remains a mystery." At the minimum, they had to raise no suspicions in Hess's mind and also encourage him to come to England, and come he did.[141] The "fingerprints" on the Hess file, one experienced writer assures us, are clearly those of MI6, but unfortunately he does not offer the requisite evidential citations.[142]

Based on the information received, the Kremlin's suspicion that British intelligence had lured Hess to Britain was best reflected during Churchill's visit to Moscow in October 1944 when Stalin "unexpectedly proposed" a toast to British intelligence, "which had inveigled Hess into coming to England." Hess could not have landed in Scotland "without being given signals." British intelligence, he insisted, had to "have been behind it all." Churchill protested that the government had no prior warning of Hess's journey. Stalin responded that Russian intelligence often acted without informing the government, doing so only after its mission was accomplished.

Churchill strenuously denied that British intelligence had played any role in Hess's flight.[143]

Churchill had the impression that Stalin believed that London and Berlin were involved in some deep exchanges "or plot . . . to act together in the invasion of Russia which had miscarried." Keeping in mind Stalin's experience in world affairs, Churchill was taken aback that the *Vozhd* was "silly" on this question. When it became clear that Stalin did not believe the explanations offered, Churchill fulminated that when he made a "statement of facts" within his knowledge, he expected it to be accepted. Stalin's reaction to this sharp retort was a "genial grin." Churchill let it pass.[144] "The Russians are very suspicious of the Hess episode," Churchill wrote six months later to Secretary of Air Sir Archibald Sinclair. Stalin, he divulged, had steadfastly maintained that "Hess had been invited over by our Secret Service."[145]

The Russian suspicions and desires were clear enough. From the very beginning, Russian concern about possible British-German exchanges had been aroused by Hess's unexpected arrival.[146] The embers of suspicion had been glowing since the previous summer when the NKVD had reported that the Duke and Duchess of Windsor, who were in Madrid, had established contacts with Hitler. According to the NKVD, the former king was discussing with Hitler the establishment of a new government in London and the conclusion of a peace settlement with Berlin, provided that a military alliance opposed to Soviet Russia could be cobbled.[147]

If Hess was the "line of communication" with Berlin, this line could be severed immediately by his execution. British resistance to this suggestion, however, only compounded the Russian suspicions. Should the tide of battle continue to go against the British, Hess's prolonged survival would offer a convenient conduit for the establishment of contact with Berlin for the purpose of negotiating London out of the war and leaving Russia to face Germany alone or, even worse, to face a British-German combination leading to a confrontation on a less-than-level playing field. After the German invasion in June and despite the fact that London and Moscow were now allied, this possibility continued to haunt the Kremlin's leadership.

Even if one concedes the paranoid nature of Moscow's leader and the fawning nature of his entourage, Moscow, through its persistence, convinced itself that Hess's bizarre descent on Scotland was prearranged and designed to hinder Russia. This Russian stance was maintained to the end of the war and beyond. It is clearly mirrored in Moscow's dissent from the majority decision of the International Military Tribunal at Nuremberg to impose life imprisonment on Hess, rather than the death penalty. Hess's mission to Scotland, the Russian judge maintained, "was undertaken in the hope of facilitating the realization of aggression against the Soviet Union by temporarily restraining England from fighting."[148] Only the short-lived postwar euphoria and Moscow's desire not to be impolitic can explain the use here of the nonabusive adjective "restraining."

If there had been any doubts in Stalin's mind about opening negotiations with Berlin through Dekanozov, they must have quickly evaporated following Hess's arrival in Scotland. The possibility of British-German negotiations through Hess must have convinced him as nothing else could that his initial decision to approach Berlin was absolutely correct. In fact, by doing so, he believed he had beaten the British to the punch. The immediate task that now faced Stalin, however, was to discover what the Germans wanted and how far he could go in satiating their desires without undermining Russia politically and militarily, and especially without undermining his own position in Russian affairs. If some sort of arrangement could be hammered out, or if the negotiations could be strung out until the late summer, it would obviate a German attack until the spring of the following year at the earliest. At that point the Russian rearmament program would have gone far to level the playing field.

## Berlin Embassy: The Order of Battle

It has been correctly pointed out that from the signature of the nonaggression pact in August 1939 until the German attack in June 1941, the personnel of the Russian embassy in Berlin was in continual flux. The tour of duty of senior embassy personnel was limited, and most of them were without doubt members of the Russian intelligence services.[149] Valentin Berezhkov, who served in the embassy from late December 1940 to June 1941 when he and others were exchanged for members of the German diplomatic mission in Moscow, was one of the glaring exceptions.[150] Another probable exception was the counselor of mission, Vladimir Semionov, who in the postwar period served in East Germany for a considerable length of time.[151]

Russian intelligence activities in Germany, however, "had aroused Hitler's interest," and repeatedly he demanded explanations of counterintelligence efforts from the German security organs. He had a healthy respect for the Russian intelligence services and believed them "much more thorough and probably much more successful" than those of the British or of any other state. He proved to be intuitively correct.[152]

Although Hitler's anxieties were understandable because Germany was Moscow's "main target" of interest, Stalin nevertheless preached the need for caution. He did not wish to furnish Hitler with a "pretext for creating new tensions or for an armed attack" that might be provided by the discovery of a Russian espionage network operating in Germany. Because the German Communist party had been decimated, the ability to recruit agents from within the party, as had been done in the past, was nonexistent, while Communist bodies that had survived had been penetrated by agents of the German security services. Though a handful of agents had escaped the Nazi takeover and were in tenuous contact with the Russian intelligence apparat, their successes were not of the first order. The Russian decision, therefore, was not to create extensive espionage networks in Germany but to penetrate it by establishing a network of secret intelligence centers in the functioning democracies that surrounded the Third Reich: Belgium, Denmark, and Holland, with backups in France and Switzerland. The added advantage of the networks in Belgium and Holland was that they could also be used in operations targeted against England.[153] Naturally, this policy was accelerated by Stalin's desire for closer relations with Hitler. By December 1936, Walter Krivitsky, a senior and very experienced intelligence officer operating in Europe, who initially was GRU and then transferred to the NKVD, was ordered by Stalin to "throttle down" his intelligence activities in Germany.[154]

The fall of Belgium, Denmark, Holland, and France in the spring onslaught of 1940 complicated Russian intelligence activities in Germany. Yet, even before the fall of these countries and of the Russian intelligence centers within them, the need to maintain the intelligence services within the Russian embassy in Berlin could not be avoided. These services consisted of two groups: the GRU, dealing with military or naval matters, and the larger NKVD, dealing with security matters. The NKVD, in turn, was split into intelligence and counterintelligence sections. The latter was then subdivided into the *Sovetskaia Kolonia* (the Soviet Colony), which acted as a watchdog over the Russian community in Germany; the *Emigratsiia* or EM (the Emigration), which operated among Russians who had fled to foreign countries and hoped to recruit them into the Russian intelligence services and to suborn or destroy the anti-Soviet Russian organizations they supported. There was also a foreign intelligence section whose duties included the gathering of political and military intelligence in Germany for the NKVD's Foreign Intelligence Directorate in Moscow.[155] Apparently to assist NKVD endeavors, the NKVD's premises within the embassy contained an area "specially equipped for the interrogation, torture and liquidation" of those in the embassy or the Soviet Russian community who were perceived by the counterintelligence section as opponents of the Russian regime.[156]

Naturally, the intelligence operatives enjoying "official or legal cover" as Russian embassy personnel, members of the mission who were entitled to diplomatic immunity, had no fear that German jurisdiction would ever be exercised against them. Leading the list, of course, was Ambassador Dekanozov himself, who, as we have seen, had previously been the head of the NKVD's foreign department, which dealt with intelligence activities abroad.[157] Amaiak Kobulov (code-named Zakhar), Dekanozov's other counselor of mission, had served for nine months as the NKVD chief in Ukraine until his posting to Berlin. The brother of Beria's NKVD crony, Bogdan Z. Kobulov, Amaiak Kobulov was one of "Beria's new, rapidly advancing lieutenants,"[158] and the NKVD resident.[159] Kobulov had received the Berlin posting thanks to his "good contacts" with the NKVD's leadership and despite "his meagre intelligence experience." His "lack of professional judgement," which was obvious to experienced NKVD officers, earned him little respect from that direction.[160] He apparently was a person of sartorial splendor who appeared cultivated, unlike his *muzhik* associates.[161] Like Dekanozov, he apparently was from the Caucasus,[162] but unlike Dekanozov, he gave no evidence to suggest that there was some doubt about his origins. In the postwar period, Kobulov was to continue his intelligence activities in the office of Soviet Property Abroad, an organization that later included Dekanozov, and as an official in the Gulag. Unlike Dekanozov, he at least initially survived execution when Beria fell from power in 1953.[163]

Tracing Kobulov's intelligence endeavors during his stay in Berlin would be virtually impossible. Nevertheless, here and there, information about Kobulov and his endeavors surfaces, especially regarding the subjects that he was interested in, the confidential documentation that he wanted, and the information about various personalities that he desired. Unbeknownst to Kobulov, Orests Berlings, a Latvian journalist whom he had recruited under pressure, had approached the Germans in mid-August 1940 and regularly reported on NKVD activities to an official on Ribbentrop's staff.

Hitler, however, who carefully read Berlings' reports, suspected that he feigned his role as a double agent and was in reality a "triple" agent bent on supplying disinformation. Accordingly, he desired that Berlings be closely watched so that subsequently he could be arrested. However, as the NKVD was told after the war, his activities on Germany's behalf were genuine. The mediocre Kobulov was so taken in by Berlings that he considered him a "most reliable source."[164] Along with Berlings, the Germans also controlled the Lithuanian Vitold Pakulat, whom we will soon discuss. The damage Pakulat did to NKVD operations in Germany caused Stalin to make an oblique allusion to him: Stalin succinctly observed to Cripps after the June attack that some Russian "agents in Germany had been found to be working for both sides."[165] This experience could only have reinforced Stalin's distrust of Russian controlled agents.[166]

The Germans, naturally, were quite aware of Kobulov's real function within the embassy. He "was under heavy survelliance,"[167] and his every movement was subjected to the scrutiny of the German security services. Kobulov, Berlings was admonished, was not to be contacted by telephone.[168]

Also enjoying official or legal cover was the embassy's press attaché, Lavrov (or Levrov), who, like Dekanozov and Kobulov, was a member of the NKVD. Intelligence information acquired by others, for example, by the so-called correspondents of the *Tass* news agency, was first submitted to Lavrov, who in turn conveyed it to his chief, Kobulov.[169] The military attaché, General Vasili Tupikov, as we have seen, was a member of the GRU,[170] as was his assistant Colonel Nikolai Skorniakov,[171] who dealt with air force matters. In all probability, the naval attaché, Captain Mikhail Vorontsov, was a member of naval intelligence, which was then independent of the GRU, and directly accountable to Admiral Nikolai Kuznetsov, the minister of marine and commander in chief of the navy.[172] Not to be outdone, the Russian consulates in

Germany contributed to the intelligence offensive in conjunction with the embassy.

We have already had a fleeting glimpse into the endeavors of the Russian consulate in Prague.[173] Greater substance, however, is offered by the German police, who discovered that agents of the embassy and the consul in Prague had set up twelve illegal wireless transmitters in Czechoslovakia. These activities led to the arrest of sixty people.[174] In Danzig, two of the consuls were heads of a wide-ranging spy ring. Their endeavors extended into army supply matters in Berlin and included the transmission of wireless messages to Moscow, which were largely about troop movements and locations and included crucial intelligence about troop concentrations in East Prussia and the movement of Germany's Baltic fleet.[175]

The trade delegation was also included in intelligence endeavors. Using a fictitious name and, as already recounted, operating under the cover that he was the trade delegation's inspector, Dmitri Konovalov, a colonel and an engineer, represented the GRU. Under his direct control was the source in the Škoda works code-named "Škvor"[176] and probably others, especially in Czechoslovakia. Using the cover of "trade representatives," a number of military engineers had also been seconded to work in Germany.[177]

Also operating out of the trade delegation was one "Alexander Erdberg." He and Embassy Officer Alexander Korotkov, who was an experienced NKVD intelligence operative, are one and the same. In later years, he was to be in charge of the NKVD's "illegals." When assigned to Berlin, Korotkov was instructed to maintain contact with the anti-Nazi underground and was instrumental in acquiring from Moscow spare parts for one of its transmitters. Korotkov was deeply involved in recruiting agents into anti-Nazi German espionage groups and acted as the contact man between these Berlin groups and Moscow. He supplied these groups with needed equipment, particularly wireless transmitters, as well as with funds, and he arranged their training in wireless operations, sometimes by sending them to Soviet Russia. He continued to work with the anti-Nazi German espionage groups even after his return to Moscow in the summer of 1941.[178] Intourist also contributed to the intelligence endeavors of those associated with the embassy, thanks to the activities of its Berlin director, Shakhanov, who was in "close contact with Kobulov."[179] In view of this contact, it would be safe to assume that Shakhanov, like Kobulov, served the NKVD.

Working parallel to or sometimes in close collaboration with those agents who enjoyed official or legal embassy cover and thus diplomatic immunity were other intelligence agents who can be labeled as "illegal" operatives because they carried false credentials. They were made members of legitimate Russian enterprises whose members did not enjoy diplomatic immunity so that their endeavors could be better disguised. During this period, the *Tass* news agency was one such enterprise, honed then, and subsequently, to perfection for illegal intelligence endeavors abroad. The dashing foreign correspondent with his proverbial trench coat, notebook, and camera was conventionally considered to be someone whose profession dictated unrestricted travel, unlimited inquiry, and access to all sorts of interesting people, including leading political figures, public officials, members of the business community and the professions, as well as laymen. At the same time, these very prerogatives of foreign correspondents are the lifeblood of any intelligence officer. Even in a society as well-controlled as was Nazi Germany, the enterprising foreign correspondent was more than a match for the Gestapo and other security organs. If cleverly used, the prerogatives of foreign correspondents could facilitate the discovery of information and the recruitment of human sources, especially if the so-called correspondent using these prerogatives was a well-trained and experienced member of the Russian intelligence services whose name and background were fictitious and whose proffered credentials were fraudulent.

For security reasons, *Tass* in 1941 Berlin was divided into two self-contained compartments: one reserved for the NKVD and the other for the GRU. Tarasov (né Udin or Uden), *Tass*'s masthead president in Berlin, was Jewish and represented the NKVD. He was not appreciated by the GRU in Moscow because he was Jewish, and in Berlin he was universally disliked by the Russian community. More important, he had failed in his mission by "blowing" his cover. The Germans were on to him by the spring of 1941, and following the June attack he was arrested and subjected to intense interrogation and beatings before he was included among those exchanged for the personnel of the German diplomatic mission in Moscow. The information that Tarasov acquired either directly or through informants was communicated to the press attaché, Lavrov, and then conveyed by him to Kobulov.[180]

Tarasov's other associates included Yekhosef Verkhovtsev, who clearly was not GRU; on the contrary, he was Dekanozov's "special protegé," which leads one to conclude that he was NKVD.[181] Then there was Ivan Filippov, who clearly was NKVD. In fact, he would serve as Kobulov's deputy when his own chief was in Moscow.[182] By mid-June, Filippov, not Kobulov, ran the Latvian journalist Berlings, who naturally recounted to the Germans his exchanges with Filippov.[183] Accordingly, like Tarasov, Filippov was known to the Germans as an NKVD agent, but there is no evidence that he was treated in the same manner as Tarasov following the German invasion, perhaps because he was not Jewish. Years later, Filippov, no doubt as compensation for his loyal service, would resurface as the ambassador to Luxembourg.[184]

The GRU contingent in *Tass* was headed by Colonel Ismail Akhmedov, the former acting chief of its Fourth Division (technological espionage). His prior activities have been recounted. Akhmedov had been dispatched to Berlin by Golikov to investigate the information that Germany would invade in June. This information, supplied by "Škvor," the above-mentioned source in the Škoda works in Prague, had raised Stalin's ire. Akhmedov was to replace Tarasov, whose cover, as already noted, had been compromised, and to do so before the Gestapo arrested Tarasov. Among his other assignments,

Akhmedov was to acquire data on German troop organization, as well as on their location and training. He also had to discover why the Nazi party was politically successful and how it had conquered most of Europe. Moreover, he was to delve into the struggles among the party's ruling elites and sketch their personalities and inclinations. Stalin, in particular, wanted to know the wellspring of Hitler's strength and, as already discussed, the reasons for Hess's flight to Scotland. Akhmedov was to be the resident of the GRU's Fourth Division in Germany and was to "reorganize and strengthen" its intelligence activities in the country. He would have to coordinate his work for the Fourth Division with General Tupikov, who was the GRU's chief resident in Germany, but would be independent of him in possessing his own ciphers and communication facilities.

To make it possible for Akhmedov to accomplish his tasks, a plausible "legend" had to be concocted to pass the scrutiny of the curious, especially of the German security organs. Since Akhmedov had been mentioned in the Russian press, he had to be given a new name, one that had previously never been involved in intelligence activities or been compromised abroad. The name finally chosen was Georgii Petrovich Nikolayev. In his fictitious biography, he was given a date of birth at variance with his true one, falsely credited with matriculation at a school of journalism following honorable military service, and so on. Before departing for Germany, Akhmedov was interviewed by Dekanozov while he was in Moscow in May, and after working a short time at *Tass* to learn its procedures, Akhmedov arrived in Berlin in late May 1941 as its resident correspondent and vice president.[185]

Akhmedov's GRU associate in *Tass* was Sergei Kudryavtsev (or Koudriavtzer), who in reality was also a member of the Fourth Section of the GRU. Whatever intelligence information Kudryavtsev unearthed had to be reported to Akhmedov, who was his chief. After Kudryavtsev returned to Moscow, following the June attack, he was reassigned to Ankara, again as a *Tass* correspondent, and then was transferred to Ottawa as first secretary of the embassy.[186] There, Kudryavtsev headed the embassy's GRU operations until the arrival of the military attaché, Colonel Nikolai Zabotin. Then in the spring of 1945, Kudryavtsev was again transferred, this time to London as first secretary of the embassy. His odyssey continued when he was apparently appointed to the Russian delegation at the United Nations. Using the cover name "Leon," Kudryavtsev was not unmasked in Canada until the defection of GRU code clerk Igor Gouzenko in the autumn of 1945. As Gouzenko's testimony and the exhibits of the 1946 Canadian Royal Commission of Inquiry clearly show, Dekanozov, then in Moscow, was in contact with Zabotin about his GRU operations.[187] Like Filippov, his NKVD *Tass* counterpart, Kudryavtsev was compensated for his services through his later appointment as ambassador to Cambodia.[188] In the early 1960s, he was appointed ambassador to Castro's Cuba and was implicated in helping to organize Cuban terrorist activities on the eastern seaboard of the United States.[189]

In addition to Akhmedov and Kudryavtsev, there was another GRU officer from the Fourth Division assigned to the *Tass* organization in Berlin, but unfortunately neither his true name nor his cover name has ever surfaced.[190] It would be safe to suggest that this medley of intelligence talent fielded by the NKVD and the GRU, operating out of the Russian embassy, the consulates, the trade delegation, Intourist, and *Tass,* was probably far larger than the available evidence shows. Nevertheless, beyond this well-developed intelligence network, there existed yet another network. This one was composed of anti-Nazi Germans and others, not necessarily Communists, resident in Germany and the areas it occupied. Some members of this network were illegal residents, sometimes dispatched by the Russian intelligence services with fraudulent documentation. They enjoyed no protection and reported directly to Moscow or indirectly through channels under embassy, consulate, trade delegation, Intourist, or *Tass* control.

The possibility of increasing the number of those who enjoyed legal German residence and thus might better assist in Russian intelligence operations presented itself when Germany and Russia agreed to exchange populations after the territorial adjustments that developed as a result of the 1939 nonaggression pact. Volksdeutsche established in areas acquired by the Russians, such as the Baltic states, were to be exchanged for Russians established in areas acquired by the Germans, such as Poland. Even if only a tiny percentage of these Volksdeutsche could be recruited for intelligence activity, they could prove to be enormously important to Russian intelligence since they came from all walks of life and would be dispersed throughout Germany but unsuspected by the German security organs. The leverage for recruitment, however, was meager. The NKVD could try to buy these people or to intimidate them by threatening to bar their departure from the country or to hold as hostage their relatives left behind. Once the recruits reached Germany, however, most soon divulged to the German authorities what had occurred.

One such Volksdeutscher was a Lithuanian, Vitold Pakulat, whose assignment was to establish a wireless transmitter and a "safe house" for illegal Russian agents. Once in Germany, Pakulat contacted the security organs and then the Russian embassy. Pakulat was kept under constant police surveillance. Following Russian orders, he set up his wireless transmitter and also acquired a small hotel, which was used by Russian agents on their way through Berlin. In addition, his Russian control officer instructed him to make "contacts with skilled workers in war industries" in order to "obtain pertinent information." He was to set up secret locations—"letter boxes"—where documentation for other agents could be deposited.[191] The damage that Pakulat caused Russian intelligence can be well imagined. The Volksdeutsche recruitment operation was conducted by the NKVD, but the GRU also participated tangentially. Akhmedov informs us that he recruited some Volksdeutsche, including some Jews who obviously could not go to Germany and hence emigrated to Great Britain or the United States. Golikov was delighted with his success at recruitment.[192]

Records of the detailed activities of these legal and illegal resident informants who contributed data to the Russian intelligence services in Germany during this period rarely surface. When they do, they attract our attention only for a moment and then quickly disappear. Nevertheless there are enough examples of what these informants did to suggest that their networks were sizeable in number and their activities were wide in scope. The story of the Lithuanian Pakulat and the assignments given to him by Russian intelligence demonstrate these activities. Operating out of the Trade Delegation, Korotkov handled some of these informants, as did the GRU's Konovalov, who ran the Czech informant Škvor. One of Korotkov's informants may have been the Foreign Ministry's Rudolf von Scheliha, who had been recruited in the 1930s for mercenary rather than ideological reasons when he served as the counselor of the Warsaw embassy. Scheliha, in turn, had brought into the Foreign Ministry Ilse Stöbe, who had acted as the "cutout" with his control officer in Warsaw. As a member of the ministry's press section, Stöbe, codenamed "Alte" (the Old One), had good reason to see the *Tass* man in Berlin to whom she gave Scheliha's data. The *Tass* man then conveyed the data to the commercial attaché. The extent of damage Scheliha wrought on the Germans "is difficult to assess, but it was undoubtedly grave."[193]

Kobulov appears to have rashly used his apartment as a quasi-espionage marshalling yard. He "looked for assistants among foreign correspondents in Berlin"—Berlings was a case in point—and through his activities, extended his reach into occupied Poland and Czechoslovakia.[194] Danzig offered Kobulov the opportunity to set up an illegal wireless transmitter serviced by an operator of the Russian Embassy. This network, according to the German police, dealt with informants culling political and economic intelligence information.[195] These informants and their operations in Germany and elsewhere include names such as the Rote Kapelle, the Schulze-Boysen group, and the Harnack group.[196]

If their collective activities and those of the NKVD and the GRU in Germany in no way affected the thinking in Moscow, the reason is to be found in the methods of information distribution and analysis in the Russian Embassy in Berlin. Sometime in January or February 1941, Ambassadors Dekanozov, Umansky and Sergei Vinogradov in Ankara were directed by Stalin and Molotov to coordinate the intelligence activities of the NKVD, GRU, and Naval Intelligence within their respective diplomatic missions. These intelligence organs then had to submit all "first-hand information" to the ambassador in question before conveying it to Moscow.[197] The ostensible purpose of the instruction was clear enough—to prevent rivalry among the intelligence services—but in practical terms, this rule gave the NKVD control over the GRU abroad. NKVD already enjoyed this control at home because the ambassadors were predominantly NKVD men.[198]

In Berlin, therefore, Dekanozov was the hub of the intelligence wheel that directed the intelligence organs, and before forwarding anything to Moscow, he vetted the material they culled. Umansky in Washington was likewise an NKVD agent and in his extended career had been the director of *Tass* and the head of the Foreign Ministry's Press Department before his assignment to Washington.[199] The inscription of Vinogradov's name on the order assigning Umansky to Washington and Umansky's wartime activities in Ankara raise the suspicion that like the other two he was NKVD.[200]

In view of Dekanozov's niche in the Kremlin's hierarchy and within Stalin's inner circle, it is difficult to believe that he would have accepted the data garnered by the intelligence services and the implications of increasing danger that flowed from this data. His initial actions reflected Stalin's stance. As we have seen, in April Dekanozov casually dismissed General Tupikov's warning that German troops were being concentrated along the border as a figment of the imagination.[201] It was a wise dismissal in view of Stalin's rejection of all data supplied by the Rote Kapelle and of the instructions sent to the embassy on April 5 that the volume of information pointing to a German attack was a "deliberate disinformation campaign" against Soviet Russia.[202]

Dekanozov's comments to Akhmedov during their May discussion in Moscow that he was convinced that Germany would not attack Soviet Russia and that Akhmedov would have plenty of time to settle into his Berlin routine further indicated Dekanozov's commitment to the Stalinist line that Nazi Germany was not to be feared, at least for the remainder of 1941.

Considering Dekanozov's somnambulant attitude, one can well imagine the comments appended to the intelligence information that he forwarded to Moscow. His editing of the embassy's political reporting, morever, can be documented. His paramount position in the embassy on both political and intelligence matters had an upas tree effect on the embassy's work. This poisonous influence is best exemplified in a report written at the end of May, though ordered weeks before, that analyzed and summarized all data that had reached the embassy about German preparations for war against Soviet Russia. A group headed by Embassy Counselor Semionov had taken on the assignment, and its report, sprinkled with pertinent quotations from *Mein Kampf,* had concluded that the Germans had completed the practical steps necessary for invasion. The inference could not be avoided: Nazi Germany was primed to attack Soviet Russia whenever it chose to do so. Dekanozov, however, would not allow this line of thought. Fearful that such an unequivocal conclusion would not be to Stalin's liking, Dekanozov moderated the text that Semionov and his associates had written.[203] He also communicated this negative stance toward General Tupikov, the military attaché, who daily reported to Moscow on the Wehrmacht's military preparations. The embassy's military, Dekanozov warned, was "greatly exaggerating the threat."[204]

However, within the edited reports that called German invasion plans rumors, there was a March 16 letter from Dekanozov to Molotov that clearly discussed evidence of a massive German buildup on the Russian border and other news of German war preparations. Again in April, Dekanozov sent a special report to Moscow in which he stated that every day brought "rumours and all kinds of evidence of a future collision between Germany and the USSR for an attack on the Soviet Union." Faced with the increasing evidence unearthed by the intelligence services, he began to waiver in his commitment to the inviolable principle that the Germans were not to be feared for the remainder of the year. He even went so far as to say that Germany intended to "attack the USSR as early as during their present war with Britain."[205]

German intelligence reliably reported the inexplicable statement of Dekanozov to Mrs. Semionov that the children of Russian nationals residing in Berlin would return home.[206] Hitler's desire for verification of this report was confirmed in mid-June, as well as the fact that the exodus would include both preschool toddlers and school-age children.[207] Despite Dekanozov's endeavors to reduce the Russian community in Berlin, the flood of Russian arrivals in Berlin, including children and pregnant wives, continued unabated.[208] Regardless, a "depressed" Dekanozov, the Germans ascertained, held it probable that Hitler wanted to go to war with Russia and had advised the Russian-born wife of a Chinese diplomat to depart quickly from Berlin.[209] Dekanozov's depressed state persisted and was noted in the Wilhelmstrasse as late as June 20.[210]

On June 13 Dekanozov sent a telegram to Molotov outlining Germany's policy that gave Greece to Italy as "Lebensraum" in the Mediteranean and forced France into a struggle against Britain in North Africa. These moves were designed to shift the German struggle against Britain "onto the shoulders of its vassals" and to allow Germany to concentrate its forces in Europe. Later, Dekanozov annexed a letter to Molotov with a map from Germany's largest mapmaker, the Hebler Geographic Institute. The map showed the Ukrainian, Belorussian, Transcaucasian, and Baltic republics "as separated from the USSR by a thick green line."[211]

On June 15, Dekanozov again telegrammed Molotov. In addition to corroborating information about German troop movements, Dekanozov added a "new element." "This troop concentration is no longer regarded as Germany's demonstration to compel the USSR to make concessions,"[212] Dekanozov confirmed. Whatever the risk Dekanozov was running by reporting this information to Moscow, it was clearly less than the alternative risk of leaving an unprepared Russia to succumb to a German invasion. Given his career and character, only this impending German armageddon could have forced him to take up the role of messenger. Even in this dire situation, despite his position and the public closeness the *Vozhd* had shown him, Dekanozov does not appear to have attempted to contact Stalin directly.

Golikov also passed to Stalin information that Hitler was moving large groups of forces to the eastern front. However, like that of Dekanozov, Golikov's context was always carefully tailored. His material supporting Stalin's position was sent in one box under the heading "from reliable sources."

Material supporting a less sanguine analysis of German intentions was relegated to another box, entitled "from doubtful sources." Golikov had squared the circle and fulfilled his duty by letting Stalin know the worst. Should a scapegoat later be sought, he could claim to have told all, even though he had sent his message in such a way as to avoid a potentially fatal contradiction of the *Vozhd*. Golikov, like others of his ilk, was able to act as both a window and mirror for Stalin, allowing the light of reality in while still allowing the *Vozhd* to bask in his own reflection.[213]

If Gresham's law of intelligence, as practiced by Stalin, applied in Moscow, it initially also applied to Dekanozov in Berlin. In the few remaining weeks of peace, Soviet Russia was like a cyclops, limited in its vision to begin with, and then rendered totally blind by the self-inflicted wound caused by its political-ideological mind-set.

# 6

# The Ultimate Deception

## The Meissner-Dekanozov Discussions

Dekanozov returned to Berlin on May 14,[1] the very day on which the Foreign Office's Ivone Kirkpatrick interrogated Rudolf Hess in Scotland for the second time.[2] The impression of the NKVD's Filippov was that German-Russian relations had improved during the preceding weeks and that Dekanozov's return to Berlin confirmed this improvement.[3]

During Dekanozov's two-week stay in Moscow, the Russian intelligence services mounted a disinformation operation. By planting a whole series of allegedly official Russian reports through Ponschab in Harbin, they assiduously attempted to exert an indirect influence on the outcome of any forthcoming discussions with the Germans.

On May 3, when Dekanozov had been in Moscow for only a few days, Ponschab reported a circular message from the Russian capital dispatched on May 1 to its diplomatic missions abroad. The message stressed that greater propaganda efforts had to be made against the landing of German troops in Finland. Should Germany invade Russia's sphere of influence to the South, an allusion to Turkey, Iran, Afghanistan, and Iraq, Russia would threaten Germany's to the North. The 1939 nonaggression pact was predicated, the message emphasized, on the neutrality of Sweden and Turkey. Though the surviving version of the message is garbled and pieces of its text are missing, the "pitch" of the message is clear enough: Moscow was prepared to work with Berlin when Germany fully respected Russia's interests. However, should Berlin intend to conclude with Ankara a treaty that excluded Moscow, then Russian protests would have to be lodged. If Turkey were attacked, Russia would not assist it militarily; Russia's riposte would be to occupy Finland and threaten Sweden.[4]

The point made, Ponschab again contacted Berlin three days later on May

6, the very day Stalin assumed the prime ministership. The Russians, he reported, had supposedly spelled out in a message to their Far East missions on May 3 how far they would countenance German penetration of Turkey and Iraq. Moscow's previous message had alluded to these states as falling within its sphere of influence. Supposedly in its May 3 message, Moscow asserted that, up to a point, the negotiations with Germany were proceeding satisfactorily. This was an allusion to economic discussions. The rub appeared to be Berlin's emphatic demand that Turkey be included in its area of interest, a demand that Moscow just as emphatically opposed. To support their case, the Germans referred to the Berlin negotiations with Molotov in November of the previous year. These talks envisaged friendly relations and mutual assistance between Germany and Turkey. Moscow, however, was of the opinion that any mutual assistance between these two states was to be restricted to the economic realm. Germany's present ploy was to pressure Turkey into an anti-British Middle East bloc, but the Turks wished to avoid this struggle, especially in Iraq, where the British had intervened militarily to thwart the pro-Axis policies of the government of Rashid Ali al Gailani. Moscow was prepared to assist Baghdad, provided it did not conclude an alliance with Berlin. Lastly, the purported message informed the Far East missions that the British had given Moscow advance notice of their troops landing at the Iraqi port of Basra, but supposedly Moscow had not yet given its consent to this landing.[5]

The latter comment was a canard evoked to impress upon the Germans that Russia's claimed political interest in Iraq was recognized even by the British. That London would inform Moscow in advance of its military operations in Iraq, or even ask for its consent, was not in the cards. As we have seen, the British opposed any possible Russian meddling in that politically sensitive area.[6] There is no creditable evidence to suggest that any such approaches were made by London to Moscow about military intervention in Iraq during this period.[7]

Russia, Ponschab went on to explain in a follow-up message, wanted to avoid any friction with Germany over control of the Middle East. Accordingly, it would not agree to any treaty with Germany establishing spheres of influence in this area. Moscow committed itself not to meddle in the Middle East and to protect its interests there by "friendly means." Indeed, Moscow would not oppose any agreement between Berlin and Ankara, provided Turkey was not forced to accede to Berlin because of military and economic pressure. Russia, however, would assist Middle East states in withstanding any imperialist pressure. Furthermore, Russia would not allow any third power to establish military bases in Turkey even if Ankara agreed, and likewise it would not allow any third power to enter the Black Sea.[8]

These messages imply that in Stalin's mind any forthcoming discussions with the Germans had to include the continued existence of the Middle East states as a buffer zone between Russia and Germany. Prior to Dekanozov's departure for Moscow, however, this had not been the case. In a conversation with the Afghan minister of economic affairs, Abdul Majid Khan, Dekanozov had talked "about frontier adjustments" between Russia and Afghanistan and appeared prepared to settle these boundary rectifications before departing for Moscow. By the time he returned to Berlin, Dekanozov's attitude had completely changed. He now maintained that "it was too late to talk about frontier adjustments." Instead, he insisted, a system guaranteeing the independence of the smaller Middle East states like Iran and Afghanistan would have to be devised.[9]

Therefore, the rumor circulating in Berlin among journalists and diplomats that Russian concessions to the Germans would be rewarded by the Germans' giving a free hand to the Russians in the Persian Gulf that could possibly lead to Russia's acquisition of Afghanistan was nothing more than whistling in the dark.[10] In view of such rumors about German-Russian relations, the American embassy in particular was suspicious. Why had Moscow not announced its policy position through *Tass,* as it inevitably did? This silence, the embassy ruminated, confirmed suspicions that something was unfolding between Moscow and Berlin.[11]

By May 11, Ponschab seemed to be able to supply a broad outline, based on a supposed circular message from Moscow on May 8, of Russia's stance in any future negotiations pertaining to Turkey. According to the Russian plan, Russian, German, and Italian areas of interest in the Middle East would be divided in a manner that would allow Turkey to remain neutral and nonbelligerent. Turkey, for example, would not allow the transit of foreign military forces nor the establishment of military bases on its territory by other states. Russia would support the "liberation movement" and concurrently would "not allow any other power to support the liberation movement" of the Asian states. Neither would Russia allow any other power to conclude treaties with Afghanistan and Iran that excluded the participation of a third power—an obvious allusion to Russia itself. In addition, Germany and Italy would lend no support to the Middle East's Islamic movement. The region's oil fields would remain under Iranian and Iraqi control, but any surplus production beyond the needs of these two states should be equally divided among Russia, Germany, and Italy. Lastly, Russia would have equal rights in the use of the Suez Canal. These were its minimum demands, Moscow insisted, and if these demands were unacceptable to Berlin, long and difficult negotiations loomed in the future.

Strained relations and conflict between both states, however, were not inevitable. Actually, this situation brought the states together rather than separating them. This cooperative attitude was clearly mirrored in the additional information that Ponschab reported to Berlin. According to Ponschab, who was supposedly using information acquired from the British embassy in Tokyo and relayed to Moscow by the Russian embassy, there were British troop concentrations in Palestine to be used to protect TransJordan and to be dispatched to occupy French-mandated Syria. The British ambassador in Tokyo, Ponschab divulged, was very worried that the Vichy French in Syria, poised to resist the British thrust, would turn to the Germans for military assistance.

Similar considerations also existed in Turkey and were spelled out by Moscow in another circular message. According to the Russian ambassador in Ankara, the rejection of Turkey's offer of mediation between Great Britain and Iraq was viewed as a victory of the anti-British sentiment prevalent in Iraq. The Turkish government found itself in a difficult situation and would maintain strict neutrality. The British had advised Turkey to occupy northern Iraq to protect the Mosul oil fields. In turn, in the hope of settling the struggle with the British, the Turks had advised the Iraqi army to withdraw northward, but the Iraqis had refused. Turkey, the circular message had observed, would not close its border with Iraq but would prevent the transit of weapons and munitions to Baghdad.

Alleged information from the State Department in Washington highlighted the Turkish cockpit. The State Department thought that a German-Turkish nonaggression pact was likely but that Ankara would not seek close ties with or positive support from Berlin. The Turks were afraid that the Russians were negotiating with the Germans about the occupation of the Straits, and the Turks feared both states. At the same time, the chance of a British victory appeared remote. Ankara, therefore, would attempt to build a Muslim bloc through discussions with other Muslim states. The failure of these negotiations would be a serious blow to the British.[12] The signal was clear enough: no matter what pressure Germany or, indeed, both powers together applied to Turkey, Turkey could not be depended upon. Its commitment to the British ran deep.

Events in Syria and Turkey were an excellent opportunity, Moscow communicated to Berlin through Ponschab, for the mutual profit of Germany and Russia, provided that the two states could cooperate politically in the Middle East. For Germany, deteriorating relations between the British and the Vichy French in Syria offered a fertile field for military and political investment; the same applied to Moscow because of its geographical proximity to Turkey and Iraq.

It was not until May 13, the eve of Dekanozov's return to Berlin, that the coda to this Russian ploy of disinformation and deception momentarily ended. As he had done so often in the past, Ponschab offered Berlin information based on instructions tendered by Moscow in a circular message to its diplomatic missions. According to these supposed instructions of May 9, although negotiations with Berlin were "proceeding normally," because of "Germany's dictatorial attitude" it had "become imperative" for Russia to warn Berlin that Moscow was "prepared to protect" its interests if—and here a cypher group was lost in transmission—they were "violated." In this type of situation, Moscow ruminated, the attitude of all other states was keenly important should a German-Russian struggle commence. Russia's diplomatic missions, therefore, had to exercise the greatest prudence. The situation was to be surveyed, and an immediate report was requested.[13] The message was clearly meant to be the stick in contrast to the carrots offered to Berlin in Ponschab's previous messages.

The second message conveyed by Ponschab on May 13 did not arrive in Berlin until the afternoon. Berlin needed to be assured of the state of Japan's relationship with Germany, but these assurances had to come from beyond the Kremlin's leadership. Accordingly, Ponschab's last piece of information for this period dealt with instructions allegedly issued on May 11 by the Comintern's leadership to the Soviet representative in Harbin. It was explained to this representative that, in order not to endanger German-Russian relations, connections had to be severed with the national movement opposed to the puppet Manchukuo state established by the Japanese in Manchuria. Likewise, the present Communist party organization in Manchuria had to be severed from the one in Russia. Because of this severance, Manchurian-Korean Communist party comrades, i.e., partisans, would henceforth be forbidden to cross into Russia without permission. The leadership of the national movement in the border area must neither supply the partisans nor have any direct contact with them. Border crossings would be "allowed only to special persons."[14] In view of Japan's special relationship with Germany, the obvious intended message was that Moscow was giving special consideration to Tokyo as a sign of its goodwill toward Berlin. Moscow was almost kowtowing to the Japanese.

Some days later, Moscow manifested this goodwill in a practical fashion. It began "substantial" westward withdrawals of troops that included artillery and tanks. These withdrawals, Steinhardt observed, "presumably were . . . from the Soviet-Korean frontier and the southern end of the Soviet-Manchukuo frontier."[15] The movement of troops and materiel out of the area appears to have continued right up to the eve of the German invasion. The evacuation route ran along the Trans-Siberian railway from the junction of Chita on the Ingoda River, 400 miles east of Lake Baikal, to Krasnoyarsk on the Upper Yenisei River far to the west. That there was "no unusual movement" further to the west of Krasnoyarsk[16] clearly shows that these troops were not being sped to eastern Poland to reinforce garrisons that were meant to repulse a German attack.

From the comments in Ponschab's messages, it appears that negotiations of a sort had already begun prior to Dekanozov's departure for Moscow. Indeed, on May 6, at a time when Dekanozov was ensconced in Moscow, Schulenburg admitted that "such conversations as are now taking place between the Soviet and German Governments did not yet deal with 'important' matters."[17] In fact, as was learned subsequently from Helsinki, the conversations dealt with "purely economic" matters.[18] On the Russian side, discussions were conducted by Aleksei Krutikov, the deputy minister of foreign trade,[19] who was in Berlin at this time.[20] His German counterpart was Karl Schnurre, a senior official of the Wilhelmstrasse's Economic Policy Department.[21]

It is conceivable that Otto Meissner, Dekanozov's counterpart in the negotiations that began after the ambassador's return to Berlin, also partook in these economic negotiations. Meissner certainly was well known to the Russian embassy, where he was a regular visitor. His constant refrain that German-Russian relations needed improvement, as well as his being considered close to the Führer,[22] no doubt enhanced his image and raised the Russian hope that something of substance could develop from these discussions.

Correctly described by the Americans after the war as a "lawyer and civil servant of the old school,"[23] Meissner has been depicted as "sly, unprincipled," and giving the "impression of being a scared rabbit, without courage or real vitality."[24] His background and his imperial and Weimar credentials were to his credit, however, for the regimes in which he had served had contained elements that at the minimum wanted correct relations with Russia. On the surface, he appeared to be the professional Weimar technocrat who had served successfully as state secretary to the Presidential Chancellery, first for the Socialist Friedrich Ebert, then for the conservative Prussian war hero, General Paul von Hindenburg, and finally for Adolf Hitler. Meissner's nimble footwork might have left some discerning Russian observers uneasy, but he also had compensating attributes that could not go unappreciated. Before his service in the Presidential Chancellery, Meissner had been a member of the Foreign Ministry and in 1918 had served as chargé d'affaires in the Ukraine. The following year, he served in the ministry's Russian Division. Moreover, because he was also multilingual,[25] his knowledge of Russian obviated the need for an interpreter in his discussions with Dekanozov and helped minimize the possibility of any leaks, since the Russian kept to the line that he knew no German. Thus, Meissner was knowledgeable about Russian matters. After 1933, his service with Hitler gave him expertise in European issues.[26] His Russian connection never lapsed, for his "spoiled but smart" son, Hans, was serving under Ambassador Schulenburg.[27] As the French ambassador succinctly put it, Meissner was at home under any form of government.[28]

The use of an NKVD man like Dekanozov (someone who had never been in the West, let alone served for a long time in the Foreign Ministry) for important substantive discussions was not an unusual procedure in Stalinist statecraft. Two years before, Litvinov, who was Jewish, had been dismissed and Molotov had been appointed foreign minister. Litvinov's dismissal was perceived in Berlin as a signal that Moscow was prepared to begin substantive negotiations.[29] Discussions of this policy change, which inevitably led to the 1939 nonaggression pact, were initially broached not through established diplomatic channels but through what Göring called "certain intermediaries," probably a euphemism for the NKVD.[30]

Depending on the requirements for each particular episode of diplomatic negotiation, the procedure followed by Moscow could vary. For example, Moscow could use a circuitous rather than a direct approach, making matters appear informal and unofficial rather than formal and official. The one inflexible element was that the negotiating surrogate had to have Stalin's abiding confidence, something the NKVD enjoyed, "Georgian special agents"[31] in general, and Dekanozov in particular.[32]

The removal from the negotiations of someone as shallow as Ribbentrop[33] must have also buoyed spirits in Moscow as a sign that Berlin was serious in its desire to arrive at a settlement of the two nations' outstanding political differences. The number of people who were "in the know" about the negotiations could not have exceeded "two or three of the highest Nazi officials."[34] Obviously, this included Hitler and Meissner. Though Ribbentrop was undoubtedly aware of the details of the negotiations, he does not appear to have revealed as much. Hitler was going to have his invasion come what may, any last minute Russian surrender notwithstanding.

During his meetings with Dekanozov, Meissner was no doubt exposed to the labyrinth of Moscow's negotiating technique best described to Steinhardt by his Finnish counterpart, who had had over fifty conferences with Stalin and Molotov. The length of the minister's comments is exceeded only by the insight they provide into the statecraft of the Stalinist regime. In negotiating with the Russians, the Finn observed that "he had learned that prestige meant more to them than anything else; that their invariable policy was to obtain what they could for as little as possible, and then ask for more; that they never sacrificed immediate gains for considerations of the future; that they paid no attention to what was said, but only to what was done; that they endeavored to be paid a high price for what they realized they must do anyway; and that they were impervious to ethical or humanitarian factors, [or to] those of abstract justice, being influenced exclusively by practical and realistic considerations."[35]

Political negotiations, of course, are the method through which states seek consensus, which in turn is legitimized through treaty arrangements. The success or failure of political negotiations in large measure depends upon the spirit of compromise and goodwill that motivates the discussants. In these negotiations, insincerity was rampant in both camps. Both nations were negotiating for time, but for different reasons. No sooner had the discussions begun than A-54 in Prague, the well-positioned Thummel, warned Czech military intelligence in London that the talks were nothing more than a mechanism to court delay.[36] He was, of course, correct.

For the Germans, the negotiations were a deception operation mounted to gain time in order to fine-tune the Wehrmacht's invasion plans and its order of battle. No doubt the Germans were hopeful that the negotiations would raise doubts about the validity of any intelligence data picked up by the British and other intelligence services. The ongoing negotiations would lead to the dismissal of the intelligence data on the grounds that German military preparations against Russia were meant only to "squeeze" Moscow and force it to accept whatever demands Berlin was insisting upon. It was a clever ploy that worked well until mid-June when the British intelligence community finally convinced itself that the German military preparations were no squeeze but the real thing—a prelude to invasion.

For the Russians, the negotiations were likewise a deception operation mounted to come to some sort of arrangements that would momentarily satiate the Germans and obviate their need to attack. If fancy footwork could get Moscow through the summer and autumn, the possibility of a German attack would recede. Should the circumstances force Moscow to accept an unsatisfactory arrangement, its foot-dragging would become obvious only with time, after which the Russian winter would help avert any German military riposte well into the late spring or early summer of 1942. By then, thanks to Moscow's rearmament program, Russia would be in a better position to field a creditable, modern, and well-trained military force that would match the military forces Germany could muster. Even if a German attack never developed, Russia would still have an advantage. Should the Americans intervene in the war and together with the British defeat Nazi Germany, Russia could then extend its military and political influence and possible control into Eastern and Central Europe. As Stalin noted to Churchill during the war, he thought he might secure an additional six months before Hitler attacked.[37]

The meetings between Meissner and Dekanozov occurred almost on a weekly basis and concluded sometime in early June.[38] Intuitively, Berlin's journalistic and diplomatic circles were convinced that these secret negotiations were in progress.[39] At the minimum, Meissner and Dekanozov must have met about four times after Dekanozov's return to Berlin on May 14. It was Sir Stafford Cripps, the British ambassador in Moscow, however, who knew with almost pinpoint accuracy what had developed in these negotiations. Crucial political discussions, he informed Steinhardt, had been in progress in Berlin between Dekanozov and the Germans since May 13, and although Cripps had been unable to confirm the information, "he had been given to understand that Turkey and Iran, and to a less extent Iraq, were the subject of the discussions." The negotiations notwithstanding, the Russians, he emphasized, would find unacceptable any German entrenchment in Iraq. Since it was the consensus of Moscow's diplomatic corps—including Cripps—that German-Russian discussions were not taking place in the Russian capital, Steinhardt leaned to the view that Hitler or Ribbentrop had lost confidence in Schulenburg, and Stalin had lost confidence in Molotov. As a result, the discussions had been transferred to Berlin, whereas in the past they would have been held in Moscow.[40]

Schulenburg himself admitted that he had no standing among the Nazi leaders.[41] But Stalin had not lost confidence in Molotov. Of course, the negotiations could have been conducted in Moscow, but that would have necessitated the recall of Schulenburg. Indeed, so removed was Schulenburg from the ruling Nazi circles in Berlin and the negotiations unfolding there that he could in all sincerity state as late as June 11 that he "doubted any negotiations were in fact taking place." His attempt to "promote peaceful relations" between the two states and "his firm opposition" to a German invasion of Russia, as well as "his present 'isolation' indicated a German intention to attack," he revealed to his Rumanian counterpart.[42]

The problem for Berlin, however, was that any attempt to replace Schulenburg with a "real Nazi would be a sure sign of a change in policy," Edward Coote of the Foreign Office's Northern Department had observed earlier.[43] It would have undermined, at least from the German perspective, the whole deception operation, which was predicated on Meissner's spinning out the discussions with Dekanozov until sometime in June, by which point the German army would be prepared to attack. Christopher Warner of the Northern Department thought that if discussions were taking place, Stalin must have very reluctantly agreed to the German capital as the venue.[44] Schulenburg's fall from grace may partially explain why the negotiations were held in Berlin, but more likely, Stalin wanted the discussions there because Dekanozov's role as his mouthpiece would minimize the possibility of leaks. Initially, Warner found it "rather improbable" that Schulenburg, who, he claimed, had done "so well in Moscow," had been frozen out of the discussions.[45] Subsequently, however, Warner had second thoughts on the matter and offered the very plausible suggestion that with "Dekanozov being Stalin's man," situating secret discussions in Berlin "might actually suit Stalin since it might enable him to keep matters from his colleagues in Moscow."[46]

Assuming that Warner was right, and certainly Stalin would have informed at the most only a very narrow grouping within the Politburo, one can suggest that for security reasons the channel of communication between Stalin and Dekanozov would have been outside the cipher communication facilities normally used by Russian diplomatic missions abroad and by the Ministry of Foreign Affairs. It is more likely that the cipher communication system employed by Stalin and his Berlin minion was the one constituted years before in Stalin's private secretariat/secret chancellery.[47] It is unclear where Cripps acquired the accurate information he shared with Steinhardt that, since May 13, Dekanozov had been having discussions in Berlin that touched on Middle East matters. Information about these discussions had filtered into the British Foreign Office on May 13 from the Finnish minister in London, but he did not mention the Middle East nor that Berlin was the venue.[48] Similar details were lacking in the information supplied to the British ambassador in Stockholm by the secretary-general of the Swedish Foreign Ministry,[49] nor were they given to Cripps by the Swedish ambassador in Moscow.[50] In the Foreign Office's papers, there is no such detailed information reported by Cripps to London or the reverse.

This lack of detail leads to the suspicion that what Cripps imparted to Steinhardt was information possibly acquired from a live source controlled since 1933 by MI6. The secret nature of the Meissner-Dekanozov discussions and the details offered by Cripps to Steinhardt would have been known only to a very narrow spectrum of very senior Russian officials. One of them would have been the longtime minister of foreign trade and Politburo member, Anastas Mikoyan, one of Stalin's supplicating survivors, whose deputy, Aleksei Krutikov, as we have seen, was involved with the economic aspects of the Berlin negotiations. The question, however, is whether the possible source who supplied Politburo documentation to MI6 and was supposedly a "senior member" of Mikoyan's staff was unmasked prior to June 1941.

It is claimed that thanks to the information supplied in the mid-1930s by the Foreign Office's Donald Maclean, the Cambridge-educated and NKVD-recruited agent, a British-controlled source within the Russian Foreign Ministry was compromised. Allegedly, this source was then "turned" by the NKVD and fed "false information" back to the British. It is possible that the agent unmasked by Maclean was also fortuitously identified to the NKVD by the traitor, Anthony Blunt, soon after his arrival in MI5's B Division (counterespionage) in the autumn of 1940.[51] The problem, however, is that the source compromised by Maclean in the mid-1930s was in the Foreign Ministry, while Blunt's source was supposedly traced in the 1940s to Mikoyan's office.

If the agent compromised by Maclean was distinct from the one in Mikoyan's office, it is likely that the latter was arrested after June 1941. Blunt would not have been given any of the agent's reports or known the agent's true name; at the most he might have known his code name. Accordingly, the only information that Blunt could have conveyed to his NKVD controller would have been details of the type of information to which the agent had access. His controller, "Henry," then conveyed Blunt's information to Moscow. "Henry" was also known as Anatoli Gromov and, later, as Professor Nikitin of the Moscow Institute of History, but his true name was Anatoli Gorski. In Moscow, the NKVD would have ascertained which Russians had access to this material and then narrowed the circle of suspects and identified the agent. This process would have taken some time.

The existence of this invaluable agent from 1933 was conceivably alluded to in September by Stalin's ambiguous comment that Russian agents in Germany had been doubled; Cripps reported to London, "perhaps this was true of our agents also."[52] This MI6-controlled agent, assuming that he had not aroused suspicions and appropriate NKVD countermeasures, should be seriously considered by anyone delving into British policy toward Soviet Russia during this eight-year period. This agent is especially important because he appears to have had access to highly sensitive material. For example, one could suggest that information regarding General Tupikov's July 1940 warning that Berlin was preparing an attack, which came to the attention of MI6,[53] was acquired through this agent. This report was likely to have been discussed in the Politburo and was thus available to him as a senior member of Mikoyan's staff. His possible operations and the information he supplied, assuming it was unfettered, undoubtedly gave London numerous advantages in parrying Moscow's thrusts.

Dekanozov applied himself to the negotiations with all the commitment one would expect from a protegé of Stalin and Beria. The telltale sign that something was afoot was that upon his return from Moscow Dekanozov dropped out of the diplomatic social scene. This was a glaring move that attracted attention because, after his posting to Berlin, Dekanozov unlike "his predecessors [had] initiated some contacts with his colleagues."[54] Moreover, he had opened up the Russian embassy to "large receptions"—among the hosts of which was Counselor of Mission Semionov—and partook in the official diplomatic life "on a grand scale in order to make contacts."[55] Dekanozov's disappearance from Berlin's diplomatic scene was of sufficient interest to the State Department that this news was brought to the attention of Lord Halifax for transmission to the Foreign Office.[56]

Everything had gone smoothly in the negotiations. There were, however, minor squalls. On May 15, the Germans proved evasive in replying to Russian complaints, initially raised on April 22, about German overflights. Moscow awaited Berlin's reply, Sobolev told Schulenburg, and "referred gravely to the fact that border violations by German planes were continuing and were still frequent."[57] On this same day, General Zhukov stepped forward and proposed a preemptive strike on the German forces poised across the frontier. Minister of Defense Timoshenko had attached his signature of approval to Zhukov's plan. Zhukov correctly contended that the mounting German forces had the capacity to execute a surprise attack. To prevent this and to deny the Germans the strategic initiative, General Zhukov proposed that the Red Army be deployed and commanded to attack the German forces when they commenced their own deployment, a moment when the German forces would be unable to organize or coordinate moves between their various services. In essence, Zhukov was not proposing the opening of general hostilities but rather a military thrust with limited strategic goals, beginning with an attack restricted to German forces concentrated in Poland and terminating with the occupation of Poland and East Prussia. An advance into Germany itself was not proposed, nor would Finland or Hungary be attacked. Rumania might be attacked if conditions allowed it.[58]

Zhukov's planned attack was really a defensive one, predicated on an offensive operation to be terminated after the acheivement of its limited goals. Its success, he no doubt thought, would guarantee Russia's security into the foreseeable future. Seeing that he was on the threshold of the Meissner-Dekanozov negotiations and feeling perhaps guardedly optimistic that some sort of new arrangement with the Germans could be hammered out, Stalin naturally could countenance no such attack plan, even one with limited goals. Zhukov's plan was stillborn. Its existence would not be known until decades later.

Likewise dismissed but for different reasons were the May 15 comments of Karl Bomer made at a reception at the Bulgarian legation in Berlin. Bomer, who was close to Goebbels and worked in the foreign press division of his Propaganda Ministry, had exclaimed while inebriated that within two months Stalin would be dead and the Wehrmacht would crush the Red Army more quickly than it had the French. Germany would show the Communists that

Hitler, not Stalin, was running Europe.[59] The NKVD's Filippov, the erstwhile *Tass* correspondent, soon learned about the remarks and about Bomer's arrest for his indiscretion.[60] In Moscow, Bomer's loose tongue would have been viewed as an act cleverly staged by Berlin to increase the pressure on the Kremlin and thus extract greater Russian concessions in the upcoming Meissner-Dekanozov discussions.

It was in this atmosphere that the messages from Sorge in Tokyo on May 13, 15, 19, and 22, already cited,[61] arrived in Moscow to warn of the German attack. It was expected that these warnings would have an impact. However, whatever slim possibility existed that they might influence the movers and doers in the Kremlin was undermined by Sorge in his message of May 22 that stated that any German attack would begin "without a declaration of war or an ultimatum."[62] Surely any such message would have been dismissed as the warning of a madman or even worse as disinformation planted on Sorge by the British, assuming he had not already been turned into a British agent. Had not Stalin made it absolutely clear to all who needed to know that any German attack would be preceded by an ultimatum and followed by a declaration of war?[63] How could Sorge say otherwise?

In the negotiations that now commenced, Meissner was more than a match for Dekanozov. In his admissions made during postwar interrogation by the Americans, Meissner disclosed nothing about this mutual deception operation that was played with such consummate skill on the German side.[64] According to Berezhkov, the negotiations centered mostly on the state of German-Russian relations and the prospects of further cooperation if nothing untoward occurred. Dekanozov complained that German deliveries to Russia had virtually ceased, while Russia continued its shipments of oil, grains, strategic metals, and materials like rubber that went far to assist Germany to circumvent the British naval blockade. Meissner conceded to Dekanozov that this was the case but promised that the situation would reverse itself once the British were defeated.[65]

Undoubtedly acting on instructions, Meissner kept on assuring Dekanozov that Hitler was on the verge of drawing up new "important proposals for cooperation with the USSR" that would shortly be presented by Berlin to Moscow to help strengthen the relations between the two states. Analogous information had already reached the Russian embassy from other sources. Dutifully, Dekanozov reported Meissner's comments to Moscow. It was pure disinformation, of course, but it kept the Kremlin in an optimistic frame of mind, for it appeared that success was right around the corner and "reinforced Stalin's conviction that there would be no war in the immediate future."[66]

The reaction in Moscow revealed this sense of confirmed optimism. When approached by the Japanese ambassador on the eve of the negotiations, Molotov contended that the rumors that there was a German plan for an upcoming attack on Soviet Russia resulted from Anglo-American "propaganda."

Otherwise, he added, relations between Moscow and Berlin were "excellent."[67] Vyshinsky put in his oar some days later when he described Russian-German relations as "very friendly." He insisted that the possibility of any difficulties between the two countries was nil, but he observed that if a clash did occur Russia could defend itself unaided and pointed out that it had done so successfully against a dozen countries in the past,[68] alluding to the civil war and to foreign intervention following the Bolshevik Revolution.

In view of this Russian euphoria, the report on May 22 of Colonel Vasili Khlopov, the assistant military attaché in Berlin, was undoubtedly dismissed as mischievous information planted on the colonel by his sources. Khlopov's warning was that an attack was reportedly set for June 15, but alternately might begin the first days of June.[69]

The most bizarre attempt to warn the Kremlin of the upcoming German attack unfolded in Moscow on May 19.[70] The bearers of the warning were no less than the anti-Nazi German ambassador, Count Schulenburg, and his counselor of mission, Gustav Hilger. The Kremlin's pattern of rejecting all incoming intelligence was best reflected in Stalin's reaction to this warning. Schulenburg, who exemplified the prerevolutionary Russophile German diplomat and was committed to peace between the two states,[71] experienced unsatisfactory interviews in April with Ribbentrop in Vienna and with Hitler in Berlin. To the former, Schulenburg had emphasized the "importance of coming to an understanding" with London and had urged him to make a "sweeping peace proposal" through King Gustav of Sweden. Ribbentrop, who listened "soberly," did not commit himself.[72] The Führer had bared his annoyance to Schulenburg during the creation of the last-minute Russian-Yugoslav Friendship Pact of April 5. All attempts by Schulenburg to explain Moscow's actions, especially in the Balkans, were waved off by Hitler, who viewed Russia's involvement in Yugoslavia as "an example of the political unreliability of a state." In an obvious attempt to turn Hitler's attention toward a negotiated settlement of whatever demands he might wish to raise with the Russians, Schulenburg expressed his conviction that Stalin was prepared to offer Germany additional concessions. Despite his obvious hostility, Hitler, in the record of this conversation, does not appear to have alerted Schulenburg to any German military designs against Russia.[73] Indeed, Schulenburg divulged that Hitler had specifically assured him that he did not intend to wage war against Soviet Russia. By the time Schulenburg arrived in Moscow on April 30, however, he apparently knew that Hitler had lied to him and that the dogs of war would be unleashed; Schulenburg said so to Hilger when he met him at the airport.[74]

Schulenburg's social standing and functional position in the anti-Nazi circles that he frequented make it safe to suggest that someone alerted him to Barbarossa after his interview with Hitler but before his arrival in Moscow. Schulenburg's depressing message, however, did not discourage Hilger.

Schulenburg hoped that peace might still be saved if Moscow could be persuaded to take the initiative and enmesh Hitler in exchanges that would undermine, at least for the moment, his justification for a military response against Russia. Fortuitously, Dekanozov was in Moscow. Ostensibly, he was there to attend the May Day parade, but, as we have seen, he was there for reasons of the highest political import rather than for any ceremonial occasion.

Hilger concluded that Dekanozov must be contacted and made aware of Berlin's designs. To be creditable, however, any discussion with Dekanozov required Schulenburg's presence, but the ambassador was reluctant to attend. He correctly pointed out that both Hilger and he could be tried for treason if the purpose of the meeting with Dekanozov were leaked. Hilger countered that the stakes were too high and said that they should not allow concern for their own safety to deter them from this extraordinary move. Schulenburg finally yielded to Hilger's arguments and gave his permission for a secret meeting with Dekanozov. The arrangement was for Dekanozov to attend a private luncheon at Schulenburg's residence. Accompanying Dekanozov was Vladimir Pavlov, Molotov's interpreter and the chief of the Foreign Ministry's German section.

Over lunch, Schulenburg and Hilger attempted to show Dekanozov the serious situation that had developed. It was possible, Schulenburg observed to Dekanozov, that nothing like this had ever happened in the history of diplomacy. Repeatedly Schulenburg and Hilger recommended that Moscow contact Berlin before Hitler attacked. Their efforts led nowhere. In a scene that borders on the surreal, Dekanozov kept asking them "with maddening stubbornness" whether they were speaking at the behest of the German authorities, even though from the inception of the discussion they had made it clear that they were acting on their "own responsibility and without the knowledge of [their] superiors."[75] If the Germans were not speaking to him officially, Dekanozov argued, he would be unable to convey their comments to the government's ranking officials. They would have to speak to Molotov, he kept saying. He had no authority to listen to their declarations. Only Molotov could hear them out.

It was obvious that Dekanozov "could not imagine" that Schulenburg and Hilger "were knowingly and deliberately incurring the greatest danger for the purpose of making a last effort to save the peace."[76] Dekanozov must have believed that on Hitler's orders they were attempting to entice Moscow to act in a manner that would harm its prestige and interests.

As the conversation unfolded, Schulenburg and Hilger came to realize that Dekanozov "had no comprehension of the good will" that moved them. If Dekanozov believed that they were acting on Hitler's orders, then their move, Hilger felt, had no chance of success and would only confirm Moscow's thoughts on the matter: Hitler was only "bluffing." Such a confirmation would explain Stalin's reaction to this warning and to many others he had received. The prediction of the same invasion date by varied sources must have strengthened Stalin's suspicions that all this information had been planted by the Germans.[77] With all this in mind and in view of the background and experience and political culture from which Dekanozov had sprung, especially considering the eerie world of the *Vozhd* in which he had been nurtured, Dekanozov's reaction to the Germans across the table from him is perfectly understandable.

Years later, Pavlov voiced the opinion that this warning had been nothing more than attempted "blackmail"—Beria's leitmotif, reflecting Stalin's negative attitude. At the time, however, someone obviously had had doubts, for Pavlov contacted Schulenburg's secretary, Gebhardt von Walther, described as "sleek, sharp" and "with a mind as nimble as a weasel's." Because von Walther had also attended the private luncheon, Pavlov inquired "how the conversation should be understood." Schulenburg's comments, von Walther assured Pavlov, should be taken as spoken.[78]

But despite Dekanozov's stance, the substance of the conversation and the warning conveyed by the two Germans were forwarded to Stalin. A special meeting of the Politburo was called, but with the Meissner-Dekanozov discussions then in full swing, the warning was predictably dismissed by the *Vozhd* on the ground that "disinformation" had reached the ambassadorial level, an episode faithfully recorded in Mikoyan's unpublished memoirs.[79]

In the postwar period, to explain away this appalling blunder, Molotov insisted with mind-boggling stubbornness that Schulenburg and Hilger had merely "hinted," not warned, about the German attack. What they had said "were only rumors," he explained. But it was incorrect, he continued, that no attention had been paid to what the two German diplomats had said. Had orders been given to the military? No, that would have been provocation, Molotov responded.[80] With that retort, his sand castle of alleged disinformation toppled in the first wave of questions.

Fortunately for Schulenburg, his behavior on this occasion never came to the attention of Berlin. As discreet as his luncheon with Dekanozov had been, Schulenburg was indiscreet in observations that he apparently made to his diplomatic counterparts in Moscow about Germany's attitude toward Russia. Comments reported by his Turkish counterpart about a purported conversation between Schulenburg and the Rumanian ambassador, Grigore Gafencu, were particularly damaging.[81] Naturally, Schulenburg vigorously defended himself and denied what had been reported to Berlin,[82] but in view of his luncheon interview with Dekanozov, one is moved to give credence to the information received by Berlin. Luckily for the ambassador, the complainant was Ernst Woermann, the director of the Foreign Ministry's Political Department. Clearly, the matter had been kept within the Foreign Ministry's "family circle" and not shared with the Gestapo or other state or party security services.

Concurrently, Moscow's euphoric attitude and Stalin's view of the unfolding world scene were best reflected by Maisky in London, who appeared unimpressed by the persistent reports of an upcoming German invasion. He dismissed any war in the East as "far from imminent" and asserted that the possibility of such a war was a topic that he felt inordinately monopolized the West's attention. If differences did exist between Moscow and Berlin, he observed to Beneš, then the Western powers could be assured that his country would do everything possible to resolve them amicably and without conflict.[83] In Moscow, Stalin calmly dismissed warnings by Austrian Communists of the continuing German military build-up. He had received "many such signals," Stalin told the Bulgarian, Georgi Dimitrov, the head of the Comintern, but "saw no grounds for particular disquiet."[84]

Moscow's faith in the inevitable success of the Meissner-Dekanozov negotiations was clearly reflected in early June when Maisky reported that the Foreign Office had informed him that a Russian national had been incarcerated by Franco's Spain and sentenced to thirty years' confinement for her assistance to the defeated Loyalists. Maisky suggested an exchange of some sort or another arrangement. He expected Moscow to turn to the Red Cross to effect an exchange or to instruct him to approach the Foreign Office and ask for British mediation. To his surprise, Maisky was informed that Moscow had approached Berlin, and from the tone of the communication, it was clear that Moscow thought its appeal would succeed. By this point, however, Maisky was more sensitized to the changing situation. Given that the increasingly hostile signs from Germany suggested that something was afoot, he found such a request for Berlin's assistance incomprehensible.[85]

Unlike Meissner, who was closemouthed in postwar defeat, Hitler during the heady days of wartime victory was both candid and loquacious. He took credit, he told his Nazi cronies in mid-May 1942, "for the fact that we succeeded in making the Russians hold off right up to the moment when we launched our attack." How was this achieved? By "entering into agreements which were favourable to their interests."[86] The Meissner-Dekanozov discussions were an important part of this deception ploy.

## Striving for Agreement

Hitler's 1942 admission, therefore, makes it possible to trace with some certainty exactly what was entailed in the negotiations that began in mid-May and continued into the early days of June 1941. As we have gathered from Cripps's comments to Steinhardt and Dekanozov's to Afghan Minister of Economic Affairs Abdul Majid Khan, as well as from Ponschab's messages to Berlin, the Middle East states were important topics of discussion between the two negotiators. Specifically, guarantees for the independence of Afghanistan and Iran, as Dekanozov admitted to Abdul Majid Khan, would have to be improvised.

The catch in any such negotiations was that, though both states had contiguous borders with Soviet Russia, they were far beyond Germany's reach and clearly fell within the British sphere of influence and control. Iraq was separated from Soviet Russia by an extensive Iranian and Turkish land mass, while Germany's attempted penetration of Iraq on behalf of the anti-British revolutionary government of Rashid Ali al Gailani had been checked by a British military riposte.

No doubt alerted by the same information that Cripps had imparted to Steinhardt about the substance of the Berlin negotiations, Eden pressed home his intelligence advantage in early June. London's response to the threat by Rashid Ali, he cautioned Maisky, was an example of Britain's "determination to maintain" its position in the Middle East, including Afghanistan and Iran. Britain "had no intention of allowing [its] interests in those countries to be attacked or undermined." London realized, he explained, that Berlin was attempting in every possible manner to undercut British interests in the Middle East and, by doing so, was attempting to bring Britain's and Russia's interests into conflict. With goodwill and no misunderstanding between London and Moscow about their respective positions, there was no reason why Berlin should succeed in stirring up ill will between the two states in the Middle East. Alluding to Russia, Eden emphasized that his country intended to maintain its present rights and interests in the area, simultaneously "disclaiming any intention to enlarge these interests at the expense of any third Power." Eden assumed that Moscow had resolved to pursue an analogous policy. Should both states adopt this line, it would be impossible for Berlin to succeed in any mischief making in the region. If Moscow assured London that it intended to pursue a similarly peaceable Middle East policy and if Moscow did not intend to join Berlin, then the relationship between London and Moscow would be improved, and consideration could be given to what subsequent action should follow.[87] Moscow could not have failed to understand Eden's message: because of its commitment to the region, London would resist any attempt to tamper with the *status quo,* which is exactly the policy that the Kremlin wanted Berlin to accept.

Turkey, however, possessed the requisite requirements to force a political agreement: it had contiguous borders with Russia and with Germany in Thrace following Germany's occupation of Greece and Bulgaria. Just as important, British and German influence in Turkey were coequal. Moscow's desire reflected in Ponschab's messages to Berlin was that Turkey remain a neutral and a nonbelligerent. In line with Hitler's admission that Germany had concluded agreements that were favorable to Russia's interests in order to keep it at bay until the moment of attack, Berlin lulled Moscow by concluding with Ankara on June 18, only days before the invasion, a treaty pledging respect for the integrity and inviolability of their respective territories.[88] But there were some who saw through this ploy and considered the treaty as furnishing "flank protection for an attack on Russia," among whom was the Greek minister in Budapest.[89]

Then, closer to home, the Russians had also to worry about issues both economic and territorial in nature with military implications in the latter. These worries are somewhat difficult to trace, and knowledge about them, with rare exceptions, is based on reports whose authenticity is difficult to establish. But even though some of these reports were clearly planted by the Germans, they are so persistent and from so many different quarters that some credence must be given to them. Krutikov conducted the economic discussions, Schnurre observed, "in a notably constructive spirit" that helped "settle satisfactorily difficult points" raised by previous agreements dealing with the delivery of a number of products, including the transit through Russia of raw rubber from Asia.[90] These negotiations, as Schnurre admitted to the Finns, went quite easily and presented no real problems "as the Russians agreed to all German demands without demur."[91]

The Ukrainian question, however, was another matter. During this period, there were continuous reports and rumors that Germany wanted to exploit the region.[92] German threats to occupy the Ukraine if Russia discontinued its aid had been reported by J. Edgar Hoover as early as mid-April, whereas Germany promised that, if Russia continued to supply aid, Germany would "respect Russia's present land boundaries."[93] In Bern in early May, the British military attaché noted that "all preparations for the invasion of the Ukraine" would be ready by the end of the month. His source, "Max," thought the invasion certain but believed that there was at the minimum "an even chance" that Stalin would not resist.[94]

From Berlin about a week later, high military sources, unidentified to the American chargé d'affaires, claimed that an ultimatum would shortly be given to Moscow demanding that it "turn over" the Ukraine for Germany's full exploitation but not for its political control.[95] Concurrently, the American ambassador in Rome reported the German decision to invade Russia "in order to obtain control of the Ukraine," using an invasion plan based on a pincer movement through Turkey and Russia itself.[96] Japanese circles in Rome, however, believed that these threats were being deliberately planted by Berlin in the hope that they would "so impress Moscow" that it would "yield readily to [the] German demands without fighting." These same Japanese sources, however, agreed that, should the Russians refuse to comply, a German military drive into Russia would undoubtedly occur.[97] During this May period, similar information was reported to the Foreign Office "that German plans for the invasion of [the] Ukraine were worked out to the last detail" and were in the possession of the Portuguese.[98]

Belatedly, even in June, the British ambassador in Chungking could report that the Chinese diplomatic missions in Berlin and Bucharest had noted "with persistence" that Berlin had been pressing Moscow "to grant a lease of the Ukraine and threatened occupation" of the region if its demand was resisted.[99] About a week later, the Moscow rumor was a reported "agreement guaranteeing the Ukraine harvest to Germany for the next three years" with some autonomy for the Ukraine, a condition that was pointed out to the

Foreign Office and that in theory was already available to all republics under the constitution.[100] This same day, June 15, Lord Halifax reported from Washington, no doubt on the basis of information supplied by the State Department, that the Vichy Foreign Ministry had received many reports of an "impending attack on the Ukraine."[101] Four days later, Sumner Welles concluded that Berlin's reported demands to Moscow "would virtually make the Ukraine into a German protectorate."[102]

What has been cited is only a sampling of the numerous reports and rumors pertaining to the Ukraine that circulated during this period. Suffice it to say that the Ukraine was unquestionably an important topic of discussion in the Berlin negotiations between Meissner and Dekanozov. The Germans no doubt pressed the matter for all it was worth, although they knew that Stalin would not bend on the issue. But in line with Hitler's admission of May 1942, Berlin fell short, except perhaps obliquely, of uttering any threats. The German ploy was simple enough: keep the Russians at bay and agree to matters favorable to Moscow's interests so as not to alert it to the upcoming attack. Accordingly, Stalin rejected German desires in the Ukraine, and he voiced his rejection both privately through surrogates and publicly to those who could read the political hieroglyphics of the Stalinist press.

In Berlin, the NKVD's excited Filippov, who ostensibly worked for *Tass*, shook his fist, threatening that this was what the Germans would get, not the Ukraine. He argued that the Ukrainian rumor was a deliberate attempt by the German hierarchy to re-test German-Russian relations. Filippov viewed the whole scenario as a German provocation and a total fabrication. Moscow had not the slightest thought, he exclaimed, of delivering its best land and the Ukrainian populace to the Nazis. Germany would not see as much Ukrainian soil "as fits under a fingernail." The embassy had received instructions from Moscow on how to conduct itself on this question, Filippov admitted.[103]

Maisky's comments in London were more measured, as one would expect the words of a long-serving ambassador to be. He emphasized to Eden that his country had no desire to become a belligerent, but neither would it yield on matters that it considered vital. "He derided reports that Russia would surrender the Ukraine." Under no condition, Maisky insisted, would Russia relinquish any of its territory to another state, and it was incorrect to suppose that Moscow's "policy was one of peace at any price." The Soviet Union, he assured Eden, "wanted peace, but in certain circumstances they were prepared to fight."[104]

Similar warnings, but more elliptical in phrasing, were echoed by Ambassador Alexander Bogomolov, who had been posted to Vichy. He confided to Gaston Bergery, Vichy's pro-Nazi ambassador in Moscow, that Russia "would welcome good commercial relations with Germany but that she would have no part in any new order in which Germany would be the prime beneficiary and Russia would be one of the hewers of wood and the drawers of water." In fact, Bogomolov added that his country "would use force if necessary to resist [an] attempt by Germany to integrate her into the German new order."[105] The Soviet Union rejected the principle of the "dominance of Europe by any one power."[106]

The public version of the story appeared in *Pravda* on May 25 under the heading "Nonsense or Simply Lies." On the surface, it was a sharp attack seemingly aimed at the Finnish press, but it was really an oblique message to the Germans. The article took to task a Berlin report that had appeared in the Helsinki newspaper *Sanomat,* which contended that the possible conclusion of a treaty between Germany and Russia would provide for German lease of the Ukraine. The *Pravda* piece urged Finnish journalists to mature and to "use their heads."[107]

All this said and done, the Russians realized that the Germans could not be totally spurned and that their desire for uncontrolled access to the resources of the Ukraine had to be satisfied in a manner that fulfilled their needs but kept the Ukraine under total Russian control. The solution that presented itself was easy enough: the Russians needed to continue to supply the Germans with whatever they were entitled to under their economic agreements and then some, a process that the Russians had begun as early as March, well before Stalin's treaty commitment to Belgrade on the eve of the German invasion of Yugoslavia.

In March, Schnurre pointed out, the number of deliveries of all products "rose by leaps and bounds." The Russians agreed "at relatively favorable prices" to a grain contract that the Germans had struggled hard to conclude. In addition, transit of Germany-bound supplies through Siberia continued unimpeded. At Berlin's request, Moscow placed at its disposal special freight facilities that were used to convey rubber from the Manchurian frontier to Germany. Despite "an initial lag [in January and February] Russian deliveries at the moment are considerable," a pleased Schnurre observed in early April.[108] The estimate for May was that oil exports to Germany jumped to 73,000 tons. Considering the export figures for May and the previous four months, one realizes that oil exports during the first three weeks of June were probably near 100,000 tons, for Moscow admitted that it had shipped 318,300 tons of oil to Germany up to the moment of the attack.[109]

Accordingly, through the spring months and up to the day of the invasion, there echoed day and night the clickety-clack of endless Russian freight trains heading west. These trains were loaded with grain, petroleum, manganese ore, and other nonferrous and precious metals.[110] By late May, according to the Foreign Office's Cavendish-Bentinck, Trans-Siberian rail traffic heading for Germany had leaped from an average of 80 freight cars per day to 110, an increase of about 40 percent.[111]

Russia's largess was also bestowed on Finland, which had attracted the NKVD's interest in the fall of 1940, as well as in March of 1941, following the arrival of German troops on Finnish ground.[112] Since it was clear that

Moscow harbored no real hope of detaching Helsinki from Berlin, Stalin's decision in early June to supply 20,000 tons of wheat to Finland, despite its arrears under their current commercial treaty,[113] can be interpreted only as an attempt to curry favor with Berlin. Any Finnish shortfall in wheat necessitated the aid of German stores, but German assistance was reduced to 30,000 tons, thanks to Stalin's largess and to Swedish promises.[114]

The next German stratagem in the Meissner-Dekanozov discussions was to raise demands that no government, let alone one being run by Stalin, could accept without casting Russia as a belligerent state and thus compromising its role as a neutral power. As the Russians candidly admitted to the Swedes, there was "ever increasing German pressure for larger deliveries [of oil] including far reaching demands for so-called collaboration, meaning German control in the Caucasian territories," to wit, demand for control of the Baku oil fields. The demand, the British observed from Stockholm, appeared "to exceed the limits even of Russian appeasement policy."[115] Even though Berlin knew the Kremlin would reject such a demand, raising it served the German purpose. Doing so helped the Germans prolong the negotiations into early June, when they were adjourned *sine die,* leaving everything unsettled and open-ended as the Kremlin pondered what to do and how to do it, and as Berlin's countdown to the invasion continued unimpeded.

Germany's purported designs on the Caucasian territories were reported by the American embassy in Berlin as early as April. This date clearly shows that the demand for these territories was a carefully placed building block in the German deception campaign, devised at least a month before the Meissner-Dekanozov discussions commenced.[116] Similar reports about the Caucasian territories were filed with Washington and London in May and June.[117] An addendum to Berlin's alleged desire to control the Caucasian areas was the oft-repeated report that Berlin sought permission for German forces and material to transit Russian territory in order to attack British forces east of Suez, namely in Iran or India, and that it wanted Russian forces to join this attack.[118] With German forces gathering on Russia's frontier, the news of the request for such permission for the transit of German forces, as we shall see, would be fed to British intelligence,[119] no doubt in the hope that this disinformation would help obscure any connection between the congregating German forces and an attack on Russia.

Although such reports continued to trickle into London and Washington until as late as mid-June, the American military attaché in Moscow, Major Ivan Yeaton, who knew the local scene well, reported on May 24 that "reliable information" indicated that the Kremlin would not sanction German troop transit across Russian territory.[120] In the Communist Party organ *Bolshevik,* whose political pronouncements were authoritative, the Kremlin then flashed its own signal rejecting any such arrangements. In the late May issue, a leading editorial entitled "For the Glory of the Fatherland" ruminated that every attempt to involve Soviet Russia "in the chain of imperialistic intrigue" had completely collapsed, as had every attempt "to bind it even indirectly to the policy of one of the belligerents or another." This comment was a not too subtle allusion to the perceived German pressure for transit rights and for Russian commitment to assist a German attack against British forces east of Suez. The war, the *Bolshevik* continued in a slap at Nazi Germany, had shown the "rottenness of the bourgeois ideology" by its espousal of racial superiority. This lifeless ideology belonged to classes that had perished. Notions of state inequality and of the oppression and domination of one group by another separated nations. They caused the debilitation and breakdown of imperialistic multinational states.[121] Apparently, the significance of the editorial eluded Cripps, but it did not elude Steinhardt, who, in reporting it, noted its "rather striking statements."[122] The impasse that developed after the Kremlin's sidestepping of the German desires for transit rights and for Russian participation in any attack on British forces undoubtedly led to the adjournment of the Meissner-Dekanozov discussions *sine die*. In the days to come, the question that puzzled the Kremlin was how these discussions could be renewed.

Moscow's maneuvers before the Meissner-Dekanozov discussions and the goals it wanted to achieve in these exchanges were illuminated in the purported Russian reports relayed by Ponschab to Berlin. Likewise, the purported Russian reports that Ponschab relayed to Berlin during the discussions partly clarify how Moscow went about attempting to achieve its goals. On May 18, by which point the discussions had started, Ponschab supplied to Berlin a supposed report from the Russian ambassador in Tokyo in answer to the circular inquiry posed by Moscow on May 9, which solicited the attitude of other states should a German-Russian war breakout.[123] According to the ambassador, "all leading personalities" held the view that, since Soviet Russia was specifically excluded from the obligations assumed by Japan under the Tripartite Pact, Japan was not obligated to intervene should a German-Russian struggle commence. The message that Moscow was attempting to convey by this spurious report was clear enough: in any conflict with Berlin, Moscow had no need to worry about its eastern flank and could concentrate its political and especially its military attention westward against any attacking German forces.

In view of Stalin's suspicions that Hess's arrival in England was perhaps the first groping step in an attempt to concoct an Anglo German alliance against Russia, the alleged report of the Russian ambassador in Berlin on May 12 is of particular interest. Hess, the ambassador claimed, had been dispatched to England in order to confuse British public opinion. Though Moscow held that it did not share the ambassador's view, it had to ascertain whether Berlin was "not seeking some sort of understanding with England." The Anglo-Americans maintained that Hess's action was anti-Soviet. Certainly, Moscow falsely noted, Hess had met Leon Trotsky in 1937, a meeting that was followed by Trotsky's plot against the Moscow regime. The Hess rendition of this story was, of course, a way of cautioning Berlin that Moscow was sensitized to a possible anti-Russian coalition fabricated through Hess and that assurances that such a coalition was not in existence would have to be forthcoming to allay Moscow's suspicions.

Several days later, Ponschab's report continued, word was received from the Russian ambassador in London that for several reasons the British government had ordered the occupation of French-mandated Syria. The first reason was the Vichy French-German agreement concluded on May 5–6, according to which war material controlled by the armistice commission was to be moved to Iraq and the Germans were to allow landing facilities in the country. The second reason was the British need for more direct contact with Turkey, most of which had been disrupted by the recent fighting in Iraq. In addition, the British, the ambassador predicted, also planned the occupation of West Africa and Somaliland (Somalia). Because Moscow wanted to maintain the Middle East states as independent buffers between itself and the Germans, it saw the alacrity of the British riposte in Syria and Iraq as an oblique sign that London would move even more quickly should there be a direct threat to Turkey, Iran, or Afghanistan. London's planned action in West Africa and Somaliland certainly showed that the British were not inert when it came to protecting what they perceived to be their vital interests, interests that included Syria and Iraq.

The ambassador's report from London on May 15 was matched by two messages filed that same day about the United States. These communications were likewise included in the same long message that Ponschab sent to Berlin. The first of these messages spoke of Washington's need to prepare American "public opinion for participation in the war," to remove the impression that Britain had been defeated in the Balkans, and to render encouragement to the British and the Chinese. Despite urgent British pressure, however, because of their unpreparedness, the Americans planned to defer "active intervention" in the struggle. But they would not defer should the British collapse in the Middle East, for Washington felt bound to intervene in the struggle in order to prevent England's surrender. In fact, the British were preparing to dispatch available troops to the Far East should Russia increase its activity in the Middle East. They also intended to occupy Dakar in French Senegal as a naval station for the American fleet.

The ambassador's message ensured that the Americans were committed to the Chinese and especially to the British. The warning was clear enough: should Moscow encroach on the Middle East, it would provoke the British to ship troops to the Far East to protect their interests in that region. Any Japanese riposte to that move might in turn produce an American reaction, and the circle of conflict would enlarge enormously. This would lead to an American-British alliance, a situation to be avoided by both Berlin and Moscow.

The second message tried to show that Washington's animus toward Berlin was also being directed toward Moscow. Washington had forbidden the export to Russia of petroleum and other materials in the fear that Moscow would attack London. When queried about this possibility at the State Department, the Russian ambassador had responded that his country would remain absolutely neutral and seek only to protect its own interests. Any rumors that Moscow wanted to invade Iran and Afghanistan were utterly false, although Russia was ready to assist these states if they asked for help. Indeed, if Washington did not lift its export ban, Russian troop withdrawal from the Far East would continue.[124]

It goes without saying that no such interview ever occurred in Washington. This second message reinforced the first: Moscow was not interested in the Middle East and, like Berlin, shared the hostility of the United States. Moscow's threat to continue troop withdrawal in the Far East would embolden the Japanese and pose a threat to the British that would be in Germany's interest, but this advantage would be offset by the increased possibilities of American intervention. The Russians hoped that the Germans would deem it best to keep the Middle East quiescent and to undo the American export ban by allowing Russia to play the role of the neutral in name as well as in fact.

Moscow's attention returned to the Middle East question several days later on May 21 when messages supposedly conveyed by it on May 17 and 18 were related by Ponschab to Berlin. The May 17 message dealt specifically with Iran. It maintained that "military circles" in that country insisted on fighting the British with Russian assistance, provided that Moscow did not demand from Tehran territorial compensation, military bases, or a portion of the oil fields. On the other hand, influential individuals surrounding the Crown Prince of Iran pressed for the maintenance of Iran's neutrality in agreement with Turkey, Afghanistan, Egypt, and Saudi Arabia. The Shah shared this view but did not object to the delivery of military supplies from Iraq. Russia would support military circles opposed to the British, even if a coup d'état proved necessary. In view of this stance, it was important for Russian diplomatic missions to ascertain the opinion of Iranians living "abroad and instruct them to support the anti-British struggle."[125] Moscow must have surmised that the specter of a Russian descent on Iran, during which Russian troops would be assisted by certain members of the Iranian military to expel the British, and would also be well beyond the radius of German attack, was a scenario that could not appeal to elements in Berlin. The intent of Ponschab's message, however, was clear enough: the dissociation of both Russia and Germany from Iran and from other areas in the Middle East was in both states' joint interests.

The second message ideologically supported the first in the sense that it expressed no sympathy for German and Japanese imperialism. It did this by explaining a Russian plan that would use the war among the imperialist states to induce Asian nations to rise up and annihilate British imperialism. Moscow worried over its efforts "not to strengthen imperialist Germany and Japan."

The task of Asian Communists in this plan was twofold: to cause uprisings in the oppressed nations against the imperial powers and to expel all those who had collaborated with these powers. The war, Moscow held, would result in the complete independence of the Asian states, although Moscow claimed it had "no ambitions to acquire colonies in Asia."[126] The *quid pro quo* was blatant: if Germany desisted from moving into the Middle East, Russia would do the same in Asia.

No doubt to allow time for some of the disinformation imparted by these messages to sink in, Moscow released nothing more for Ponschab to relay to Berlin until May 24. On that date, he conveyed two alleged Moscow reports dated May 22, both of which dealt with American actions and intended to show, despite certain policy differences between London and Washington over the Arab world, the continuing American hostility toward Germany. According to the Russian ambassador in Washington, after discussions with the Democratic party, President Roosevelt had decided that in order to assist the British, American naval and air forces in the North Atlantic would be sent to the Indian Ocean and the South Pacific area. If necessary, troops would be dispatched to Australia and South Asia. The military expenses for this assistance would not be charged to the British, while their payments for the delivery of American goods could be in cash or credit. Moreover, as a result of repeated government negotiations with American industry, controls would be set on prices and profits in an attempt to thwart any inflationary spiral in the United States. Lastly, the Moscow report ineptly noted, Russian intelligence had reported that London planned to "drag" Washington into the "war by sinking American merchant ships."[127]

The messages also discussed the policy differences between London and Washington in the Arab world. London, for example, wanted TransJordan's Amir Abdullah, a British ally, to receive the northern area of Arabia and to fight King Ibn Saud of Saudi Arabia. The Americans conversely insisted that the whole of Arabia be placed under King Saud's control, provided that all of it joined the struggle against Germany. The Americans also wanted the Italian and French possessions in North Africa to join the struggle. This plan was connected with Asia's Pan-Islamic movement, which included India. London, however, was opposed to a Pan-Arab union that did not want to change its present anti-British stance.[128] In short, all was not well between the British and Americans in the Middle East. Precipitous moves and changes in the area, political or military, might go far to bring London and Washington together and to undermine what appeared to be a widening geopolitical rift.

A week went by before the alleged American-British differences in the Arab world were again used in the Russian disinformation scheme. On May 31, Ponschab relayed to Berlin, on the basis of a message from Moscow on the 24th, that the Russian ambassador in Washington had reported that the British had caved in to the Americans on policy in Arabia. Although Ponschab's communication was slightly garbled, it made clear that London had agreed to Washington's interventions but had insisted on making Amir Abdullah ruler of TransJordan and Palestine. Should America agree to this condition, Britain would not oppose placing Iraq and the Port of Aqaba in TransJordan under King Ibn Saud's rule and would hand over to him the French oil fields at Mosul in northern Iraq. The Russian ambassador's American informant expected that the Arab national movement would fail. The negotiations with King Saud would be conducted by President Roosevelt's son. Accordingly, it appeared from this alleged information from Washington that the American involvement in the Arab world was outpacing British involvement and that an entirely new and powerful actor would soon make his presence felt in the Middle East. This message merely confirmed the previous ones, and it also warned that German involvement in the Middle East spelled trouble and should be avoided.

The next two alleged messages from Washington included by Ponschab in his communication to Berlin supplied further evidence of a hardening anti-German attitude and a possible attack by the Americans. In a supposed circular to American diplomatic missions in the Far East, Secretary of State Cordell Hull assured them that no credence should be given to rumors that Washington did not plan to transfer units from the Atlantic to the Pacific Fleet. Such rumors, which conveyed a bad impression to the Chinese and to the Dutch, were to be denied. In fact, the Pacific Fleet was then being strengthened through the addition of new ships, especially submarines that had been built for service in the area.

In addition to this circular, Ponschab reported another message from Hull, the issue date of which was unknown but the obvious purpose of which was to raise German fears of direct American involvement in the war. In this supposed second circular, the notion was conveyed that, although the government in Washington had advised the introduction of a convoy system, the military had opposed it. In fact, political consultants thought that the convoy system was not effective and therefore insisted "on [a] direct attack on Germany." Accordingly, the convoy system would not be implemented.[129] The themes of these spurious messages and of those that had preceded them were now familiar: American hostility toward Germany and Russia and the dangers that lurked should Germany seek a niche for itself in the Middle East.

The six remaining messages that Ponschab relayed to Berlin during the month of June continued the charade. With the negotiations between Meissner and Dekanozov rapidly reaching an impasse, purported Moscow messages were planted with Ponschab on June 2 and 3 for transmission to Berlin. The first one recounted a May 26 message to Russian diplomatic missions worldwide. It related the instructions issued to the Washington embassy to spread the rumor that Moscow would not quietly accept any joint Anglo-American action the purpose of which was to monopolize the high seas under the pretext of protecting maritime commerce. Indeed, Moscow could not recognize such an Anglo-American move and would fight it in every way possible, even armed resistance. For the moment, Moscow did not want to make any official pronouncement; therefore, the embassy had to emphasize through its agents that Russia would support any state that resisted this Anglo-American move. The concluding comment of this message was a not too subtle hint to Berlin that both the Germans and the Russians had a medley of interests in this matter.

On May 27, the day following the transference of this message, the Ministry of Foreign Trade supposedly sent a message of its own to the Comintern, Ponschab also reported. It argued that the Anglo-American strategic plan was the destruction of Europe's industry by bombing and its development in Canada and the United States, where it would be safe from attack. The industry that would remain in Britain would therefore only be able to fulfill the immediate needs of the British population and of the defense of the realm. The difficulty of supplying the colonies from Canada and the United States would apparently be handled by the establishment of support facilities in India, where conditions were more propitious than in Australia. Should this plan be executed, Moscow explained, it would benefit Russia; the destruction of Europe's industry meant Russia "would achieve a superior position." However, the establishment of any contemplated base in India that would strengthen the domination of the British colonies was dangerous for Russia. To put it succinctly, the task of the Comintern was to induce India's peasants and workers to execute a "revolutionary social freedom movement" that would destroy this Anglo-American industrial plan.[130]

The purpose of this observation was no doubt to assure Berlin that, though certain Anglo-American actions might in the end benefit Moscow, the convergence of German and Russian interests was far more beneficial for ideological and other reasons and justified continued support of the 1939 nonaggression pact by both nations. Certainly, the alleged report of the Russian embassy in Tokyo on May 29, also communicated by Ponschab in his message to Berlin, supported continued cooperation. Tokyo's belief was that President Roosevelt's offstage, *ad hominem* comments represented "a political declaration of war against Germany" that would in time be manifested militarily. Therefore, the message claimed, the Japanese navy had been strengthened in preparation for hostilities, intending to control American and British shipping in the western Pacific. Accordingly, Japan would dispatch many warships to its mandated islands in the Pacific.[131]

The second message of June 3 continued the theme of American hostility directed against both Russia and Germany. In particular, the message discussed a purported circular of May 29 that divulged that worsening relations between Russia and the Anglo-Americans evoked the fear that pressure would be increased on Communists residing in those countries. As a result, all Russian diplomatic missions were "requested to institute suitable measures." Officially, Moscow would attempt to "maintain normal relations" with Washington and to eschew "hostile activity," although Moscow had no other option than to "push for an outbreak of the revolution" in order to hinder Washington.[132]

Ponschab also included in his message the alleged reports of May 29 and 30 from the Russian ambassador in London. These continued the discussion of American hostility directed against Germany. The Anglo-Americans, the ambassador reported, had decided to establish in Washington a joint staff for handling military operations. The Department of War was determined to send a mechanized division to West Africa. However, before this step was taken, the navy would be dispatched to West African ports and nearby islands in order to conceal the intended invasion and sudden attack. The alleged report of May 30 continued the canard and again warned Berlin about the Middle East cockpit. According to the ambassador, Washington had offered London support in Turkey, provided that the British, without regard to Russian and French opposition, occupied the line from Iraq to Syria and thus restored the prior connection with Turkey. Moreover, London was to warn Moscow that Britain was prepared for the military defense of its Middle Eastern interests through "warlike interference" in either Iran or Iraq. Finally, Washington promised London that it would deliver the necessary supplies, and London accepted the American offer and was vigorously engaged in making the necessary preparations.[133]

A four-day lull followed. Then on June 7, Ponschab again contacted Berlin and relayed two messages from Moscow allegedly sent on June 5. The first, though slightly garbled, dealt with a report from the Russian ambassador in Washington that the American military and naval authorities opposed President Roosevelt's desire to enter the war. These authorities, the report claimed, believed that the necessary preparations had not been completed and that several months of preparation were still needed. The British ambassador was said to be "perplexed" by this attitude and had declared that under present conditions his country could not hold out against Germany for longer than one month if the United States did not enter the struggle.[134] Roosevelt, it was believed, would take steps to have the army and navy agree to his policy stance. The navy's patrols were being extended into the South Pacific.

The second message of that day noted that the British army was poised to attack Syria, which was controlled by the Vichy French. Syria was invaded several days later by combined British and Free French forces. The situation in the Middle East, Moscow observed, was "extremely dangerous." It had to be assumed that London had promised Syria and northern Iraq to Ankara, provided that Turkey maintained a "strict neutrality." The invasion of Syria would allow the British to get closer to Russia's southern borders, threatening Russian interests. Because of this fear, Ankara and Baghdad had been warned that Moscow would take "decisive measures" if either of them cooperated with London.[135] The purpose of this spurious information passing through Ponschab corresponded to those of the messages that had preceded it: to emphasize American hostility toward Germany that might soon lead to armed confrontation, as well as to emphasize the volatile nature of the Middle East and the dangers that awaited Germany should it decide to embroil itself in the region.

Then there was another four-day lull. Finally, on June 11, Ponschab again sprang into action and relayed to Berlin information fed to him by Moscow. The Middle East was once more the topic of discussion, as reflected in an alleged Moscow message of June 8. Because of the invasion of Syria by British and Free French forces, the attitude of diplomatic circles had to be closely monitored. The British and Turks were not in step, Moscow claimed, and London had declared Syria's neutrality in the expectation that Syria would receive Arab sympathy. Britain clung to its decision to destroy France in the hope that Syria would receive American assistance in West Africa. In fact, Moscow had information that German forces were on the verge of invading Egypt. Because British and Free French action in Syria threatened Russian interests, Moscow closely followed what was occurring on its southern frontier.[136]

The next day, June 12, Ponschab transmitted the last of his messages. These two messages clearly reveal that at this point the Meissner-Dekanozov discussions had lapsed. The carrot once offered to the Germans by the Russians was now replaced with a stick. The first message, supposedly sent on June 8, to Russia's diplomatic representatives in the Far East informed them that the pact between Germany and Japan explained Japan's and Manchukuo's (Manchuria's) extremely inflexible attitude toward Russia. This inflexibility appeared predicated on forcing a more cooperative attitude in Moscow by keeping it permanently occupied with both its western and eastern frontiers. Russia, the message observed, would no doubt collaborate with these two powers on the problems that mutually interested them, but it would "resolutely resist" Germany's and Japan's "intimidation." Moscow, the message claimed, in no way feared a peace settlement between London and Berlin or an attack by Germany on Russia—a claim that was a monumental lie. The task set before Russia was to find ways and means of hindering German and Japanese advances in South Asia while maintaining good relations with the two powers. Due to America's lack of preparedness, the message claimed, Russia had to hold German forces, as well as Japanese initiatives, in check.[137]

The second alleged message that Ponschab transmitted to Berlin on June 12 spoke of a June 2 communication relayed by Moscow to consulates and embassies in Tokyo, Harbin, and Shanghai. The communication, said Ponschab, requested that firms that had had transit difficulties be informed that the Ministry of Transport had to curtail movements, including boxcars on the Siberian railways from Manchuria to Vladivostok, because the Russian railways were "overburdened with internal transport." The availability of boxcars heading east was likewise curtailed. This condition, they were informed, was "temporary and [would] be lifted in about two weeks." As a temporary measure, new goods would not be accepted for shipment in order to reduce the accumulated backlog.[138]

Several weeks before, movement from west to east had likewise been hindered when Moscow passed a decree prohibiting the transit of German war material through Russia to Japan.[139] The signal being flashed by Moscow was clear enough: transit across Russia—which provided access to commodities like rubber[140] that could only be furnished from the east—could be easily disrupted or even cut off, creating disastrous repercussions for the German war effort. In their attempt to bring the Germans to their senses and to conclude the Meissner-Dekanozov discussions successfully, this issue was one of the few pressure points that the Russians could press, and press they did. In addition, one could suggest that this pressuring concurrently flashed a signal to Berlin that Moscow was conserving its rolling stock and that any German attack would find the Russian railways more than capable of expeditiously transferring troops and materiel from Russia's eastern to its western frontiers.

These Ponschab messages no doubt buttressed comments made by Dekanozov to Meissner during the negotiations and, supported by the comments in *Pravda* and the authoritative *Bolshevik,* formed an integral part of Moscow's deception operation meant to influence the Germans in the unfolding Berlin negotiations. Based on largely invented data, these messages covered the gamut of disinformation: they touched upon the dangers for Berlin of encroaching in the Middle East, Washington's support of London, Washington's hostility toward and likely assault on Berlin, and so on. If these messages, which started in March and reached their crescendo in May-June, failed to influence or dissuade Hitler from attacking the Russians, it was not for want of trying. As already discussed, Hitler was committed to the invasion and no deception *cum* disinformation ploy made by Stalin or anyone else could change his mind.

## London: Revised Intelligence Estimates

The movement of German forces into Finland, initially noted by British intelligence in late April,[141] continued to hold British attention during the first week of May. In addition, the British were attracted by the troop movements between Germany and northern Norway, especially those to the port of Kirkenes, in proximity to the Russian border. These movements into northern Norway, it was observed, perhaps reflected Berlin's anxiety to protect the Petsamo nickel mines or, as reported by one source, presaged an attack on Iceland. Alternatively, the troop movements into northern Norway might be part of the political pressure to which Soviet Russia was being subjected.

Concurrently, British intelligence observed, it had been "reliably reported" that Rumanian forces had been "withdrawn and civilians evacuated" from the frontier with Russia to make way for German forces. Should hostilities commence, the Rumanians would occupy Bessarabia after the Germans had conquered it and would hold onto the area while German forces continued their advance.[142]

On May 5, MI14, the War Office branch on military intelligence for Germany, reported that vague information persisted that German forces were moving into Moldavia. Then there were other indications that Berlin was preparing for hostilities against Russia, some reports offering August as the probable date for the upcoming attack. Yet Cripps in Moscow maintained that Germany was making every effort to suppress all suggestions that an attack was contemplated, possibly because Berlin felt that German propaganda had overdone it.[143]

By the second week of May, thanks to MI14, British perceptions about the German-Russian conflict of interests were better focussed.[144] The War Office's weekly intelligence summary observed that data had been received confirming that the Germans were steadily strengthening their forces along the entire length and breadth of the Russian frontier from Norway in the north to the Black Sea in the south; the War Office suggested that Germany's preparations for military operations against Soviet Russia would soon be completed.

It had been reported that contingents of the Schutzstaffel, Hitler's murderous elite guard of the Nazi party, were being formed from among emigrants of the Ukraine and the Baltic States and that pro-German governments were being planned for these areas. Divers quarters, some probably German-inspired, emphasized the "inevitability of a clash between Germany and Russia *eventually,*" but they differed as to the probable date of the confrontation. Though June and July were mentioned as the earliest dates, the War Office, for unexplained reasons, discounted these reports as overly "optimistic." In fact, the War Office thought it probable that Berlin had not yet decided whether Moscow was to be "persuaded by threats to comply with German wishes or should be attacked."[145] That the War Office's intelligence summary was the accepted official British line was reflected in its acceptance by the Chiefs of Staff in their weekly resumé.[146]

Both before and after these MI14–War Office intelligence estimates had been made, Enigma decrypts revealed a continuous and increasing eastward movement of German air force units. In fact, for the first time, these decrypts stumbled across the code name Barbarossa. Though difficulties were encountered in exactly plotting German army movements through Enigma decrypts, there was no doubt that most of these movements were being directed toward the Russian frontier.[147] It was probably at this point that the Joint Intelligence Committee, chaired by the Foreign Office's Cavendish-Bentinck, unilaterally forecast that between June 20 and 25 a German attack would be launched against Soviet Russia. All intelligence mandarins, as well as the Chiefs of Staff, thought that the committee had gone mad.[148]

The War Office's weekly intelligence summary for the third week of May, however, confirmed through several sources that the Germans were continuing to strengthen their forces along the Russian frontier and that troops being pulled from the Balkans might well be headed for Poland. These actions, however, were offset by reports that hinted at a German-Russian rapprochement. Indeed, some reports suggested that German threats had succeeded and that Moscow had succumbed to arrangements allowing Berlin to control the flow of supplies from Russia.

Interestingly, the War Office observed that German propaganda, which had lately been popularizing war, was now stressing German-Russian cooperation. Then there came several mixed reports. One piece of information was that Hitler was still undecided about whether to achieve his desires by "suasion or military action," while another piece of information, which perhaps provided the "true solution to the problem," was that military action would be chosen if suasion did not show results by late May.[149] The military offered information confirming what the War Office had noted, that German troop movements into Kirkenes in Norway equaled one division and that there had been troop movements from the Baltic ports that tended to suggest that German forces in Norway and Finland were being further strengthened.[150]

On the basis of evidence that was obviously acquired from Enigma decrypts, especially those describing the movement of German air force units, air force intelligence concluded on May 23 that Berlin's aims were to "obtain full control of Russian resources" as a counterweight to Washington's assistance to London. Such a German step was unavoidable because Berlin realized that an early defeat of England was not in the cards. Indeed, it was becoming increasingly obvious that if Moscow failed to offer Berlin its full cooperation, Hitler would then "satisfy German requirements by [a] military occupation" of western Russia.[151]

The strong possibility remained that a display of German force would be needed to guarantee Moscow's acquiescence to Berlin's demands. Because of this possibility, for a short period of time, the transferred German air force units would be held either facing the Russian frontier or in Germany itself so that they could rapidly be deployed. This period of time, it was felt, would be during June; consequently, Germany's western defenses would be considerably undermined.[152]

Several days later, MI14 reported that an attack on Russia was unlikely until the tail end of June, by which time the German armor damaged in Greece and Yugoslavia would be repaired. In an allusion to data acquired from Enigma decrypts, MI14 noted that although German troop reinforcements in Poland continued, mechanized equipment and other supplies used in the Balkan campaign would "have to be overhauled before any large-scale operation is undertaken." Concurrently, rumors that a German attack on Russia was imminent had given way to reports, perhaps floated by the Germans, that there were ongoing German-Russian discussions. Naturally, MI14 was unaware that these rumors alluded to the Meissner-Dekanozov talks unfolding in Berlin. Nor could it confirm the blatant disinformation planted by Berlin that an agreement had actually been reached with Moscow, especially in delimiting Middle East spheres of influence, or the story that German forces gathering in Lwow (Lvov) in Poland would transit Soviet Russia to Iran with Moscow's consent.[153]

All this information finally propelled the War Office to conclude in its weekly intelligence summary for late May that Berlin was "making vast preparations for offensive action against Russia [while] coincidentally" negotiating with Moscow. The concentration of military might on Russia's frontier was "evidently to reinforce the argument" that the flow of Russian supplies to Germany be increased and that German forces be permitted transit through Russia to Iraq, as far as northern Iran. The Wilhelmstrasse, the War Office correctly observed, favored an arrangement with Moscow. The War Office was only partially correct in its observation that the Wehrmacht mistrusted the Russians and favored war. The War Office's opinion that Hitler was undecided on the matter was, of course, totally incorrect.[154]

The final word came on May 30 from the Joint Intelligence Committee under Cavendish-Bentinck, who had assumed Cassandra's mantle months before. The committee reported that it could be logically argued that Germany's next move following its capture of Crete could be against Egypt. This, however, would not likely be the case, for all the available evidence pointed to Germany's next move being directed against Russia in an "attempt to enforce her demands on the Soviet by means of a threat of force which can immediately be turned into action."[155] The likely date for such an action was late June.

The committee then listed the German actions that had driven it to conclude that such an action would occur: the German preparation along the entire Russian frontier of a "network of signal communications for large-scale operations"; the movement of air force unit ground staffs from the Balkans to re-forming areas in eastern Germany, from which these units could be quickly moved to the Russian frontier; and lastly, the movement of operational units from the Balkans to bases in eastern Germany for refitting. These moves, the committee concluded, had been made to allow any operations decided upon to begin along the Russian frontier by the latter half of June.

The continued fighting in Crete, however, had delayed this deployment. The air force preparations were similar to those that had preceded earlier campaigns. All these preparations, it was thought, could "only portend such drastic demands on the Soviet Government" that Hitler doubted their acceptance and was "therefore prepared to implement his threats of force by actual operations."[156] In support of its stance, the committee also pointed to other moves made by Berlin, for example, the buildup of Germany's military forces in northern Norway and especially in Poland and East Prussia, including armored and mechanized divisions.

The committee warned, however, that it could not fix upon the moment when German pressure would be exerted on the Russians or the exact instant when actual attack would occur. This knowledge would crystallize only when large concentrations of German armored and mechanized divisions and air force units were clearly established on the Russian frontier. For the moment, indications were that the air force deployment needed to "implement any threat to Russia cannot now be completed before the end of June." Should Moscow meet Berlin's demands without a struggle, the committee's estimate was that it would take the Germans from two to four weeks to transfer the Luftwaffe to its next theater of operations.[157]

The Chiefs of Staff Committee endorsed the Joint Intelligence Committee's report,[158] and on that same day, May 31, the War Office warned the Middle East command that it had "firm indications" that the Germans were concentrating large forces against Russia. Under German threat, the Russians would be pressured to make concessions that would be detrimental to British interests. Should Moscow refuse to acquiesce to the demands, the Germans would attack. Russian resistance, however, might be very much influenced if Moscow thought that any submission to Berlin would provoke an attack by London on the Baku oil fields. To be creditable, any such threat required British control of the Mosul oil fields in Iraq before any Russian or German riposte was possible. Immediate action, therefore, had to be taken to acquire control of Mosul, and the War Office queried whether this action might be taken through some sort of airborne operation.[159] Such an operation proved unnecessary, for on the very day this message was sent an armistice was concluded, the pro-German government of Rashid Ali al Gailani in Baghdad was ousted, and the British military occupied all major Iraqi cities including Mosul.[160]

Foreign Office Permanent Under Secretary Cadogan agreed with the Chiefs of Staff that Germany was "*prepared* to attack Russia," but he also believed that the Russians would knuckle under and "sign on the dotted line."[161] Grudgingly, by late May 1941, important British leaders, both in and out of the British intelligence establishment, were coming to the conclusion, almost against their better judgment, that the Germans were prepared to attack Russia should their demands be rejected.

Being a practical people but feeling overwhelmed by the empirical evidence that faced them, the disbelievers in London became believers. Unfortunately, they failed to give sufficient consideration to Hitler's lack of commitment to a peaceful settlement. However, Brigadier E. O. Skaife of the Foreign Office's Political Intelligence Department had raised this issue as early as May 12 when he said that war or peace for Russia depended "on whether the player whom M. Stalin is facing shows restraint in the game."[162] British intelligence and, indeed, experienced people like Cadogan thought that Hitler would show restraint. They and Moscow erred by underestimating the possibility that, contrary to Germany's self-interest, the key actor in the unfolding drama would show no restraint. Attacking the Russians when the British were not yet vanquished and dividing the German forces in the field were actions contrary to all military doctrine. The British model was both rational and Clausewitzian; however, it did not afford proper weight to the deciding factor, Hitler's irrationality.

# 7

# *Nakanune* On the Eve

## London: Reaching Out

By the beginning of June, German rail traffic in the direction of Russia's western borders had increased to "such an extent that it became obvious even to the layman that large-scale troop concentrations were taking place."[1] For the next three weeks, the steady movement of German forces continued unabated and was not accelerated until the invasion date approached. Armoured units held at a distance, for example, were rushed into the line only hours before the attack,[2] along with recently arrived troops that had taken part in the Greek campaign.[3]

In early June, Generals Timoshenko and Zhukov called on Stalin and presented diverse information reporting the upcoming German assault. Stalin pointed to his own documentation. His information was almost identical in content to that of Timoshenko, but it was mottled by reports from Golikov. Timoshenko observed years later that Golikov knew Stalin's view that there would be no war in the coming months and, in an attempt to please him, had completely ignored the accuracy and the trustworthiness of Timoshenko's information. In an allusion to Sorge, not devoid of obscenity and complaint, the *Vozhd* waxed hot and heavy about what trust could be placed in Sorge and especially in his information that a German attack would be launched on June 22.[4] Stalin's firm belief that the Germans would not attack thus explains the warning issued to Timoshenko, Zhukov and the General Staff, and the commanders of the military districts along the border that they would be held personally responsible for any untoward events caused by rash actions of their troops. They were all explicitly admonished not to move any forces forward without the *Vozhd*'s personal approval.[5] In addition, Stalin "failed to authorize all urgent or decisive defense measures along the frontier" in the fear that such measures could be used as a pretext to justify an attack, General

A. I. Yeremenko tells us.[6] For example, when the commander of the Kiev Special Military District, who believed an invasion was imminent, suggested that 300,000 people be evacuated from the border regions, that defensive positions be prepared, and that anti-tank obstacles be put in place, Moscow's firm reply was that any such action "would be a provocation." None of this suggested work "should be undertaken at the borders," Moscow observed, so that Berlin could be denied "any pretext for the initiation of military action against us."[7] When this same commander, General M. P. Korponos, ordered his forces to occupy forward, but uncompleted, frontier fortifications, Zhukov admonished him to revoke the order immediately since it might provoke a German attack and also to report back who had ordered this arbitrary step. Zhukov's intervention has been credited to Beria—which is plausible in view of the role he played as his master's watch-dog.[8]

Among the information that Stalin ignored or rejected during these June days were the following items: the NKVD reported that all women of the British embassy had to be ready to depart for Iran by June 22 and that Steinhardt was packing and examining roads east of Moscow, odd activities for an ambassador not scheduled to depart for a vacation or recalled from his post; the naval attaché in Berlin disclosed that a German invasion was scheduled for the period of June 20–22; "Ramzai"—Sorge in Tokyo—sent information about German strategic, operational, and tactical plans targeted against the Red Army and subsequently followed this with a report that the invading German army would attack at dawn on June 22 along a broad front and would be composed of nine army corps consisting of 150 divisions.[9] Stalin had also been informed of the German embassy's instructions to prepare for an evacuation, Schulenburg's packing of his personal belongings, the return to Berlin of the wives, children, and members of the German embassy staff, and the burning of the archives in the embassy's basement.[10] On June 4, a report from the intelligence section of the Headquarters of the Western Special Military District stated that, based on "reliable sources from the secret service," German military preparations "for war against the USSR lately, and especially since May 25," had been "intensified." The report included a discussion of the secret mobilization of officials to work in occupied Soviet territory and courses for parachutists' training for sabotage missions in Belorussia. Also included was the interrogation report of Frentsel Jozef Jozefovich, who had crossed the Soviet border on June 4, "from which it is plain that the German army intended to attack the USSR imminently."[11]

Stalin's persistent policy of accommodation, particularly his continuing and satisfactory delivery of raw materials and his "endeavoring to do everything to prevent a conflict with Germany," did not go unnoticed or unappreciated in Berlin.[12] Stalin's activity to prevent conflict was best reflected in the information of the acting German military attaché, Colonel Hans Krebs, who pointed out to Schulenburg that on June 3, Georgii Malenkov, supported by Stalin, had opposed a draft directive by the Army's Military Council to its political commissars that stressed the themes of vigilance and the immediate danger of war. Malenkov had vigorously attacked the draft directive on the grounds that it was formulated in unsophisticated terms, as if war would begin the following day. Because of Stalin's "genius-like leadership," Malenkov argued, war posed no threat to Russia now or in the future. Naturally, in view of Stalin and Malenkov's opposition the draft directive was not issued. Stalin's stance, according to Krebs, was supported by most of Stalin's entourage, including Beria, Molotov, Voroshilov, and Zhdanov. The latter, in particular, repeatedly emphasized his previously expressed view that Germany could not and would not fight a two-front war.[13]

Timoshenko's and Zhukov's attempt to warn Stalin was then repeated by the NKVD. On June 6, as the Meissner-Dekanozov discussions were petering out, Stalin was alerted that there were now four million German troops poised on Russia's western frontiers.[14] This data could not have come as a surprise to him, for in early May the GRU had brought to his attention the rapid increase in the number of German divisions on the border to 107, which, combined with Rumanian and Hungarian forces, equaled approximately 130 divisions. Likewise the NKVD gave the nature of and pinpointed the disposition of the German divisions.[15] The excellent intelligence reports, whether NKVD or GRU, on the increasing troop concentrations[16] were buttressed by the Russians' observations through field binoculars of the continuing German military buildup along the frontier.[16]

The German buildup became a topic of conversation in London on June 2 when Eden observed to Maisky that, according to information available to the British government, it was clear that Berlin was concentrating diverse military formations against Russia. Maisky asked whether Eden was convinced that the information he had imparted about these German formations was accurate. Naturally without alluding to the Enigma decrypts or agents' reports, Eden correctly responded that it "was always difficult to be absolutely certain on these matters," but that the information he had offered to Maisky "was given in good faith" and the British government believed it was exact. Maisky conceded that the information might be correct and that these German forces were indeed on Russia's western borders, but "he found it very hard to believe" that the Germans were contemplating an attack against his country.[18]

Like the *Vozhd,* Maisky was assuming that, at least in this situation, Hitler would conduct a rational foreign policy. Maisky rightly pointed out that any attack on Russia would be a major undertaking. He emphasized, and Eden had the feeling that he was perhaps "trying to convince himself as he went along," that the Russian military was well equipped and that, because of past experience, the Ukrainians would be hostile to the Germans. After citing other factors that appeared detrimental to an attack, Maisky found it difficult to believe that a German offensive was in the offing and credited the border formations to "part of a war of nerves." Eden agreed that this might well be the case. The Soviet government, Maisky continued, "did not attempt to deduce the purpose" for which the Germans were preparing these border concentrations. Eden thought it "quite possible" that Berlin hoped by this action to force Moscow to make "concessions that it was not in [its] national interest to give."[19] In the remaining weeks, the notion that Berlin's concentrations on the border were nothing more than a contribution to a war of nerves became one of the Kremlin's favorite lines used to explain away the incoming intelligence. This line was a poor substitute for a close sifting and analysis of the data.

With the British intelligence community convinced that the Germans were prepared to do battle with the Russians, and with German troop concentrations obvious to everyone except the Kremlin's leadership, Eden decided to recall Cripps for consultation. The future development of Russian policy, Eden explained to Cripps on June 2, the same day he saw Maisky, was of "such importance" that he wanted Cripps to return to London as soon as possible, provided he had no strong objections.[20]

Upon his departure from Moscow, however, Cripps gave Vyshinsky the impression that he doubted that he would return. Cripps's comment "created considerable surprise," Maisky observed to Eden, who responded that he knew nothing about what Cripps had said and that he thought there was some sort of misunderstanding.[21] Eden explained that Cripps had been asked to return for awhile for talks and that it was the Foreign Office's habit to seek contact with very distant diplomatic missions in this manner. He pointed out that Cripps had not visited London since his appointment to Moscow in June of the previous year. Accordingly, the subsequent British radio announcement that Cripps's recall was a perfectly normal step had been "designed to quiet" the Russian government.[22]

Appearing reassured by Eden's comments, Maisky hoped that during Cripps's stay in London a plan might be devised to improve Anglo-Russian relations. Maisky was convinced that such a plan could be formulated. The downside of this conversation was Maisky's admission that he had received no reply to Eden's prior inquiry about the Middle East and the relations between the two states in respect to recent developments in the area. Berlin had denied an Italian radio announcement that Russia and Germany had reached a military accord; Maisky thought that on this occasion Berlin's denial of any accord was genuine. The Germans knew, he observed, that his country would resent what had been disseminated by the radio broadcast.[23]

Mistrustful of Eden and his assurances, Maisky immediately made arrangements to see Sir Walter Monckton, the director of the Ministry of Information, to ascertain why Cripps had been recalled. Monckton assured him that he had heard nothing that led him to believe that Cripps had contemplated remaining in England and surrendering his ambassadorial post.[24] Confidence, however, was in short supply everywhere. In his comments to the cabinet, Eden noted that despite Maisky's remarks "it did not follow" that a German-Russian military accord had not been reached. Alluding to his conversation with Maisky on June 2, he divulged that the ambassador had not been "shocked" when he was told that Germany had plans for attacking his country. The Foreign Office's view, Eden admitted, continued to be that "Russia would make substantial concessions rather than fight Germany."[25] It was a view shared by decision makers in many political centers around the world.

The Swedes, however, did not share this view, as Cripps soon discovered when he arrived in Stockholm on his way to London. On the night of June 7, the secretary-general of the Swedish Foreign Ministry, Erik Boheman, informed Cripps and his counterparts from Helsinki and Stockholm that during the previous "forty-eight hours he had become quite convinced" that on or about the 15th of the month Berlin "would force a political showdown" with Moscow. It could go either way. Boheman's British guests were unable to "discover what new information" had moved him to form this opinion, but they thought Boheman was aware among other things of the disclosure of the Swedish businessman, Birger Dahlerus, who was close to Herman Göring.[26] Dahlerus had received a somewhat "cryptic message" from Göring that seemed to indicate that Germany would attack Russia on about the 15th.[27] Dahlerus's credibility in the Swedish Foreign Ministry was undoubtedly high, for on the urging of Göring, whom he had first met in 1934, Dahlerus had made a last-minute mediation effort in 1939 to avoid the outbreak of the war.[28]

The Swedish minister to London, Björn Prytz, admitted that he had never known Boheman to speak as positively about anything as he had spoken about this question. Although Boheman had not shared with Prytz the information on which he based his stance, Prytz felt sure that it had to be "very reliable."[29] Concurrently, Boheman expressed similar views to the Americans.[30]

Boheman, it appears, then had another conversation with Cripps. He divulged that his latest information was that June 21 would be the exact date of the German attack. He had this information, he noted, from an unimpeachable source whom, of course, he could not reveal.[31] Cripps thought the report was all part of a German bluff. Boheman strongly disagreed. He foresaw a massive German strike, stretching from the Baltic in the north to the Black Sea in the south, commencing on June 20 at the earliest and June 25 at the latest.[32]

Why was Boheman so adamant that a German attack was forthcoming in the latter part of June? The answer is simple enough. Aside from the reports of Swedish diplomats and service attachés and other information flowing into Stockholm, the Swedes had also intercepted German telephone conversations; most important, they had unraveled the German cypher, thanks to the Uppsala University mathematician Arne Beurling. His yeoman efforts were made possible by the abundant data culled from tapped landlines leased to Berlin to connect Sweden with Germany and Norway, including lines connecting Oslo and Copenhagen to Berlin, as well as Oslo to Trondheim, Narvik, and Stockholm, and Stockholm to Helsinki.[33]

Subsequent information given by Dahlerus to the Americans after he had met Göring in Berlin, information doubtlessly also furnished to the Swedish

Foreign Ministry, tangentially buttressed Boheman's comments to Cripps.[34] On his arrival in London, Cripps informed Minister of Economic Warfare Hugh Dalton, who was also the coordinator of the Special Operations Executive that dealt with "ungentlemanly warfare," that he thought that Moscow eventually would be at war with Berlin.[35] After the German attack on June 22, Cripps scribbled his thanks to Boheman for this information, which he admitted had changed his mind and thus made it possible for him to brief the British cabinet correctly.[36] Churchill also gave his thanks in October when Boheman was in London. Boheman's advice to Cripps, the prime minister admitted, "had saved 'dear Stafford' from making a misleading report to the Cabinet." Equally important, Boheman's information had confirmed the views held by British intelligence.[37] The German attack was no surprise to the Swedes and, thanks in part to Swedish information, neither was it to the British.

Cripps's unexpected departure and the impression that he had conveyed to Vyshinsky that his return from London was uncertain fortuitously coincided with the termination of the Meissner-Dekanozov discussions. Stalin's mind-set and the fawning and sycophantic nature of his entourage caused suspicion to become father to the thought: Moscow's inability to conclude an acceptable arrangement with Berlin and Cripps's recall were undoubtedly seen as the first steps leading to Anglo-German discussions targeted against Russia,[38] which were perhaps initiated through and certainly lubricated by Hess's presence in England.

Events and rumors in London contributed to this Russian belief: Lord Simon, one of the old appeasement stalwarts, Maisky learned, was the person who would question Hess. A rumor campaign to unnerve the Russians about Germany policy was sponsored by the Foreign Office. There appeared to be evidence implying that Washington was pressuring Churchill and Eden to consider any German peace offer favorably; the recently appointed American ambassador, John Winant, was recalled to Washington for consultations. All these activities and perhaps others again triggered public speculation, first raised by Hess's flight to Scotland, that peace discussions were in the offing. At the minimum, Moscow believed that London might signal Berlin that Britain would be neutral should Germany assault Russia.[39]

Looking at its situation in this light, the Kremlin had to move quickly. Its first step was to assure London that it was not involved in any negotiations with Berlin directed against British interests. Accordingly, the ever-faithful Maisky was activated, and on the morning of June 10, he called on Eden to assure him on the basis of their prior conversation that no military alliance existed between his country and Germany, nor did Moscow contemplate such an alliance. Furthermore, Maisky put forth, Moscow was not negotiating "any new agreement, either economic or political," with Berlin.[40] Since the Meissner-Dekanozov discussions had adjourned only days before, this comment was technically correct.

Maisky admitted that perfectly normal informal diplomatic talks on economic matters might be in progress, but he denied any large-scale discussions for a comprehensive economic arrangement. His government's relations with Germany, Maisky emphasized, were governed by the 1939 nonaggression pact. He thought this situation was good, and in his view, it showed that there was room for Anglo-Russian conversations. When Eden raised the question of Middle East matters, Maisky said that he hoped he would be able to supply some information presently. On the question of German troop concentrations along Russia's western frontiers, Maisky noted that, if such concentrations existed, London should seek the explanation for their existence in the lack of discussions for an agreement between his country and Germany. Moscow had no anxiety about these troop concentrations, he explained. Eden admitted that London knew no more than Maisky about these portentous concentrations. Then he made the commitment that, if Germany and Russia clashed, the British government was prepared to take whatever countermeasures it could to institute air strikes against western areas occupied by the Germans. Maisky nodded that he understood but refrained from any comment.[41] The interview appears to have gone well.

Since Maisky was often ill informed by Moscow, Eden observed to the American chargé d'affaires, Eden found it very difficult to accept Maisky's comments "at face value." Eden admitted, however, no doubt on the basis of intelligence information that Maisky had received "precise instructions to give him the statement" that no military or economic agreement existed between Russia and Germany. The German military concentrations along the Russian border, Eden thought, were meant to pressure Moscow; Berlin held the "belief that Stalin, if pressed hard enough, would give in to any German demand." But Eden was inclined to believe that Berlin had made up its mind to invade come what may and to get what it wanted.[42]

On the following night, Wednesday June 11, Cripps arrived in London, and by the morning of the next day British press comments implied that there was a noticeable deterioration in German-Russian relations.[43] That Cripps's arrival was immediately followed by these press comments was obviously an ill omen in Maisky's mind, and that night, June 12, Maisky called on Iverach McDonald, the diplomatic correspondent of the *Times* of London. Maisky deplored the newspapers' comments, which he credited to "a Foreign Office stunt." An "official campaign" like this, he declared, would have just the opposite effect in Moscow: cold relations would turn colder. Maisky "seemed a little hurt" when McDonald held to the line that the Foreign Office did not approve of stories having to do with German-Russian relations. By common agreement, he explained, the press had avoided the subject for some time, but the news could no longer be suppressed, and the Foreign Office had to accept the responsibility of newspapers toward their readers. McDonald was puzzled that Moscow should be so sensitive to a few newspaper stories, the majority of which were very objective, and concurrently pretend to ignore the German troops concentrations on Russia's western frontiers. Moscow applied different standards, he added, when comparing British and German actions.

Maisky, however, was convinced that Germany would not attack his country. No doubt repeating Moscow's heartfelt beliefs, he argued that Germany never struck until it had encircled its intended victim, a situation that had not yet developed; that the strength of the Red Army was known; and lastly, that by defeating England, Hitler would terminate the war and could then settle with Russia. His country did not expect a crisis with Germany, Maisky assured McDonald. The military forces perched on the borders "were mere embroidery," and Moscow, as always, had faith in the fundamentals of its own strength. If Maisky was anxious about anything, it was whether Cripps would return to Moscow.[44]

This same night, Churchill had a meeting with Eden and Cripps to discuss the situation in Russia and Russia's relations with Germany in particular. They agreed that Eden was to send for Maisky and suggest certain proposals to him.[45] Eden and Maisky met on the evening of June 13, but as on a previous occasion, Maisky was accompanied by his youngish embassy counselor, Novikov, whose task no doubt was to play the role of duenna.

Eden began by noting the increasing German military concentrations along Russia's western borders. He did not wish to prophesy about the purpose of these concentrations. Nevertheless, there were possibilities about which he could comment: the concentrations could be part of a war of nerves, or they might portend an attack on Russia. London knew nothing, but in light of these formidable military formations, the British government had to consider a clash between Germany and Russia and thought it proper to inform Moscow of certain steps that London could take should such a clash occur, although it fully understood that Moscow might think such a colllision very remote.

Eden now expanded on the commitment that he had made to Maisky in their previous chat of June 10. Should hostilities break out, London, Eden explained, was prepared to dispatch to Russia a military mission composed of officers whose recent experience in fighting the Germans might be useful to the Russian military. London would be prepared to consider Moscow's "economic needs"[46] and, depending on Japan's position, to discuss certain technical issues such as routing and transport on the Trans-Siberian Railway and possibly via the Persian Gulf. Boldly, Maisky queried whether these facilities, especially economic aid, would be available only if his country clashed with Germany. Eden quite rightly responded that he could not suppose that Moscow would want the military mission unless it thought that an attack was imminent. Economic assistance would obviously be forthcoming at the expense of Britain's own effort, and while London would be willing to give such assistance if Germany and Russia were at war, this effort could not be expected of a belligerent power like Britain for the benefit of a neutral power like Russia. Maisky saw the point.

Maisky then asked for details, based on British reports, about the German concentrations along the border. Eden was prepared to approach Churchill and the military with this question to see what could be done. He did not wish to give a casual response, for the matter was technical, and he was not qualified to handle it in detail. Maisky thought it would be useful if this information could be supplied quickly, for it always proved useful to compare one's own reports with those of others. Maisky was sure that London exaggerated these frontier concentrations, and he rejected the possibility that Germany would attack Russia. He appeared to regard the concentrations, Eden observed, "as part of a war of nerves."[47]

When Maisky observed that Eden's message presupposed "intimate collaboration" between their two countries, and asked if the conditions for collaboration were present, Eden replied that, on the basis of the information available, the situation that faced the Russians "was one of the utmost urgency." The two options that London faced, Eden explained, were either to say nothing to Moscow until the clash it foresaw occurred and hostilities commenced or to convey to it in advance and in a candid manner what London's attitude would be. The British government thought the latter option "was the fairer course," though it realized that Moscow might not agree with London's diagnosis of the danger that Russia faced.[48]

The conversation then turned to Maisky's chat with McDonald on the previous day. Eden pointed out that what McDonald had said was correct. Maisky had to realize, he continued, that the American press and newspapers in other parts of the world had for some time been discussing the German troop concentrations, and that he could not expect the British press to ignore what was occurring. Maisky said he understood the matter, but he feared that the type of newspaper reports published the previous day would not be understood and, indeed, would be resented in Moscow. He pressed Eden to do what he could to reduce publicity and especially speculation about events in his country and Moscow's reaction to them.

Despite Eden's offer of future assistance, the discussion had not gone well. It was "somewhat stiff throughout," Eden observed to Lacy Baggallay, the chargé d'affaires in Moscow. Eden credited this stiffness in part to the presence of Novikov and to "his knowledge, as well as M. Maisky's, that [he] should have preferred to see the Ambassador alone."[49]

At this point, in view of Maisky's request for British reports about the increasing German concentrations along the border, Eden called the Foreign Office's Victor Cavendish-Bentinck, the chairman of the Chiefs of Staff Joint Intelligence Committee, into his office to talk with Maisky. It proved to be an unsuccessful session. Cavendish-Bentinck spent twenty fruitless minutes attempting to convince Maisky that a German invasion was being prepared. He argued that the assault would occur either on June 22 or June 29. Cavendish-Bentinck was personally partial to June 22.[50] Several days later on June 16, Cadogan at the Foreign Office gave Maisky additional details on the

German military concentrations along the Russian frontier.[51] The data from these briefings, however, do not appear to have had any impact on the Kremlin's stance. By now, with knowledge of the invaluable material culled from the Enigma decrypts, Eden, unlike Maisky, was a true believer in the German plan to attack. A German invasion of Russia was "imminent," and Churchill and Cripps shared this opinion, Eden assured the American chargé d'affaires after the interview with Maisky.[52]

Naturally, Maisky did not accept Cadogan's information as absolutely correct. Military intelligence data, Maisky pointed out, was not always 100 percent accurate. Moreover, London was interested in a German-Russian confrontation and might purposefully exaggerate information so that it would have a greater impact on Moscow. All of these considerations caused Maisky to discount what Cadogan had told him. On the other hand, the information Cadogan had imparted was "so serious" and "so precise and concrete" that it seemed to Maisky that it would cause Stalin to pause and immediately force him to double check these British reports and to instruct the Russian military to be on alert.[53]

## Kick Start

Eden's approaches to Maisky on June 10 and 13, however, and the commitments he made on behalf of the British government had come too late. Even if these warnings had occured earlier, there is serious doubt that Stalin would have paid any attention to them. Leaving aside his innate hostility to London and his instinctive distrust of all information flowing from that quarter, the reality Stalin faced was Berlin's omnipotence on the continent of Europe. Its ability to strike at Russia was in no way circumscribed physically. The only restraint on Hitler was the seemingly obvious one of self-interest: no state, even a powerful Germany, facing as implacable a foe as Great Britain would divide its forces in the field by striking in another direction and taking on an added opponent. Moreover, Eden's commitments commenced only if Germany attacked Russia. As desirable as these commitments were, they did nothing to fend off the increasing German political and military pressure building up against Russia. The only way to keep the Germans at bay, to assuage them politically, was to negotiate a revision of the 1939 agreement. If these negotiations could begin, and if they could be extended through August, the likelihood of a German attack, even if the negotiations proved fruitless, would diminish considerably because of the approaching winter.

Then again, what was Moscow to make of the persistent rumor, which surfaced as early as May 25, that the Germans were making a special effort to produce a large number of Soviet Red Banner flags with the hammer and sickle for Stalin's and Molotov's forthcoming visit to Germany to meet Hitler and Ribbentrop?[54] If the rumor was created as a German ploy to allay Russian suspicions, which it appears it was, and was a piece of deception *cum* disinformation circulated after the collapse of the Meissner-Dekanozov negotiations, it certainly was planted at a propitious moment and had an unexpected impact. Did the rumor imply, the Kremlin must have asked itself, that additional exchanges were still feasible and that German-Russian negotiations should recommence despite the seeming failure of the Meissner-Dekanozov discussions? Had not Meissner assured Dekanozov during their exchanges that Hitler was on the verge of "drawing up further important proposals for cooperation" with Soviet Russia? Understandably, such a comment by Meissner only "reinforced Stalin's conviction that there would be no war in the immediate future."[55] Obviously, what was needed was a way to kick start new Meissner-Dekanozov discussions and discover Hitler's important proposals, provided they had been formulated. The well-used ploy adopted to fulfill this need involved the sending of less than official and formal signals on the night of June 13, concurrent with Eden's chat with Maisky and Novikov.

The instrument initially chosen for this communication, as it had been so often in the past, was the well-worn *Tass* communiqué. This time, it was diffused through the medium of Radio Moscow on the night of June 13 and repeated in the morning papers the following day. To spotlight the communiqué's significance, Molotov, in an unusual step made on the night of its release, personally handed Ambassador Schulenburg a copy of the message.[56] Certainly in the Russian embassy in Berlin the communiqué was viewed as a renewed attempt by Stalin to probe German intentions.[57]

According to the communiqué, even before Cripps had arrived in London, but particularly after his arrival, rumors had appeared in the British and foreign presses about the imminence of war between Germany and Russia. These rumors claimed that Berlin had presented territorial and economic demands to Moscow; that negotiations were in progress between the two states for the establishment of new and closer agreements between them; that because Moscow had rejected these demands, Berlin had begun concentrating troops on Russia's western borders for an inevitable invasion of Russia; and lastly, that Russia likewise was supposedly concentrating troops at the border and had increased its preparations for a clash with Germany.

Despite the unlikelihood of these rumors (the communiqué continued alluding to London as a possible source for the rumors), "responsible circles in Moscow" deemed it necessary to delegate *Tass* to proclaim that the rumors were clumsy concoctions persistently repeated and "spread by forces hostile" to both states, "forces interested in the further expansion and spreading of the war." [58] *Tass* was authorized to deny these rumors; thus it followed that no negotiations were taking place between Russia and Germany. According to Moscow's information, Berlin likewise was scrupulously executing the strictures of the 1939 nonaggression pact. Therefore, it was the opinion of Russian circles that rumors that Germany intended to terminate the 1939 agreement were without foundation.

Furthermore, it had to be assumed that the transfer to eastern and northeastern Germany of troops that had recently completed the military operations in Greece and Yugoslavia had no bearing on Russian-German relations.

On the basis of its consistent policy of peace, Russia fulfilled and intended to fulfil the provisions of the 1939 nonaggression pact; therefore, rumors that Moscow was preparing for a war with Germany were "false and provocative." The summer muster of Red Army reservists and the plans for upcoming maneuvers were nothing more than the yearly ritual of the training of reservists and the testing of the railroad system. Any attempt to depict these measures as hostile to Germany, *Tass* concluded, was, to say the least, ridiculous.[59]

Some of Stalin's thoughts about this *Tass* communiqué were revealed in his conversation with Admiral Kuznetsov earlier that day at a point when the communiqué had not been officially released, though it was available to senior officials. When informed by Kuznetsov that because German ships had been withdrawn from Russian ports and that he wanted to withdraw Russian ones from German ports, Stalin denied the request. Had not Kuznetsov read today's *Tass* communiqué, he queried, denying the provocative rumors of an imminent German attack? There was provocation everywhere, Stalin observed. All of Moscow's enemies, as well as its false friends, were attempting to embroil it with Hitler in order to further their own interests.[60] Timoshenko did not fare any better when he asked Stalin's permission to order the forces on the border to be alerted and the advance units to be deployed according to defensive plans. Stalin responded that he would mull over this request.[61] Obviously, since the communiqué was about to be released, this was not the time to rock the boat.

In the army, the political cadres were instructed to emphasize in their lectures that any war talk was provocation and that the communiqué proved that there existed no Russian disagreement with Berlin. Thanks to Stalin's stance, Russia was assured, peace was secured well into the future. *Tass* denounced rumors of war as provocation.[62] Foreign reactions to the communiqué soon surfaced. In London, Andrew Rothstein, the *Tass* representative, brazenly complained to the Foreign Office's News Department that the press in general had not given the communiqué the same prominence that it had given the original rumors. It was all an attempt to minimize the communiqué's importance, he observed, threatening to send Moscow a strongly worded message on this matter.[63] Eden's concern was understandably different. He was "surprised," Eden wrote to Maisky, by the reference to Cripps in the communiqué and by the explicit connection made between his arrival and the rumors of German troop concentrations along Russia's borders. He asked for any explanation that Maisky could offer. Was Eden to attach "particular importance" to the mention of Cripps's name in the communiqué? he asked. Eden reminded Maisky that he had discussed the question of German troop concentrations with him on the basis of data that had not come from Russia itself. This discussion had occurred even before Cripps had returned to London.[64]

Maisky's sophistic response was that the *Tass* communiqué "merely related the facts as they existed." It was undeniable that the British press following

Cripps's return gave great import to the circulating rumors alleging an impending German invasion of Russia. In fact, press reports claimed that in his talks with Churchill, Cripps had voiced the opinion that a clash between Russia and Germany was "unavoidable" in the immediate future.

Maisky noted that in his conversation with Eden on the night of June 13, before the communiqué appeared, he had drawn Eden's attention to the "unfortunate press campaign." To Maisky's regret, the campaign had continued, even though during their conversation of June 5 Eden had intimated his desire to see the press desist from speculation on Russia's "policy and position" in connection with Cripps's return.[65] Indeed, Eden had admitted in their conversation of June 13 that such a press campaign was in full swing, but Eden had justified it on the ground that a similar campaign was already being waged in the American press.

To Eden's question whether special importance was to be attached to the mention of Cripps's name in the communiqué, Maisky could reply only that the communiqué refrained from expressing any opinion on the role played by Cripps in the appearance of the press rumors. The communiqué restricted itself to noting that the increase in the rumors and in the British press speculations happened to coincide with Cripps's return to London.[66]

Cripps himself was less than tolerant. When Maisky asked him when he was returning to Moscow, Cripps plucked up the *Tass* communiqué and told Maisky "quite frankly and forcibly" that in his view the communiqué "was intended as a direct personal attack upon [himself]." He railed that no such precedent could be cited and that it had been issued to appease Germany. Cripps doubted the value of his returning to Moscow. In the atmosphere that Moscow had generated, he felt he could do no useful work.[67]

The chargé d'affaires in Moscow, Baggallay, likewise found unacceptable the communiqué's "unpardonable reference" to Cripps. In particular, he had difficulty reconciling the import of the communiqué with the ruling elite's determination to go to great lengths to avoid a German attack, as well as with their need to keep the military and the populace working at the fever pitch required to support the ongoing military and industrial effort by pointing to some potential enemy, real or imagined. In fact, at recent party meetings, Germany, under varying disguises, had often been cast as that enemy.[68]

During Cripps's absence from the embassy, Baggallay called on Vyshinsky, ostensibly because he wanted to make his acquaintance. Baggallay raised the question of the communiqué and asked why Cripps's name had been coupled with *Tass*'s denial of reports that concerned Russia and Germany and that could be traced in origin to various capitals. The communiqué had merely related fact, Vyshinsky insisted, and had done so very carefully. It had not offered a cause-and-effect relationship—a *post hoc propter hoc* sequence. The observation it made was that after Cripps arrived in London the British press gave more space to these reports than they had previously. Perhaps this was because Cripps's arrival had "stimulated their imagination." He just did not know, Vyshinsky observed.

Baggallay did not dispute the communiqué's grammar, but the "fine distinction" between *post hoc* and *propter hoc* would not be understood by most people, he argued. Indeed, why had the Russians singled out Cripps's arrival and the press's comments from many other relevant facts?

Vyshinsky retorted that, in drafting communiqués, one could not consider their effects on the average person. When pressed by Baggallay, however, Vyshinsky was willing to admit that he could see that this communiqué's wording might annoy Cripps and Baggallay. Still, to the question of why the two things were singled out, Vyshinsky responded, "why not."[69]

Immediately preceding his description of this conversation, Baggallay had inserted in his report a message that he had ascertained from a "good source": in the factories, lectures to the workers on the international situation—lectures that had been recently bellicose in tone and clearly aimed at the Germans as the enemy—had become much milder and were stressing the possibility of friendship between the two states. If Baggallay's source was correct, Edward Coote of the Northern Department minuted, then it was a clear indication that the Russians were "preparing to climb down." The salient question, however, was "will Hitler let them?"[70]

A senior official in the Vichy Foreign Ministry thought that the *Tass* communiqué was so unequivocal in praising "Germany's 'loyal' attitude as to make it 'a really extraordinary document.' " It appeared, he observed, that Moscow was striving to construct a strong moral case for itself in anticipation of a German attack.[71] In Berlin, the communiqué was a sensation of the first order among foreign circles already nervous and uncertain about Hitler's intentions.[72] It left the Russian journalists sanguine. Not so for their Hungarian and Rumanian counterparts, who reckoned that in the foreseeable future there was a 99 percent probability of open hostilities.[73] The Swedish minister saw in the communiqué "feelings of anxiety and weakness in Moscow in the face of the German threat."[74] The American embassy, however, correctly interpreted the communiqué as allowing Moscow to manifest its fears of conflict with Berlin but saw its chief importance as Moscow's "evidence of a new readiness to negotiate."[75]

German reciprocation to this readiness, however, was not forthcoming. In the Baltic, a Russian airplane was shot down by German warships escorting troop transports.[76] Luftwaffe circles in Berlin received the communiqué "with great irony." They stressed that the communiqué was devoid of value.[77] Privately, the communiqué was noted in the Wilhelmstrasse,[78] but publicly and officially, a deafening silence followed its release.[79] Because of this silence, Steinhardt in Moscow conveyed a copy of the communiqué directly to the embassy in Berlin for its information.[80]

The Russians did not let the cat out of the bag until about a week after the German invasion. Solomon Lozovsky (né Dridzo), former head of the Red International Unions and deputy foreign minister, who was subsequently shot by Stalin, insisted that the communiqué of June 14 "was an attempt to force Germany to make it clear once and for all whether she intended to fulfil" the 1939 nonaggression pact. Had the communiqué been published in Germany's controlled press and in that of the occupied countries, Lozovsky explained, it would have meant that Berlin would abide by the 1939 treaty. If the reverse proved to be the case, it signaled that Germany intended to break the pact. It was not printed; therefore, Moscow discovered that Berlin was on the verge of becoming an enemy.[81]

As we will see, this line of reasoning was an *ex post facto* rumination, for there is not a shred of evidence that the Kremlin had made any such deductions. The communiqué, Stalin's biographer correctly notes, which "disoriented not so much the fascists as the Soviet people, had only one specific aim," namely, to entice Hitler to commence new negotiations. If the negotiations had been dragged out through June, July, and August, the Fascists would not have unleashed a war, for the hard Russian winter would have been right round the corner.[82] This admission was forty-seven years in coming.

The comment of General Nikolai F. Vatutin, Zhukov's deputy, shows that, like the masses, the Russian military were fed the same bowl of porridge, that the purpose of the communiqué was to test Germany's real intentions.[83] In the atmosphere created by Stalin's firm belief that the Germans would agree to negotiations, any information of an impending German attack did not fall on fertile ground. For example, an urgent and special intelligence report to Stalin and Molotov from Berlin was rejected. This report stated that military preparations for an invasion had been completed and an attack could be expected at any moment. Who the sources were, where did they work, what was their reliability, and how did they manage to acquire such secret data were questions Stalin asked Vsevolod Merkulov, Beria's deputy, and Lieutenant-General Pavel Fitin, who, like his immediate predecessor Dekanozov, was director of the NKVD's Foreign Department. Merkulov was a Chekist thug with an instinct for survival, while Fitin was able but prudent. After some perfunctory questioning, the *Vozhd* turned to both men and expounded the view that except for Wilhelm Pieck (who years later became president of East Germany) no Germans could be trusted. Was that clear? Stalin asked. That was clear, Fitin wisely answered. Stalin pressed for more precise information, demanded that the report be checked, and told Fitin to contact him again. Years later, Fitin speculated that Stalin's dismissal of the report was based on the notion that the German sources who had supplied the data were not Communists but Nazi party members and Wehrmacht officers and that, possibly, the report was a disinformation ploy. Before a reply to Stalin's questions was received from Berlin, the Germans had attacked.[84]

In all probability, this particular report was the one that was released by Moscow several years ago. The NKVD's source for the report's information was someone at Luftwaffe headquarters in Berlin, most likely Lieutenant Harro Schulze-Boysen, a member of the Rote Kapelle. The report, verified by Fitin, arrived in the Kremlin no later than June 16. On the accompanying memorandum sent with the report to Merkulov, Stalin scribbled a vulgar expletive about the source and his mother. He was no source, the *Vozhd* insisted. On the contrary, he was a *"disinformer."*[85] Even a marginal scribble by Stalin like this one would not have been contradicted in the best of times. Nevertheless, a draft reply attempting to respond to Stalin's queries and offering a tight analysis of the current situation led nowhere since the survivalist Merkulov refused to sign the document. In a clear allusion to Stalin, Merkulov noted that those further up the command structure knew how to analyze matters far better than Fitin or himself.[86]

Because of the anxiety along the border, on June 14, the day the *Tass* communiqué was released, Timoshenko, accompanied by Zhukov, called on Stalin and spoke to him of the need to put the troops on full alert. Stalin objected that their proposal to alert, mobilize, and move the troops to face the Germans meant war. Did both of them, Stalin asked, understand this or not? When Stalin asked how many divisions were on the western borders and was told there were close to 150, he asked if that was not sufficient. According to Moscow's information, he maintained, the Germans did not have as many troops along the border. Zhukov observed that the GRU had reported that Wehrmacht units were fully manned and had assumed a wartime stance. Moreover, German divisional strength was anywhere from 14,000 to 16,000 troops, while the Russian divisions, even those composed of 8,000 men, were only about half as strong. Stalin's rejoinder was that intelligence data could not be believed in every instance.[87] The twenty-four hours that had elapsed since he had rejected Kuznetsov's and Timoshenko's proposals had not manifestly changed his interpretation of the situation. What was needed, Stalin insisted, was a response from Berlin that would break the logjam in negotiations, and Stalin was not going to take any step that might jeopardize Hitler's response.

Indeed, the release of the communiqué on June 14 buttressed Molotov's bravado that had been first displayed to Yugoslavia's Gavrilović in April. Stalin was extremely sure that militarily the Red Army was a creditable deterrent against any attack by the Wehrmacht and that the receipt of a response to the communiqué from Berlin was only a matter of time. When Admiral Kuznetsov shared his suspicions about German behavior, particularly about the movement of German merchant ships, Molotov fended him off with the observation that "one would have to be a fool to attack us."[88] If Molotov had been the proverbial fly on the wall in the inner chambers of British intelligence, his attitude would have been far less cavalier.

## London's Prediction: Invasion

The release of the *Tass* communiqué on June 14 coincided with the conclusions of British intelligence that Germany would soon invade Russia.

Based on the data available to British intelligence, which in many respects was less complete than that accumulating in Moscow,[89] the prognosis of British intelligence was readily accepted by Churchill and the government. Early signs that an invasion was in the offing came from Enigma decrypts, especially those relating Luftwaffe activities: requests for maps of the Baltic states, Poland, and northwestern Rumania; a conference between Luftwaffe commanders and intelligence officers; evidence of troop assembly areas for attack to the rear of the Bessarabian frontier and of Berlin's plans to use Moldavia as the jump-off point in any invasion. Rail movements in Poland, although not totally understood, left little doubt that Luftwaffe and Wehrmacht units were being deployed along the length and breadth of the frontier. Reinforcements in northern Norway revealed by Enigma decrypts, as well as the transfer of Luftwaffe units from France and Greece to the east, provided additional indications that an attack was being prepared.

On May 31, the Government Code and Cypher School surveyed the data furnished by the Enigma decrypts. What in the past had been a probability of a German plan to spring a surprise attack had now turned into a "virtual certainty." The move, for example, of a prisoner-of-war cage to Tarnow in Poland, which is east of Cracow, looked "more like business than bluff." Though German involvement in a prolonged struggle on two fronts would be "rash," the explanation that presented itself was that Germany did not expect an extended Russian campaign. The British concluded that the enormous concentrations of German forces in the east and the German expectation of a quick victory and attainment of a paramount position in Europe and Asia might explain the endless troop trains moving from the Balkans to Germany's eastern-most frontiers.[90]

Despite the accumulating evidence, Czech General Moravec was informed that the War Office did not completely share the view that a German invasion of Russia was inevitable.[91] This attitude was partly reflected in the War Office's observation on June 2 that there were signs that the German preparations had not been completed. Indeed, the War Office bought the deception ploy of the Meissner-Dekanozov conversations by noting that it appeared probable, as reported by one well-positioned source, that wide-ranging negotiations were unfolding between Berlin and Moscow, especially for increased food and raw material deliveries by the latter. Moreover, two sources suggested that Hitler was still undecided about whether it was advantageous to "use suasion or force to gain his ends." Hitler's indecision perhaps existed, the War Office continued, and the ongoing military preparations were "on such a scale as to give him complete freedom in his choice." However, there were indications that if Germany did use force, it would not do so before mid-June.[92] Perhaps to redress the balance, MI14 on the following day, June 3, penned a neat note to a paper on German activities and possible intentions. It pointed out that the continuing train movements east suggested that Berlin intended to be in a position to implement its threat if Moscow "should prove obdurate."[93]

The War Office's stance, which reflected its inability to believe that Hitler would open a second front when still faced with the first one, was finally put on paper in its weekly intelligence summary. Though it thought that German preparations for an attack "must be practically complete," it ruminated that these very preparations might "still be used merely to ensure" Russian compliance with the German demands being made in the negotiations believed to be in progress. Only if Moscow declined Berlin's desires did military action appear likely.[94] The Chiefs of Staff appear to have raised no objections to this reasoning, and the War Office's view was repeated verbatim in their weekly résumé for May 29–June 5.[95]

By June 7, however, the missing pieces in the puzzle of whether Germany would attack Russia had been discovered through Enigma decrypts. These pieces included the Luftwaffe's order of battle in Russia. Moreover, the calculation was made that more than two thousand planes had been committed to the campaign. The Government Code and Cypher School judged that without a doubt Germany was planning a huge military operation in which Poland and East Prussia would be the staging areas for the attack. The transfer of certain Luftwaffe units led to the surmise that the Germans would be prepared by June 15. Concurrently, a marked increase in the Luftwaffe's wireless telegraph activity contributed to the notion that an armed attack was not far off.

The data and the certainty of the decrypters, however, were offset by the reaction of Whitehall's intelligence community. They juxtaposed the presented evidence against the established assumption that Berlin and Moscow were negotiating. Since this assumption was supported by diplomatic sources, Whitehall understandably made a different analysis of the clues furnished by the Enigma decrypts. For Whitehall's intelligence community, each additional piece of data spelling out Germany's military preparations was further proof of Berlin's determination to have its way in the negotiations. While the probability could not be dismissed that Germany's determination would lead to invasion, Whitehall likewise feared that Moscow might knuckle under to the German pressure. Not until June 9 did the Foreign Office swing behind the notion of a German invasion.[96]

In the following days, evidence of German military preparations for a strike against Russia steadily accumulated. Aside from the continuous reports about troop movements and concentrations in Moldavia and Poland, there surfaced reports of troop movements in northern Norway and Finland. Several sources suggested that hostilities would begin about mid-June, but the War Office observed that this depended on the outcome of the ongoing German-Russian negotiations. Nevertheless, the scale of the German preparations seemed so extensive that Berlin appeared to be insuring that its demands on Moscow would be accepted, "either by threat of military action or, if necessary, by force."[97]

By June 12, the Joint Intelligence Committee felt confident enough to write that the most recent evidence in hand divulged that Hitler had decided to eliminate Soviet Russian obstruction and intended to attack. Hostilities, therefore, appeared "highly probable," and though it was "premature" to predict a date for their outbreak, it remained the opinion of the committee that matters would likely crystallize during the second half of June.[98] It was at this point on June 10 and 13, that, as we have seen, Eden had his two probing conversations with Maisky. Eden gave Maisky intelligence data and drew from him the assurances that Germany and Russia were not involved in political negotiations and that there would be no alliance between them.

On June 14, Churchill, unlike his counterpart in Moscow, was convinced by the evidence and concluded that Hitler was about to launch an attack on Soviet Russia. "From every source at my disposal," he informed President Roosevelt, "including some most trustworthy, it looks as if a vast German onslaught on Russia was imminent." The German forces were deployed on the Russian frontier from Finland in the north to Rumania in the south, and the arrival of air force and armoured units was being completed. Should hostilities break out, Churchill continued, London would give Moscow every encouragement and whatever assistance it could spare, for it viewed Hitler as the foe who had to be vanquished.[99]

Washington was less charitable. Eden was informed that it would not approach Moscow and that it would treat any approaches made by Moscow "with reserve" until such time as Soviet Russia satisfied the United States that it was not engaged in maneuvers in order to obtain unilateral "concessions and advantages for itself." Furthermore, Washington would reject Moscow's suggestions to make concessions merely to improve the atmosphere between the two states. Washington would insist on strictly *quid pro quo* arrangements for any assistance that it was willing to render. It would not sacrifice principle in order to improve American-Russian relations and would encourage Moscow to understand that the United States considered improved relations between the two states to be as important to Moscow as they were to Washington. Indeed, an improvement might be even more important to Moscow than to Washington. As far as was practical, Washington would base its relations with Moscow on the reciprocity principle.[100]

As one would expect, Steinhardt was foursquare in support of this policy stance. Because his Moscow experiences had helped mold his perceptions of the Soviet regime, his observations are not without interest. The "psychology of the individuals who are conducting Soviet foreign policy," he noted, had long since convinced him that "they do not and cannot be induced to respond to customary amenities, that it is not possible to create 'international good will' with them, that they will always sacrifice the future in favor of an immediate gain, and that they are not affected by ethical or moral considerations, nor guided by the relationships which are customary between individuals of culture and breeding." On the contrary, their psychology recognized "only firmess, power, and force" and reflected "primitive instincts and reactions entirely devoid of the restraints of civilization." It was Steinhardt's opinion that the Kremlin had to be "dealt with on this basis and on this basis alone."[101]

His experience was that, whenever the State Department or the embassy made concessions to the Kremlin or approached it in a friendly fashion, the Kremlin's reaction was to receive these gestures "with marked suspicion and a disposition to regard them as evidence of weakness." When America's attitude was less flexible, the Kremlin regarded Washington's "demeanor as evidence of self-confidence and strength" and promptly assumed a more conciliatory tack, which increased Washington's prestige. This "reciprocal application of unpleasant measures" led the Kremlin to show neither resentment nor bitterness toward the Americans. Steinhardt cautioned, however, that, as with "all primitive people," it was important that any retaliation should not proceed beyond a point where it may be construed as "provocation." Every American action must be identifiable as a retaliation for some action that Moscow had taken or had failed to take. If they were clearly identifiable, it did not appear that such retaliation would generate further retaliation. In fact, the "retaliation" frequently resulted in a "relaxation or complete withdrawal of the action which provoked the retaliation."[102] The long and the short of it was that Stalin's attempt to placate Berlin had led him to take policy stances and to use self-defeating statecraft practices that only estranged Washington, Steinhardt, and others. Only a German thrust across the frontier could reverse this estrangement, and as the British knew, it was only days away.

Churchill's secret communication of June 14 to President Roosevelt soon came to the attention of the NKVD, thanks to an agent code-named "Karmen" who had access to the American embassy in Moscow.[103] The sensitive nature of Churchill's message and the steps that would have been taken to protect its contents suggest that "Karmen" was either running a senior officer of the embassy's staff or somehow had short-circuited the embassy's security procedures to acquire a copy of the message's text. Nevertheless, as one would expect, "Karmen's" information had no visible impact on the Kremlin's movers and doers. Who "Karmen" was is unknown, but we will encounter this resourceful NKVD agent again.

An estimate made by Loy Henderson, the State Department's assistant chief of the European Affairs Division, was that the odds were ten to one against a German attack. This estimate propelled an irritated Eden to observe to Lord Halifax that, on the contrary, London had good reason to believe that Hitler wished "to put an end once and for all to the Soviet Union as a potential menace to Germany and intends to force the issue now."[104]

By June 16, MI14 reported that political indications pointed to an upcoming crisis in German-Russian relations occurring by June 20. It still appeared, MI14 noted, that Germany anticipated "the necessity to use force," possibly because Berlin felt certain that Moscow could not acquiesce to the "very drastic demands" it intended to make.[105] Should the Germans present an ultimatum and the Russians reject it, the War Office observed two days later, it was "reasonable to expect that a German attack [would] follow without any delay."[106] The next day, June 19, the Chiefs of Staff related the remorseless build-up of German forces along the Russian frontier.[107]

Understandably, in view of Stalin's track record, there were those in Whitehall, as well as elsewhere, who were uncertain about whether the Russians would resist if the Germans increased the pressure or if they attacked.[108] By the early morning hours of June 22, events ended all speculation. The information gathered by the intelligence services and especially the clues offered by the Enigma decrypts pointing to a German invasion proved accurate. Equally important, they were accepted by London's decision makers as presaging an attack.

## From Deception to Attack

In view of what Khrushchev referred to as "Stalin's pathological suspicions"[109] why did the *Vozhd* express even guarded optimism after the termination of the Meissner-Dekanozov discussions? There was, as we have seen, Meissner's fabrication that Hitler was on the verge of drawing up important proposals for cooperation with Moscow, as well as the story of Stalin and Molotov's upcoming visit to Germany to meet Hitler and Ribbentrop. Equally important was that as early as November 1940, when Molotov was in Berlin, Hitler had cleverly planted the notion that any difficulties between the two sides could be tackled only at a summit conference. Though Hitler's comment does not appear in the documentation published about the Berlin Conference, Berezhkov, who was Molotov's interpreter, was present when the comment was made and when Molotov reported it to Stalin. Struck by the idea, the *Vozhd* "quite clearly hoped for arrangements to be made for such a meeting, at which, perhaps, he would be able to sort things out with Hitler." Berezhkov is also convinced that the notion of a summit conference "played a very important part in Stalin's misperceptions over the months that followed."[110] Meissner's story of important proposals from Hitler, the rumors of Stalin and Molotov's upcoming visit to meet Hitler and Ribbentrop, and the notion of a summit conference, worked together to deceive Stalin up to the day of the attack and the days immediately thereafter.

In Stalin's mind, discussions with Hitler were not only possible but probable, provided that an indirect, unofficial, informal, and symbolic request for such discussions was made by the Russians. This request occurred in the *Tass* communiqué of June 14. Obviously, in Stalin's view, it would have been a political gaffe of the first order to ignore the rumors that high level discussions might soon crystallize. For Stalin, reaching out to grasp the lifeline Hitler was apparently offering in a rapidly deteriorating political atmosphere appeared the height of realism. Indeed, one might suggest that Stalin's assumption of the prime ministership in early May could have been perceived by the *Vozhd* as absolutely necessary since it put him at least functionally on par with Hitler, a prerequisite for any summit meeting.[111] Both the direct and indirect evidence appears to support Berezhkov's view.

Berlin's ominous silence, therefore, about the *Tass* communiqué of June 14 and its lack of response to Ponschab's intercepts, the latest reported to the Wilhelmstrasse on June 12, called for Stalin to make an immediate probe. The skeletal outline of this inquiry was reported by Steinhardt on June 19. According to the ambassador, a report he had received, which he was "unable to confirm," held that German-Russian negotiations were taking place in Berlin "through the medium of a Soviet representative of no particular rank or standing." Moreover, these negotiations were unknown to Schulenburg and the German embassy in Moscow or to Dekanozov and the Russian embassy in Berlin.[112] In view of Schulenburg's pariah status in Berlin, which was probably known to the Kremlin, his exclusion from any such exchanges rings true. Considering Dekanozov's close relationship with Stalin and Beria, his exclusion from the Kremlin's plan is harder to accept. But reports of his activity during this period would appear to substantiate Steinhardt's information.

Dekanozov's request to call on State Secretary Weizsäcker on June 18 caused anxiety within Hitler's chancellery. Was Stalin, the members of the chancellery feared, going to throw in the towel and concede virtually everything? They decided that Hitler and Ribbentrop would have to "vanish" from Berlin—so they could not be reached.[113] Indeed, private railroad cars had been put under steam at the marshalling yards should just such a situation arise—should some conciliatory gesture by Moscow appear to satisfy Berlin's desires.[114]

The chancellery need not have worried, for Dekanozov's conversation with Weizsacker was remarkably anodyne. The few questions Dekanozov brought up were of "lesser importance" than those expected, Weizsäcker noted to Ribbentrop, and were followed by a query about Weizsäcker's recent trip to Budapest and an insignificant exchange about Hungary, Rumania, and Syria. The ambassador took his leave, the state secretary observed, "without anything whatever having been said about German-Russian relations," and conducted the conversation "with complete unconstraint and in a cheerful mood."[115]

Considering the ongoing German military buildup, Berlin's silence on the recent *Tass* communiqué, and the rumors sweeping Europe about German-Russian relations, one would think that during an appointment requested by Dekanozov questions of greater substance, especially about the relations between the respective states, would have been the order of the day. It could be suggested that the "freezing out" of Dekanozov can be traced to his changing stance on the likelihood of a German attack. On June 21, Beria complained to Stalin, as he had previously, that Dekanozov was "bombarding" him with reports that Hitler was preparing to attack Soviet Russia and that the attack would commence the following day, June 22. Dekanozov's change in stance, as we have seen, had certainly begun to occur by late May or early June,[116] but it was a tack that displeased Beria, who naturally wanted to keep in tandem with Stalin's thinking on the matter. Beria insisted, as he had previously, that the *Vozhd* should recall Dekanozov from Berlin and punish him.[117] Dekanozov's high profile, however, precluded his recall during a tense period in German-Russian relations. His removal as ambassador and his execution were out of the question. Only the attack of June 22 vindicated Dekanozov's stance. It can be suggested, if secret negotiations indeed took place, that the dispatch of the special Russian emissary was an attempt to bypass Dekanozov, perhaps because of his handling of the Berlin negotiations with Meissner and because his recent reporting generated no confidence in Moscow.

Uncertainty remains regarding who could have given this information to Steinhardt? If the information were true, it would have been a closely guarded secret within the innermost sanctum of the Kremlin. It could be that the information was available to Anastas Mikoyan and was thus obtainable by Gibson's alleged source, who worked in Mikoyan's office. Assuming that the information was from Gibson's source, its communication back to London would have been through MI6 channels. That this type of documentation continues to be closed to researchers may help explain why it is not to be found in the Foreign Office Archives at the Public Record Office in London.

If Steinhardt received this information through the British, it was in line with previous British practice to share with him information throwing light on German-Russian negotiations. But Cripps, as we have seen, was in London, not Moscow, during this period. Certainly, if the information about the special Russian emissary to Berlin had been acquired from some source other than a British one, Steinhardt would have immediately reported it to the British embassy in Moscow, in view of the close cooperation between the two embassies and despite Cripps's dislike of him.[118] However, the Foreign Office Archives yield no information that Steinhardt made such an approach.

Steinhardt pointed out to Secretary of State Cordell Hull that he would have hesitated to transmit the information that had been given to him, "were it not for the fact that similar means [of covert negotiation] had been resorted" to by Moscow on previous occasions.[119] Steinhardt was alluding to an apparent Russian attempt in February 1940 to use a relatively unknown Estonian attorney to explore the possibilities of arranging a peace settlement to terminate the so-called Winter War between Finland and Russia. For many years, the attorney had represented Soviet Russia's legal interests in his country. This 1940 maneuver was a veritable replay, Steinhardt observed to Hull, of the initial approach made to the Estonians in 1919 that led to the peace treaty between Estonia and Russia. On that occasion, the approach was made by "relatively unknown individuals occupying no official position whose activities could be readily disavowed" by Moscow. Though Steinhardt did not enlarge on his discussion of the subject, what his Estonian counterpart described as the Kremlin's "underground approach,"[120] the use of informal, unofficial agents, had been well honed by the late 1930s as a tool of Russian statecraft. The method was used, as we have seen, in relations with Germany following Hitler's rise to power,[121] and the strong circumstantial evidence is that a special agent was sent by the Kremlin to Berlin on this occasion and that Cripps was subsequently alerted to this agent's mission.

When the Kremlin's alleged emissary arrived in Berlin is unknown, but clearly, the emmisary must have arrived sometime after it became apparent that the Germans were going to ignore the *Tass* communiqué. When he left Berlin is also unknown, but presumably he did so before June 22, the day the Germans attacked. Though his exact movements are unknown, his probable assignment was to arrange a high-level meeting with the Germans as soon as possible. The purpose of this meeting was to expedite the convening of the summit conference that had been hinted at by Hitler during the 1940 Berlin conference, and seemingly dangled before Moscow in the late May rumor that Stalin and Molotov would be coming to Germany for high-level discussions with Hitler and Ribbentrop.

On June 20, General Franz von Halder, the Wehrmacht's Chief of Staff, after visiting Rumania, Hungary, and Slovakia the previous two days, wrote in his diary that Molotov had wanted to see Hitler on June 18,[122] the very day on which Dekanozov had his anodyne conversation with Weizsäcker. Where Halder got this information goes unrecorded. There is no doubt, however, that this comment in Halder's diary written in the Gabelsberger system of shorthand is genuine and not an *ex post facto* addition, which would be very difficult to insinuate into a shorthand diary.

The comment was accepted as genuine by the Americans who translated the diary after the war, by others who have reproduced various edited versions of the seven notebooks that comprise the diary, and by the Germans who published a definitively edited multivolume edition in the 1960s. However, there is not a shred of evidence that any such proposal was tendered either through Dekanozov, who "was engaged in no important conversations with the Wilhelmstrasse," or through Schulenburg, who "did no last minute negotiating with the Kremlin leaders."[123] The only plausible explanation is that the proposal was tendered through the Kremlin's special emissary.

The Kremlin's expectation that there would be some sort of discussions with the Germans was divulged by Cripps to Steinhardt some days after the attack: The Russians "had been taken by surprise," he observed to the American, because "they had considered the German moves as preparation for negotiations which the Russians felt confident they could prolong sufficiently to cover their final preparations."[124] Since no such information would have been forthcoming from the Russians to any ambassador, let alone a British ambassador, Cripps's comments possibly stemmed from the information supplied by Gibson's alleged source and from the knowledge that Moscow's hopes for negotiations through its special emissary in Berlin never crystallized.

Molotov's belief, however, that negotiations were in the offing, as well as Stalin's admonition that there should be no provocative moves made on the Russian side and that provocative ones by the Germans should be avoided,[125] go far to explain Molotov's subsequent cryptic comments about and Stalin's sluggish response to the increasing German military threat being reported from all directions. Steinhardt summarized the whole problem in his succinct postwar comment that many had attempted to warn Stalin and Molotov, "but they wouldn't listen."[126]

In the guardedly optimistic setting of the Kremlin, it was a conditioned reflex to ignore the mounting evidence of a German attack. For example, no heed was paid to Cripps's warning to Maisky in London on June 18 that before the middle of July or "perhaps much earlier" there would occur either a German-Russian conflict or Russia's complete capitulation to Germany. Though Maisky tried to convince himself and Cripps that Russia could hold off the Germans, Cripps did not think that Maisky succeeded in convincing himself and knew that he certainly did nothing toward convincing Cripps.[127] A similar warning made by Cripps on the 21st that an attack would occur on the following day or by June 29th at the latest was likewise ignored.[128]

Nor was attention paid to the concurrent warning of Ambassador Schulenburg's secretary, Gebhardt von Walther. Apparently sent to Berlin "to pry out all the information he could get" and to report to Schulenburg personally,[129] von Walther admonished Steinhardt, probably on Schulenburg's instructions, to institute an immediate evacuation of all American women and children who could not withstand a severe blow.[130] Their evacuation soon commenced.[131] "Karmen," the resourceful NKVD agent in the embassy, reported that von Walther had also assured American journalist Alice-Leone Moats that the German attack would commence on June 21. Perhaps suspicious of "Karmen's" real role in the embassy, Moats, looking directly at "Karmen," exclaimed that "everyone [was] already tired of warning the Russians."[132]

As we have seen, German plans to evacuate the Moscow embassy and the burning of its archives there were already known to the Russian intelligence services.[133] Von Walther himself publicly and symbolically conveyed the invasion warning when he evacuated his beloved boxer by air. Suspended from the dog's collar, the air ticket reading "Berlin" vastly simplified the task of "Ernst," the NKVD agent who reported von Walther's initiative.[134] The intelligence services' decryption of a coded message on June 19 to the Italian ambassador in Rome was likewise ignored. Schulenburg's "personal impression," he admitted confidentially to his Italian counterpart, was that a war was unavoidable and that it could commence within several days, perhaps by Sunday, June 22.[135]

Moscow's mind-set at this time is best reflected in reactions to Maisky's suggestion to his superiors on June 20 that a Russian steamer be routed not to Murmansk, the natural port of return from London, provided a German threat did not exist, but to Vladivostok via the Panama Canal. The response, which arrived after the attack but was dated June 21, insisted that the steamer proceed to Murmansk. Naturally, the invasion obviated the instruction.[136] The insistence that the steamer proceed to Murmansk was a leap of faith in view of the disappearance by June 16 from Russian waters of all German ships[137] and of the information received in Moscow four days later that Russian vessels were being denied permission to depart from German ports[138] and that all radio communication with these vessels had abruptly and inexplicably terminated.[139]

During this period, Molotov had a talk with the Japanese ambassador, General Yoshitsugu Tatekawa, who attempted to engage him on the subject of Russian-German relations. While waiting for the expected call from Berlin, Molotov was calm. Any alarm, he indicated, was unwarranted, and "if there were any 'differences' [with Berlin] it was his function to smooth them out." Tatekawa's impression was that, while Moscow perhaps anticipated demands from Berlin, it assumed that they would be of such a nature that they could not be met but that Moscow was confident about its ability to handle the situation.[140]

In a subsequent conversation with the Turkish ambassador, Ali Haydar Aktay, Molotov seemed less sanguine as he patiently waited for the phone call inviting him to proceed to Berlin. When asked about his views on the general situation, Molotov responded that the question was difficult to answer because the present "situation was confused and uncertain." He limited himself to reiterating the substance of the *Tass* communiqué of the previous week: there were no ongoing German-Russian negotiations, and Russia was under no threat. Haydar noted that he did not observe in Molotov "any trace of anxiety."[141] This was probably true, but Berlin's silence and the mounting evidence left other Russian movers and doers disconcerted and uneasy.

One of these was the NKVD's "Karmen," who along with "Loyal" had penetrated the American embassy and boldly queried why no one had reacted to all the information he had conveyed ("Diamond" and "Georgi" had certainly penetrated the British embassy, while "Hawk," in all likelihood, and Gerhard Kegel certainly had penetrated the German embassy). "Karmen" asked what was occurring. He wanted his reports placed into the hands of the "highest authorities" and demanded that this be done since he was a "Chekist," as well as a "Soviet man" who valued his Motherland's "destiny." Like so many others, he no doubt thought his intelligence information was being intercepted by higher-ups and denied to the *Vozhd*. As late as June 21, however, Beria would hear none of "Karmen's" complaints. Because of their "systematic disinformation," "Karmen" and the other agents, Beria wrote, were to be ground "into the labour camp dust as the abettors of international provocateurs wishing to make us argue with Germany. Strongly warn the others," Beria insisted.[142]

Likewise this same day, only hours before the German attack, Beria, who had excoriated Dekanozov, also excoriated the military attaché in Berlin, General Tupikov. Tupikov's crime was to insist, based on his sources, one of whom appears to have been in Goebbels' Propaganda Ministry, that the German attack would commence the following day, June 22. However, he and the NKVD, Beria assured Stalin, firmly remembered the *Vozhd*'s framework of analysis: Hitler would not attack Russia in 1941.[143]

If Beria had the power and the nerve to denounce the well-informed Tupikov, it only followed that "Otto" (the GRU's Leopold Trepper) would meet the same fate. "Otto's" message was that the Wehrmacht had concluded the transfer of its forces to the Russian frontier and that on the following day, June 22, there would be a surprise attack. The message, however, was dead before it arrived. General Ivan Susloparov, the military attaché in Vichy who transmitted the message, added the editorial comment that he did not trust Trepper.

Even without the general's comment, the message would have been rejected for it did not dovetail with Stalin's Weltanschauung. Ascertain who the "author of this provocation is and punish him" (presumably Trepper), Stalin minuted in red ink.[144] The "big boss," Trepper discovered after the attack, was amazed that someone as experienced as Trepper had "allowed himself to be intoxicated by English propaganda." The *Vozhd* was convinced that a war with Nazi Germany would not begin before 1944.[145] Obviously in this atmosphere and mind-set, Maisky's report at 9 P.M. that Cripps had warned him that the Germans would attack the following day, June 22,[146] was summarily dismissed as blatant British disinformation and provocation.

Punishing the anxiety-ridden and defenseless "Karmen," Trepper, and other agents was one thing; fending off the anxiety-ridden General Zhukov was another. On the evening of June 18, a young German soldier deserted. He had struck an officer and feared for his life, and he claimed that his father was a Communist. He divulged that at 4:00 A.M. on June 22 the Germans would attack along the length and breadth of the German-Russian frontier. If this did not occur by 5:00 A.M. and he was lying, the soldier volunteered, he should be shot. German provocations like this one, the area commander observed, should not be believed. Only because of the insistence of the reporting officer was it agreed that troops in the area could be moved forward since they would be shielded by a forest canopy. General Konstantin Rokossovsky, commander of the Ninth Mechanized Corps in the Ukraine, was worried by everyone's excessive fear of provoking the Germans. He correctly held that this fear was detrimental to the Red Army's combat readiness along the frontier.[147]

This particular troop redeployment based on personal initiative was unique. Red Army units in the frontier regions had not been moved to their forward defensive positions out of fear that such action would provoke a conflict.[148] Border troops were not put on alert. Mechanized units were posted ten kilometers from the frontier. Ammunition was reduced to a few days' supply. Only lightly armed patrols were allowed to operate. Anti-aircraft fire against unidentified aircraft was prohibited, and Russian aircraft were expressly forbidden to operate within twenty kilometers of the border lest they prove provocative.[149] From Minister of Defense General Timoshenko on down the line, everyone was warned that he would be held personally responsible for any untoward action made by the troops. Everyone was strictly forbidden to move any military units to advance positions without a green light from Stalin himself.[150]

Because of the Kremlin's hostility to the receipt of any such deserter information, Khrushchev tells us, forwarding the news of the young German soldier to the Kremlin would have engendered fear in the heart of the sender, no matter how cleverly he packaged the message.[151] The notion of provocation, which was the buckle of Stalin's belt of erroneous assumptions and beliefs about Germany's political and military policies, persisted, fortunately for Berlin, until the moment of the attack and even beyond. Stalin's was an incredible stance that has had few, if any, equals in twentieth-century statecraft.

Nevertheless, after a three-day delay, late on the night of June 21, Zhukov was informed by the Kiev Military District of the desertion and of the information that the projected attack was set for 4:00 A.M.[152] Zhukov immediately reported the deserter's story to the minister of defense, General Timoshenko, and to Stalin. Stalin instructed Zhukov to come to the Kremlin with Timoshenko.[153] Because the GRU's Golikov reported directly to Stalin, Zhukov was probably unaware that Golikov had been informed from Sofia on the previous day, June 20, that a German attack would begin either on the 21st or the 22d. Indeed, in the late afternoon of June 21, before Zhukov had received the message about the deserter, Golikov was informed by Sorge in Tokyo that the German ambassador had told him that a German-Russian clash was "inevitable." Germany's present military edge provided an opportunity, according to the ambassador, to destroy the Red Army, Europe's last great land force; the Russians, he added, were not defensively ready any more than the Poles had been in September 1939.[154]

Before hurrying to the Kremlin with his deputy and Timoshenko in tow, Zhukov composed a draft directive alerting the Red Army to a possible German attack. For the first time, Stalin appeared worried, which was understandable in view of the messages that Golikov had received from Sofia and Sorge. Perhaps the soldier's desertion was nothing more than a provocation, Stalin suggested. No, the generals replied, they thought his revelations were accurate. Members of the Politburo now trooped in. Timoshenko proposed that a directive be issued to alert the army along the frontier. After Zhukov had read his draft, Stalin objected that to issue such an order was premature. Perhaps the questions could be peacefully settled, Stalin ruminated. He wanted to issue a pithy directive pointing out that any attack might begin with provocative moves by the German army. Troops along the border had to avoid provocations in order to prevent complications.

Zhukov and his deputy then drew up a revised draft. It was re-read to Stalin, who then checked it again, amended it, and gave it to Timoshenko for his signature. For the next forty-eight hours, the directive warned, a sudden German attack was possible and might commence with provocative moves. These provocative incitements might generate serious complications and were to be avoided. Nevertheless, all troops were to be ready for combat to ward off any sudden blow made by Germany or its allies. Aside from the precise defensive steps that were ordered, the various commands were admonished that no other measures could be taken without specific orders. At thirty minutes past midnight on June 22, the order was flashed to all army commands and a copy was forwarded to the naval authorities.[155] Concurrently, Stalin appears to have contacted Khrushchev "warning him to be alert," for information had reached him that Germany might attack on June 22.[156]

Thirty minutes before the order was transmitted, another defection was reported by the Kiev military. This time a German sergeant major, Alfred Liskov, who considered himself a Communist, had deserted. During interrogation, Liskov revealed that German troops had been moved up to their take-off points on the frontier and that an attack would begin in the early morning hours of June 22.[157] In view of the information offered by the two deserters, there could be no doubt in the minds of Zhukov and the military that an attack was only hours away. But there was still some doubt in the Kremlin. In the Ukraine, the army commander, General Rodian Malinovsky, was somewhat confused by the order. Can we open fire, he asked, if the Germans invade? Moscow's response was immediate: do not fall prey to provocation, and do not open fire.[158] Moscow's hesitation created a scene that bordered on the surreal. At the very moment the directive was being formulated, the scheduled train from Berlin innocently chugged through Brest-Litovsk on its way to Moscow. To the German forces entrenched along the River Bug and waiting for the order to open fire and advance, the train's passage "was a weird moment."[159]

Frantically, Moscow made official, formal, and direct attempts to contact Berlin, to convene a conference, and to commence the discussions to which the Nazi leadership had adroitly eluded during the preceding weeks. On the morning of June 21, the Berlin embassy was instructed to approach the Wilhelmstrasse and convey a statement proposing an exchange of views on the state of Russian-German relations. The Germans were to be informed that Moscow was aware of the troop concentrations along the frontier and that any military step could lead to dire consequences. The statement's main point, however, was that Moscow continued to hope that a clash could be averted and was prepared to commence discussions about the situation that had developed. Despite repeated attempts to contact Ribbentrop and Weizsäcker, Berezhkov was politely fended off. Concurrently, Moscow telephoned the embassy to urge that the matter be expedited.[160]

While Berezhkov telephoned the Wilhelmstrasse every thirty minutes, in Moscow at 9:30 P.M. Molotov unexpectedly summoned Schulenburg to his office. He informed him that Dekanozov had been instructed to contact the Wilhelmstrasse over the continuing German violations of Russian airspace first addressed by Moscow on April 22. Obviously, Molotov used these overflights as a pretext to broach the general subject of German-Russian relations. He noted indications that Berlin was dissatisfied with Moscow. There were even rumors of war; that Berlin did not respond to the *Tass* communiqué and that the German press did not publish it fed these rumors. Moscow could not fathom the reasons for Berlin's dissatisfaction. If the Yugoslav question was the source of this dissatisfaction, Molotov felt that his earlier explanations had cleared up the matter, which, by this time, was water under the bridge. Molotov asked Schulenburg what had contributed to this present state of affairs between their respective states. Schulenburg nimbly sidestepped the query: he could offer no response because he lacked the necessary information to do so but would convey Molotov's concerns to Berlin. Molotov wondered whether the rumors might not have substance. German businessmen had left the country while the embassy's women and children had returned to Germany. This remark embarrassed Schulenburg. His unconvincing riposte was that Moscow's harsh climate made this the usual time for summer vacations to Germany. In fact, not everyone had departed. Hilger's wife, he lamely but correctly noted, was still in town. Molotov shrugged his shoulders.[161] Tactfully, however, he avoided mentioning that the hundreds of German engineers working in Leningrad on the unfurnished cruiser *Lutzow*, bought by Moscow in late 1939, had by June 15 all returned to Germany.[162] The interview had led nowhere and obviously had been embarrassing to both sides.

At about 1 A.M. June 22, the substance of this interview was conveyed to the Russian embassy in Berlin. The questions that Molotov posed to Schulenburg were listed, and Dekanozov was instructed to approach Ribbentrop or his deputy immediately and to raise these very same questions.[163] Unknown to Moscow, at the very moment that Molotov met with Schulenburg, Dekanozov was finally able to see Weizsäcker. He handed him a note referring to the previous unanswered Russian complaint of April about German violations of Russian airspace. In the interim, despite repeated protests, 180 additional overflights had occurred. The possibility that these airspace violations were accidental, the note emphasized, was precluded by their systematic nature and because German aircraft had often penetrated Russian airspace to a depth of 100 to 150 kilometers and beyond. The Russian government expected that the necessary steps would be taken to end these violations of Russia's airspace.

With the German attack only hours away, Weizsäcker was unwilling to make any concessions. Since he knew none of the details nor the alleged protests that the Russians had filed, he disingenuously replied, he would refer

Dekanozov's note to the appropriate offices. Weizsäcker insisted, however, that his information spoke of large-scale violations of German airspace by Russian aircraft. It was Germany, not Russia, that had grounds for complaint. Dekanozov's attempt to respond to Weizsäcker's remarks was cut short. The German observed that, because their opinions differed and because he had to await the views of his government, it was wise not to delve into the question at this time. The German reply would follow later. Dekanozov agreed and departed.[164] He would soon return to the Wilhelmstrasse.

Not until 3 A.M., about two hours after Molotov described to the Berlin embassy his conversation with Schulenburg, did the Wilhelmstrasse finally contact Berezhkov. It was obvious that there was no connection between Ribbentrop's invitation to the Russians to come to his office immediately and Berezhkov's frantic calls for an interview. Since Dekanozov had to be roused from his bed, Berezhkov replied that their arrival would be delayed. The Reich minister's personal car was at their disposal and was already parked outside the embassy entrance, came the curt response. The interview at 4 A.M. proved to be vintage Ribbentrop: he was frenzied and highlighted by what appeared to be his controlled inebriation. Before Dekanozov could read the statement that Moscow had dispatched, Ribbentrop began to recite a litany of real or imagined complaints about Moscow's actions, culminating with the declaration that German troops had crossed the Russian frontier an hour before.[165]

This kind of German behavior was not new. Others had already preceded Dekanozov along this familiar road "strewn with all the shopworn lies and fabrications at which Hitler and Ribbentrop had become so expert and which they had concocted so often before to justify" previous aggression.[166] The American embassy correctly observed that it was standard practice for the Germans in this type of situation to act in the manner they had, informing the party attacked and the world community of the "reasons and excuses for Germany's action." The other party was always accused of terminating its agreements with Germany and of violating its own neutrality. The Germans also made it clear that Berlin had "resorted to force without a formal declaration of war." This avoidance of one of the tenets of international law, according to the embassy, was based on the military consideration that such action obviously gains "the initial advantage of surprise." It was believed that Germany desired "to avoid the onus of formally declaring war," both because of the stipulations of the Kellogg-Briand Pact, which renounced war as an instrument of national policy, and "in order to fasten war guilt on its enemies for posterity in any German dictated peace."[167]

Dekanozov was enraged. Allegedly, he exclaimed that the German action was "unprovoked aggression" against his country and that Berlin would pay a heavy price for its duplicity.[168] He bowed routinely and left, contrasting his entrance into the office minutes before when he had offered his hand to Ribbentrop.[169] Why these rapid German actions seemed to have taken Dekanozov by surprise is a mystery in view of his pessimistic reports to Moscow that Berlin would attack that very day. These reports, as we have seen, had infuriated Beria.

Perhaps Dekanozov had banked his warning fires in order to keep Beria at bay and to attenuate his rage. It is also possible that Dekanozov might have been instructed by Moscow to mend his ways. He certainly was circumspect in his dealings with the NKVD's Filippov earlier the previous day, June 21. Dekanozov, Filippov felt, did not take seriously the queries raised by the foreign correspondents about rumors of an impending German attack on Soviet Russia. Instead, he asked Filippov for his thoughts on the matter. In view of the many facts in Dekanozov's possession, Filippov replied, these rumors had to be taken seriously. Dekanozov retorted that there was no need to panic; panic was exactly what Russia's enemies wanted. The problem was distinguishing between what was truth and what was propaganda.[170]

On this same day, June 21, Dekanozov dismissed the information brought to him that Germany would attack the next day. The information had been acquired by the longtime chief of the Associated Press Bureau in Berlin, Louis Lochner, whose source in the past had always proved reliable. Lochner had then apparently passed the information on to his *Tass* counterpart, Kudryavtsev, who passed it on to the GRU in Moscow. Dekanozov feigned disbelief in the information, an action that is hard to accept in view of his prior warnings, and ordered the information be forgotten. Indeed, he advised the embassy staff to attend a picnic that he had personally arranged for the following day.[171]

Molotov in his postwar ruminations tells us that Dekanozov was an "honorable" man.[172] His use of this adjective is difficult to swallow in view of Dekanozov's track record. Nevertheless, it would be fair to say that Molotov's use of "honorable" accurately characterized Dekanozov's actions in honestly reporting to Moscow what he correctly perceived as a continuing German buildup that would lead to an attack on Soviet Russia when he knew that such reportage was anathema to the entrenched Stalinist view. Naturally, the adjective's essence does not cover Dekanozov's 180-degree turn on June 21, as mirrored in his comments to Filippov and in his rejection of Lochner's information, but this change might have been triggered by threats from Moscow telling Dekanozov to curb his alarming reports and information.

The charade that occurred in Berlin was repeated in Moscow. In the same hour that Ribbentrop asked to see Dekanozov, he issued Schulenburg his instructions and ordered him to call on Molotov. Schulenburg was to destroy all cipher books and communications equipment and was admonished not to discuss the contents of Ribbentrop's message with Molotov. At 4 A.M., as Ribbentrop began his memorable performance for Dekanozov and Berezhkov, a dispirited Schulenburg, accompanied by Hilger, entered Molotov's office. Understandably in view of that night's developments, Molotov "wore a tired and worn-out expression," Hilger tells us.[173] What Hilger and Schulenburg apparently did not know was that Molotov had just attended a Kremlin meeting presided over by an ashen-faced Stalin, in which the Politburo was informed of the German attack.[174]

The gist of Ribbentrop's note was that, despite the 1939 nonaggression pact, Moscow and the Comintern had systematically attempted to undermine Germany's position throughout Europe and especially in Yugoslavia. This attempt was accompanied by a steady increase of Russian troop concentrations along the border that had triggered necessary German countermeasures. The aggressive nature of these concentrations was no longer in doubt. Moreover, there were British reports of conversations between Cripps and the Russians about closer political and military collaboration. Through these actions, Russia had broken its treaty commitments to Nazi Germany and was on the verge of attacking at the very moment Germany was involved in a life-and-death struggle with Britain. Hitler had therefore ordered the German army "to oppose this threat with all the means at its disposal."[175]

Once Schulenburg had delivered the message, there were a few moments of silence. The Russian, "visibly struggling with deep inner excitement," asked whether Schulenburg's note was to be construed as a declaration of war. The German said nothing, but his body language answered that in this situation he was helpless and could offer no answer. Then, "with a slightly raised voice," Molotov observed that Berlin's message was nothing less than a war declaration since German forces had already crossed the border into Russia and raided its cities during the last hour and a half. The German invasion, Molotov fulminated, was unprecedented. Germany had attacked a state with which it had signed a nonaggression pact. The reasons given by Berlin for the invasion were nothing more than a pretext since the message's import was based on the nonsensical notion of Russian troop concentrations on Germany's border. If Russian forces had been in that position and the Germans had been uneasy over it, then a simple communication to the Russian authorities would have been sufficient to have the troops withdrawn. The German response, however, was to unleash a war and all that war portended. Then Molotov made a final comment: "Surely we have not deserved this." Schulenburg interjected that he could say nothing beyond the instructions issued him. As Schulenburg departed, he and Molotov shook hands.[176] But then, Schulenburg was no Ribbentrop.

Years later, Molotov would deny that he had told the German diplomats that his country did not deserve to be attacked. He called the reports all "pure invention," since he obviously would never have said anything "so silly." The only people present during this conversation, he insisted, were the two Germans and his interpreter.[177] In making this categorical statement, Molotov was evidently completely unaware of Hilger's memoirs, published in 1953. No blame could be laid on the interpreter since Hilger was fluent in Russian. The words spoken by Molotov were first absorbed by Hilger in Russian and then in German as Molotov's interpreter repeated them to Ambassador Schulenburg.

In retrospect, considering the information now spaded up about Moscow's concerted efforts during May and June to bridge the gap with Berlin,

Molotov's sensitivity about this statement makes even more sense today than when Hilger first quoted it. Dekanozov's discussions with Meissner, the *Tass* communiqué of June, the likely dispatch of a secret emissary to Berlin, as well as Molotov's attempt to be received by Hitler on June 18 were all part of this concerted effort. The invasion of June 22, however, did not obviate these efforts. They were to persist and, as we shall see, recommence in the autumn as the German armies approached Moscow.

# 8

# To the Bitter End

## Don't Resist

The public reaction in Berlin to the attack "was one of almost shocked surprise since few Germans were able to believe that a campaign of such magnitude would be initiated in the east" against the Russians while the struggle in the West against the British continued unabated despite the flood of rumors that had recently focussed public interest on German-Russian relations.[1] Excluding the Kremlin's political and military leadership, Moscow and the Russian masses knew nothing of what had transpired along the frontier. People everywhere went about their usual Sunday routines. The attack went unannounced in the media, which continued its coverage of the ordinary news.[2] Then at about 11 A.M. on June 22, Moscow radio announced that Molotov would make a broadcast at about noon.[3] It was not until 12:15, eight hours after the attack, that Molotov finally announced what had occurred. In an address speckled with self-pity, he noted that the attack had not been preceded by a declaration of war, was perfidious, and had been perpetrated despite the 1939 nonaggression pact that Russia had conscientiously executed. Molotov related his early morning exchange with Schulenburg and categorically denied that the Russian military had violated the frontiers; Hitler's insistence on the contrary was a "lie and a provocation." Dipping into his Marxist ideological primer, he summed up that this "war" had been forced on Soviet Russia not by the workers, peasants, or the intelligentsia of Germany, whose sufferings could be well appreciated, but by Germany's ruthless Nazi overlords, who had enslaved Belgians, Czechs, Danes, Dutch, Frenchmen, Greeks, Norwegians, Poles, and Serbs. What had happened to Napoleon would happen to Hitler, Molotov assured the Russian people.[4] The solidarity of the working classes alluded to by Molotov was still being slavishly touted several days later by the German Communist party, which invoked what it called the indestructible bond between the German and Russian peoples, going back in history as far as the time of Chancellor Bismarck.[5] Listening to Molotov in London, Maisky asked himself why Molotov had made the radio announcement rather than Stalin.[6]

What could account for this eight-hour delay in informing the Russian masses of the attack? The State Department's attention was attracted to the fact that Germany had not formally declared war. Washington asked Steinhardt whether Moscow had formally declared war against Germany and Italy. If it had, he was to supply the text and the date. No such declaration had been issued, Steinhardt responded, either against Germany or Italy, and the legal status of German-Russian relations remained as Molotov had explained in his radio announcement. Nor had the Russians made any reference to Italy.[7]

When Zhukov contacted Stalin and informed him of what had developed and sought permission to retaliate, the only sound he could hear over the telephone was the *Vozhd*'s breathing.[8] It is claimed that for two hours after this call Stalin did not communicate with anyone.[9] Whether this was the case can be debated. But what cannot be debated is that when the Politburo convened in the early morning hours of June 22, Stalin was ashen-faced.[10] He was during this period, Khrushchev subsequently wrote, "a bag of bones in a gray tunic."[11] It was clearly beyond Stalin's comprehension to admit that he had been outsmarted by the rabble in Berlin. "He considered himself infallible," his daughter Svetlana writes, "and, whatever happened, never had any doubts in his righteousness." Her father "considered his political flair unmatchable."[12] The closest that he came to admitting that he had been taken in was his bitter comment that in the past he had "trusted" Hitler.[13] Understandably, Stalin's initial reaction was that the attack had been a provocative move made by the German military that was supposed to have been obviated by the directive issued earlier that night to the Russian military at General Zhukov's urging. This was not the moment for the Russians to play into the hands of the German military, who were to be feared more than Hitler. In comparison to his military, Hitler seemed reasonable.[14] The fact that there had been no formal declaration of war supported this view. If Hitler had sanctioned the attack, it would have been preceded by an ultimatum, and a declaration of war would have soon followed, whereas an attack instigated by the military through Ribbentrop would have avoided both of these steps. We know, of course, that none of this dovetailed with Hitler's *modus operandi*, precedent, or reality, but on the matter of Hitler's plan for Russia, as we have seen, Stalin's mind was inflexible. As Nikita Khrushchev subsequently observed in his special report to the 1956 Twentieth Communist Party Congress, "despite evident facts," Stalin "thought that the war had not yet started."[15]

Therefore, Stalin's initial ploy, based on instructions he had already issued, was to offer no real resistance until Berlin could be contacted and the unilateral action of the German military roped in by Hitler. No sooner had the

Germans started shelling than they intercepted the Russian message: "We are being fired on. What shall we do?" The reply of the headquarters unit reflected the Stalinist mind-set: "You must be insane. And why is your signal not in code?"[16]

Outside of Lemberg (Lwow), despite the German shelling and much to the surprise of the German officers, there was no counter battery fire. Only with the forward rush of the German infantry did Russian artillery fire commence. The captured Russian commander explained that he believed that the initial German salvos were artillery practice rounds that had overshot their target and landed beyond the frontier. His strict orders to avoid border incidents explained why he did not respond to the initial shelling until the infantry advance made it obvious to him that a war had started.[17]

In Minsk, General I. V. Boldin was reminded by Defense Minister Timoshenko that no military riposte was to be made against the Germans without Moscow's knowledge. Stalin, Timoshenko observed, had specifically forbidden any artillery attacks against the German forces. When Boldin remonstrated, Timoshenko insisted that there was to be "no air reconnaissance more than thirty-five miles [56 kilometers] beyond the frontier." Boldin's argument that the tactical situation required greater military commitment did not sway Timoshenko from his negative stance.[18] The Russian naval authorities likewise restrained themselves.[19]

It was not until 7:15 A.M., more than three hours after the attack, that the first directive signed by Timoshenko, Zhukov, and Malenkov was issued by the Red Army's General Staff. An odd directive, it said nothing about a state of war between Soviet Russia and Germany. In line with Stalin's mind-set, it reflected Moscow's indecision about whether or not Russia was faced with war. Indeed, it appeared to suggest a situation that was less than war. It spoke only of "unprovoked bombing raids" and other military actions, not of war. Ripostes against the Germans were to be limited to attacking and liquidating them in areas "where they have violated the Soviet border." Until further notice, however, the Red Army's forces were not to cross the frontier. The air force, especially, was to locate and attack German aircraft and troop concentrations, but air attacks in particular were not to exceed a depth of 100 to 150 kilometers inside German territory, except for the cities of Königsberg and Memel. Until additional orders were issued, the directive specifically prohibited flights over Finland and Rumania,[20] both of whom had joined the German attack.

The directive, it has been observed, is hardly "a military document," but "rather bears the stamp of Stalin's hand."[21] It "reads very strangely"[22] and, in retrospect, contains the "ring of bitter travesty,"[23] but today, because its basic premise is now understood, it makes more sense than when it was issued on June 22, 1941.

Probably sometime after 7:15 A.M., when the first directive was issued by the Red Army's General Staff, Stalin made his move. The initial fighting had disrupted international radio communications, but their resumption allowed Stalin to approach the Wilhelmstrasse constantly and directly. Concurrently, Tokyo was likewise approached and asked to act as an intermediary between Russia and Germany.[24] In the postwar period, Molotov, intent on not tarnishing further the *Vozhd*'s image, let alone his own, predictably denied that any approach had been made to Hitler once the invasion had commenced.[25] The empirical evidence supporting the occurrence of such an approach, however, is incontestable. Naturally, in view of the euphoric atmosphere in Berlin, no response was made to this Russian initiative; what the Japanese reaction was is unknown.

That Vyshinsky knew of these frantic attempts to approach Berlin and Tokyo is obvious from his conversation with the British chargé d'affaires on the morning of the attack. Acting without instructions, Baggallay called on Vyshinsky. He thought that Vyshinsky would agree that their respective positions had altered in the course of the night. Whether London and Moscow liked it or not, they were now mutually interested in defeating Germany. In such a situation, one would think that Vyshinsky would have readily agreed with Baggallay; instead he "gave a cautious assent." As Baggallay later observed to Steinhardt, Vyshinsky "responded somewhat dryly 'perhaps.' "[26]

When queried by Vyshinsky, Baggallay admitted that at the moment he had no specific plan in mind, but he reminded Vyshinsky that on June 10 and 13 Eden had offered assistance to Maisky if Russia were attacked. Baggallay presumed that Moscow was now studying this possibility of aid if it had not done so before the attack. Vyshinsky appeared "exceedingly nervous," Baggalay noted to London. He rationalized that "this may have accounted for a degree of caution which might seem excessive in anyone but a Soviet official." On matters of detail, Vyshinsky appeared willing to do whatever he could.[27] If Vyshinsky was nervous, his condition probably had more to do with the possibility that Stalin's approaches to Berlin and Tokyo might fail than it did with the customary caution of a Soviet official. If Stalin's efforts failed, then what Baggallay said would occur: like it or not, London and Moscow would be forced into an alliance. That it should come to this after more than twenty years of ideological and political hostility between Moscow and London, especially with Churchill now at the helm of Britain, was unimaginable to Vyshinsky, not to mention to Stalin and all the others in the Kremlin. Obviously, Stalin's dialectic had failed the Kremlin's leadership at a crucial hour.

Hoping, no doubt, that Berlin would respond to his overtures and that it would restrain its military and revert to the *status quo ante,* Stalin held fast to his position and waited. Because he wished to avoid the rapturous scenes that had greeted the outbreak of the First World War, which, if repeated, might undermine his approach to Berlin, there were no popular patriotic demonstrations anywhere. In Moscow there was "none of the enthusiasm," reported the British embassy, that one might have expected in the "capital of a country engaged in [the] biggest war of its history." There were, for example, "no patriotic demonstrations organised or otherwise, on a large scale." Moreover, resolutions adopted by factory meetings had "little real significance."[28]

Any high profile activity during this period was likewise not in Stalin's interest if he wanted his approach to Berlin to bear fruit. Stalin's desire to avoid publicity might in part explain why his name disappeared from the newspapers[29] and why it was Molotov who addressed the nation on the 22nd rather than Stalin himself. The British embassy incomprehensibly attributed Molotov's radio address to the fact that Russians found Stalin's "pronounced" Georgian accent "somewhat comic." That Stalin "should not have issued any personal call to the people [was] more difficult to understand."[30] Naturally, Stalin's approach to Berlin was unknown in the Foreign Office, but its suspicions were aroused. Edward Coote of the Northern Department found it both "strange" and "rather ominous" that there had been so muted a response to the attack in Moscow "and stranger still that Stalin should not have given tongue."[31] The "point about Stalin is perhaps rather sinister," minuted Christopher Warner in agreement.[32]

In view of Stalin's stance and of the atmosphere in Moscow, Baggallay was not approached by the Russians, nor did they express any desire to discuss with him the possibility of Anglo-Russian cooperation in the struggle that had begun.[33] Neither did Stalin respond to Churchill's radio address of the 22nd, in which he promised whatever aid possible to Russia and its people.[34] Likewise, in London an impatient Maisky waited for instructions to establish a plan for cooperation, instructions that did not arrive.[35]

It was not until the afternoon of the 23rd that the Russian naval authorities requested to see the British naval attaché.[36] By this point, it must have been obvious even to Stalin that the German attack was no unauthorized, military-sponsored foray, but a full-fledged Nazi-inspired invasion. Indeed, in a directive issued at this time, Stalin ordered the capture of Lublin and permitted the "crossing of the border" from the Baltic to the Hungarian frontier and "action in disregard of the border."[37]

The request to see the naval attaché was soon followed by an agreement to exchange British and Russian military missions.[38] When Cripps arrived in Moscow on the 27th with economic and military missions in tow, he immediately presented them to Molotov, whom he described to Steinhardt as "pale, nervous and obviously shaken." Though this was the first time Cripps had seen or spoken to Molotov in several months, the Russian "gave no indication of having anything to say either to Cripps or [to] the members of the Missions." With Russia invaded and fighting for its life, Molotov's behavior was certainly bizarre; his strange behavior had the "result that the interview ended without any effort by Molotov to discuss the objectives of the Missions or anything else." Thanks to Cripps's endeavors, the missions were later put into contact with the pertinent authorities.[39]

### Where is the Boss?

The British military mission had expected to be received by Stalin rather than Molotov. In fact, during this period the *Vozhd* had virtually vanished and the great question that circulated in Moscow was one of his whereabouts.[40] As we have seen, in the hours immediately after the attack, Stalin appeared ashen-faced.[41] The enormity of what had occurred and his inability to elicit a response from Berlin to his approach on the morning of the 22nd must have contributed immeasurably to his mental anguish. We are reliably informed that he "simply lost control of himself and went into psychological shock."[42] That this was so is attested to by his daughter, Svetlana, who writes of his "deep depression" once the attack had commenced.[43]

The assertion, however, that for ten days the Kremlin was "leaderless" does not stand up to scrutiny.[44] On the surface at least, Stalin appeared to be functioning. On the day before the attack, he kept thirteen appointments in his office. After news of the invasion on the 22nd, he talked to Molotov at 5:45 A.M. and continued meeting senior personnel until 4:45 P.M. During this day, he had twenty-nine interviews. Starting with an appointment on the 23rd with Molotov at 3:20 A.M., he continued meetings until 1:25 A.M. on the 24th. During this twenty-two-hour period, he met a total of twenty-one people. On the 24th, he had twenty interviews; on the 25th, he had twenty-nine interviews; on the 26th, he had twenty-eight interviews; and on the 27th, he reached his zenith for this period with a total of thirty interviews. On the 28th, he slipped perceptively back to twenty-one interviews.[45]

During these seven days, Soviet Russia suffered losses of such magnitude that one would be hard-pressed to point to another state that in an equal time span experienced a similar fate. By June 24, the cities of Brest-Litovsk, Kaunas (Kovno), and Vilnius (Vilna) had fallen to German forces. Dvinsk fell two days later; Libau and Minsk, the capital of Belorussia, fell on the 28th, followed by Riga on the next day. The loss of men and materiel was enormous. Corps units and whole army groups had been annihilated, thousands of tanks and guns had been destroyed, and thousands more had been captured. The air force was virtually destroyed as a fighting entity, and hundreds of thousands of troops were taken prisoner. In a functioning democracy, responsibilty for this incredible debacle would rightly have been laid at Stalin's door.

It was not, however, until the 29th that Stalin began to unravel and to lose control of himself under the impact of the preceding days' events. Leaving the Ministry of Defense with Beria, Molotov, Voroshilov, and Zhdanov, he loudly exclaimed: "Lenin left us a great inheritance and we, his heirs, have fucked it all up!" Molotov stared at Stalin in amazement but, emulating the others, held his tongue.[46]

That same day Stalin was visited at his dacha by Beria, Mikoyan, Malenkov, Molotov, Voroshilov, and the academician Nikolai Voznesensky. They had resolved to propose to Stalin that a National Defense Committee be created to assume all state power. Molotov cautioned the others that Stalin was so prostrated that he was indifferent to everything, devoid of initiative, and not at all well. When they entered the gloomy dacha, Stalin asked why they had come. Both the look on his face and the question were strange. Molotov explained the need for a National Defense Committee headed by Stalin himself in order to "ensure rapid decision-making" and somehow get the country moving. Stalin appeared surprised, raised no objections, and agreed to establish the committee and preside over it.[47]

Despite this exchange, the National Defense Committee chaired by Stalin was not decreed until the following day and was not made public until July 1, when its establishment was reported in *Pravda*.[48] During the two days of June 29 and 30, Stalin did not appear in public or at his office; he resumed appointments sometime on July 1.[49] If Stalin's "state of depression was obvious"[50] at this time, Stalin undoubtedly reached his lowest point during these last two days of June.

Then at 6:30 A.M. on July 3, without a prior announcement, Stalin, sitting before a radio microphone in the Kremlin, addressed the nation. The speech was repeated throughout the day by announcers and to pedestrians through loudspeakers. Its text was posted everywhere. By the end of the day, everyone knew what Stalin had said.[51] His frank admission of territorial losses and the continuing German advance required that he explain how Germany had achieved such remarkable military successes within such a short time. The plausible explanation he offered was that as a belligerent state Germany was fully mobilized, at the ready, awaiting only the signal to start hostilities. This readiness he contrasted to the state of Russian forces that still had to be mobilized and proceed to the frontiers. Naturally, he did not mention the accurate warnings of an impending attack that he had received from both Russian and foreign sources.

The 1939 nonaggression pact that had allowed Hitler to commence the Second World War Stalin justified as a measure that had given Russia a year-and-a-half opportunity to prepare itself to fend off any intended German attack should Berlin risk it despite the pact's strictures. As Molotov had done in his speech, Stalin could not avoid dipping into his ideological primer to describe the struggle in class terms: one between Soviet Russia's peoples and Nazi Germany's armed forces. Russia's aim in this war was not only to eliminate the dangers facing the country but also to aid all Europeans suffering under the Nazi yoke. Fortunately, Soviet Russia would have "loyal allies in the peoples of Europe and America," including the people of Germany suffering persecution from the Nazis. Soviet Russia's freedom war would merge with that of the peoples of Europe and America. Almost as an afterthought, Stalin mentioned British and American declarations of governmental aid, offers that could only "evoke a feeling of gratitude in the hearts of the peoples" of Soviet Russia.[52] The address was pure Stalin and fitted the necessity to zag after having zigged in August 1939 with the signature of the nonaggression pact.

Steinhardt reported that those who listened to the address stated that Stalin was "greatly agitated and spoke with obvious emotion."[53] A young Moscovite girl who also listened to Stalin that morning remembered years later that "he spoke in an unsteady voice and one could hear clinking sounds as he reached with trembling hands to pour water from a pitcher into his glass."[54] Unlike Molotov's speech, which had "made a good impression," Maisky thought that Stalin's address had not been up to snuff. It was delivered in " 'a dull colourless voice' with Stalin 'often stopping and breathing heavily,' " giving the impression that he "was at the end of his strength."[55] Stalin's depressed state at this time was, of course, unknown to the people listening to the broadcast. Probably, he was still in the throes of his depression. As the days wore on, however, slowly his depression lifted, but his troubles did not disappear.

## The Bulgarian Connection

In the weeks that followed Stalin's radio address, Russia's military situation steadily worsened. Several days after the speech, Ostrov, Pskov, and Porkhov were captured on the northern front. By mid-July, Smolensk fell, followed by Tallinn (Reval). August saw the fall of Novgorod, the overrunning of large areas of the Ukraine, and the capture of Dniepropetrovsk. By early September, Leningrad (Saint Petersburg) was blockaded and Kiev had fallen. The German advance toward Moscow accelerated in October with the capture of Orel followed by that of Kaluga, Kalinin, Odessa, and Kharkov. In the Kremlin, despite the *Vozhd*'s treaty commitment made to the British on July 12 that both states would "neither negotiate nor conclude an armistice or treaty of peace [with Germany] except by mutual agreement," the *Vozhd* wanted to disengage Russia from the war and save what he could of his own position and of the Communist party, as well as of Lenin's legacy. But in view of the July 12 treaty arrangement, Stalin's problems were how he should approach the Germans and what he should offer to satiate Berlin.

Any message to Berlin, however, would have to be expedited through a secure channel trusted by the Germans. Of all the inhabitants of wartime Moscow, the Bulgarian minister, Ivan Stamenov, fitted the bill: he represented a neutral state, had played a role in helping to arrange the exchange of the German and Russian diplomatic missions, and enjoyed gilt-edged credentials in Berlin. As the representative of a neutral state, he looked after German, Hungarian, and Rumanian interests in Soviet Russia.[56] Accordingly, he was even more isolated in Moscow than his Japanese counterpart; in Sofia, however, he had King Boris's support, which was no doubt generated by his previous service in the royal court.[57]

As early as July, the Foreign Office told Cripps that on "good authority"—perhaps that of a decrypt—a senior Bulgarian official had remarked that it was very much in Germany's interest for Stamenov to remain in Moscow because Berlin "counted on his being a valuable source of information."[58] When Cripps suggested to Stalin that it would be wise to send Stamenov home on the grounds that he was "little more than a German agent," Stalin seemed to concur and "intimated that the Soviet authorities had come to the same conclusion."[59] Despite this admission, Stalin allowed Stamenov to remain in Moscow. No one knew what future use could be made of him.

Stalin's biographer suggests that the approach to Berlin was made through Stamenov in July 1941,[60] the very period during which Cripps complained about him. Khrushchev, on information subsequently supplied to him by Beria and Malenkov, asserted that this approach "probably" occurred in 1942.[61] In actual fact, a peace feeler might well have been conveyed through Stamenov not in July but in October 1941 as the Wehrmacht forced its way toward Moscow. This date is attested to by Stamenov's junior in the Bulgarian diplomatic mission, Dimitar Peyev, who "became aware of the secret deal" at that time.[62]

Indeed, General Zhukov apparently admitted that on October 7, 1941, he met Stalin with Beria present. Though the NKVD chief was silent throughout the interview, Stalin was very pessimistic about the unfolding situation. Then suddenly he began to ruminate about what had occurred in 1918: Lenin had left a Communist state and had ordered that it should be enhanced in every way possible. But his instructions had not been carried out. The Germans were now headed for Moscow, and the necessary forces to defend the city were not to be had. Russia needed a respite from the struggle as much as it had in 1918 when it signed the Brest-Litovsk Peace Treaty with Germany. Accordingly, Stalin instructed Beria to investigate the possibilities of another Brest-Litovsk arrangement with the Germans. Toward this end, the *Vozhd* was willing to cede Lithuania, Latvia, Estonia, Moldavia, Belorussia, and part of the Ukraine. In view of what the NKVD knew about Stamenov, Beria assigned agents to contact him and ask that he act as the intermediary who would convey Stalin's peace feeler to Berlin.[63] According to Beria, when Stamenov met Stalin, the *Vozhd* said nothing. Apparently, only Molotov spoke to the Bulgarian and asked him to approach Berlin. Molotov supported the proffered arrangement as another Brest-Litovsk.[64] As one would expect, Molotov's disingenuous postwar comment was that after the battle of Moscow no armistice was proposed.[65]

Much of what Zhukov divulged dovetails with what Stamenov admitted when he was questioned in Sofia by a senior official of Moscow's procurator office following Beria's arrest in 1953. In particular, Stamenov supplied the code names of Beria's intermediaries, who had also been unearthed in Moscow.[66] The assertion, even if true, that Stamenov refused to assume the role of intermediary and claimed that Russia would still win even if the Red Army fell back to the Urals[67] does not exculpate the *Vozhd* from making the attempt.

Conveying Stalin's offer to Berlin was not without risk. What if the Germans leaked the offer or stated outright that it had been made? Cleverly,

Beria took countermeasures to prevent such a move. His disinformation took the form of a public and official denial of a German armistice offer that, of course, had never been made. There was "not an iota of truth in reports" of a suggested German armistice, Deputy Foreign Minister Lozovsky assured the Moscow press corps. He dismissed any such offer as the "usual German propaganda . . . meant to confuse issues." Concurrently, Beria's disinformation people were busy in neutral capitals far removed from Moscow. To buttress Lozovsky's comment, British diplomatic missions in Ankara, Bern, Cairo, Lisbon, and Madrid apparently reported "various peace proposals and overtures" that were believed to be connected with some sort of German peace offensive. Naturally, Berlin emphatically denied the report that it had offered Moscow an armistice. To believe that Germany had "asked for an armistice at the very moment she had beaten the adversary down to his knees is both absurd and laughable," Berlin responded.[68] Beria, however, had so muddied the waters of international diplomacy that any German release about a peace feeler from Stalin would have been greeted with derision and universally dismissed as a cheap countershot devoid of substance.

Nevertheless, Berlin's reaction that any German-offered armistice was both "absurd and laughable," reflected its optimism. As German forces closed in on Moscow, victory appeared to be within Berlin's grasp. Since the complete prize of a conquered Russia was virtually assured, why would they settle for anything less? If Stalin attempted a peace feeler, it generated no response, let alone an acceptance.

## Future Imperfect

Those raised in the values of open and pluralistic societies find it difficult to fathom the leader and the leadership in Soviet Russia who helped make Barbarossa a German success. (One can suggest that there are limits to the explanations that can be offered about this phenomenon by social scientists, limits that would probably not appreciably expand if submitted to cogitation by psychotherapists.) As in Stalin's Russia, political elites in democratic societies have occasionally gone beyond the limits that the political culture allowed; such behavior will no doubt be repeated in the future. The saving grace of democratic societies is that even when power is highly centralized it is inevitably shared with others. Under the rubric of "others" fall not only the political culture and the values of the society as they are reflected in the polity's constitutional and political makeup, including the structure and composition of its political parties, but also the visibly political nongovernmental groups and even those not visibly political groups whose existence and influence in society cannot be easily ignored.

This complex democratic structure of restraint did not exist in Soviet Russia, especially during the 1939–1941 period. Using Marxist terminology, one might argue that the Communist superstructure imposed on Russian society in the years following the revolution led unhesitatingly to the new regime's adoption of a political culture and values analogous to those of the preceding tszarist superstructure, despite the radical alteration of the economic base from which the New Jerusalem of the working class was supposed to grow. As absolute as the tsars had been, they paled in comparison to those who wielded power in the allegedly classless society of the workers' paradise. Initially under Lenin and more so under Stalin, power in Soviet Russia was centralized; certainly by 1939, power was shared with no one. As befits a modern totalitarian society, this system destroyed not only the political lives but also the private lives of its citizens.

Yet, at the same time, there are limits to every regime. Even at the apex of the system, information did get through on such a central question as relations with Germany that, at a minimum, implicity challenged Stalin's view. The impending catastrophe was simply too great to hide. The *Vozhd*'s power lay in his ability to effectively monopolize the interpretation of all the information coming into Moscow, though this is not to underestimate the tremendous amount of slavish self-censorship exercised by those below him, out of a desire to live if nothing else. Nor is this meant to diminish the strenuous efforts Stalin made to keep those around him divided and ignorant of all that was happening. Stalin called the tune, and ignorant or not, everyone hummed along.

The sycophantic nature of Stalin's entourage, which was cemented by the purges, reinforced an atmosphere in which criticism of or a stance at variance with the faultless leader could be lethal, as, for example, Air Force General and GRU Director Ivan Proskurov discovered. Few had the courage of a Novobranets. Even Aesopian language, which had saved many a Greek or Roman, offered no protection, although Dekanozov and others, perhaps out of duty or perhaps out of fear of being blamed if catastrophe struck, did make notable attempts to keep Moscow informed. Within Hitler's immediate circle, aside from the 1934 killing of Ernst Roehm, the cutting down to size of the Sturmabteilung to assuage the Wehrmacht, and the execution of those implicated in the 1944 plot to assassinate Hitler, everyone was safe. But within the *Vozhd*'s immediate circle, no one was safe, as so many of Stalin's associates discovered.

In this intimidating setting, Stalin's monopolization of security intelligence naturally went unchallenged. Equally important, all intelligence information was prepared for him by NKVD and GRU officials sensitized to his views by the removal and demise of their predecessors. Wisdom dictated that these officials avoid trouble and please Stalin, and please him they did. Accordingly, they do not appear to have made any serious and sustained efforts to sift incoming intelligence data in an analytical fashion. Their reports were puerile or outright hostile to the agents or sources that supplied the security information. Sorge and the information he supplied are a case in point. This problem was compounded by Stalin's insistence that raw security intelligence material and periodic intelligence reports not be forwarded directly to him. Incoming security intelligence was to be edited or summarized by the intelligence staff, and Stalin was to be presented only with the facts and the sources from which they were derived. The problems caused by this deplorable situation became especially acute as June 22 approached and as the warnings became more frantic, witness the gyrations of Beria and Dekanozov, until the latter developed second thoughts in the weeks immediately preceding the attack.

Military intelligence, as it was controlled by General Golikov, fared no better. Indeed, one might argue it was even worse, for Chief of Staff Zhukov and Minister of Defense Timoshenko were excluded from the security intelligence distribution list. This exclusion was probably due more to Stalin's machinations than to Golikov's, but it certainly removed the buckle from the belt of Russian army preparedness. Stalin's control of security data gave him enormous advantages over his Politburo associates, as well as over the military; if information is power, Stalin certainly had power in this context as he had it in all others. Unlike victorious generals tumultuously received in Rome, Stalin did not have a slave whispering repeated admonitions to remember that he was but a man. What is clear from all this, as *sui generis* as it was, is that caution should be used by all watchers of the intelligence scene, especially by optimists who believe that the safety of a state can, to a marked degree, be secured by an effective, wide-ranging information-gathering capacity.

Stalin's ascent of the greasy pole of political power in Soviet Russia over the assorted bodies of friends and foes left him with hubris and ingrained hostility. Stalin's hubris was belief in his own infallibility, his righteousness, and what he considered, his daughter tells us, his unmatchable political flair. It manifested itself in his insistence that he serve as his own intelligence analyst; in his conviction, which was intuitive and devoid of empirical fact and/or historical evidence, that a German attack would be preceded by an ultimatum followed by a declaration of war; in his perception, despite all prior indications, that it was senior German officers rather than Hitler himself who might unleash an attack; and so on.

In tandem with this hubris, Stalin's hostility was all-pervasive. He appears to have viewed the Germans with a particular respect and to have perceived Hitler as a worthy opponent, someone who did not really approach his own high talents but who could be controlled with proper management. On the other hand, his deep-seated hostility toward Great Britain was enormous. During the interwar years, Britain had been Soviet Russia's most implacable foe. Though British sagacity and security intelligence-gathering were formidable, he bestowed upon them an omnipotence that was well wide of the mark. This attitude explains Stalin's alacrity in crediting the British with the most diabolical strategems and scribbling such words as "provocation," "deception," "disinformation" on all incoming British security information. In view of Churchill's long-held hostility toward the Communist system, his fortuitous prime ministership beginning in the spring of 1940 did little to assuage Stalin's Anglophobia.

As the preceding pages show, the successful execution of Barbarossa had absolutely nothing to do with a failure of the Russian intelligence and diplomatic services in uncovering the German intention to attack. These services, along with the non-Russian sources who had conveyed their data to Moscow, had clearly reported the German intention. Accordingly, the evidence contradicts the assertion that in 1940–1941 GRU officers in particular "were clearly of low caliber, demoralized and running around like headless chickens in the wake of Stalin's purges of the 1930s."[69] Nor is there any substance to the assertion that these same purges had so denuded the NKVD of experienced personnel that the commencement of war found Russia "virtually" devoid of a "strategic secret service."[70]

If anything, Stalin and the Kremlin's decision-making elites were faced by a surfeit, rather than a paucity, of information about a probable upcoming German attack. Indeed, though Moscow would like to convey the impression that preponderantly this security data originated with agents, its guarded admission would appear to show that sizeable amounts of data were acquired through the intense decryption activities of the Russian intelligence services.[71] The failure of Stalin and the Kremlin's governing elite was not one of intelligence-gathering but of its proper analysis and integration of intelligence data into policy formulation. As nothing else can, Stalin's performance makes clear the notion that the lack of political acumen on the part of the decision-maker can negate even the best intelligence capability and analysis. The situation Stalin created reflects the conundrum faced by all intelligence services: what difference does it make how good you are if your information and advice are ignored?

Stalin's entourage, terrified to question his wisdom, accepted without demur his thesis that Hitler and the ruling Nazi elite would never attack Russia and expose the Third Reich to a two-front war. Just such a two-front war had contributed to Germany's defeat in the First World War, and Stalin firmly believed that Berlin had learned its lesson. What he failed to see, as indeed so many others did, was that the conduct of foreign affairs in Nazi Germany was often a high-risk operation. National interests and rationality, which often go hand in hand, were not connected in Hitlerian Germany.

How Stalin persevered in his belief that Hitler would play a rational role remains a mystery in view of the mounting evidence to the contrary after Hitler's assumption of power in 1933 and certainly after the outbreak of the war in 1939. Likewise, how Stalin came up with the notion of the paramount role of the German military in decision making and with the certainty that a declaration of war would be preceded by the delivery of a German ultimatum, is also a mystery. Not every individual abberation is open to empirical investigation and solution. In fairness to Stalin, one cannot help noting that, with the exception of Cavendish-Bentinck, the British likewise suffered from the affliction of believing that Hitler would never fight a two-front war. But, unlike Stalin, they at least had sufficiently open minds to accept the empirical evidence, especially that furnished by the Enigma decrypts: what at one point had seemed virtually impossible was not only possible but probable by June 22.

Of the deception ploys mounted by both sides, clearly those most successful were the German ones. If successful deceptions are measured in their effectiveness, in their ability to convince and manipulate the perceptions of the opponent's decision makers to gain competitive advantage, then German deceptions during this period achieved, if they did not exceed, their assigned tasks. Beginning in November 1940, with Hitler's comments to the Russians during the Berlin negotiations that a future German-Russian summit conference might be possible to straighten out subsequent difficulties, the Germans played their cards with consummate skill. Planted in November and supplemented by other actions, the idea of a summit conference was watered and fertilized and shaped into a hedged maze that inevitably led to the Meissner-Dekanozov discussions of May–June 1941. The Germans certainly never meant these discussions to succeed but to terminate *sine die.*

Stalin's appetite was whetted by the planted German rumors that a summit conference was in the offing in Berlin to pick up where the Meissner-Dekanozov discussions had failed. Along with the increasing political and military pressure of the Germans, these rumors in all likelihood led to the dispatch to Berlin of the unidentified agent who was reported by Steinhardt and who broached Molotov's desire to talk to Hitler. This particular ploy of a summit conference, planted with Molotov in November 1940, was the key ingredient in a cleverly concocted formula of deception that did so much to lull Stalin into rejecting as British-inspired the assortment of incoming security intelligence that warned of a German attack.

Concurrently, as we have seen, the Russians, who were no novices when it came to deception operations, mounted an imaginative deception scheme in far-off Manchuria. More complex than that of their Nazi German opponents, it might have had some impact on Berlin if Hitler's commitment and desire to invade Russia had not superseded virtually any and all incoming security data. This supersedence explains why Ponschab's messages were filed away and ignored. However, even after five decades, the manner in which the Russian deception operation was mounted is not absolutely clear in all respects. Clearly, Moscow's spurious messages were fed to Berlin through Ponschab. The question is: how did Ponschab acquire them? Based on the evidence of Ponschab's administrative assistant, they apparently came to Ponschab through the Abwehr agent, Ivar Lissner. Beyond Lissner, the trail is shrouded in mist. But in view of the people with whom Lissner cavorted in Harbin, the trail would appear to lead back to the White Russian community and, in all likelihood, beyond that community to the imaginative practitioners of the NKVD.

The edifice that Stalin built in 1939, grounded on the nonaggression pact and on the notion that a new world war between the Anglo-French and the Germans was manna from heaven, collapsed with Germany's victory in Europe in the spring of 1940. Stalin was beside himself with anger, as Khrushchev tells us.[72] Stalin made an enormous miscalculation in believing that a new world war would be partly a repetition of the previous one; he foresaw a war in which the opponents would exhaust themselves politically, militarily, and economically, and Soviet Russia would walk in and pick up the pieces. Until the German attack in June 1941, this policy had led to Russia's political and military isolation on the continent. By this policy's failure, Moscow was forced to succumb to wishful thinking as the rumors and empirical evidence showed the increasing possibility of a German attack.

All along the line, Stalin had committed one policy failure after another, whether in accepting the terms of the 1939 nonaggression pact or in being completely taken in by the German deception operations first foisted on him during the Berlin negotiations of November 1940 and terminating with the discussions of May–June 1941. In view of the warnings issued by the Russian intelligence services, especially by their operatives abroad, awareness of what had occurred and the discussion and dissemination of these policy failures by Moscow's ruling elite were not in the *Vozhd*'s interest.

This miserable track record of policy and intelligence failures partially explains the hostile reception accorded intelligence operatives when they returned from abroad. Stalin could ill afford to have the Leopold Treppers of the world ruminating about their recent experiences with Moscow and the neglect shown their warnings. The incarceration of such agents in the Gulag was an unavoidable necessity.[73] Loyal to the bitter end, Sándor Radó attributed his imprisonment to being " 'one of the victims of the cult of personality,' a victim of the Stalinist era."[74]

Regarding Sorge, the Japanese deputy minister of defense, General Kyoji (Keoji) Tominaga, alleged that between Sorge's sentencing in late 1941 and his execution in November 1944, while Japan and Russia were not at war with each other, the Japanese on three occasions had proposed to the Russian embassy in Tokyo that the two states make an exchange of Sorge for an imprisoned Japanese. The Russians' response on all occasions was that Richard Sorge was unknown to them. If Sorge had not been unmasked by the Japanese, and if he had returned to Soviet Russia after the war, as a non-Russian he would have suffered the same fate as those non-Russians who were liquidated in the prewar purges of the NKVD and the GRU—Theodore Maly, Ignace Reiss, and so many others.[75] In Sorge's case, Stalin was not open to charity; too many of Sorge's accurate reports had been ignored, and the risk was too high to have him surface in wartime Moscow. He was left to his fate, though he was immortalized by the Soviets on a postage stamp years later. If what General Tominaga said was true, and there is no reason to doubt him, Moscow could ill afford to have him testify at the postwar Tokyo War Crimes

Trial. Accordingly, though Tominaga was called as a witness, the Russians refused to bring him before the tribunal on the ground that he was "under investigation on charges of war crimes" in Russia.[76]

If there is one phenomenon that pervades Russian statecraft, especially during the period covered by this work, it is the role, direct and indirect, assigned to the Russian intelligence services in the conduct of foreign relations. The intensity of their involvement is in direct proportion to the importance of the target selected. Because Nazi Germany was correctly perceived in the Kremlin as the immediate enemy, the activities of the intelligence services directed against Germany were all-pervasive, as exemplified by the NKVD-GRU component of the Russian embassy in Berlin. Direct participants in diplomatic negotiations at important "out stations," such as Berlin and Washington, were tested NKVD men, such as Dekanozov and Umansky, while someone like Maisky in London, who was a former Menshevik and thus suspect, could be controlled through close surveillance. Even those intelligence operatives of lower silhouette who seemingly played lesser, although often not unimportant, roles were in all likelihood used in 1939 as conduits to convey to Moscow Berlin's feelers about a possible nonaggression pact.

The interrelationship between the intelligence services and the conduct of foreign relations has, of course, been intimate in many political cultures. In the case of Russia, however, especially under the Communists, this relationship was deep and pervasive and beyond a mere cheek by jowl relationship. Its deep roots were historical, political, and cultural. It is so much a part of the fabric of the Russian political scene that the tumultous events of 1917, rather than demolishing it, raised the relationship to even higher levels than before.

Not anticipating the German attack was not a failure of intelligence but was a failure of Stalin and his system. Despite the enormous and immediate nature of the threat and the fact that many people in Moscow knew what was happening both on the border and in Berlin in June 1941, no defense was mounted. For all the difficulties in analyzing Hitler's intentions, it is clear, painfully clear in the hours just before and after the attack, that Stalin had deceived himself. Unfortunately, he was the only one in Moscow who mattered. No amount of hagiographic papering has been able to hide the magnitude of the *Vozhd*'s failure.[77] Stalin's unfettered hubris led him to the mistake of keeping his friends close but his enemies closer.

# Notes

## Abbreviations

| | |
|---|---|
| AA | Australian Archives, Canberra |
| BL | Bodleian Library, Oxford University |
| CB | Carlisle Barracks, Carlisle, Pennsylvania |
| CC | Churchill College Library, Cambridge University |
| CU | Butler Library, Columbia University |
| *DGFP 1918–1945* | Germany. Auswärtiges Amt, *Documents on German Foreign Policy, 1918–1945* (Washington, D.C.: Government Printing Office, 1949) |
| FDR Library | Franklin Delano Roosevelt Library, Hyde Park, New York |
| FO | Foreign Office records, Public Record Office, London |
| *FRUS* . . . | U. S. Department of State, *Foreign Relations of the United States* . . . (Washington, D.C.: Government Printing Office . . .) |
| HIA | Hoover Institution Archives, Stanford, California |
| HLRO | House of Lords Record Office, London |
| LC | Manuscripts Division, Library of Congress |
| LSEP | London School of Economics and Political Science |
| NA | National Archives, Washington, D.C. |
| *NCA* | *Nazi Conspiracy and Aggression* (Washington, D.C.: Government Printing Office, 1946) |
| PRO | Public Record Office, London |
| *TMWC* | International Military Tribunal, *Trial of the Major War Criminals before the International Military Tribunal, Nuremberg, 14 November 1945–1 October 1946* (Nuremberg, 1947–) |

| | |
|---|---|
| *TWCT* | International Military Tribunal for the Far East, *The Tokyo War Crimes Trial,* ed. R. John Pritchard, Sonia Magbanua Zaide, and Donald C. Watt (New York: Garland Publishing, 1981), 22 vols. |
| US Army Intelligence and Security Command | United States Army Intelligence and Security Command, Fort Meade, Maryland |
| UY | Borthwick Institute of Historical Studies, University of York, England |

## Chapter 1: Perceptions and Deceptions

1. Germany. Auswärtiges Amt, *Nazi-Soviet Relations 1939–1941; Documents from the Archives of the German Foreign Office* (Washington, D.C.: Government Printing Office, 1948), p. 74.

2. Nikita Khrushchev, *Khrushchev Remembers,* ed. and trans. Strobe Talbott (Boston: Little, Brown, 1970), pp. 134, 166; Nikita Khrushchev, *Khrushchev Remembers: The Glasnost Tapes,* trans. and ed. Jerrold L. Schecter and Vyacheslav V. Luchkov (Boston: Little, Brown, 1991), p. 54.

3. On Stalin's fears of a German-Japanese coalition see, A. I. Eremenko, *V nachale voiny* (Moscow: Nauka, 1964), p. 48.

4. Khrushchev, *Khrushchev Remembers,* pp. 128–129.

5. Eduard Beneš, *Memoirs of Dr. Eduard Beneš* (London: Allen and Unwin, 1954), pp. 138–139. On "little gnome," see Harold Nicolson, *Diaries and Letters of Harold Nicolson,* ed. Nigel Nicolson (New York: Atheneum, 1967), vol. 2, p. 155.

6. Georgii Zhukov, *Vospominaniia i razmyshleniia* (Moscow: Novosti, 1969), p. 244.

7. John Erickson, "Threat Identification and Strategic Appraisal by the Soviet Union, 1930–1941," in *Knowing One's Enemies; Intelligence Assessment Before the Two World Wars,* ed. Ernest May (Princeton: Princeton University Press, 1984), p. 404n.

8. He added up British and German casualties "not in two columns, but in a single column," Ambassador Maisky noted to a foreign diplomat [Llewellyn Woodward, *British Policy in the Second World War* (London: H. M. Stationery Office, 1970), vol. 1, p. xliv]. See also Beria's alleged quoting of Stalin saying that, with war in Europe, Soviet intelligence priorities should be refocused on exacerbating conflicts inside and between various states, in Pavel Sudoplatov and Anatoli Sudoplatov with Jerrold L. Schecter and Leona P. Schecter, *Special Tasks* (New York: Little, Brown, and Company, 1994), p. 100.

9. George F. Kennan, *Russia and the West Under Lenin and Stalin* (Boston: Little, Brown, 1960), pp. 287–288.

10. Aleksandr M. Nekrich, "Stalin and the Pact with Hitler," *Russia* no. 4 (1981): 46.

11. Lord Balfour of Inchrye, Moscow Diary 1941, entry of Wed., Oct. 1, HLRO.

12. Record of Conversation with [Konstantin] Oumansky [by the Australian Minister], May 1, 1941, FO/371/29501.

13. Davidson to Sargent, Mar. 1, 1941, FO/371/29464.

14. See Donald Cameron Watt, *How War Came: The Immediate Origins of the Second World War, 1938–1939* (London: Heinemann, 1989), passim.

15. Feliks I. Chuev, *Sto sorok besed s Molotovym: iz dnevnika F. Chueva* (Moscow: Terra, 1991), p. 20.

16. *DGFP 1918–1945,* ser. D, vol. 7, pp. 245–247.

17. D[onald] Cameron Watt, "[John] Herbert King: A Soviet Source in the Foreign Office," *Intelligence and National Security* 3, no. 4 (October 1988): 62–82. Also, see John Costello, *Mask of Treachery* (New York: Morrow, 1988), pp. 174, 181–182, 279–280, 345–347; and Neil Balfour and Sally Mackay, *Paul of Yugolslavia* (London: Hamish Hamilton, 1980), p. 170.

18. William L. Shirer, *The Rise and Fall of the Third Reich* (New York: Simon and Schuster, 1960), pp. 665–666.

19. Franz Halder, *Kriegstagebuch* (Stuttgart: Kohlhammer, 1962), vol. 1, p. 107 and vol. 2, pp. 32, 49–50. Also, see *NCA,* vol. 3, p. 620; vol. 5, pp. 734–735, 740–741; and Supplement B, pp. 1635–1637, as well as Walter Warlimont, *Inside Hitler's Headquarters, 1930–1945* (New York: Praeger, 1964), pp. 111–114.

20. Khrushchev, *Khrushchev Remembers,* pp. 128–129, 134, 166; Khrushchev, *Khrushchev Remembers: The Glasnost Tapes,* p. 54; "Marshal Zhukov on Soviet Leadership on the Eve and in the Early Days of War," A[gency] P[ress] N[ovosti], *Military Bulletin* (Moscow), Special Issue, no. 20 (25), 012SDO–871009–GA–l (Oct. 1987): 2. Also, see Mikhail Heller and Aleksandr M. Nekrich, *Utopia in Power: The History of the Soviet Union from 1917 to the Present* (New York: Summit, 1986), p. 351.

21. Dmitri Volkogonov, *Stalin: Triumph and Tragedy* (London: Weidenfeld and Nicolson, 1991), p. 370.

22. Gabriel Gorodetsky, *Stafford Cripps' Mission to Moscow 1940–1942* (Cambridge: Cambridge University Press, 1984), p. 6. On Rothstein and his father, see Andrew Boyle, *The Fourth Man* (New York: Diall/James Wade, 1979), pp. 36–37, and Costello, pp. 88, 94–97, 175, 183, 215.

23. *DGFP, 1918–1945,* ser. D, vol. 8, pp. 166, 214.

24. On the description of Schulenburg, see Valentin Berezhkov, "Stalin's Error of Judgement," *International Affairs* (Moscow) no. 9 (September 1989): 24–25 and Steinhardt (Moscow) to the Sec. of State, no. 240, Feb. 9, 1941, File 740.0011 European War 1939/8225, RG 59, NA. Also, see Carl E. Schorske, "Two German Ambassadors: Dirksen and Schulenburg," in *The Diplomats 1919–1939,* ed. Gordon A. Craig and Felix Gilbert (Princeton: Princeton University Press, 1953), pp. 477–511.

25. *DGFP, 1918–1945,* ser. D, vol. 9, pp. 474–475, 548–550, 561, 572–574, 577–578, 581–583, 589, 595–596, 599–601, 606–607, 627–629, 687–688; vol. 10, 3–4, 12–13, 21, 26, 37–38, 77, 126, 156, 238, 264–267, 332–341, 466, 483–484, 502, 510, 576–590; vol. 11, 1, 8–10.

26. David Low, *Low on the War: A Cartoon Commentary of the Years 1939–41* (New York: Simon & Schuster, 1941), p. 15.

27. Dusty Sklar, *Gods and Beasts: The Nazis and the Occult* (New York: Crowell, 1977), passim.

28. Adolf Hitler, *Mein Kampf* (New York: Reynal and Hitchcock, 1940), pp. 398, 406, and passim.

29. *DGFP 1918–1945,* ser. D, vol. 10, p. 323. Also, see Davidson to Sargent, Mar. 1, 1941, FO/371/29464.

30. Halder, vol. 2, pp. 320, 337–338. Also, see Robert Cecil, *Hitler's Decision to Invade Russia 1941* (London: Davis-Poynter, 1975), pp. 153–166.

31. Ulrich von Hassell, *The Von Hassell Diaries 1938–1944* (Garden City, New York: Doubleday, 1947), pp. 198–199, 207.

32. Shirer, p. 373.

33. A. Rossi [Angelo Tasca], *Deux ans d'alliance Germano-Sovietique* (Paris: Fayard, 1949), pp. 149–150.

34. *DGFP 1918–1945,* ser. D, vol. 10, pp. 429–432; vol. 11, pp. 64–65, 66–68, 73–74, 287–289, 318, 335, 424–425, 458–459, 461–462, 467–469, 510, 650, 788–789, 838–839, 879–881, 883–884, 1002, 1013–1015, 1044–1045, 1072–1073; vol. 12, pp. 59–60, 191–194.

35. Ibid., ser. D, vol. 11, 113–125, 132–133, 142–143, 164–165, 179–180, 187–189, 195–196, 204–205, 224, 268.

36. Rossi, pp. 170–171.

37. Nikolai G. Kuznetsov, *Nakanune* (Moscow: Voenizdat, 1969), p. 325.

38. *DGFP 1918–1945,* ser. D, vol. 11, pp. 187, 195–196, 224, 268, 291–297, 317, 327–328, 334–335, 353–354, 432, 438–439, 508–510, 521–522, 533–550, 562–570, 581.

39. Ibid.

40. Valentin M. Berezhkov, *S diplomaticheskoi missiei v Berlin, 1940–1941* (Moscow: Novosti, 1966), p. 47. See also Winston S. Churchill, *The Second World War* (Boston: Houghton, Mifflin), 1949, vol. 2, p. 586.

41. Churchill, vol. 2, p. 584.

42. [Rudolf] L[ikus], Confidential Reports, Nov. 13 and 14, 1940, Microfilm T120, Serial 36, Frames 25933, 25938–25939, German Foreign Ministry Archives, NA.

43. [Rudolf] L[ikus], Confidential Report, Nov. 22, 1940, Microfilm T120, Serial 36, Frame 25040, German Foreign Ministry Archives, NA.

44. Chuev, p. 27.

45. Gordon Wright, *The Ordeal of Total War 1939–1945* (New York: Harper and Row, 1968), p. 35.

46. *DGFP 1918–1945,* ser. D, vol. 11, pp. 714–715, 1124–1125.

47. Ibid., ser. D, vol. 11, p. 1156.

48. Warlimont, pp. 114–115, 135–148; Germany. Kriegsmarine Oberkommando, *Fuehrer Conferences on Matters Dealing with the German Navy 1940* (Washington, D.C.: U.S. Navy Department, 1947), vol. 2, pp. 41, 70–71.

49. *Fuehrer Conferences,* vol. 2, p. 71.

50. *Fuehrer Conferences,* vol. 1, p. 4.

51. Germany. Auswärtiges Amt, pp. 260–264.

52. Over the years the Russian state security service has undergone many organizational and name changes as its powers and responsibilities ebbed and, more often, flowed. The history of Soviet intelligence begins shortly after the October Revolution on December 20, 1917, with the creation of the All-Russian Extraordinary Commission for Combating Counter-Revolution and Sabotage *(Vecheka).* On February 6, 1922, it became the GPU (State Political Administration). This became the OGPU (Unified State Political Administration) on November 15, 1923. Political changes brought important organizational changes in 1934 when the GUGB (Main Administration for State Security) and an All-Union NKVD (People's Commissariat for Internal Affairs) were created. The GUGB's responsibilities included foreign intelligence,

and it was integrated into the latter's structure. On February 3, 1941, the NKGB (People's Commissariat of State Security) was created, separate from the NKVD, and it became the center for state security activity. Almost a month after the German attack on Russia, this arrangement was ended, and the situation reverted to the GUGB's being under the NKVD. While not underestimating the importance of these changes, for clarity, the term "NKVD" will be used throughout this period to describe Soviet intelligence. See Amy W. Knight, *The KGB: Police and Politics in the Soviet Union* (London: Allen & Unwin, 1988), pp. 35, 315; John J. Dziak, *Chekisty: A History of the KGB* (Lexington: D. C. Heath, 1988), pp. 184–185.

53. Pyotr Grigorenko, *Memoirs* (New York: Norton, 1982), p. 117.

54. Ibid.

55. The acronym GRU stands for *Glavnoye Razvedyvatelnoye Upravlenie* (Main Intelligence Directorate of the General Staff). While Soviet military intelligence has gone through organizational and name changes, for clarity, the term "GRU" will be used throughout. The GRU has been correctly described as the "most professional of all Soviet intelligence services," with "high professional standards, competence, and efficiency in intelligence matters" [Barton Whaley, *Codeword Barbarossa* (Cambridge: MIT Press, 1973), p. 194]. Also, see Viktor Suvorov (psued.), *Inside the Aquarium* (New York: Macmillan, 1986), pp. 5–6 and [Elizabeth Poretsky], "Soviet Military Intelligence: Comments on the Book 'Handbook for Spies' " (Santa Monica, California: Rand Corporation, August 12, 1949, revised October 12, 1949), RM-207a, pp. 5–6.

56. Grigorenko, *Memoirs,* pp. 117–118; Pyotr Grigorenko, *The Grigorenko Papers* (London: Hurst, 1976), p. 48; Viktor Suvorov (pseud.), *Soviet Military Intelligence* (London: Hamish Hamilton, 1984), pp. 24, 178; Ismail Akhmedov, *In and Out of Stalin's GRU: A Tatar's Escape from Red Army Intelligence* (Frederick: University Publications of America, 1984), p. 127.

57. Volkonogov, *Stalin,* p. 375.

58. Hallawell to Seeds, May 30, 1939, FO/371/23684; Suvorov, *Soviet Military Intelligence,* p. 178; Akhmedov, p. 127.

59. I. V. Uspensky, "Shto Skazal Doktor Kleist v 1939 Godu," *Voenno-istoricheskii zhurnal,* no. 12 (1991). 21n. 1, and Arkady Vaksberg, *The Prosecutor and the Prey* (London: Weidenfeld and Nicolson, 1990), p. 222.

60. V M. Kulish, "U poroga voiny," *Komsomolskaia pravda,* Aug. 24, 1988: 3.

61. Suvorov, *Soviet Military Intelligence,* pp. 22–24; Khrushchev, *Khrushchev Remembers,* pp. 154–155; Erickson, "Threat Identification and Strategic Appraisal by the Soviet Union, 1930–1941," p. 410; Akhmedov, pp. 109–120; Otto Preston Chaney, *Zhukov* (Norman: University of Oklahoma Press, 1971), p. 64.

62. F. H. Hinsley et al., *British Intelligence in the Second World War* (London: H. M. Stationery Office, 1979), vol. 1, p. 433.

63. Suvorov, *Soviet Military Intelligence,* pp. 30, 178–179; *Pravda,* Aug. 1, 1980: 3; *New York Times,* Aug. 1, 1980: B4; *Times* (London), Aug. 8, 1980: 12; Gabriel Gorodetsky, "Filip Ivanovich Golikov," in *Stalin's Generals,* ed. Harold Shukkman (New York: Grove Press, 1993), pp. 77–88.

64. Khrushchev, *Khrushchev Remembers,* p. 194n.; Gorodetsky, "Golikov," p. 79.

65. Anthony Read and David Fisher, *The Deadly Embrace: Hitler, Stalin and the Nazi-Soviet Pact 1939–1941* (New York: Norton, 1988), p. 617.

66. Vladimir Petrov, *"June 22, 1941"; Soviet Historians and the German Invasion* (Columbia: University of South Carolina Press, 1968), p. 257.

67. Heller and Nekrich, p. 362. Also, see Petrov, p. 254.

68. Read and Fisher, *The Deadly Embrace,* p. 618.

69. A[ndrei] Grechko, "25 let tomu nazad," *Voenno-istoricheskii zhurnal,* no. 6 (1966): 8.

70. Khrushchev, *Khrushchev Remembers,* p. 194.

71. Grigorenko, *Memoirs,* p. 117.

72. Ibid., pp. 115, 117–120. See also V[asili] Novobranets, "Nakanune voiny," *Znamia,* no. 6 (June 1990): 165–192.

73. Petrov, p. 253. Also, see Zhukov, pp. 233, 247; and "Marshal Zhukov on Soviet Leadership," pp. 8–9.

74. "Marshal Zhukov on Soviet Leadership," pp. 8–9; Zhukov, p. 247.

75. Petrov, p. 257; and [Anonymous], "Sovetskie organy gosudarstvennoi bezopasnosti v gody Velikoi Otechestvennoi Voiny," *Voprosy istorii* no. 5 (May 1965): 27.

76. Khrushchev, *Khrushchev Remembers,* pp. 133, 174.

77. Erickson, "Threat Identification and Strategic Appraisal by the Soviet Union, 1930–1941," p. 421.

78. Amy Knight, *Beria: Stalin's First Lieutenant* (Princeton: Princeton University Press, 1993), pp. 7–8, 57–62, and passim.

79. Walter Laqueur, "The Strange Lives of General Skoblin," *Encounter* 72, no. 3 (March 1989): 17; Walter Laqueur, *Soviet Realities* (New Brunswick: Transaction Publishers, 1990), p. 103, and Volkonogov, *Stalin,* p. 317.

80. Erickson, "Threat Identification and Strategic Appraisal by the Soviet Union, 1930–1941," p. 420; and John Erickson, *The Road to Stalingrad* (Boulder: Westview, 1984), p. 88.

81. Alexander Orlov, *Handbook of Intelligence and Guerrilla Warfare* (Ann Arbor: University of Michigan Press, 1963), p. 10.

82. Vaksberg, pp. 218–219.

83. [Rudolf] L[ikus], Confidential Report, Apr. 11, 1941, Microfilm T120, Serial 36, Frames 26015–26016, German Foreign Ministry Archives, NA.

84. Zhukov, p. 250.

85. Niels Erik Rosenfeldt, *Knowledge and Power. The Role of Stalin's Secret Chancellery in the Soviet System of Government* (Copenhagen: Rosenkilde and Bagger, 1978), passim. On Proskrebyshev, see Volkonogov, *Stalin,* pp. 155–156, 203–204, 268–269, 318, 330–331.

86. *FRUS, 1941,* vol. 1, p. 808; Robert E. Sherwood, *Roosevelt and Hopkins* (New York: Harper and Brothers, 1948), p. 335; Lord Balfour, Moscow Diary 1941, entry of Wed., Oct. 1, HLRO.

87. *FRUS, 1941,* vol. 1, p. 808; Sherwood, p. 335.

88. Embassy of the Union of Soviet Socialist Republics, Washington, D.C., *Information Bulletin* no. 128 (Mon., Dec. 15, 1941): 2.

89. *Pravda,* June 22, 1989: 3.

90. Khrushchev, *Khrushchev Remembers,* p. 129.

91. See Louis Rotundo, "Stalin and the Outbreak of War in 1941," *Journal of Contemporary History,* Vol. 24, No. 2 (April 1989), pp. 280–283. Note Stalin's views on the role of technology and the state of the German military in Dmitri Volkogonov,

"The German Attack, the Soviet Response, Sunday, 22 June 1941," in *Barbarossa: The Axis and the Allies,* ed. John Erickson and David Dilks (Edinburgh: Edinburgh University Press, 1994), pp. 78–79.

92. On the matter of a vigorous riposte and no fear of a German attack see discussions in this chapter, p. 17, and Chapters 3, p. 76, and 7, p. 193.

93. Berezhkov, *S diplomaticheskoi missiei,* p. 50.

94. Andrei Gromyko, *Memories* (London: Hutchinson, 1989), p. 38.

95. *Outline History of the U.S.S.R.,* trans. George H. Hanna (Moscow: Foreign Languages Publishing House, 1960), p. 319.

96. Harrison E. Salisbury, *The 900 Days: The Siege of Leningrad* (New York: Harper and Row, 1969), pp. 57, 70.

97. *FRUS. The Conference at Cairo and Teheran 1943,* p. 513.

98. Cecil, p. 113.

99. Ibid.; Hans von Herwarth [Bittenfeld] and S. Frederick Starr, *Against Two Evils* (New York: Rawson, Wade, 1981), p. 197. "The supplies from the Russians," it was noted in the Wilhelmstrasse, "have heretofore been a very substantial prop to the German war economy." Moreover, transit across Siberia was the only economic tie with Afghanistan, China, Iran, Japan, Latin America, and Manchuria (*DGFP 1918–1945,* ser. D, vol. 11, pp. 221–223). Also, see *DGFP 1918–1945,* vol. 12, pp. 19–21.

100. Germany. Auswärtiges Amt, p. 76.

101. Khrushchev, *Khrushchev Remembers,* pp. 167–168.

102. Erickson, "Threat Identification and Strategic Appraisal by the Soviet Union, 1930–1941," pp. 419–420.

103. Record of Conversation with Oumansky [by the Australian Minister], May 1, 1941, FO/371/29501. Somewhat analogous comments were voiced a week later by Umansky's Russian counterpart in Stockholm, who thought that Russia might be Germany's next victim, but the Red Army was prepared and the air force was formidable [Mallet (Stockholm) to the Foreign Office, no. 272, May 7, 1941, FO/371/29501]. On the Stalin-Churchill exchange of October 1944, see Record of Talks at the Kremlin at Supper on October 18th 1944 at 1 A.M., PREM3/434/7, PRO.

104. Ibid.

105. Walter Duranty, *The Kremlin and the People* (New York: Reynal and Hitchcock, 1941), pp. 188–189.

106. Svetlana Alliluyeva, *Only One Year* (New York: Harper and Row, 1969), p. 392.

107. Churchill, vol. 4, p. 493.

108. Petrov, p. 257.

109. Read and Fisher, *The Deadly Embrace,* p. 619.

110. Khrushchev, *Khrushchev Remembers,* p. 166; Khrushchev, *Khrushchev Remembers: The Glasnost Tapes,* p. 55; "Marshal Zhukov on Soviet Leadership," p. 2. Also, see Heller and Nekrich, p. 311.

111. Vojtech Mastny, *Russia's Road to the Cold War: Diplomacy, Warfare, and the Politics of Communism, 1941–1945* (New York: Columbia University Press, 1979), p. 34.

112. Whaley, pp. 251–252.

113. Cited in *Deception Operations: Studies in the East West Context,* ed. David A. Charters and Maurice A. J. Tugwell (London: Brassey's, 1990), p. 4.

114. Erickson, "Threat Identification," p. 419.

115. *NCA,* vol. 3, pp. 849–850.

116. Ibid.

117. Hinsley et al., vol. 1, p. 434.

118. *NCA,* vol. 5, pp. 734–735.

119. "Marshal Zhukov on Soviet Leadership," p. 4; Volkonogov, *Stalin,* pp. 399–400. Also, see Elena Rzhevskaya, "V tot den, pozdnei oseniun," *Znamia* no. 12 (Dec. 1986): 169; Robert Conquest, *Stalin: Breaker of Nations* (London: Weidenfeld and Nicolson, 1991), p. 234; and *Pravda,* June 20, 1988: 3.

120. "Marshal Zhukov on Soviet Leadership," p. 9.

121. Whaley, pp. 247–248.

122. Ibid., pp. 248–250.

123. Ibid., pp. 260, 262, 263.

124. On the impact of Goebbels's article in the *Volkischer Beobachter* on foreign circles in Berlin, see [Rudolf] L[ikus], Confidential Report, June 14, 1941, Microfilm T120, Serial 36, Frames 26075–26077, German Foreign Ministry Archives, NA.

125. Whaley, pp. 170–187, 247–266; Hans von Greiffenberg, Deception and Cover Plans, MS. # P–O44a; Erhard F. J. Raus, Strategic Deception, MS. # P–O44b; and Harald Weberstedt, Public Deception Regarding the Russian Campaign, MS. # P–O44c, Box 98, RG 338, NA; Charles Cruickshank, *Deception in World War II* (Oxford: Oxford University Press, 1979), pp. 207–212; Pavel A. Zhilin, *Kak fashistskaia Germaniia gotovila napadenie na Sovetskii Soiuz* (Moscow: Mysl', 1970), pp. 150–154; Zhukov, pp. 241–242; Svein Lorents Myklebust, *The Greatest Deception in the History of Warfare: Hitler's Deceptive Operations in the Months Prior to the Attack on Russia in June 1941* (Ann Arbor: University Microfilms International, 1982), passim; Hinsley et al., vol. 1, p. 448.

126. [Anonymous], "Sovetskie organy," pp. 23–24, 27.

127. Khrushchev, *Khrushchev Remembers,* p. 138.

128. On "deceiver" and "deceived" see Edward Jay Epstein, *Deception: The Invisible War between the KGB and the CIA* (New York: Simon and Schuster, 1989), pp. 215–216.

129. "Marshal Zhukov on Soviet Leadership," p. 8.

130. Petrov, p. 183.

131. *DGFP 1918–1945,* ser. D, vol. 8, p. 92.

132. Ibid., ser. D, vol. 8, p. 103.

133. N. N. Voronov, *Na sluzhbe voennoi* (Moscow: Voen, 1963), p. 175; and Ivan V. Tiulenev, *Cherez tri voiny* (Moscow: Voenizdat, 1960), p. 138.

134. Shirer, passim.

135. Erickson, "Threat Identification," p. 422.

136. Baggallay (Moscow) to Eden, no. 49, Mar. 9, 1942.

137. Erickson, "Threat Identification," pp. 418–423. Also, see Earl F. Ziemke, "Soviet Net Assessment in the 1930s," in *Calculations: Net Assessment and the Coming of World War II,* ed. Williamson Murray and Allan R. Millett (New York: Free Press, 1992), pp. 209–210; and Zhukov, p. 232. On demands and ultimatum, see Baggallay (Moscow) to Eden, no. 49, Mar. 9, 1942, and the enclosure, Political Review of Events in the Soviet Union during 1941, FO/371/3302/6; Breckinridge Long Diary, June 30, 1941, LC; Whaley, pp. 50–51, 117–118, 223, 241–242; Von

Hassell, *The Von Hassell Diaries*, p. 200; and W. Averell Harriman and Elie Abel, *Special Envoy to Churchill and Stalin 1941–1946* (New York: Random House, 1975), p. 80. "Churchill, the great optimist, wanted to believe that Russia was next on Hitler's list, and thought he could prove it," an investigator of this period has written, "while Stalin, because of his unpreparedness, chose to believe what Hitler wanted him to believe" (Myklebust, p. 269).

## Chapter 2: War and Rumors of War

1. [Anonymous], "Sovetskie organy gosudarstvennoi bezopasnosti v gody Velikoi Otechestvennoi Voiny," *Voprosy istorii* no. 5 (May 1965): 27. Also, see "Iz istorii Velikoi Otechestvennoi Voiny. Nakanune voiny (Dokumenty 1940–1941)," *Isvestiia TsK KPSS* no. 4 (April, 1990): 199, 202; and Franz Halder, *Kriegstagebuch* (Stuttgart: Kohlammer, 1963), vol. 2, pp. 9, 17, 39–40.

2. Pavel A. Zhilin, *Kak fashistskaia Germaniia gotovila napadenie na Sovetskii Soiuz* (Moscow: Mysl', 1970), p. 218. Also, see "Iz istorii Velikoi," 199–200. For the MI6 report see F. H. Hinsley et al., *British Intelligence in the Second World War* (London: H.M. Stationery Office, 1979), vol. 1, p. 433.

3. "Iz istorii Velikoi," p. 219. It would appear that the December report of General Tupikov misled Leopold Trepper, part of GRU operations in Western Europe. Trepper claimed that his associate in Tokyo, Richard Sorge, code-named "Ramzai," "immediately" warned Moscow after the Barbarossa directive was issued [Leopold Trepper, *The Great Game* (London: Michael Joseph, 1977), pp. 125–126]. How Sorge, sitting in the German embassy in Tokyo, could have so quickly acquired a copy of Directive 21, with the very tight security exercised over the document, goes unexplained. There is no evidence to warrant Trepper's claim. See Gordon W. Prange et al., *Target Tokyo. The Story of the Sorge Spy Ring* (New York: McGraw-Hill, 1984), p. 322. What Sorge did report on November 18, before the Barbarossa directive was issued, was the possiblity of a German attack against Russia. On December 28, after the Barbarossa directive was issued, he reported the formation of a forty-division reserve force based in Leipzig. See V. D. Danilov, "Sovetskoe glavnoe komandovanie v preddverii velikoi otechestvennoi voiny," *Novaia i noveishaia istoriia* no. 6 (1988): 17–18; and Ovidii Gorchakov, "Nakanune, ili tragediia Kassandry," *Nedelia* no. 42 (Oct. 17–23, 1988): 12.

4. [Anonymous], "Sovetskie organy," p. 27.

5. Nikolai Kuznetsov, "Voenno-Morskoi Flot nakanune Velikoi Otechestvennoi Voiny," *Voenno-istoricheskii zhurnal* no. 9 (1965): 67–68. By March 9 the NKVD learned from Berlin through its agent in the Air Ministry, Lieutenant Schulze-Boysen, of the successful and accelerating aerial photography of Russian military installations, especially of the naval base at Kronstadt. "Iz istorii Velikoi," p. 206.

6. Trepper, p. 126. Schulze-Boysen's report did not arrive in Moscow until March 24. See "Iz istorii Velikoi," p. 207; for the code name, see p. 202.

7. Kuznetsov, "Voenno-morskoi flot," p. 68. These and other similar events and warnings are also discussed in A. V. Basov, *Flot v Velikoii Otechestvennoi Voine, 1941–1945* (Moscow: Nauka, 1980), pp. 58–69.

8. Kuznetsov, "Voenno-morskoi flot," p. 68. For some of the intelligence data on Bulgaria see "Iz istorii Velikoi," p. 202.

9. Valentin M. Berezhkov, *S diplomaticheskoi missiei v Berlin, 1940–1941* (Moscow: Novosti, 1966), p. 79.

10. Nikolai G. Kuznetsov, *Nakanune* (Moscow: Voenizdat, 1969), pp. 324–325.

11. Georgii Zhukov, *Vospominaniia i razmyshleniia* (Moscow: Novosti, 1969), pp. 248–249. On the report of March 9, see "Iz istorii Velikoi," p. 219. Germany's desire to capture Russia's grain and energy resources was initially voiced by the first secretary of the Greek Legation in Moscow, believed by his minister, and reported by Russian counterintelligence in early 1941. See ibid., p. 205.

12. David Kahn, *Hitler's Spies: German Military Intelligence in World War II* (New York: Macmillan, 1978), pp. 454, 601n.

13. "Iz istorii Velikoi," p. 216.

14. Barry A. Leach, *German Strategy Against Russia 1939–1941* (Oxford: Clarendon Press, 1973), p. 91; Albert Seaton, *The Russo-German War 1941–45* (London: Arthur Barker, 1971), pp. 43–49; Paul Leverkuehn, *German Military Intelligence* (New York: Praeger, 1954), pp. 155–161; Lauran Paine, *German Military Intelligence in World War II* (New York: Stein and Day, 1984), pp. 152–153.

15. "Iz istorii Velikoi," passim.

16. Gorchakov, "Nakanune, ili tragediia Kassandry," *Nedelia* no. 42, p. 12.

17. Helmuth Greiner, *Die Oberste Wehrmachtführung 1939–1943* (Wiesbaden: Limes, 1951), pp. 312–313.

18. Germany. Wehrmacht, Oberkommando der Wehrmachtführungsstab, *Kriegstagebuch 1 August 1940–31 Dezember 1941,* ed. Percy Ernst Schramm (Frankfurt am Main: Bernard and Graefe, 1965), vol. 1, p. 120; Halder, vol. 2, p. 120.

19. Mikhail Gorokhov, "From the NKVD to the Polish Army," Box 1, David Dallin Papers, CU.

20. Hinsley et al., vol. 1, pp. 435–436.

21. Čestmir Amort and I. M. Jedlička, *Hledá se Zrádce X* (Prague: NVSPB, 1968), pp. 149–151. Thummel's activities are also discussed, although not as fully, in Rudolf Ströbinger, *Stopa Vede k Renému* (Prague: Lidova Demokracie, 1966), pp. 92–105. Also, see Janusz Piekalkiewicz, *Secret Agents, Spies & Saboteurs* (Newton Abbot: David and Charles, 1976), pp. 132–140. On the German engagement and incitement of emigré Russians and Ukrainians, see the Czech Intelligence Reports no. 6 (Nov. 2–7, 1940), no. 9 (Nov. 25–Dec. 2, 1940), and no. 10 (Dec. 2–9, 1940), FO/371/24292; and Robert Bruce Lockhart, *The Diaries of Sir Robert Bruce Lockhart,* ed. Kenneth Young (London: Macmillan, 1980), vol. 2, p. 97. On the Russian knowledge of the emigrés see, "Iz istorii Velikoi," p. 199. For discussion of the "walk-in," see William Hood, *Mole* (New York: Norton, 1982), p. 33. Additional background on Thummel can be found in Jan G. Wiener, *The Assassination of Heydrich* (New York: Grossman, 1969), pp. 61–69 and František Moravec, *Master of Spies* (Garden City, New York: Doubleday, 1975), passim. On Beneš's suspicions and a possible Canaris connection, see Callum MacDonald, *The Killing of SS Obergruppenführer Reinhard Heydrich* (New York: The Free Press, 1989), pp. 55, 71; and *Dokumenty z historie československé politiky 1939–1943. [Acta Occupationis Bohemiae & Moraviae],* ed. Libuše Otáhalová and Milada Červinková (Prague: Academia, 1966), vol. 1, pp. 187–188; as well as Nigel West, *MI6: British Secret Intelligence Service Operations, 1909–1945* (New York: Random House, 1983), p. 93.

22. Hinsley et al., vol. 1, p. 436n; F. H. Hinsley, "British Intelligence and Barbarossa," in *Barbarossa: The Axis and the Allies,* ed. John Erickson and David Dilks (Edinburgh: Edinburgh Universiy Press, 1994), pp. 46–47.

23. Amort and Jedlička, p. 145.

24. Eduard Beneš, *Memoirs of Dr. Eduard Beneš* (London: Allen and Unwin, 1954), p. 150; and Moravec, pp. 91–92.

25. Beneš, p. 137; and Ivan Maisky, *Vospominaniia Sovetskogo posla: voina 1939–1943* (Moscow: Nauka, 1965), p. 152, as well as Josef Korbel, *The Communist Subversion of Czechoslovakia, 1938–1948* (Princeton: Princeton University Press, 1959), p. 78.

26. Bruce Lockhart, Soviet Approaches to Dr. Beneš: Suggested Return to Moscow of Dr. [Zdenek] Fierlinger, the Former Czechoslovak Minister to the U.S.S.R., May 17, 1940, FO/371/24856.

27. Alexander Cadogan, *The Diaries of Sir Alexander Cadogan,* ed. David Dilks (London: Cassell, 1971), p. 363.

28. Maisky, p. 125. Also, see Maisky's comments in Amort and Jedlička, p. 136.

29. Bruce Lockhart, Soviet Approaches to Dr. Beneš, May 17, 1940, Lothian (Washington) to the Foreign Office, no. 758, May 18, 1940 and no. 748, May 22, 1940, Foreign Office to Lothian, no. 931, May 29, 1940, Bruce Lockhart, Record of Conversation with M. Fierlinger, Former Czechoslovak Minister to Russia, June 12, 1940, and the attached minutes, FO/371/24856.

30. Moravec, pp. 188, 190; Edward Taborsky, *President Edvard Beneš; Between East and West 1918–1948* (Stanford: Hoover Institution Press, 1981), p. 137; Detlef Brandes, *Die Tschechen unter Deutschem Protektorat* (München: Oldenbourg, 1969), vol. 1, pp. 185–186.

31. Robert Bruce Lockhart, *Friends, Foes, and Foreigners* (London: Putnam, 1957), pp. 133, 137–138; Amort and Jedlička, p. 135; and Otáhalová and Červinková, vol. 1, pp. 139–140, 147, 185, 197; Beneš, pp. 146, 164n. 9; Lockhart to Sargent, Mar. 12, 1941, FO/371/29480.

32. Foreign Office to Cripps, no. 234, Mar. 21, 1941, Cripps (Moscow) to the Foreign Office, no. 264, Mar. 24, 1941, Sargent to Lockhart, Mar. 28, 1941, Lockhart to Sargent, Mar. 28, 1941, and the attached minutes, FO/371/29537; Bruce Lockhart Diary, Sun., Mar. 9, 1941, Mon. Mar. 10, 1941, and Sat., Apr. 26, 1941, HLRO; Lockhart to Sargent, [late April 1941], FO/371/29480; [Lockhart] to Beaverbrook, Sept. 10, 1941, D/339, Beaverbrook Papers, HLRO; Lockhart, *Friends, Foes, and Foreigners,* pp. 137–138.

33. Otáhalová and Červinková, vol. 1, pp. 104–105.

34. Moravec, p. 128n.

35. Amort and Jedlička, pp. 135–136.

36. Piekalkiewicz, p. 143.

37. Amort and Jedlička, pp. 151 and 275n. 119.

38. Moravec, pp. 45–57, 88–89, 92–95. Also, see Beneš, p. 41.

39. Richard A. Woytak, *On the Border of War and Peace: Polish Intelligence and Diplomacy in 1937–1939 and the Origins of the Ultra Secret* (Boulder: Eastern European Quarterly; New York: Distributed by Columbia University Press, 1979), p. 22.

40. Amort and Jedlička, pp. 51–53, 133–134.

41. See Beneš, p. 85.

42. Robert Bruce Lockhart Diary, Thurs., Jan. 23, 1941, HLRO.

43. MacDonald, p. 71.

44. Moravec, pp. 95, 143–146, 148–149, 151–153. On Dansey see Patrick Howarth, *Intelligence Chief Extraordinary: The Life of the Ninth Duke of Portland* (London: Bodley Head, 1986), p. 119 and Anthony Read and David Fisher, *Colonel Z: The Life and Times of a Master of Spies* (London: Hodder and Stoughton, 1984), pp. 275–277. For the £50,000 sterling, see Otáhalová and Červinková, vol. 1, p. 85. In an article, general in scope, Moravec's deputy confirms much of what Beneš, Maisky, and Moravec have written. See Emil Strankmuller, "Čs. Ofenzívní Zpravodajství od Března 1939," *Odboj a Revoluce* (Prague) 8, no. 1 (1970): 210–219.

45. John Costello, *Ten Days to Destiny* (New York: Morrow, 1991), pp. 447, 453–454, and 580n. 36.

46. Peter Wright, *Spycatcher* (New York: Viking, 1987), p. 352. Equally ungenerous are the comments of Edward Jay Epstein, *Deception: The Invisible War between the KGB and the CIA* (New York: Simon and Schuster, 1989), who categorizes Beneš as an agent of Russian influence, someone "secretly in the debt . . . if not the pay" of Moscow (p. 254).

47. Alexander Orlov, *Handbook of Intelligence and Guerrilla Warfare* (Ann Arbor: University of Michigan Press, 1963), pp. 6–7, 10, 12. See also Chapter 1, p. 14.

48. Otáhalová and Červinková, vol. 1, p. 185.

49. Ivan Pfaff, "Prag und der Fall Tuchatschewski," *Vierteljahrshefte fur Zeitgeschichte* 34, no. 1 (1987): 95–134; Dmitri Volkogonov, *Stalin: Triumph and Tragedy* (London: Weidenfeld and Nicolson, 1991), pp. 317–324; Walter Laqueur, "The Strange Lives of General Skoblin," *Encounter* 72, no. 3 (March 1989): 11–20; Walter Laqueur, *Soviet Realities* (New Brunswick: Transaction Publishers, 1990), pp. 99–109; Walter Schellenberg, *The Schellenberg Memoirs* (London: Deutsch, 1956), pp. 46–49; Gunter Peis, *The Man Who Started the War* (London: Odhams, 1960), pp. 76–102; Beneš, p. 47n. 8; Moravec, pp. 91–92; John Erickson, *The Soviet High Command* (London: Macmillan, 1962), pp. 433–436; Paul W. Blackstock, *The Secret Road to World War Two: The Soviet Versus Western Intelligence 1921–1939* (Chicago: Quadrangle Books, 1969), pp. 287–295; Winston S. Churchill, *The Second World War* (Boston: Houghton Mifflin, 1948) vol. 1, pp. 288–290 and n.; Wilhelm Hoettl, *The Secret Front. The Story of Nazi Political Espionage* (London: Weidenfeld and Nicolson, 1953), pp. 79–87; John J. Dziak, *Chekisty: A History of the KGB* (Lexington: Lexington Books, 1987), pp. 96–97; Geoffrey Bailey (psued.), *The Conspirators* (London: Gollancz, 1961), pp. 118–224; Robert Conquest, *The Great Terror* (London: Macmillan, 1968), pp. 219–221; Robert C. Tucker, *Stalin in Power: The Revolution from Above, 1928–1941* (New York: Norton, 1990), pp. 381–384. For a different view of the Tukhachevsky affair, see Pavel Sudoplatov and Anatoli Sudoplatov with Jerrold L. Schecter and Leona P. Schecter, *Special Tasks* (New York: Little, Brown, and Company, 1994), pp. 87–96.

50. Amort and Jedlička, p. 134.

51. Kurt Glaser, *Czecho-Slovakia: A Critical History* (Caldwell, Idaho: Caxton, 1961), pp. 70–73.

52. William L. Shirer, *The Rise and Fall of the Third Reich* (New York: Simon and Schuster, 1960), p. 843n. Also, see William Russell, *Berlin Embassy* (London: Michael Joseph, 1942), pp. 52–53.

53. John V. H. Dippel, *Two Against Hitler: Stealing the Nazis' Best-Kept Secrets* (New York: Praeger, 1992), passim.

54. Cordell Hull, *Memoirs* (New York: Macmillan, 1948), vol. 2, p. 968.

55. Walter Laqueur and Richard Breitman, *Breaking the Silence* (New York: Simon and Schuster, 1986), p. 282n.

56. Barton Whaley, *Codeword Barbarossa* (Cambridge: MIT Press, 1973), p. 38 and fn.

57. Ibid., pp. 38–39. Also, see Hull, vol. 2, p. 968.

58. Hans von Herwarth [Bittenfeld] and S. Frederick Starr, *Against Two Evils* (New York: Rawson, Wade, 1981), pp. 177–178. As to the purveyors of "legends," aside from Whaley, already cited, see William Stevenson, *A Man Called Intrepid* (London: Macmillan, 1976), pp. 206–207. On his American friends, see Herwarth and Starr, passim and Charles E. Bohlen, *Witness to History 1929–1969* (New York: Norton, 1973), pp. 69–88.

59. Anthony Read and David Fisher, *The Deadly Enemies: Hitler, Stalin and the Nazi-Soviet Pact 1939–1941* (New York: Norton, 1988), p. 605.

60. A handwritten message by the source in German, and addressed to the Embassy of the United States, dated 27.12.40, MID File 2016–1326–7, Military Intelligence Division Correspondence, 1917–1941, Box 634, RG 165, NA.

61. Adolf A. Berle Diary, Jan. 26, [1945], Box 216, FDR Library.

62. Hull, vol. 2, p. 968.

63. Laqueur and Breitman, p. 282n.

64. Hull, vol. 2, p. 968.

65. Military Intelligence Division, War Department, General Staff, Report 17,875, Jan. 17, 1941 by Colonel B. R. Peyton, MID File 2016–1326/7, Military Intelligence Division, Correspondence, 1917–1941, Box 634, RG 165, NA.

66. Ibid.

67. Ibid.

68. Ibid.

69. Hull, vol. 2, p. 968.

70. Ibid.; Sumner Welles, *The Time for Decision* (New York: Harper, 1944), pp. 170–171.

71. Adolf A. Berle Diary, Jan. 26, [1945], Box 216, FDR Library; Memo. of Con. (Oumansky, Welles), June 26, 1941, File 740.0011 European War 1939/12914, RG 59, NA; *FRUS, 1941,* vol. 4, p. 742; Arkady Vaksberg, *The Prosecutor and the Prey* (London: Weidenfeld and Nicolson, 1990), p. 218.

72. Welles, p. 171.

73. Adolf A. Berle Diary, Jan. 26, [1945], Box 216, FDR Library; Adolf A. Berle, *Navigating the Rapids 1918–1971,* ed. Beatrice Bishop Berle and Travis Beal Jacobs (New York: Harcourt Brace Jovanovich, 1973), p. 518; Loy W. Henderson, *A Question of Trust: The Origins of US-Soviet Diplomatic Relations: The Memoirs of Loy W. Henderson,* ed. George W. Baer (Stanford: Hoover Institution Press, 1986), p. 500.

74. Berle, *Navigating the Rapids,* p. 518. Also, see Ladislas Faragó, *The Broken Seal* (New York: Random House, 1967), p. 197. It is highly unlikely that Umansky on his own initiative would have approached Thomsen with this information. More likely he was instructed by Moscow to convey it to Thomsen, in order to show that Moscow had no doubts about Berlin's fidelity to the 1939 pact. At the same time, Moscow may have wished to signal Berlin that, should there have been substance to this information, they were alerted by it.

75. Ruth R. Harris, "The 'Magic' Leak of 1941 and Japanese-American Relations," *Pacific Historical Review* 50, no. 1 (February 1981): 82 and n. 15.

76. Henry Morgenthau Diary, Sept. 19, 1940, pp. 76–77, Box 307, FDR Library.

77. Document 514, Dec. 3, 1941, Box 12 (FBI Reports nos. 503–560), Office File 10b, Department of Justice, FDR Library.

78. Forrest Davis and Ernest K. Lindley, *How War Came* (New York: Simon and Schuster, 1942), p. 175.

79. Berle, *Navigating the Rapids,* p. 374. After the German attack in June 1941, Berle opposed the proposal to allow Russian engineers into American defense plants producing secret weapons. "In point of fact, the engineers they have wished to let into the plants," he wrote, "are the same ones who were doing espionage for Russia and Germany until six weeks ago" (Ibid). Also, see Raymond E. Lee, Journal (typescript) entry October 30, 1941, pp. 1–2, U.S. Army Military History Institute, CB.

The FBI was equally opposed to the proposal that Russian experts should be given a "free hand to inspect" industries engaged in armaments manufacture. It hoped that London would adopt a similar stance. The Russians would be treated "on a strictly reciprocal basis," Lord Halifax was informed, so as to induce them to allow British examination of armaments industries and other installations in which London was interested [Halifax (Washington) to the Foreign Office, no. 3708, Aug. 7, 1941 and Foreign Office to Washington, no. 4599, Aug. 18, 1941, FO/371/29562].

During this period Nazi-Communist collaboration on intelligence matters was not restricted to the United States. In the course of the negotiations that led to the 1939 pact, a warm NKVD-Gestapo camaraderie was manifested publicly (Volkonogov, *Stalin,* p. 387, and Herwarth [Bittenfeld] and Starr, p. 165). In partitioned Poland, for example, the Gestapo and the NKVD closely cooperated to combat the Polish resistance movement [see Tadeusz Bor-Komorowski, *The Secret Army* (London: Gollancz, 1951), pp. 46–47]. Likewise, about "800 German and Austrian communists" who had fled to Soviet Russia "were handed over to the tender mercies of the Gestapo" [Jonathan Lewis and Phillip Whitehead, *Stalin: A Time for Judgement* (London: Methuen, 1990), p. 117]. Some of them who were Jews were quietly surrendered by the NKVD at Brest-Litovsk to the German security services. See Margarete Buber, *Under Two Dictators* (London: Gollancz, 1950), pp. 162–166; F. Beck and W. Godin, *Russian Purge and the Extraction of Confession* (New York: Viking, 1951), pp. 126–127; Alexander Weissberg, *The Accused* (New York: Simon and Schuster, 1951), pp. 502–506; and Viktor A. Kravchenko, *Kravchenko versus Moscow; The Report of the Famous Paris Case* (London: Wingate, 1950), pp. 205–206. For a NKVD boast that information was being exchanged with the Gestapo see Evgeni Gnedin, "Sebia ne poteriat," *Novy Mir* no. 7 (July 1988): 196–197.

Cooperation between the German and Russian militaries had manifested itself early. Captured Polish soldiers of German background or born in areas incorporated into Nazi Germany were swapped by the Russians for Ukrainians and Belorussians captured by the Germans [Jan Karski, *Story of a Secret State* (Boston: Houghton Mifflin, 1944), pp. 25–33]. In the period before the attack on Soviet Russia, the Germans, in negotiations with the French Communist party, "had reached the stage of discussing permission to let *L'Humanite* appear." In Norway and Belgium "Communist periodicals were briefly allowed" to circulate (Conquest, *The Great Terror,* p. 218n).

80. Hoover to Berle, June 25, 1941, and the attached memorandum, June 24, 1941, File 740.0011 European War 1939/12631, RG 59, NA.

81. Gabriel Gorodetsky, *Stafford Cripps' Mission to Moscow, 1940–1942* (Cambridge: Cambridge University Press, 1984), p. 248.

82. Peyton to the A[ssistant] C[hief] of S[taff], G-2 [Intelligence], War Department, Washington, D.C., Feb. 10, 1941, no. 17,965, Folder: 4000–Germany, Records of the War Department, General and Special Staffs, Box 1096, RG 165, NA.

83. Breckinridge Long Diary, Feb. 21, 1941, LC. For the edited version, see Breckinridge Long, *The War Diary of Breckinridge Long,* ed. Fred L. Israel (Lincoln: University of Nebraska, 1966), pp. 182–184.

84. Henry C. Cassidy, *Moscow Dateline 1941–1943* (Boston: Houghton Mifflin, 1943), p. 76.

85. *FRUS, 1941,* vol. 1, p. 712.

86. Ibid., vol. 1, p. 714.

87. Ibid., vol. 1, pp. 713–714.

88. *DGFP 1918–1945,* ser. D., vol. 12, p. 285.

89. Heinrich Brüning, *Briefe und Gespräche 1934–1945* (Stuttgart: Deutsche Verlags-Anstalt, 1974), pp. 344–345 and nn.; and Dippel, pp. 5–6, 12, 17–18, 47.

90. Military Intelligence Division, War Department, General Staff, Report 17,875, Jan. 17, 1941 by Colonel B. R. Peyton, MID File 2016–1326/7, Military Intelligence Division, Correspondence, 1917–1941, Box 634, RG 165, NA.

91. See earlier in this chapter, p. 37.

92. Brüning, p. 345n. On Bohlen's postwar admission, see Laqueur and Breitman, p. 282n. Also see Breckinridge Long Diary, Mar. 11, 1941, LC. On Respondek also see Whaley, pp. 38, 93, 150, 277n. Brüning had "asserted" that the documents examined by him were "authentic," Long noted after the conversation (B[reckinridge] L[ong], Memo. Mar. 7, 1941, Folder: 4000–Germany, Records of the War Department, General and Special Staffs, Box 1096, RG 165, NA).

93. Breckinridge Long Diary, Mar. 11, 1941, LC. The pertinent translated documents can be found in Folder: Germany, President's Secretary File, Box 4, FDR Library.

94. Franklin D. Roosevelt, *F. D. R.: His Personal Letters, 1928–1945,* ed. Elliott Roosevelt (New York: Duell, Sloan, and Pearce, 1950), vol. 2, p. 1130; F[ranklin] D. R[oosevelt], Memo. for the Sec. of State, Mar. 7, 1941, Folder: Cordell Hull 1941–1942, President's Secretary File Box 93, FDR Library; E[dwin] M. W[atson], Memo. for the President, Mar. 5, 1941, Hull to the President, Mar. 5, 1941 and Mar. 13, 1941, Folder: Germany, President's Secretary File, Box 4, ibid.

95. Halifax (Washington) to the Foreign Office, no. 1047, Mar. 7, 1941, FO/371/26518.

96. Long, *The War Diary,* pp. 188–189. For a synopsis of the document, see Military Intelligence Division, War Department, General Staff, no. 18,018, Feb. 24, 1941, by J. R. Lovell, Folder: 4000–Germany, Records of the War Department, General and Special Staff, Box 1096, RG 165, NA. Also, see Military Intelligence Division, War Department, General Staff, no. 18,019, Feb. 24, 1941, by J. R. Lovell, MID File 2016–1297/181, Military Intelligence Division, Correspondence, 1917–1941, Box 633, RG 165, NA.

97. Hoyer-Millar (Washington) to Hopkinson, June 17, 1941, and Hopkinson to [Alexander] Hardinge, June 26, 1941, FO/371/26521. Hinsley, "British Intelligence and Barbarossa," p. 51.

98. *FRUS, 1941,* vol. 1, p. 723.

99. [General Yoshitsugu] Tatekawa (Moscow) to Harbin, no. 5, Mar. 14, 1941, SRDJ no. 010455, Box 12, RG 457, NA. On unravelling the code see Ronald William Clark, *The Man Who Broke Purple* (London: Weidenfeld and Nicolson, 1977). Based on "anonymous" sources, erroneous assertions have been made that during this period Welles had engaged in personal diplomacy to "wean" Russia from Germany by alerting Moscow of the impending German attack. To accomplish this, he supposedly showed Umansky copies of the intercepted Japanese messages, as well as memoranda from the Army's Signal Intelligence Service that contained clear references to Magic. It is contended that this action by Welles led to the Germans' becoming aware that the Americans had unraveled the Purple code (Faragó, pp. 196, 412). Unfortunately, this claim was accepted uncritically (Whaley, pp. 42–46). Welles was not without fault. Nevertheless, he was an intelligent and experienced diplomatic officer. Since he had been warned by the Federal Bureau of Investigation of Umansky's conversations with the German chargé d'affaires, Hans Thomsen, it borders on the absurd to claim, without specific evidence, that Welles would have made available to Umansky Magic decrypts or memoranda by the Army's Signal Intelligence Service. German knowledge of Magic (*DGFP 1918–1945,* ser. D, vol. 12, p. 661), it has been plausibly argued, probably came from the failure of the British embassy in Washington to transmit Magic material given to it by Welles in a high level secure code (Harris, pp. 83–84). Fortunately, and much to the relief of the cryptologists of the Army's Signal Intelligence Service, the Japanese ignored the German warning that the Americans could read the Purple code (Whaley, pp. 43–46).

100. Memo. from the Royal Greek Legation, Washington, Mar. 19, 1941, File 740.0011 European War 1939/9288, RG 59, NA; *FRUS, 1941,* vol. 1, p. 723n. Also, see Wilhelm M. Carlgren, *Swedish Foreign Policy during the Second World War* (New York: St. Martin's Press, 1977), p. 101.

101. Greek Note to the Foreign Office, Mar. 11, 1941, FO/371/29779.

102. *FRUS, 1941,* vol. 1, pp. 133–134.

103. [Greek] Foreign Ministry, *1940–41 Greek Diplomatic Documents* [in Greek] (Athens, 1980), p. 151 and n.

104. Gunnar Hagglof, *Samtida Vittne 1940–1945* (Stockholm: Norstedt, 1972), pp. 96–97.

105. Sterling (Stockholm) to the Sec. of State, no. 199, Apr. 25, 1941, File 740.0011, European War 1939/9969, RG 59, NA.

106. O'Malley (Budapest) to the Foreign Office, no. 140, Mar. 6, 1941, FO/371/26518.

107. Mallet (Stockholm) to the Foreign Office, no. 133, Mar. 7, 1941, FO/371/26518.

108. Minutes by A[lexander] C[adogan], Mar. 11 and Mar. 28, 1941, FO/371/26518.

109. Breckinridge Long Diary, Apr. 4, 1941, LC.

110. Memo. of Con., [Long, Brüning], Apr. 4, 1941, Folder: Germany, Breckinridge Long Papers, LC.

111. [Brüning] to [Long], Apr. 10, 1941, Folder: 4000–Germany, Records of the War Department, General and Special Staffs, Box 1096, RG 165, NA.

112. These documents can be found in the folder: Germany, President's Secretary File, Box 4, FDR Library, and Report Three, End of April, 1941, Folder: 4000

Germany, Records of the War Department, General and Special Staffs, Box 1096, RG 165, NA.

113. B[reckinridge] L[ong] to [Watson], May 12, 1941, Folder: 4000 Germany, Records of the War Department, General and Special Staffs, Box 1096, RG 165, NA; E[dwin] M. W[atson], Memo. for the President, May 12, 1941, Hull to the President, May 12, 1941, C[ordell] H[ull], Memo. for the President, June 5, 1941, Welles to the President, July 7, 1941, Folder: Germany, President's Secretary File, Box 4, FDR Library.

114. Hoyer-Millar (Washington) to Hopkins, June 17, 1941, FO/371/26521.

115. Hopkinson to Hardinge, June 26, 1941, FO/371/26521.

116. Vladimir Petrov, *"June 22, 1941"; Soviet Historians and the German Invasion* (Columbia: University of South Carolina Press, 1968), pp. 180–181.

117. United States. Congress. Committee on the Investigation of the Pearl Harbor Attack, *Pearl Harbor Attack,* Hearing before the Joint Committee on the Investigation of the Pearl Harbor Attack, 79th Congress, 1st sess., pt. 34 (Washington, D.C.: Government Printing Office, 1946), pp. 190–191.

118. See John Erickson, *The Road to Stalingrad* (Boulder: Westview, 1984), pp. 77, 80, 89.

119. See Chapter 1, p. 17.

120. *DGFP 1918–1945,* ser. D, vol. 11, pp. 1066–1069.

121. For German troop movements through December 1940, see "Iz istorii Velikoi," pp. 199–204.

122. Paul Paillole, *Services Speciaux 1935–1945* (Paris: Laffont, 1975), pp. 336–337.

123. David J. Dallin, *Soviet Espionage* (New Haven: Yale University Press, 1955), p. 209.

124. Sándor Radó, *Dora Jelenti* (Budapest: Kossuth Könyvkiadó, 1972), p. 135.

125. Laqueur and Breitman, p. 101; Hinsley, "British Intelligence and Barbarossa," p.48.

126. Bor-Komorowski, pp. 56–63.

127. Hinsley et al., vol. 1, pp. 445–446. German troop movements east were brought to the attention of the Foreign Office even earlier by the Polish government-in-exile (Polish Ministry of Foreign Affairs to the Foreign Office, Jan. 16, 1941, FO/371/29479). Others have erroneously reported that it was only in March 1941 that the Polish resistance informed the government-in-exile of the German troop concentrations along the Russian frontier. See, for example, Churchill, vol. 3, p. 390, and Jan Ciechanowski, *Defeat in Victory* (Garden City, New York: Doubleday, 1947), p. 24. The movement of German troops east until the moment of the attack was continuously reported by the Polish resistance, which showed ingenuity, tenacity and enormous courage. See *Armia Krajowa w Dokumentach 1939–1945,* ed. Halina Czarnocka et al. (Londyn: Studium Polski Podziemnej, 1970), vol. 1, pp. 516–520, 539–543, 548–549, 550–551; Stanislaw Mikolajczyk, *The Rape of Poland* (New York: McGraw-Hill, 1948), p. 11; The Countess of Listowel, *Crusader in the Secret War* (London: Christopher Johnson, 1952), pp. 77–97.

128. Berezhkov, *S diplomaticheskoi missiei,* p. 80.

129. Danilov, p. 18, and Gorchakov, "Nakanune, ili tragediia Kassandry," p. 12.

130. Hinsley et al., vol. 1, p. 445.

131. Future Operations (Enemy) Planning Section, Jan. 8, 1941, in Chiefs of Staff Committee (41) 23, Jan. 9, 1941, CAB/80/25, PRO. On the short history of the Future Operations Enemy Planning Section, see Wesley K. Wark, "British Intelligence and Operation Barbarossa, 1941: The Failure of the F.O.E.S.," in *In the Name of Intelligence: Essays in Honor of Walter Pforzheimer,* ed. Hayden B. Peake and Samuel Halperin (Washington: NIBC Press, 1994), pp. 499–512.

132. No. 54, MI14, Military Indications of German Intentions Towards Russia, Jan. 17, 1941, WO/190/893, PRO.

133. No. 13B, Future Axis Strategy in Europe and the Middle East, Feb. 6, 1941, WO/190/893, PRO.

134. Chiefs of Staff Committee, Weekly Resumé, no. 75, Jan. 30–Feb. 16, 1941, CAB/80/25, PRO.

135. Minute by F[itzroy] H. R. Maclean, Jan. 15, [1941], FO/371/29479.

136. Hoare (Bucharest) to the Foreign Office, no. 38, Jan. 9, 1941, FO/371/29500.

137. *DGFP 1918–1945,* ser. D, vol. 11, pp. 1122, 1124, 1144, 1156, 1172.

138. Mallet (Stockholm) to the Foreign Office, no. 35, Jan. 11, 1941 and the attached minute by F[itzroy] H. R. Maclean, Jan. 15 [1941], FO/371/29479.

139. Sterling (Stockholm) to the Sec. of State, no. 58, Jan. 25, 1941, File 740.0011 European War 1939/7909, RG 59, NA.

140. W. M. (41) 20, Feb. 24, 1941, CAB/65/21, PRO.

141. Ministry of Economic Warfare, Trans-Siberian Railway: Freight Rates, Apr. 3, 1941, FO/371/29497.

142. Air Ministry, Weekly Intelligence Survey, no. 85, Apr. 16, 1941, AIR/22/74, PRO.

143. Mallet (Stockholm) to the Foreign Office, no. 72, Jan. 26, 1941, Clark-Kerr (Chungking) to the Foreign Office, no. 89, Feb. 19, 1941 and Cripps (Moscow) to the Foreign Office, no. 153, Feb. 21, 1941, FO/371/27956.

144. Air Ministry, Weekly Intelligence Survey, no. 99 (July 23, 1941), AIR/22/74, PRO.

145. Air Ministry, Weekly Intelligence Survey, no. 79 (Mar. 5, 1941), no. 83 (Apr. 2, 1941), no. 86 (Apr. 23, 1941), and no. 92 (June 4, 1941), AIR/22/74, PRO; Cripps (Moscow) to the Foreign Office, no. 63, Mar. 27, 1941, FO/371/29497. Also, see *DGFP 1918–1945,* ser. D, vol. 12, pp. 282–283, 474–475.

146. Hoare (Madrid) to the Foreign Office, no. 418, Mar. 7, 1941, FO/371/29500.

147. Franz von Papen, *Der Wahrheit eine Gasse* (München: List, 1952), p. 528.

148. Cripps (Moscow) to Halifax, Nov. 26, 1941, FO/371/29506.

149. Feliks I. Chuev, *Sto sorok besed s Molotovym: iz dnevnika F. Chueva* (Moscow: Terra, 1991), pp. 28–29.

150. *DGFP 1918–1945,* ser. D, vol. 11, pp. 630, 855.

151. Chuev, pp. 28–29.

152. Vaksberg, p. 353n. 2.

153. Liudas Dovydenas to the writers, November 6, 1989.

154. [Hoover] to Donovan, Jan. 27, 1942, File 10532, OSS Papers, RG 266, NA.

155. Walter Bedell Smith, *My Three Years in Moscow* (Philadelphia: Lippincott, 1950), p. 43.

156. Ernst von Weizsäcker, *Erinnerungen* (München: Paul List, 1950), p. 306 and Papen, p. 528.

157. Ismail Akhmedov, *In and Out of Stalin's GRU: A Tatar's Escape from Red Army Intelligence* (Frederick: University Publications of America, 1984), p. 140.

158. Weizsäcker, p. 306.

159. Liudas Dovydenas to the writers, November 6, 1989.

160. On "legend," see Henry S. A. Becket, *The Dictionary of Espionage* (New York: Stein and Day, 1986), p. 101. On Dekanozov's (Protopopov's) bogus background, see Schulenburg (Moscow) to Berlin, no. A/5120/40, Nov. 26, 1940, Microfilm T120, Serial no. 104, Frame Nos. 112718–112719, German Foreign Ministry Archives, NA. In early 1921, a Madame Olga Fonov, the daughter of Katon and Barba Protopopov, born in 1850 in Astrakan and residing in Switzerland, became a subject of interest to American military intelligence because of her professed "bolshevik ideas." Military intelligence decided that she would be "carefully watched." What relationship there was, if any, between Olga Protopopov Fanov and Dekanozov (Protopopov) is unclear, but if there was one it might partially help to explain his desire to develop a legend. MID File 10058–Y-27/1, Military Intelligence Division Correspondence, 1917–1941, Box 2297, RG 165, NA.

161. In 1942 at Dekanozov's suggestion, the NKVD's Vladimir Proletarsky (né Shorokhov), who had been assigned to Stockholm, changed his name to Vladimir Petrov. Dekanozov considered Proletarsky as "too militant" a name for someone posted to an embassy abroad. Petrov defected in Australia in 1954 ("Personal History of Vladimir Mikhailovich Petrov," CRS A6283/XR1/80, p. 1, AA).

162. Amy Knight, *Beria: Stalin's First Lieutenant* (Princeton: Princeton University Press, 1933), pp. 21–22, 91, 104.

163. Albert N. Tarulis, *Soviet Policy Toward the Baltic States 1918–1940* (Notre Dame: University of Notre Dame Press, 1959), pp. 201–215; Erich F. Sommer, *Das Memorandum* (München: Herbig, 1981), pp. 107–126; V. Stanley Vardy, "Aggression, Soviet Style, 1939–40," in *Lithuania Under the Soviets 1940–1965: Aggression Soviet Style 1939–1940,* ed. V. Stanley Vardy (New York: Praeger, 1965), pp. 50–55; Read and Fisher, *Deadly Enemies,* pp. 466–469. Also, see Juozas Urbsys, *Atsiminimai* (Chicago: Lithuanian National Foundation, 1988), pp. 89, 94, 98–99, and Liudas Dovydenas, *Mes Valdysim Pasuali* (Woodhaven, New York: Romuva, 1970), vol. 1, p. 15 and vol. 2, pp. 271, 272, 274, 277, 415.

164. Akhmedov, pp. 140, 145.

165. Vaksberg, p. 353n. 2.

166. M. Loginov, "Kul't lichnosti chuzhd nashemu stroiu," *Molodoi kommunist* no. 1 (January 1962): 53–54; and A[leksei] Roshchin, "V narkomindele nakanune voiny," *Mezhdunarodnaia Zhizn,* no. 4 (April 1988), p. 126; Liudas Dovydenas, *We Will Conquer the World* (New York: Romuva, 1971), p. 12; Akhmedov, p. 140; and Tarulis, p. 239. Someone interrogated by Dekanozov in 1940 has recalled that it "was useless to speak to him of anything human; the human being did not exist for him, only a 'subject under investigation' " (A. Grigoriev, "Investigative Methods of the Secret Police," in *The Soviet Secret Police,* ed. Simon Wolin and Robert M. Slusser (New York: Praeger, 1957), p. 211.

167. [Hoover] to Donovan, Jan. 27, 1942, File 10532, OSS Papers, RG 226, NA.

168. Knight, *Beria,* pp. 202–203, 218.

169. Seeds (Moscow) to Halifax, no. 143, May 12, 1939, FO/371/23685.

170. *FRUS. The Soviet Union, 1933–1939,* p. 771.

171. Roshchin, p. 125; and *FRUS. The Soviet Union, 1933–1939,* pp. 770–772.

172. [Hoover] to Donovan, Jan. 27, 1942, File 10532, OSS Papers, RG 266, NA. Hoover's assertion that Dekanozov backed the 1939 nonaggression pact is supported by Ivan Filippov, a senior NKVD officer, whose "cover" was *Tass* correspondent in Berlin. See Woermann (Berlin) to Schulenburg, Nov. 29, 1940, Microfilm T120, Serial 1447, Frame 3648987, German Foreign Ministry Archives, NA. On Filippov see Whaley, pp. 84, 90, 160, 181.

173. See Chapter 1, p. 17.

174. *FRUS, 1940,* vol. 1, p. 588.

175. Cripps (Moscow) to Eden, Mar. 5, 1941, FO/371/29498, PRO.

176. *FRUS, 1941,* vol. 1, p. 606.

177. Ulrich von Hassell, *Die Hassell-Tagebücher 1938–1944,* ed. Klaus Peter Reiss (Berlin: Siedler, 1989), p. 522n 103.

178. *FRUS, 1940,* vol. 1, p. 587.

179. Woermann (Berlin) to Schulenburg, Nov. 29, 1940, Microfilm T120, Serial 1447, Frame 364987, German Foreign Ministry Archives, NA.

180. Cripps (Moscow) to the Foreign Office, no. 1032, Nov. 25, 1940, and the attached minute by F[itzroy] H. R. Maclean, Nov. 28, 1940, FO/371/24855.

181. Cripps (Moscow) to Eden, Jan. 26, 1941, FO/371/29500. Also, see Cripps (Moscow) to Halifax, Nov. 26, 1940, FO/371/29506. On Cripps's personality, see Harold Nicolson, *Diaries and Letters of Harold Nicolson,* ed. Nigel Nicolson (New York: Atheneum, 1967), vol. 2, 241.

182. Cripps (Moscow) to the Foreign Office, no. 68, Jan. 25, 1941, and Knatchbull Hugessen (Angora) to the Foreign Office, no. 195, Jan. 27, 1941, as well as the minute by F[itzroy] H. R. Maclean, Jan. 29 [1941], FO/371/29777.

183. [Hoover] to Donovan, Jan. 27, 1942, File 10532, OSS Papers, RG 226, NA.

184. Memo. of Con. (Oumansky, Welles), June 26, 1941, File 740.0011 European War 1939/12914, RG 59, NA. See also Vaksberg, p. 218.

185. *FRUS, 1942,* vol. 3, p. 587.

## Chapter 3: Echoes

1. *DGFP 1918–1945,* ser. D, vol. 11, pp. 126–128, 136–137, 144–146, 260–261, 276–277, 279–280, 684–690, 921–922, 1002–1003, 1060, 1076, 1080–1081, 1104–1114, 1160–1161, 1171–1172, 1185–1186, 1210–1211, 1216–1217, 1236–1237.

2. Ibid., vol. 11, pp. 1122–1125, and vol. 12, pp. 195, 213–216; and Joachim von Ribbentrop, *The Ribbentrop Memoirs* (London: Weidenfeld and Nicolson, 1954), pp. 155–156. Also, see *Soviet Documents on Foreign Policy,* ed. Jane Degras (London: Oxford University Press, 1953), vol. 3, pp. 482–483.

3. *DGFP 1918–1945,* ser. D, vol. 12, pp. 182, 195, 213–216.

4. John J. Dziak, *Chekisty: A History of the KGB* (Lexington: D. C. Heath, 1988), p. 41.

5. James E. McSherry, *Stalin, Hitler, and Europe* (New York: World Publishing Co., 1970), vol. 2, p. 229.

6. John J. Dziak, "Soviet Deception: The Organizational and Operational Tradition," in *Soviet Strategic Deception,* ed. Brian D. Bailey and Patrick J. Parker (Lexington: Lexington Books, 1987), p. 9; Dziak, *Chekisty,* p. 110; McSherry, 229, 300–301n. 5.

7. Reiner Rohme [August Ponschab], *Die Marionetten des Herrn* (Stuttgart: Rentsch, 1960); J. W. M. Chapman, "The Polish Connection: Japan, Poland and the Axis," *Proceedings of the British Association for Japanese Studies,* ed. Peter Lowe and Gordon Daniels (Sheffield: Sheffield University Press, 1977), vol. 2, pt. 1, p. 68; Herbert O. Yardley, *The American Black Chamber* (Indianapolis: Bobbs-Merrill, 1931), pp. 279–281; and The Countess of Listowel, *Crusader in the Secret War* (London: Christopher Johnson, 1952), pp. 38–39.

8. West German Foreign Ministry to the writers, Aug. 18, 1989; and David Kahn, *The Codebreakers* (New York: Macmillan, 1967), p. 1083n. 650.

9. Summary Report on German Intelligence Activities in China, Mar. 1, 1941, Box 28, Folder 152, RG 226, NA.

10. Christopher Andrew, *Her Majesty's Secret Service* (New York: Viking, 1986), pp. 259–338; Richard H. Ullman, *Anglo-Soviet Relations, 1917–1921* (Princeton: Princeton University Press, 1972), vol. 3, pp. 265–314; James Barros, *Office Without Power: Secretary-General Sir Eric Drummond 1919–1933* (Oxford: Clarendon Press, 1979), p. 120; Yardley, pp. 239–249.

11. Robert J. Lamphere and Tom Shachtman, *The FBI-KGB War: A Special Agent's Story* (New York: Random House, 1986), pp. 78–86, 91, 96–97; Peter Wright, *Spycatcher* (New York: Viking, 1987), pp. 180–182.

12. Kahn, *The Codebreakers,* p. 1083n. 650. See also Germany. Reichsluftfahrtsministerium. Forschungsamt, *Breach of Security: The German Secret Intelligence File on Events Leading to the Second World War* (London: Kimber, 1968), p. 17.

13. *DGFP 1918–1945,* ser. D, vol. 12, p. 793n.

14. These decrypted circular messages are to be found in Microfilm T120, Serials 104 and 105, German Foreign Ministry Archives, NA. The assertion that there are "no fewer than 105" of these intercepts that cover the limited period of May-June 1941 and that are "preserved but almost forgotten" in German and American national archives is not supported by the archival evidence. As has been pointed out, Ponschab did not have the staff, facilities, training, or expertise to be involved in any such decryption operation. For the assertion, see Barton Whaley, *Codeword Barbarossa* (Cambridge: MIT Press, 1973), p. 297n. 83.

15. Ponschab (Harbin) to Berlin, no. 42, May 18, 1941, Microfilm T120, Serial 105, Frame 113437, German Foreign Ministry Archives, NA.

16. Georg Korter to the writers, Mar. 7, 1991.

17. John J. Stephan, *The Russian Fascists: Tragedy and Farce in Exile 1925–1945* (New York: Harper and Row, 1978), pp. 52, 317–319.

18. See Chapter 2, p. 35.

19. Stephan, *The Russian Fascists,* pp. 52, 317–319.

20. The most abundant and fruitful material on Ivar Lissner, including translations of his Japanese interrogations, is to be found in File XE 232422, US Army Intelligence and Security Command. German comments about Lissner's Spielmaterial ploy are rendered in Summary Report on German Intelligence Activities in China,

Mar. 1, 1946, pp. 34, 62–63, 76, Box 28, Folder 152, RG 226, NA. See also Ivar Lissner, *Vergessen aber nicht vergeben* (Frankfurt: Ullstein, 1970), passim; Heinz Hohne, *Der Krieg im Dunkeln* (München: Bertelsmann, 1985), pp. 304, 435–440; and F. W. Deakin and G. R. Storry, *The Case of Richard Sorge* (London: Chatto and Windus, 1966), pp. 303–309, 312, 214, 332, 333, 335. On Rodzaevsky, see Stephan, *The Russian Fascists,* pp. 52, 317–319. For the episode at the Toyko War Crimes Trial, see *TWCT,* vol. 4, pp. 7601–7602.

21. McSherry, p. 296n. Also, see *DGFP 1918–1945,* ser. D, vol. 12, p. 793n.

22. Ponschab (Harbin) to Berlin, no. 6, Mar. 6, 1941, Microfilm T120, Serial no. 104, Frame Nos. 113116–113117, German Foreign Ministry Archives, NA.

23. Georg Korter to the writers, Mar. 7, 1991. Tangential evidence supporting Korter's claim that Harbin's Russian Consulate General staff was about seventy is the Harbin report to the British embassy in Tokyo, following the invasion, that fifty-four women and children of the Russian staff had been evacuated. See Craigie (Tokyo) to the Foreign Office, no. 1140, July 8, 1941, FO/371/27881.

24. Ponschab (Harbin) to Berlin, no. 6, Mar. 6, 1941, Microfilm T120, Serial no. 104, Frame Nos. 113116–113117, German Foreign Ministry Archives, NA.

25. Winston S. Churchill, *The Second World War* (Boston: Houghton Mifflin, 1951), vol. 3, pp. 97, 233; Anthony Eden, *The Eden Memoirs: The Reckoning* (London: Cassell, 1965), pp. 205, 208; and Llewellyn Woodward, *British Policy in the Second World War* (London: H. M. Stationery Office, 1970), vol. 1, pp. 530, 551.

26. *FRUS, 1941,* vol. 1, pp. 930, 933–934, 935, 936–940; and Joseph Edward O'Connor, "Laurence A. Steinhardt and American Policy toward the Soviet Union, 1939–1941" (Unpublished Ph.D. dissertation, University of Virginia), pp. 161–165. Also, see William L. Langer and S. Everett Gleason, *The Undeclared War 1940–1941* (New York: Harper, 1953), pp. 335–345.

27. *FRUS, 1941,* vol. 1, p. 162; and Gabriel Gorodetsky, *Stafford Cripps' Mission to Moscow 1940–1942* (Cambridge: Cambridge University Press, 1984), p. 102.

28. *DGFP 1918–1945,* ser. D, vol. 12, pp. 250–251. On Sweden's attitude toward the transit of German troops, see W. M. Carlgren, *Swedish Foreign Policy during the Second World War* (New York: St. Martin's Press, 1977), pp. 94–99.

29. Nikolai G. Kuznetsov, *Nakanune* (Moscow: Voenizdat, 1969), pp. 343–344.

30. Georgii Zhukov, *Vospominaniia i razmyshleniia* (Moscow: Novosti, 1969), pp. 248–249.

31. See Vladimir Petrov, *"June 22, 1941"; Soviet Historians and the German Invasion* (Columbia: University of South Carolina Press, 1968), pp. 250, 253, 254, 257. It should be noted that veracity of reporting was not one of Golikov's strong points. It has been observed that during the battle on the Voronezh front "it proved to be impossible to form an objective picture from the reports" filed by Golikov [Sergei Shtemenko, *Generalnyi shtab v gody voiny* (Moscow: Voenizdat, 1968), p. 109 and also p. 99].

32. Roy Medvedev, *Let History Judge,* rev. ed. (New York: Columbia University Press, 1989), p. 739.

33. Chapter 2, p. 44.

34. R[ichard] B[utler], An untitled memorandum of conversation, Mar. 18, 1941, FO/371/29479.

35. Chiefs of Staff Committee, Weekly Résumé, no. 80, Mar. 6–13, 1941, no. 81, Mar. 13–20, 1941, and no. 82, Mar. 20–27, 1941, CAB/80/26, PRO.

36. No. 33A, Summary of MI14, Indication Files, Mar. 25, 1941, WO/190/893, PRO.

37. J. M. A. Gwyer, *Grand Strategy* (London: H. M. Stationery Office, 1964), vol. 3, p. 82.

38. Chiefs of Staff Committee, Weekly Résumé, no. 83, Mar. 27–Apr. 3, 1941, CAB/80/27, PRO.

39. "Iz istorii Velikoi Otechestvennoi Voiny. Nakanune voiny (Dokumenty 1940–1941)," *Izvestiia TsK KPSS* no. 4 (April 1990): 201, 214.

40. Donald McLachlan, *Room 39, Naval Intelligence in Action 1939–1945* (London: Weidenfeld and Nicolson, 1964), pp. 242–243; Cavendish-Bentinck to Gaselee, Nov. 12, 1941, FO/371/29491; and Patrick Howarth, *Intelligence Chief Extraordinary: The Life of the Ninth Duke of Portland* (London: Bodley Head, 1986), p. 152.

41. The purported message of March 15 is recounted in the dubious volume by Pierre Accoce and Pierre Quet, *A Man Called Lucy 1939–1945* (New York: Coward-McCann, 1967), pp. 86–87. On Foote, see Alexander Foote, *Handbook for Spies,* 2nd ed. (London: Museum Press, 1964). On Radó, see Sándor Radó, *Dóra Jelenti* (Budapest: Kossuth Könyvkiadó, 1972).

42. Hans Rudolf Kurz, *Nachrichtenzentrum Schweiz* (Frauenfeld and Stuttgart: Huber, 1972), pp. 32–33; Radó, pp. 58, 212; *The Rote Kapelle: The CIA's History of Soviet Intelligence and Espionage Networks in Western Europe, 1936–1945* (Frederick: University Publications of America, 1979), pp. 177, 345.

43. Ibid., p. 345.

44. Ibid., pp. 224–225, as well as pp. 344, 349. Also, see Nigel West, *Unreliable Witness* (London: Weidenfeld and Nicolson, 1984), pp. 66–67.

45. David Dallin, *Soviet Espionage* (New Haven: Yale University Press, 1955), pp. 192–194; František Moravec, *Master of Spies* (Garden City, New York: Doubleday, 1975), pp. 171–172; Anthony Read and David Fisher, *Operation Lucy* (London: Hodder and Stoughton, 1980), pp. 87–88; Jon Kimche, *Spying for Peace: General Guisan and Swiss Neutrality* (New York: Row, 1962), pp. 89–91.

46. On the rapidity, scope, volume, and accuracy of Rossler's information, see Accoce and Quet, pp. 9–10, 59, 154; West, *Unreliable Witness,* pp. 54–57; Kimche, p. 93. For Swiss intelligence in Germany, see Dallin, *Soviet Espionage,* p. 192; and Kimche, p. 74. On Swiss intelligence, also see Józef Garliński, *The Swiss Corridor: Espionage Networks in Switzerland during World War II* (Toronto: Dent, 1981), pp. 6–11. For a different version of the Lucy case, see the controversial work by Pavel Sudoplatov and Anatoli Sudoplatov with Jerrold L. Schecter and Leona P. Schecter, *Special Tasks* (New York: Little, Brown, and Company, 1994), pp. 140–146.

47. See Chapter 2, p. 47.

48. See earlier in this chapter.

49. *DGFP 1918–1945,* ser. D, vol. 12, pp. 160, 180–181, 203.

50. Ibid., pp. 195, 213–216 and Steinhardt (Moscow) to the Sec. of State, no. 456, Mar. 9, 1941 File 740.0011 European War 1939/8893, RG 59, NA. Also, see Degras, vol. 3, pp. 483–484.

51. Woodward, vol. 1, p. 531.

52. *DGFP 1918–1945,* ser. D, vol. 12, pp. 230–232.

53. Ibid., p. 231n.

54. J. B. Hoptner, *Yugoslavia in Crisis 1934–1941* (New York: Columbia University Press, 1962), pp. 218–221; and Neil Balfour and Sally Mackay, *Paul of Yugoslavia* (London: Hamish Hamilton, 1980), pp. 226–229, 273.

55. Cripps (Moscow) to the Foreign Office, no. 289, Mar. 31, 1941 and Palairet (Athens) to the Foreign Office, no. 639, Apr. 5, 1941, FO/371/29479. Also, see MacVeagh (Athens) to the Sec. of State, no. 184, Section 2, Apr. 5, 1941, File 740.0011 European War, 1939/9657; and Steinhardt (Moscow) to the Sec. of State, no. 757, Apr. 12, 1941, File 740.0011 European War, 1939/9901, RG 59, NA. Another view of events is that Hitler's remarks were fabricated by elements inside the Yugoslav government to facilitate the upcoming negotiations with Moscow. Prince Paul's subsequent denial of the story in 1968 is cited in support of this version. See Dušan Biber, "The Yugoslav *Coup D'Etat,* 27 March 1941," in *Barbarossa,* pp. 34–37.

56. *FRUS, 1941,* vol. 1, p. 315.

57. *FRUS, 1941* vol. 2, p. 973. Also, see Eden, p. 220.

58. Leigh White, *The Long Balkan Night* (New York: Scribner's 1944), pp. 175–176.

59. Campbell (Belgrade) to Athens, no. 253, Mar. 30, 1941, FO/371/29479.

60. Halifax (Washington) to the Foreign Office, no. 1436, Apr. 2, 1941, ibid.

61. Constantine Fotitch, *The War We Lost* (New York: Viking, 1948), p. 58. Also, see Vladimir Dedijer, *Tito* (New York: Simon and Schuster, 1953), p. 134.

62. In Belgrade on March 20, Prince Paul lunched with the former German ambassador, Ulrich von Hassell. The prince mentioned his secret meeting with Hitler, but made no mention of Hitler or of Hitler's comment that he would invade Russia. Prince Paul, of course, could not have been aware that the ambassador was a leader in the anti-Nazi conspiracy. The only elliptical comment was that perhaps a German-Russian clash "might constitute a bridge toward an understanding [by Germany] with the west" [Ulrich von Hassell, *The Von Hassell Diaries 1938–1944* (Garden City, New York: Doubleday, 1947), pp. 175–177].

63. *FRUS, 1941,* vol. 1, p. 315.

64. Cripps (Moscow) to Eden, no. 123, Sept. 27, 1941, FO/371/29491 and Baggallay (Moscow) to Eden, no. 49, Mar. 9, 1942, FO/371/33026.

65. Campbell (Belgrade) to the Foreign Office, no. 1003, Nov. 26, 1940, and Campbell (Belgrade) to the Foreign Office, no. 1079, Dec. 9, 1940, FO/371/25034. Also, Campbell (Belgrade) to the Foreign Office, no. 50, Jan. 11, 1941, FO/371/30228.

66. Minutes by L[aurence] Collier, Apr. 2, 1941 and A[lexander] C[adogan], Apr. 3, 1941, FO/371/29479.

67. Lane (Belgrade) to the Sec. of State, no. 141, Mar. 4, 1941, File 740.0011 European War 1939/8769, RG 59, NA. On the Hitler-Inonu correspondence, see *DGFP 1918–1945,* ser. D, vol. 12, pp. 187–188, 201–203.

68. Murray to Berle, Mar. 8, 1941, File 740.0011 European War 1939/88769, RG 59, NA.

69. Ilija Jukić, *The Fall of Yugoslavia* (New York: Harcourt Brace Jovanovich, 1974), pp. 48, 52.

70. *Dokumenty z historie československé politiky 1939–1943. [Acta Occupationis Bohemiae & Moraviae],* ed. Libuše Otáhalová and Milada Červinková (Prague: Academia, 1966), vol. 1, pp. 186–187. See also Eduard Beneš, *Memoirs of Dr. Eduard Beneš* (London: Allen and Unwin, 1954), p. 150; and Moravec, p. 191.

71. Campbell (Belgrade) to the Foreign Office, no. 394, Mar. 12, 1941, FO/

371/29779. On Gavrilović's keenness, see Campbell (Belgrade) to the Foreign Office, no. 405, Mar. 12, 1941, FO/371/29780 and Gavrilović to the Foreign Ministry, no. 115, Mar. 14, 1941, Box 14, Prince Regent Paul of Yugoslavia's Papers, Bakhmeteff Archive, CU. On Tupanjanin and British intelligence, see Jukić, p. 60. As to his subsidy, see the minute by P[hilip] Nicols, Mar. 11, 1947, FO/371/29779. Also, see David A. T. Stafford, "SOE and British Involvement in the Belgrade Coup d'État of March 1941," *Slavic Review* 36, no. 3 (September 1977): 410–411.

72. Gavrilović to the Foreign Ministry, no. 111, Mar. 9, 1941, and no. 115, Mar. 14, 1941, Box 14, Prince Regent Paul of Yugoslavia's Papers, Bakhmeteff Archive, CU.

73. Cripps (Moscow) to the Foreign Office, no. 215, Mar. 12, 1941, FO/371/29779; and Gavrilović to the Foreign Ministry, no. 115, Mar. 14, 1941, Box 14, Prince Regent Paul of Yugoslavia's Papers, Bakhmeteff Archive, CU.

74. Vladimir Vauhnik, *Memoires eines Militärattachés* (Buenos Aires, Palabra Eslovena, 1967), pp. 147–150, 154–155; Hoptner, pp. 232–233, 281–283; Frank C. Littlefield, *Germany and Yugoslavia 1933–1941* (Boulder: East European Monographs; New York: distributed by Columbia University Press, 1988), pp. 103, 125–126. Hans Oster was an anti-Nazi and a member of the officer corps before the First World War. His warnings to the Yugoslavs had been preceded by warnings to the Danes, Dutch, and Norwegians of the coming German attacks. See Jacobus Beus, *Tomorrow at Dawn!* (New York: Norton, 1980).

75. Walter Schellenberg, *The Schellenberg Memoirs* (London: Deutsch, 1956), pp. 190–198. On the Forschungsamt, see Germany. Reichsluftfahrtsministerium. Forschungsamt, p. 17. It would be safe to suggest that it was the Forschungsamt that in July 1940 intercepted and decrypted Ambassador Gavrilović's conversations in Moscow with diplomatic counterparts and senior Russian officials. See *DGFP 1918–1945,* ser. D, vol. 10, pp. 321–324.

76. *DGFP 1918–1945,* ser. D, vol. 12, pp. 232–233, 255–258, 269–270, 281–282, 291–294, 303–304, 312–315, 323, 335–338, 353.

77. Cripps (Moscow) to the Foreign Office, no. 270, Mar. 24, 1941, FO/371/30206; Henry C. Cassidy, *Moscow Dateline 1941–1943* (Boston: Houghton Mifflin, 1943), p. 11; and Grigore Gafencu, *Prelude to the Russian Campaign* (London: Muller, 1945), p. 144.

78. Stafford, passim.

79. Hoptner, p. 259n.; King Peter II, *A King's Heritage* (New York: Putnam's 1954), pp. 81–82.

80. *Pravda,* Apr. 1, 1941: 5; and Cripps (Moscow) to the Foreign Office, no. 294, Apr. 2, 1941, FO/371/30228.

81. *DGFP 1918–1945,* ser. D, vol. 12, pp. 383–385, 421–422, 431, 452; Hoptner, p. 284.

82. Steinhardt (Moscow) to the Sec. of State, no. 455, Mar. 9, 1941, File 740.0011 European War 1939/8892, RG 59, NA.

83. Degras, vol. 3, p. 484. Also, see *FRUS, 1941,* vol. 1, p. 611.

84. Moravec, p. 191. Also, see Beneš, p. 150.

85. *DGFP 1918–1945,* ser. D, vol. 12, p. 427n.

86. Ibid, p. 1064.

87. See earlier in this chapter, p. 63.

88. Gavrilović to the Foreign Ministry, no. 133, Mar. 23, 1941, Box 14,

Prince Regent Paul of Yugoslavia's Papers, Bakhmeteff Archive, CU; and Lampson [Cairo] to Belgrade, no. 651, Mar. 21, 1941, FO/371/30253, Cripps (Moscow) to the Foreign Office, Nos. 259, 260, and 285, Mar. 22, 23, and 29, 1941, FO/371/30228.

89. Gavrilović to the Foreign Ministry, no. 169, Apr. 4, 1941, Box 14, Prince Regent Paul of Yugoslavia's Papers, Bakhmeteff Archive, CU.

90. Gavrilović to the Foreign Ministry, no. 154, n.d., nos. 169 and 170, Apr. 4, 1941, Box 14, Prince Regent Paul of Yugoslavia's Papers, Bakhmeteff Archive, CU.

91. Ibid.

92. Ibid.

93. Ibid.; Lane (Belgrade) to the Sec. of State, no. 297, Apr. 1, 1941, File 740.0011 European War 1939/9549; Steinhardt (Moscow) to the Sec. of State, no. 645, Apr. 1, 1941, File 740.0011 European War 1939/9537, and Steinhardt (Moscow) to the Sec. of State, no. 656, Apr. 2, 1941, File 740.0011 European War 1939/9561, RG 59, NA; Campbell (Belgrade) to the Foreign Office, no. 604, Apr. 2, 1941, FO/371/30208; Cripps (Moscow) to the Foreign Office, no. 318, Apr. 6, 1941, FO/371/29544; *FRUS, 1941,* vol. 1, pp. 300–302; Hoptner, pp. 276–280; Cassidy, pp. 10–11. For the treaty, see Degras, vol. 3, pp. 484–485.

94. War Cabinet 38 (41) Apr. 7, 1941, CAB/65/18, PRO.

95. King Peter II, p. 91.

96. Cassidy, p. 11.

97. On the question of the time sequence, see *FRUS, 1941,* vol. 1, p. 301; and Hoptner, p. 285.

98. [Rudolf] L[ikus], Confidential Report, Apr. 7, 1941, Microfilm T120, Serial 36, Frame 26012, German Foreign Ministry Archives, NA.

99. Ponschab (Harbin) to Berlin, no. 14, Apr. 5, 1941, Microfilm T120, Serial 104, Frame Nos. 113257–113258, German Foreign Ministry Archives, NA.

100. *DGFP 1918–1945,* ser. D, vol. 12, pp. 451–452.

101. Cripps (Moscow) to the Foreign Office, no. 309, Apr. 6, 1941, FO/371/29544.

102. *FRUS, 1941,* vol. 1, p. 136.

103. Steinhardt (Moscow) to the Sec. of State, no. 703, Apr. 7, 1941, File 740.0011 European War 1939/9712, RG 59, NA; and Cripps (Moscow) to the Foreign Office, no. 318, Apr. 6, 1941, FO/371/29544.

104. Minute by L[aurence] Collier, Apr. 7 [1941], FO/371/29544.

105. War Cabinet 38 (41) Apr. 7, 1941, CAB/65/18, PRO.

106. *DGFP 1918–1945,* ser. D, vol. 12, p. 484.

107. Alexander Werth, *Russia at War 1941–1945* (London: Barrie and Rockliff, 1964), pp. 117–118; and Steinhardt (Moscow) to the Sec. of State, no. 699, Apr. 7, 1941, File 740.0011 European War 1939/9715, RG 59, NA. On the Russian demarche to Hungary, see Degras, vol. 3, pp. 485–486; and Steinhardt (Moscow) to the Sec. of State, no. 759, Apr. 13, 1941, File 740.0011 European War 1939/9908, RG 59, NA.

108. Steinhardt (Moscow) to the Sec. of State, no. 708, Apr. 8, 1941, File 740.0011 European War 1939/9728, RG 59, NA.

109. Steinhardt (Moscow) to the Sec. of State, no. 730, Apr. 10, 1941, File 740.0011 European War 1939/9872, RG 59, NA.

110. Steinhardt (Moscow) to the Sec. of State, no. 736, Apr. 11, 1941, File 740.0011 European War 1939/9894, RG 59, NA.

111. Steinhardt (Moscow) to the Sec. of State, no. 769, Apr. 14, 1941, File 740.0011 European War 1939/9951, RG 59, NA.

112. Steinhardt (Moscow) to the Sec. of State, no. 784, Apr. 16, 1941, File 740.0011 European War 1939/10029, RG 59, MA.

113. *DGFP, 1918–1945,* ser. D, vol. 12, pp. 490–491.

114. Morris (Berlin) to the Sec. of State, no. 1365, Apr. 9, 1941, File 740.0011 European War 1939/9825, RG 59, NA.

115. Ponschab (Harbin) to Berlin, no. 16, Apr. 9, 1941, Microfilm T120, Serial 104, Frame Nos. 113283–113284, German Foreign Ministry Archives, NA.

116. Ibid.

117. Ibid.

118. Ponschab (Harbin) to Berlin, no. 17, Apr. 11, 1941, Microfilm T120, Serial 104, Frame Nos. 113293–113294, German Foreign Ministry Archives, NA.

119. *FRUS, 1941,* vol. 1, p. 302.

120. Ibid., p. 311.

121. Baggallay (Moscow) to Eden, no. 49, Mar. 9, 1942 and the enclosure Political Review of Events in the Soviet Union during 1941, FO/371/33026.

122. *FRUS, 1941,* vol. 1, p. 313.

123. "Iz istorii Velikoi," p. 209.

124. Cripps (Moscow) to the Foreign Office, no. 309, Apr. 6, 1941, FO/371/29544.

125. *FRUS, 1941,* vol. 1, p. 135.

126. [Rudolf] L[ikus], Confidential Report, Apr. 8, 1941, Microfilm T120, Serial 36, Frame 26013–26014, German Foreign Ministry Archives, NA.

127. Interrogation of Gustav Hilger, Department of State Special Interrogation Mission under Dewitt C. Poole, RG 59, NA. Also, see Gustav Hilger and Alfred G. Meyer, *The Incompatible Allies. A Memoir-History of German-Soviet Relations 1918–1941* (New York: Macmillan, 1953), p. 326.

128. *FRUS, 1941,* vol. 4, p. 960.

129. *DGFP 1918 1945,* ser. D, vol. 12, pp. 666–669

130. Milovan Djilas, *Conversations with Stalin* (New York: Harcourt, Brace and World, 1962), p. 65.

131. Cripps (Moscow) to the Foreign Office, no. 320, Apr. 8, 1941, FO/371/29479.

132. *FRUS, 1941,* vol. 1, p. 302; and see also Cripps (Moscow) to the Foreign Office, no. 318, Apr. 6, 1941, FO/371/29544. Also, see "Iz istorii Velikoi," p. 209. Former NKVD officer Pavel Sudoplatov, in his controversial memoirs, alleges that the NKVD, with the assistance of the Ministry of Foreign Affairs, had at this time "formally recruited, as our agent, the Yugoslavian ambassador to the Soviet Union, Gavrilovich." According to Sudoplatov's account, he and another NKVD officer ran Gavrilović, whom they suspected was "playing a double game in the interest of the British" because Gavrilović was in weekly contact with British officials in Moscow. See Sudoplatov and Sudoplatov, pp. 118, 124.

133. Cripps (Moscow) to the Foreign Office, no. 365, Apr. 16, 1941 and the minute by L[aurence] Collier, Apr. 18 [1941], FO/371/29479.

134. *FRUS, 1941,* vol. 1, p. 315 and Steinhardt (Moscow) to the Sec. of State, no. 703, Apr. 7, 1941, File 740.0011 European War 1939/9712, RG 59, NA.

135. *FRUS, 1941,* vol. 1, p. 135.

136. Harold Nicolson, *Diaries and Letters of Harold Nicolson,* ed. Nigel Nicolson (New York: Atheneum, 1967), vol. 2, p. 155.

137. Minute by E[dward] O. Coote, Apr. 18, [1941], FO/371/29479.

138. [Anonymous], "Sovetskie organy gosudarstvennoi bezopasnosti v gody Velikoi Otechestvennoi Voiny," *Voprosy istorii* no. 5 (May 1965): 27; *Trud,* Dec. 19, 1967: 1.

139. Winston S. Churchill, *The Second World War* (Boston: Houghton Mifflin, 1950), vol. 4, p. 493.

140. "Marshal Zhukov on Soviet Leadership on the Eve and in the Early Days of War," A[gency] P[ress] N[ovosti], *Military Bulletin* (Moscow), Special Issue, no. 20 (25), 012SDO-871009–GA-1 (Oct. 1987): 8.

141. *NCA,* vol. 4, p. 277.

142. M[artin L.] van Creveld, "The German Attack on the USSR: the Destruction of a Legend," *European Studies Review,* Vol. 2, no. 1 (January 1972), p. 83.

143. Ibid, pp. 70–71, 83–86; and Martin L. van Creveld, *Hitler's Strategy 1940–1941: The Balkan Clue* (Cambridge: Cambridge University Press, 1973), pp. 173–175, 182–183.

144. See earlier in this chapter, p. 57.

145. *DGFP 1918–1945,* ser. D, vol. 12, pp. 376–383, 386–394, 403–409, 413–420, 453–458.

146. Degras, vol. 3, pp. 486–487.

147. *DGFP 1918–1945,* ser. D, vol. 12, pp. 495–496, 502, 536–537, 546–547, 642–643.

148. Ibid.

149. Otáhalová and Červinková, vol. 1, pp. 202–203.

150. Gallienne, Conversation with M. Helfand, Apr. 14, 1941, FO/371/29501.

151. Gordon W. Prange et al., *Target Tokyo. The Story of the Sorge Spy Ring* (New York: McGraw-Hill, 1984), p. 326.

152. Prange et al., pp. 23–28, 273–275; Chalmers Johnson, *An Instance of Treason: Ozaki Hotsumi and the Sorge Spy Ring* (Stanford: Stanford University Press, 1964), passim; Charles A. Willoughby, *Shanghai Conspiracy: The Sorge Spy Ring* (New York: Dutton, 1952), pp. 33–39, 103–116, 208–213.

153. Prange et al., pp. 148, 152, 185, 220, 223, 274–275, 325, 337, 360, 377, 398–99, 403–404; Johnson, pp. 113, 133–134, 197; Willoughby, p. 110.

154. Deakin and Storry, p. 224.

155. Prange et al., pp. 325, 337; and Deakin and Storry, p. 224.

156. Prange et al., p. 148; and Johnson, p. 214n.

157. Prange et al., p. 487; Johnson, pp. 113, 180, 199; Willoughby, pp. 124–125, 277–278.

158. *FRUS, 1941,* vol. 4, p. 953.

159. *DGFP 1918–1945,* ser. D, vol. 12, pp. 536–537, 570.

160. *FRUS, 1941,* vol. 4, p. 957.

161. Prange et al., pp. 322–329.

162. *FRUS, 1941,* vol. 4, p. 953.

163. Ibid., pp. 954–955.

164. *The Price of Admiralty: The War Diary of the German Naval Attaché in Japan, 1939–1943,* ed. and trans., J. W. M. Chapman (Rips, Sussex: Saltire Press, 1984), vol. 3, p. 260n. 13.

165. *DGFP 1918–1945,* ser. D, vol. 12, p. 537; Ernst Köstring, *General Ernst Köstring: Der militärische Mittler zwischen dem deutschen Reich und der Sowjetunion 1921–1941,* ed. Herman Teske (Frankfurt am Main: Mittler und Sohn, 1966), pp. 300–301; Moscow Chancery to the [Northern] Department and the enclosure, Apr. 18, 1941, FO/371/29480; John Scott, *Duel for Europe: Stalin versus Hitler* (Boston: Houghton Mifflin, 1942), pp. 236–237; Cassidy, pp. 8–9.

166. Moscow Chancery to the [Northern] Department and the enclosure, Apr. 18, 1941, FO/371/29480.

167. *FRUS, 1941,* vol. 4, p. 959.

168. Lockhart to Sargent, [Apr. 30, 1941?], FO/371/29480.

169. Interrogation of Ambassador Paul Otto Gustav Schmidt, Department of State Special Interrogation Mission under Dewitt C. Poole, RG 59, NA.

170. Prange et al., p. 328.

171. *DGFP 1918–1945,* ser. D, vol. 12, p. 570.

172. Ibid., pp. 306–308, 560–561.

173. Ponschab (Harbin) to Berlin, no. 19, Apr. 17, 1941, Microfilm T120, Serial 104, Frame 113323, German Foreign Ministry Archives, NA.

174. Ponschab (Harbin) to Berlin, no. 20, Apr. 18, 1941, Microfilm T120, Serial 104, Frames 113331–113332, German Foreign Ministry Archives, NA.

175. *DGFP 1918–1945,* ser. D, vol. 12, pp. 579–580, 602.

176. Air Ministry, Weekly Intelligence Survey, no. 96 (July 2, 1941), no. 92 (June 4, 1941), AIR/22/74, PRO. As to the "excellent German source," see Phillips (Rome) to the Sec. of State, no. 582, Apr. 23, 1941, File 740.0011 European War 1939/10247, RG 59, NA. The question of Russian deliveries to the Germans in April lacks consensus. Others report the delivery of 208 million tons of grain, 90,000 tons of coal, 8,300 tons of cotton, 6,400 tons of copper, steel, nickel, and other metals, and 4,000 tons of rubber acquired from third parties by Russia, along with other materials in Germany's behalf [Vitaly Rapoport and Yuri Alexeev, *High Treason: Essays on the History of the Red Army 1918–1938* (Durham: Duke University Press, 1985), p. 416n. 6].

177. Feliks I. Chuev, *Sto sorok besed s Molotovym: iz dnevnika F. Chueva* (Moscow: Terra, 1991), p. 33.

178. *Pogranichnie voiska SSSR (1939–iiun 1941),* ed. E. V. Tsybulskii, A. I. Chugunob, and A. I. Iukht (Moscow: Nauka, 1970), pp. 17–18, 375.

179. *DGFP 1918–1945,* ser. D, vol. 12, pp. 602–603. Also, see "Iz istorii Velikoi," pp. 211, 216.

180. Ponschab (Harbin) to Berlin, no. 29, Apr. 29, 1941, Microfilm T120, Serial 104, Frames 113386–113387, German Foreign Ministry Archives, NA.

181. Ibid.

182. Ibid.

## Chapter 4: Imperialist Provocation and Disinformation

1. Cripps (Moscow) to the Foreign Office, no. 89, Feb. 1, 1941 and no. 90, Feb. 2, 1941, FO/371/29463. Also, see Llewellyn Woodward, *British Foreign Policy*

*in the Second World War* (London: Her Majesty's Stationery Office, 1970), vol. 1, pp. 597–598.

2. "Iz istorii Velikoi Otechestvennoi Voiny. Nakanune voiny (Dokumenty 1940–1941)," *Izvestiia TsK KPSS* no. 4 (1990): 206–207. See also Walter Duranty, *The Kremlin and the People* (New York: Reynal and Hitchcock, 1941), pp. 185–186.

3. S. J. Taylor, *Stalin's Apologist: Walter Duranty, The New York Times' Man in Moscow* (Oxford: Oxford University Press, 1990). "His subservience to the Party Line was so complete," Duranty's illustrious contemporary Malcolm Muggeridge wrote, "that it was even rumoured that he was being blackmailed by the Soviet authorities" [Malcolm Muggeridge, *Chronicles of Wasted Time* (London: Collins, 1972), vol. 1, p. 255].

4. Cripps (Moscow) to the Foreign Office, no. 266, Mar. 24, 1941, FO/371/29464.

5. Cripps (Moscow) to the Foreign Office, no. 267, Mar. 24, 1941, FO/371/26518.

6. Cripps (Moscow) to the Foreign Office, no. 268, Mar. 24, 1941, FO/371/26518.

7. Cripps (Moscow) to the Foreign Office, no. 272, Mar. 25, 1941, FO/371/26518.

8. Mallet (Stockholm) to Eden, no. 121, Apr. 4, 1941, FO/371/29479.

9. Military Attaché (Bern) to the War Office, no. 00594, Mar. 24, 1941 and the marginal note, FO/371/29479.

10. Kelly (Berne) to the Foreign Office, no. 652, Mar. 26, 1941, FO/371/29479.

11. William Phillips, *Ventures in Diplomacy* (London: John Murray, 1955), p. 212; and Vincent Sheean, *Between Thunder and the Sun* (New York: Random House, 1943), p. 331.

12. Eduard Beneš, *Memoirs of Dr. Eduard Beneš* (London: Allen and Unwin, 1954), pp. 149–150 and 164n. 11. For other sources of information reaching Whitehall, see F. H. Hinsley, "British Intelligence and Barbarossa," in *Barbarossa: The Axis and the Allies,* ed. John Erickson and David Dilks (Edinburgh: Edinburgh Universiy Press, 1994), pp. 52–53.

13. František Moravec, *Master of Spies* (Garden City, New York: Doubleday, 1975), pp. 191–192.

14. Phillips, p. 212. See also Sheean, p. 331.

15. *Dokumenty z historie československé politiky 1939–1943. [Acta Occupationis Bohemiae & Moraviae],* ed. Libuše Otáhalová and Milada Červinková (Prague: Academia, 1966), vol. 1, pp. 201–202, 206.

16. Summary Report on German Intelligence Activities in China, Mar. 1, 1946, pp. 39–40, Box 28, Folder 152, RG 226, NA.

17. See Chapter 3, p. 60; Hinsley, "British Intelligence and Barbarossa," p. 45.

18. Winston S. Churchill, *The Second World War* (Boston: Houghton Mifflin, 1951), vol. 3, p. 354.

19. No. 35D, Summary of MI14. Indication Files, Apr. 1, 1941, WO/190/893, PRO.

20. War Office, Weekly Intelligence Summary, no. 85, Mar. 26–Apr. 2, 1941, WO/208/2259, PRO.

21. Chiefs of Staff Committee, Weekly Résumé, no. 83, Mar. 27–Apr. 3, 1941 and no. 84, Apr. 3–10, 1941, CAB/80/27, PRO.

22. Churchill, vol. 3, p. 356.

23. Ibid., p. 357.

24. Ibid., pp. 356–358. Also, see Alexander Cadogan, *The Diaries of Sir Alexander Cadogan,* ed. David Dilks (London: Cassell, 1971), p. 367. On the inability to convey Enigma information, see John Toland, *Adolf Hitler* (New York: Doubleday, 1976), p. 658n. On consulting Sir Stewart Menzies, see F. W. Winterbotham, *The Ultra Secret* (New York: Harper and Row, 1974), p. 70.

25. Cripps (Moscow) to the Foreign Office, no. 307, Apr. 5, 1941, FO/371/29479.

26. Foreign Office to Moscow, no. 297, Apr. 7, 1941, FO/371/29479.

27. Cripps (Moscow) to the Foreign Office, no. 317, Apr. 6, 1941, FO/371/29479.

28. Cripps (Moscow) to the Foreign Office, no. 320, Apr. 8, 1941, FO/371/29479.

29. Gabriel Gorodetsky, "Churchill's Warning to Stalin: A Reappraisal," *The Historical Journal* 29, no. 4 (1986): 985.

30. Curtis Keeble, *Britain and the Soviet Union, 1917–1989* (London: Macmillan, 1990), p. 369n. 14.

31. Foreign Office to Moscow, no. 321, Apr. 11, 1941, FO/371/29479.

32. Cripps (Moscow) to the Foreign Office, no. 346, Apr. 12, 1941, FO/371/29479.

33. Ibid. Also, see Cripps (Moscow) to Eden, Apr. 18, 1941 and the enclosure Cripps to Vyshinsky, Apr. 11, 1941, FO/371/29480; and Woodward, vol. 1, p. 606.

34. Gorodetsky, "Churchill's Warning to Stalin," p. 986.

35. Churchill, vol. 3, p. 359.

36. Ibid., p. 360.

37. Eden (London) to Cripps, no. 52, Apr. 16, 1941, FO/371/29465.

38. On Novikov's ascendent career, see *The Soviet Diplomatic Corps 1917–1967,* ed. Edward L. Crowley (Metuchen: Scarecrow Press, 1970), pp. 5, 11, 15, 19, 40, 129–130, 220.

39. For Webb's assessment of Maisky, see Beatrice Webb, *The Diary of Beatrice Webb 1924–1943,* ed. Norman and Jean MacKenzie (London: Virago in association with the London School of Economics and Political Science, 1985), IV, pp. 292, 301. On Maisky's need for an advisor and his fall from grace, see Alexander Nekrich, "The Arrest and Trial of I. M. Maisky," *Survey* 22, no. 3/4 (Summer/Autumn 1976): 313–320. Maisky's cultivation of Webb and others is well described in Sidney Aster, "Ivan Maisky and Anti-Appeasement," in *Lloyd George: Twelve Essays,* ed. A. J. P. Taylor (London: Hamish Hamilton, 1971), pp. 317–357.

40. Eden (London) to Cripps, no. 52, Apr. 16, 1941, FO/371/29465; and Anthony Eden, *The Eden Memoirs: The Reckoning* (London: Cassell, 1965), p. 265.

41. Churchill, vol. 3, p. 360.

42. Foreign Secretary to Prime Minister, Apr. 18, 1941, PREM 3/403/7, PRO.

43. Foreign Office to Cripps, no. 364, Apr. 18, 1941, FO/371/29479.

44. Gorodetsky, "Churchill's Warning to Stalin," p. 987. Also, see Woodward, vol. 1, pp. 607–609. For the actual memorandum, see Cripps (Moscow) to Eden, Apr. 18, 1941 and the enclosure, FO/371/29465.

45. Cripps (Moscow) to the Foreign Office, no. 381, Apr. 18, 1941, FO/371/29465.

46. Vyshinsky to Cripps, Apr. 18, 1941, FO/371/29481.

47. Minute by R. A. Butler, Apr. 25, 1941, FO/371/29465.

48. Diary of Beatrice Webb, Vols. 55–57 (1941–1943), May 23, 1941 (unpublished: LSEP), p. 7079.

49. Cripps (Moscow) to the Foreign Office, no. 383, Apr. 19, 1941, FO/371/29480.

50. Cripps (Moscow) to the Foreign Office, no. 407, Apr. 22, 1941, FO/371/29480.

51. Churchill, vol. 3, p. 360.

52. Ibid.

53. Prime Minister to Foreign Secretary and Lord Beaverbrook, Oct. 14, 1941, PREM 3/403/7, PRO.

54. Foreign Secretary to Prime Minister, Oct. 14, 1941, PREM 3/403/7, PRO.

55. Churchill, vol. 4, p. 493.

56. Woerman (Berlin) to Schulenburg, Apr. 7, 1941, Microfilm T120, Serial 1448, Frames 365324–365326, German Foreign Ministry Archives, NA; and *DGFP 1918–1945,* ser. D, vol. 12, pp. 604–605.

57. Germany. Reichsluftfahrtsministerium. Forschungsamt, *Breach of Security: The German Secret Intelligence File on Events Leading to the Second World War* (London: Kimber, 1968), p. 130.

58. Ibid., p. 17.

59. Record of Talk between Mr. Butler and Mr. Loy Henderson, Apr. 19, 1941, FO/371/29500.

60. Georgii Zhukov, *Vospominaniia i razmyshleniia* (Moscow: Novosti, 1969), pp. 243–244.

61. *Pravda,* June 20, 1988: 3.

62. Feliks I. Chuev, *Sto sorok besed s Molotovym: iz dnevnika F. Chueva* (Moscow: Terra, 1991), p. 39.

63. See Chapter 1, p. 17.

64. Churchill, vol. 4, p. 493.

65. Phillips, pp. 212–213. Also, see Sheean, pp. 331–332.

66. Valentin Berezhkov, *S diplomaticheskoi missiei v Berlin, 1940–1941* (Moscow: Novosti, 1966), pp. 69–72; Arkady Vaksberg, *The Prosecutor and the Prey* (London: Weidenfeld and Nicolson, 1990), p. 219 and Ovidii Gorchakov, "Nakanune, ili tragediia Kasssandry," *Nedelia* no. 42 (Oct. 17–23, 1988): 12.

67. Ismail Akhmedov, *In and Out of Stalin's GRU: A Tatar's Escape from Red Army Intelligence* (Frederick: University Publications of America, 1984), pp. 136–137. On Škvor and a more ominous version of Stalin's note ("This information is English provocation, find out who is making this provocation and punish him") handed to Akhmedov by Major General Panfilov rather than Golikov, see Akhmedov's testimony in United States Senate, Committee on the Judiciary, *Interlocking Subversion in Government Departments,* Hearing before the Subcommittee to Investigate the Administration of the Internal Security Act and other Internal Security Laws, 83rd Cong., 1st sess., pt. 15 (October 28, 29, November 12, 17, 18, 23, and December 2, 1953) (Washington, D.C.: Government Printing Office, 1953), pp. 1004–

1006. The British information from Škoda mentioned that aside from suspending all export orders to Russia, all future orders from Russia were to be refused. Simultaneously, Škoda had been ordered to collect from the Russians "as many payments as possible" during the next six weeks. Cadogan's minute was a pithy "Significant."

In addition, Czarist Russians and Ukrainians financed by the Germans contended that Germany would attack Russia during the summer and that by the autumn the Ukraine would be free of the Communists and would be an independent state. The information pertaining to the Škoda works came "from an authoritative source," the Foreign Office was told. Lockhart to Sargent and the minute by A[lexander] C[adogan], Apr. 22, 1941, FO/371/26548; R. H. B[ruce] L[ockhart], Office of the British Representative with the Provisional Czechoslovak Government, no. 9, Apr. 25, 1941, FO/371/26380. Also, see Lockhart to Sargeant, [Apr. 30, 1941?], FO/371/29480.

68. Akhmedov, p. 145.

69. Vaksberg, pp. 218–219; and Gorchakov, "Nakanune, ili tragediia Kassandry," p. 12. For a slightly garbled version of Susloparov's report, see Vladimir Petrov, *"June 22, 1941"; Soviet Historians and the German Invasion* (Columbia: University of South Carolina Press, 1968), pp. 169–170.

70. Akhmedov, p. 145.

71. "Marshal Zhukov on Soviet Leadership on the Eve and in the Early Days of the War," A[gency] P[ress] N[ovosti], *Military Bulletin* (Moscow), Special Issue, no. 20 (25), 012SDO-871009–GA-1 (Oct. 1987): 8. Also, see Zhukov, p. 244.

72. *Pravda,* Nov. 6, 1964: 6. Sorge's message of March 5 allegedly was a microfilm containing information from Ribbentrop to Ambassador Ott in Tokyo that gave the date of Barbarossa as mid-June. See F. W. Deakin and G. R. Storry, *The Case of Richard Sorge* (London: Chatto and Windus, 1966), p. 230; V. D. Danilov, "Sovetskoe glavnoe Komandovania v preddverii Velikoi Otechestvennoi voiny," *Novaia i noveishaia istoriia* no. 6 (1988): 18. Likewise suspect are telegrams purportedly sent by Sorge on April 11 and May 2 warning of a German attack. Textual exegeses raise suspicions that these are no more genuine than the March 5 message mentioned above. Gorchakov, "Nakanune, ili tragediia Kassandry," p. 12.

73. Deakin and Storry, pp. 228–229, Chalmers Johnson, *An Instance of Treason: Ozaki Hotsumi and the Sorge Spy Ring* (Stanford: Stanford University Press, 1964), pp. 155–156; Gordon W. Prange et al., *Target Tokyo. The Story of the Sorge Spy Ring* (New York: McGraw-Hill, 1984), p. 338. On Colonel von Niedermayer's activities, see John W. Wheeler-Bennett, *The Nemesis of Power* (London: Macmillan, 1954), pp. 127–129, 611, and 612–613n.; and Herbert von Dirksen, *Moskau-Tokio-London* (Stuttgart: Kohlhammer, 1949), pp. 133–134.

74. The Sorge Spy Ring: A Case Study in International Espionage in the Far East. Supreme Commander Allied Powers (SCAP), Civil Intelligence Section (CIS), Summary no. 23, Dec. 15, 1947. Sanitized Version Released to the Press Feb. 10, 1949, p. 41, Records of the Army Staff, Folder 15, Box 7480, RG 319, NA.

75. Danilov, p. 18.

76. The Sorge Spy Ring, pp. 9–13, 38–39; Extracts "The Sorge Spy Ring Case": Highlights from Thirty (30) Consecutive Exhibits Documenting the Sorge Case Prepared by the Military Intelligence Section GHQ Far East Command, Tokyo/Japan (n.d.), pp. 22–24, 49–55, Records of the Army Staff, Folder 21, Box 7481, RG 319, NA; An Authenticated Translation of Sorge's Own Story, Prepared and Translated by the Military Intelligence Section GHQ Far East Command Tokyo/Japan

(n.d.) from Documents of the Criminal Affairs Bureau, Ministry of Justice, Tokyo, Feb. 1942, Sorge Case Materials, pt. 3, Apr. 1942, p. 7, Records of the Army Staff, Folder 10, Box 7480, RG 319, NA; Extracts from an Authenticated Translation of the Foreign Affairs Yearbook 1942. Prepared and Translated by the Military Intelligence Section GHQ Far East Command Tokyo/Japan. Criminal Affairs Bureau, Ministry of Justice, Tokyo (n.d.), pt. 11, Summary of Radio Communications Facilities, p. 156, pt. 15, Sorge's Notes, p. 192, Folder 12, Box 7480, RG 319, NA; Johnson, pp. 164–167; Prange et al., pp. 102, 311, 502.

77. There appears to be a lack of consensus as to whether Clausen sent fifty or sixty transmissions in 1939. Since there was an increase of 6,040 word groups in 1940 over 1939, we decided to accept the lower figure of fifty transmissions for 1939. The Sorge Spy Ring, p. 50, loc. cit.; Extracts from an Authenticated Translation of the Foreign Affairs Yearbook 1942 . . . pt. 11, Summary of Radio Communication Facilities, p. 158, loc. cit.; Charles A. Willoughby, *Shanghai Conspiracy: The Sorge Spy Ring* (New York: Dutton, 1952), pp. 100, 121; Johnson, p. 167; Prange et al., pp. 268, 316, 340.

78. Prange et al., pp. 265–271.

79. "The Sorge Spy Ring—A Case Study in International Espionage in the Far East," Appendix, Feb. 9, 1949, in United States Congress, *Congressional Record,* 81st Cong., 1st sess., vol. 95, pt. 12, p. A722; Johnson, pp. 166–168, 181n.; Prange et al., pp. 313–316, 338–340, 502; Willoughby, p. 121. For Clausen's comments in postwar Tokyo, see C[ounter] I[ntelligence] C[orps] to Foreign Section, Dec. 5, 1945; and for his explanations about the question of his quasi-aborted transmissions, see Exhibit 3, Tokyo, Nov. 20, 1945, p. 3, Max Clausen Folder (XA502453) Box 31, IRR, RG 319, NA. On the Order of the Red Banner, see *Pravda,* Jan. 20, 1965: 1. On the Russian claims for May 6 and 19, 1941, see *Pravda,* Nov. 6, 1964: 6.

80. *Trud,* Dec. 19, 1967: 3.

81. See Chapter 1, p. 13.

82. See Chapter 3, p. 59.

83. Leopold Trepper, *The Great Game* (London: Michael Joseph, 1977), p. 127.

84. Vitaly Rapoport and Yuri Alexeev, *High Treason: Essays on the History of the Red Army 1918–1938* (Durham: Duke University Press, 1985), p. 348.

85. *Pravda,* June 22, 1989: 3.

86. Roy Medvedev, *Let History Judge,* rev. ed. (New York: Columbia University Press, 1989), p. 738. See also John Erickson, *The Road to Stalingrad* (Boulder: Westview, 1984), p. 89.

87. Erickson, *The Road to Stalingrad,* p. 77.

88. Rapoport and Alexeev, p. 420n. 22.

89. Alain Guerin and Nicole Chatel, *Camarade Sorge* (Paris: Julliard, 1965), pp. 87–88. See also Deakin and Storry, p. 231.

90. Prange et al., p. 341.

91. Johnson, p. 156; and Deakin and Storry, p. 231 and n.

92. Johnson, p. 156.

93. See early in this chapter, p. 89.

94. No. 38A, German Armoured Divisions, Apr. 3, 1941, WO/190/893, PRO.

95. No. 40B, Summary of MI14. Indication Files, Apr. 8, 1941, WO/190/893, PRO.

96. War Office, Weekly Intelligence Summary, no. 86, Apr. 2–9, 1941, WO/208/2259, PRO.

97. Chiefs of Staff Committee, Weekly Résumé, no. 84, Apr. 3–10, 1941, CAB/80/27, PRO.

98. No. 44B, Summary of MI14 Indication Files, Apr. 15, 1941 and no. 44C, World Situation, Apr. 15, 1941, WO/190/893, PRO.

99. Chiefs of Staff Committee, Weekly Résumé, no. 85, Apr. 10–17, 1941, CAB/80/27, PRO. On the Russian troop call-up during this period, see Military Attaché (Moscow) to the War Office, Apr. 11, 1941, FO/371/29479.

100. Foreign Office to Moscow, no. 375, Apr. 20, 1941, FO/371/29479.

101. Ibid.

102. No. 49A, Summary of MI14. Indication Files, Apr. 22, 1941, WO/190/893, PRO.

103. No. 49B, Axis Strategy, Apr. 22, 1941, WO/190/893, PRO.

104. F. H. Hinsley et al., *British Intelligence in the Second World War* (London: H. M. Stationery Office, 1979), vol. 1, p. 459.

105. Chiefs of Staff, 143rd Meeting, Apr. 22, 1941, CAB/79/11, PRO. On Cavendish-Bentinck's unease, see Chapter 3, p. 60.

106. No. 54B, MI14, German Relations with the U.S.S.R., Apr. 25, 1941, WO/190/893, PRO.

107. Ibid.

108. Ibid.

109. Ibid. On the destruction of the enemy's forces, see Carl von Clausewitz, *On War,* ed. and trans. Michael Howard and Peter Paret (Princeton: Princeton University Press, 1976), pp. 90–99. For the Petsamo nickel mines, see H. Peter Krosby, *Finland, Germany, and the Soviet Union, 1940–1941: The Petsamo Dispute* (Madison: University of Wisconsin Press, 1968). As to the Hungarian occupation of Ruthenia, see Paul Robert Magocsi, *The Shaping of a National Identity. Subcarpathian Rus', 1848–1948* (Cambridge: Harvard University Press, 1978), pp. 246–249.

110. No. 55B, Summary of MI14. Indication Files, Apr. 28, 1941, WO/190/893, PRO.

111. War Office, Weekly Intelligence Summary, no. 89, Apr. 23–30, 1941, WO/208/2259, PRO.

112. Chiefs of Staff Committee, Weekly Résumé, no. 87, Apr. 24–May 1, 1941, CAB/80/27, PRO.

113. Hinsley et al., vol. 1, pp. 460, 461.

114. Air Ministry, Weekly Intelligence Survey, no. 87, Apr. 30, 1941, AIR/22/74, PRO.

115. Hinsley et al., vol. 1, p. 460.

116. Air Ministry, Weekly Intelligence Survey, no. 88, May 7, 1941, AIR/22/74, PRO. For a discussion of other sources of British information, see Hinsley, "British Intelligence and Barbarossa," pp. 60–62.

117. Roberta Wohlstetter, *Pearl Harbor: Warning and Decision* (Stanford: Stanford University Press, 1962), pp. 3, 387.

118. See Chapter 1, p. 16.

## Chapter 5: Stalin

1. Chapter 4, p. 108.

2. *FRUS, 1941,* vol. 1, p. 165.

3. Cripps (Moscow) to Eden, no. 123, Sept. 27, 1941, FO/371/29491.

4. See Chapter 2, p. 51.

5. *FRUS, 1941,* vol. 1, pp. 805–814.

6. *Pravda,* June 20, 1988: 3.

7. John Erickson, *The Road to Stalingrad* (Boulder: Westview, 1984), pp. 88–90.

8. See Chapter 2, p. 48, and Chapter 3, p. 83.

9. *DGFP 1918–1945,* ser. D, vol. 12, p. 873.

10. Interrogation of Erick Kordt, Department of State Special Interrogation Mission under Dewitt C. Poole, RG 59, NA. See also Germany. Reichsluftfahrtsministerium. Forschungsamt, *Breach of Security: The German Secret Intelligence File on Events Leading to the Second World War* (London: Kimber, 1968), p. 123. On some of the German decrypts of Turkish messages, see ibid., pp. 131, 133–165, 182–183. For the Italian decryption, see Barton Whaley, *Codeword Barbarossa* (Cambridge: MIT Press, 1973), p. 152, and for the Russian, see "Iz istorii Velikoi Otechestvennoi Voiny. Nakanune voiny (Dokumenty 1940–1941), *Izvestiia TsK KPSS* no. 4 (1990): 207–208, 209, 211.

11. *DGFP 1918–1945,* ser. D, vol. 12, pp. 873–876. See also *NCA,* vol. 6, p. 998. On the Aktay-Cripps-Gavrilović-Diamantopoulos exchanges, see Gabriel Gorodetsky, *Stafford Cripps' Mission to Moscow 1940–1942* (Cambridge: Cambridge University Press, 1984), p. 92; and Henry C. Cassidy, *Moscow Dateline 1941–1943* (Boston: Houghton Mifflin, 1942), pp. 74–75.

12. Ismail Akhmedov, *In and Out of Stalin's GRU: A Tatar's Escape from the Red Army Intelligence* (Frederick: University Publications of America, 1984), pp. 139–140.

13. *DGFP 1918–1945,* ser. D, vol. 12, pp. 691–692, 791. See also *FRUS, 1941,* pp. 612–613.

14. *DGFP 1918–1945,* ser. D, vol. 12, p. 791.

15. [Rudolf] L[ikus], Confidential Report, May 3, 1941, Microfilm T120, Serial 36, Frame 26026, German Foreign Ministry Archives, NA.

16. Steinhardt (Moscow) to the Sec. of State, no. 896, May 2, 1941, File 701.626/61, RG 59, NA.

17. Ibid.

18. Grigore Gafencu, *Prelude to the Russian Campaign* (London: Muller, 1945), pp. 189–190.

19. Franz Halder, *Kriegstagebuch* (Stuttgart: Kohlhammer, 1962), vol. 2, p. 396.

20. Two demands Cripps did not believe the Russians would agree to were "for territorial concessions or for demobilisation" of the Red Army. Cripps (Moscow) to the Foreign Office, no. 502, May 13, 1941, FO/371/29481. Also see *FRUS, 1941,* vol. 1, p. 164.

21. "Iz istorii Velikoi," passim.

22. Ibid., pp. 219–220.

23. *FRUS, 1941,* vol. 1, p. 141.

24. *Pravda,* May 6, 1941: 1.

25. Dmitri Volkogonov, *Stalin: Triumph and Tragedy* (London: Weidenfeld and Nicolson, 1991), p. 370.

26. Alexander Werth, *Russia at War 1941–1945* (London: Barrie and Rockliff, 1964), pp. 122–123.

27. Cripps (Moscow) to the Foreign Office, no. 483, May 8, 1941, and Mallet (Stockholm) to the Foreign Office, no. 292, May 23, 1941, FO/371/29481; *DGFP 1918–1945,* ser. D, vol. 12, p. 965; Georgii Zhukov, *Vospominaniia i razmyshleniia* (Moscow: Novosti, 1969), p. 245; John Scott, *Duel for Europe: Stalin versus Hitler* (Boston: Houghton Mifflin, 1942), p. 245. See also Vladimir Petrov, *"June 22, 1941"; Soviet Historians and the German Invasion* (Columbia: University of South Carolina Press, 1968), p. 256n.; and Harrison E. Salisbury, *The 900 Days. The Siege of Leningrad* (New York: Harper and Row, 1969), p. 68n. 1.

28. Gustav Hilger and Alfred G. Mayer, *The Incompatible Allies: A Memoir-History of German Soviet Relations 1918–1941* (New York: Macmillan, 1953), p. 330 and n; Dmitri Volkogonov, "The German Attack, the Soviet Response, Sunday, 22 June 1941," in *Barbarossa: The Axis and the Allies,* ed. John Erickson and David Dilks (Edinburgh: Edinburgh University Press, 1994), pp. 78–79.

29. *DGFP 1918–1945,* ser. D, vol. 12, pp. 964–965.

30. Ibid., ser. D, vol. 12, p. 792.

31. Morris (Berlin) to the Sec. of State, no. 1762, May 6, 1941, File 740.0011 European War 1939/10680, RG 59, NA.

32. *FRUS, 1941,* vol. 1, p. 613.

33. Iverach McDonald, Untitled memorandum, June 13, 1941, FO/371/29483.

34. Hoover to Berle and the enclosed memorandum, May 9, 1941, File 861.00/11886, RG 59, NA.

35. Morris (Berlin) to the Sec. of State, no. 1766, Section One, May 7, 1941, File 740.0011 European War 1939/10703, RG 59, NA.

36. *FRUS, 1941,* vol. 1, p. 613.

37. Moscow Chancery to the Northern Department, Foreign Office, May 23, 1941, FO/371/29499.

38. Petrov, p. 257.

39. Zhukov, p. 249; and Nikita S. Khrushchev, "The Crimes of the Stalin Era," *The New Leader,* ed. Boris I. Nicolaevsky (New York, 1962), p. S37. See also Arkady Vaksberg, *The Prosecutor and the Prey* (London: Weidenfeld and Nicolson, 1990), p. 219. This incident is misdated May 19 in Ovidii Gorchakov, "Nakanune, ili tragediia Kassandry," *Nedelia* no. 43 (Oct. 24–30, 1988): 18.

40. See Roy Medvedev, *Let History Judge,* rev. ed. (New York: Columbia University Press, 1989), p. 739.

41. See Chapter 3, pp. 58–59.

42. *FRUS, 1941,* vol. 1, p. 165.

43. Cripps (Moscow) to the Foreign Office, no. 475, May 7, 1941, FO/371/29498.

44. Ibid.

45. Cripps (Moscow) to the Foreign Office, no. 475, May 7, 1941, and the attached minute by E[dward] O. Coote, May 8, [1941], FO/371/29498.

46. Cripps (Moscow) to the Foreign Office, no. 475, May 7, 1941, and the attached minute by L[aurence] Collier, May 8, [1941], FO/371/29498.

47. Cripps (Moscow) to the Foreign Office, no. 475, May 7, 1941, and the attached minute by A[lexander] C[adogan], May 9, 1941, FO/371/29498.

48. Cripps (Moscow) to the Foreign Office, no. 475, May 7, 1941, and the attached minute by A[nthony] E[den], May 9, [1941], FO/371/29498.

49. War Cabinet, May 8, 1941, CAB/65/18, PRO.

50. Schoenfeld (Helsinki) to the Sec. of State, no. 139, May 10, 1941, File 861.00/11885, RG 59, NA.

51. *DGFP 1918–1945,* ser. D, vol. 12, p. 730. See also *NCA,* vol. 6, p. 998.

52. *DGFP 1918–1945,* ser. D, vol. 12, p. 734.

53. Ibid., ser. D, vol. 12, pp. 790–792.

54. Ibid., ser. D, vol. 12, p. 793. See also *NCA,* vol. 6, p. 998.

55. Cripps (Moscow) to the Foreign Office, Nos. 486 and 488, May 9, 1941, FO/371/29500; Steinhardt (Moscow) to the Sec. of State, no. 935, May 9, 1941, File 701.5761/13, RG 59, NA; *FRUS, 1941,* vol. 1, p. 312; Harold Eeman, *Inside Stalin's Russia: Memoirs of a Diplomat 1936–1941* (London: Triton, 1977), pp. 190–191; Cassidy, p. 13; Scott, p. 242.

56. Cassidy, pp. 13–14; and Scott, pp. 242–243.

57. *FRUS, 1941,* vol. 1, pp. 311–312.

58. Cripps (Moscow) to the Foreign Office, no. 488, May 9, 1941, FO/371/29500.

59. Eeman, p. 191.

60. Mallet (Stockholm) to Eden, no. 177, May 22, 1941, FO/371/29501. On the German desire to convert their diplomatic missions in the Baltic states to consular ones, see *DGFP 1918–1945,* ser. D, vol. 12, pp. 243–244.

61. Eeman, pp. 190–191; Cassidy, pp. 14, 76; Scott, pp. 244, 257; Max Beloff, *The Foreign Policy of Soviet Russia 1929–1941* (London: Oxford University Press, 1949), vol. 2, p. 378n.

62. Vereker (Helsingfors) to Warner, May 26, 1941, FO/371/29501.

63. *FRUS, 1941,* vol. 1, pp. 141–142.

64. Cassidy and Warner to Harrison, May 9, 1941, FO/371/29500. Also, see *NCA,* vol. 6, p. 998.

65. War Office, Weekly Intelligence Survey, no. 91, May 7–14, 1941, WO/208/2259, PRO.

66. Cassidy, p. 14. See also *NCA,* vol. 6, p. 998.

67. Cripps (Moscow) to the Foreign Office, no. 486, May 9, 1941, FO/371/29500.

68. Lockhart to Sargent, May 12, 1941, FO/371/29501.

69. *Soviet Documents on Foreign Policy,* ed. Jane Degras (London: Oxford University Press, 1953), vol. 3, pp. 487–488.

70. Ibid., p. 488.

71. Beloff, vol. 2, p. 379n. On premature recognition, see Gerhard von Glahn, *Law Among Nations,* 5th ed. (New York: Macmillan, 1986), pp. 88–89. For German-Italian-Iraqi contacts, see Llewellyn Woodward, *British Policy in the Second World War* (London: H. M. Stationery Office, 1970), vol. 1, p. 580n.

72. Draft note by Sir Orme Sargent to Maisky about Iraq, May 31, 1941, FO/954/24; Sargent to the Sec. of State, May 14, 1941, FO/371/29501.

73. Minute by F[itzroy] H. R. Maclean, Jan. 28, [1941], FO/371/27666.

74. David J. Dallin, *Soviet Russia's Foreign Policy 1939–1942* (New Haven: Yale University Press, 1942), p. 296; and Beloff, vol. 2, p. 382.

75. Phillips (Rome) to the Sec. of State, no. 701, May 14, 1941, File 740.0011 European War 1939/10964, RG 59, NA.

76. *Dokumenty z historie československé politiky 1939–1943. [Acta Occupationis*

*Bohemiae & Moraviae],* ed. Libuše Otáhalová and Milada Červinková (Prague: Academia, 1966), vol. 1, p. 231.

77. Cripps (Moscow) to the Foreign Office, no. 413, Apr. 23, 1941, FO/371/29480.

78. Winston S. Churchill, *The Second World War* (Boston: Houghton Mifflin, 1951), vol. 3, p. 48.

79. William L. Shirer, *The Rise and Fall of the Third Reich* (New York: Simon and Schuster, 1960), p. 838; James Douglas-Hamilton, *Motive for a Mission* (Edinburgh: Mainstream, 1979), pp. 217–226; Earle (Sofia) to the Sec. of State, no. 240, May 13, 1941, File 862.00/4015, RG 59, NA.

80. For the German investigation, see Walter Schellenberg, *The Schellenberg Memoirs* (London: Deutsch, 1956), pp. 199–203.

81. For example, there are pages blanked out in PREM 3/219/7, PRO. In file 5188 in FO/371/29565, the papers C5251, C5253, C5301, and C5589 are closed for seventy-five years, or until the year 2017. Additional information on Hess can be found in FO/115/3544, FO/371/26565, 26566, and 30920, as well as in INF/1/912, HO/144/22492, AIR/19/564 and WO/199/3288A, all in the PRO.

82. Anthony Cave Brown, *"C": The Untold Story of Sir Stewart Graham Menzies; Spymaster to Winston Churchill* (New York: Macmillan, 1987), p. 348.

83. Churchill, vol. 3, p. 52.

84. Ivone Kirkpatrick, *The Inner Circle* (London: Macmillan, 1959), p. 180; and *NCA,* vol. 8, p. 43.

85. John Simon, *Retrospect* (London: Hutchinson, 1952), p. 263. As to Lord Simon's questioning of Hess, see Rudolph Hess—Preliminary Report, June 10, 1941, PREM 3/219/7, PRO.

86. Brown, p. 350.

87. A. J. P. Taylor, *Beaverbrook* (London: Hamish Hamilton, 1972), p. 485.

88. Eden to Cripps, no. 6, Nov. 2, 1941, CAB/66/19, pp. 234–235, PRO. Also, see W. Averell Harriman and Elie Abel, *Special Envoy to Churchill and Stalin, 1941–1946* (New York: Random House, 1975), p. 91.

89. Lee (London) in a paraphrased cablegram to the War Department, May 24, 1941, File 740.0011 European War 1939/12172, RG 59, NA.

90. Raymond E. Lee, *The London Observer: The Journal of General Raymond E. Lee 1940–1941,* ed. James Leutze (London: Hutchinson, 1972), p. 441.

91. [Lee] to Miles, Nov. 5, 1941 and the attached memorandum, Rudolf Hess Folder, File B8-0260-20, IRR, RG 319, NA.

92. Lee, p. 442.

93. Ibid., pp. 464–466.

94. Churchill, vol. 3, p. 356.

95. John Costello, *Ten Days to Destiny* (New York: Morrow, 1991), pp. 447–449.

96. Robert E. Sherwood, *Roosevelt and Hopkins, an Intimate History,* rev. ed. (New York: Harper, 1950), p. 294.

97. Schellenberg, p. 201.

98. *NCA,* vol. 8, pp. 38–46.

99. Cavendish-Bentinck to Cadogan, May 13, 1941, FO/371/26565.

100. Douglas-Hamilton, pp. 169, 292–294. On the Berlin rumors, see early in this chapter, p. 112. On racial hostility, see Chapter 1, pp. 7–8.

101. Winant (London) to the Sec. of State, no. 1907, May 13, 1941, File 862.00/4016, RG 59, NA

102. *DGFP 1918–1945,* ser. D, vol. 12, pp. 783–785.

103. Ibid., ser. D, vol. 12, pp. 783-787. On the use of Burckhardt as an intermediary, see Costello, *Ten Days to Destiny,* pp. 344, 454–455.

104. Douglas-Hamilton, p. 150.

105. See Robert Conquest, *Stalin: Breaker of Nations* (London: Weidenfeld and Nicolson, 1991), pp. 233–234.

106. Cripps (Moscow) to the Foreign Office, no. 502, May 13, 1941, FO/371/29481. See also Cripps (Moscow) to the Foreign Office, no. 413, Apr. 23, 1941, FO/371/29480.

107. *FRUS, 1941,* vol. 1, p. 314. The reduction of the Luftwaffe's sorties by 1,000 in May was incorrectly credited by the British to adverse weather and to recuperation from the successes of Royal Air Force night fighters. Air Ministry, Weekly Intelligence Survey, no. 90 (May 21, 1941), AIR/22/74, PRO.

108. Hoover to Berle, May 22, 1941, and the enclosure of May 21, 1941, File 862.00/4041, RG 59, NA.

109. Authenticated Translation of the Foreign Affairs Yearbook 1942. Prepared and Translated by the Military Intelligence Section GHQ Far East Command Tokyo/Japan. Criminal Affairs Bureau, Ministry of Justice, Tokyo (n.d.), pt. 6, p. 44; and F. W. Deakin and G. R. Storry, *The Case of Richard Sorge* (London: Chatto and Windus, 1966), p. 229n.

110. Yeaton (Moscow) in a paraphrased cablegram to the War Department, May 20, 1941, File 740.0011 European War 1939/11348, RG 59, NA.

111. See Chapter 4, p. 103.

112. *FRUS, 1941,* vol. 1, pp. 166–167.

113. Douglas-Hamilton, pp. 190–191.

114. Anthony Eden, *The Eden Memoirs: The Reckoning* (London: Cassell, 1965), p. 259.

115. Memorandum of Conversation by Sumner Welles, June 22, 1941, President's Secretary File, FDR Library.

116. Joseph P. Lash, *Roosevelt and Churchill 1939–1941* (New York: Norton, 1976), pp. 347–348.

117. Address book, May–June 1941, Box 142, Hugh Gibson Collection, Hoover Institution Archives, Stanford, California.

118. Halifax Diary, Thursday, Dec. 11, 1941, A7. 8. 9, Borthwick Institute of Historical Research, UY. Also see Alexander Cadogan, *The Diaries of Sir Alexander Cadogan,* ed. David Dilks (London: Cassell, 1971), p. 389.

119. Joseph E. Davies, Journal, June 23, 1941 and Diary, June 23, 1941, Folder, June 18–Sept. 10, 1941, Box 11, Joseph E. Davies Papers, LC.

120. Costello, *Ten Days to Destiny,* pp. 435–437. Philby's code name, according to Costello, was "Sonnchen" (Little Sun). Doubtlessly in the transliteration of the code name from German to Russian to English, a mistake developed. While Sohnchen (Little Son) makes sense in German, Sonnchen does not, especially if one keeps in mind that Philby's father was the eminent Arabist and explorer, Harry St. John Philby, thus the code name Sohnchen. On this point, see Walter Laqueur, "Disinformation," *The New Republic,* Aug. 5, 1991: 41.

121. [Rudolf Likus?], Confidential Report, May 16, 1941, Microfilm T120, Serial 36, Frame 26035, German Foreign Ministry Archives, NA.

122. Costello, *Ten Days to Destiny,* p. 441.

123. Ibid., pp. 441–442.

124. Ibid., pp. 435–437.

125. *DGFP 1918–1945,* ser. D, vol. 12, pp. 1042–1043. See also [Rudolf] L[ikus], Confidential Reports, June 13 and 14, 1941, Microfilm T120, Serial 36, Frames 26069–26070 and 26073, German Foreign Ministry Archives, NA.

126. Akhmedov, pp. 139, 146; and United States Senate, Committee on the Judiciary, *Scope of Soviet Activity in the United States,* Hearings before the Subcommittee to Investigate the Administration of the Internal Security Act and Other Internal Security Laws, 84th Cong. 2nd sess. pt. 3 (February 23, 1956) (Washington, D. C.: Government Printing Office, 1956), p. 66. Hereafter cited as *Scope of Soviet Activity in the United States.*

127. Nikita Khrushchev, *Khrushchev Remembers,* ed. and trans. Strobe Talbott (Boston: Little, Brown, 1970), p. 133.

128. Moscow Narrative, Sept. 30, 1941, D/100, Beaverbrook Papers, HLRO; Sherwood, p. 390. As to Cripps's comment, see Cripps (Moscow) to the Foreign Office, no. 502, May 13, 1941, FO/371/29481.

129. *FRUS, 1941,* vol. 1, p. 143; and Halifax (Washington) to the Foreign Office, no. 2281, May 21, 1941, FO/371/26565.

130. Ivan Maisky, *Vospominaniia Sovetskogo posla: voina 1939–1943* (Moscow: Nauka, 1965), pp. 133–134.

131. Butler to the Sec. of State, May 14, 1941, FO/371/29501.

132. Diary of Beatrice Webb, vols. 55–57 (1941–1943), May 23, 1941, p. 7080, LSEP.

133. Lee, p. 344.

134. Ivan Yeaton, Memoirs (typescript), pp. 37–38, U.S. Army Military Institute, CB.

135. A. J. P. Taylor, p. 485

136. *Pravda,* Oct. 15 and 19, 1942: 1.

137. Eden, p. 257. For the November documentation, see Douglas-Hamilton, pp. 297–300.

138. *DGFP 1918–1945,* ser. D, vol. 11, pp. 15–18, 60–61, 78–81, 129–132, 162–163; and Douglas-Hamilton, pp. 143–165.

139. Costello, *Ten Days to Destiny,* pp. 452-454.

140. Ibid., pp. 454–460, 493. On the Venlo incident, see the account by one of the MI6 participants, S. Payne Best, *The Venlo Incident* (London: Hutchinson, 1950).

141. Anthony Masters, *The Man Who Was M: The Life of Maxwell Knight* (London: Blackwell, 1984), pp. 126–128; and Donald McCormick, *17F. The Life of Ian Fleming* (London: Owen, 1993), pp. 81–97.

142. Brown, pp. 348–350.

143. Record of Talks at the Kremlin at Supper of October 18th 1944 at 1 A.M., PREM3/434/7, PRO.

144. Churchill, vol. 3, p. 5.

145. C[hurchill] to the Secretary of State for Air, Apr. 7, 1945, INF/1/912, PRO.

146. Gabriel Gorodetsky, "The Hess Affair and Anglo-Soviet Relations on the Eve of 'Barbarossa,' " *English Historical Review* 101, no. 399 (Apr. 1986): 405–420.

147. "Iz istorii Velikoi," p. 199. On the contacts between the Germans and the Duke and Duchess of Windsor during the summer of 1940, see Michael Bloch, *Operation Willi* (London: Weidenfeld and Nicolson, 1984), passim; and Philip Ziegler, *King Edward VIII: The Official Biography* (London: Collins, 1990), pp. 420–436.

148. *TMWC*, vol. 1, p. 354.

149. Adam Ulam, *Expansion and Coexistence. The History of Soviet Foreign Policy 1917–67*, 2nd ed. (New York: Praeger, 1974), p. 278n. Also, see Akhmedov, pp. 143–144.

150. Valentin M. Berezhkov, *S diplomaticheskoi missiei v Berlin, 1940–1941* (Moscow: Novosti, 1966), passim.

151. *The Soviet Diplomatic Corps 1917–1967*, ed. Edward L. Crowley (Metuchen: Scarecrow Press, 1970), pp. 4, 6, 16, 37, 143, 220.

152. Schellenberg, p. 321.

153. David J. Dallin, *Soviet Espionage* (New Haven: Yale University Press, 1965), p. 138. Also, see Leopold Trepper, *The Great Game* (London: Michael Joseph, 1977), p. 93.

154. Walter Krivitsky, *In Stalin's Secret Service* (New York: Harper, 1939), pp. 21, 214–215. On Krivitsky's move from the GRU to the KGB, see Elisabeth Poretsky, *Our Own People: A Memoir of 'Ignace Reiss' and His Friends* (London: Oxford University Press, 1969), p. 185n.; and John J. Dziak, *Chekisty: A History of the KGB* (Lexington: Lexington Books, 1988), p. 83.

155. Akhmedov, pp. 144, 208, 214. One former NKVD officer refers to Soviet intelligence having "developed a powerful network in Germany." See Pavel Sudoplatov and Anatoli Sudoplatov with Jerrold L. Schecter and Leona P. Schecter, *Special Tasks* (New York: Little, Brown, and Company, 1994), p. 138.

156. Christopher Andrew and Oleg Gordievsky, *KGB: The Inside Story of its Foreign Operations from Lenin to Gorbachev* (London: Hodder and Stoughton, 1990), p. 204. For the analogous paraphernalia in the Russian embassy in Paris, see David Irving, *Hitler's War* (New York: Viking, 1977), pp. 209–210. On this point, see also Cripps (Moscow) to Eden, no. 113, Sept. 17, 1941, FO/371/29491; and *Pravda*, Aug. 10, 1941: 4.

157. See Chapter 2, p. 40.

158. Dallin, *Soviet Espionage*, p. 132; Amy Knight, *Beria: Stalin's First Lieutenant* (Princeton: Princeton University Press, 1993), pp. 80, 91, 103, 125, 167; Michael Parrish, *Soviet Security and Intelligence Organizations, 1917–1990* (New York, Greenwood Press, 1992), pp. 77–78, 190.

159. United States Senate, Committee on the Judiciary, *Interlocking Subversion in Government Departments*, Hearings before the Subcommittee to Investigate the Administration of the Internal Security Act and Other Internal Security Laws, 83rd Cong. 1st sess. pt. 15 (October 28, 29, November 12, 17, 18, 23, and December 2, 1953) (Washington, D.C.: Government Printing Office, 1953), p. 1021. In the above hearing, his name is misspelled "Kabulov" and "Kubalov." Hereinafter cited as *Interlocking Subversion in Government Departments*. On the Kobulov brothers, also see Akhmedov, p. 143. On some of Kobulov's other activities in Berlin, see Sudoplatov and Sudoplatov, p. 114.

160. John Costello and Oleg Tsarev, *Deadly Illusions* (London: Century, 1993), p. 441n. 30.

161. [Rudolf] L[ikus], Confidential Report, Feb. 18, 1941, Microfilm T120, Serial 36, Frames 25965–25968, German Foreign Ministry Archives, NA. For a contrary view, see Erich F. Sommer, *Das Memorandum* (München: Herbig, 1981), p. 136.

162. Though not the most reliable of sources, see Thaddeus Wittlin, *Commissar. The Life and Death of Lavrenty Pavlovich Beria* (New York: Macmillan, 1972), pp. 27, 54; Sommer, p. 85; Knight, *Beria,* pp. 91, 103, 125, 167.

163. Sommer, p. 103; Knight, *Beria,* pp. 144, 167, 214; Parrish, pp. 77–78, 190.

164. On Kobulov's activities see Microfilm T120, Serial 36, passim, German Foreign Ministry Archives, NA. For the recruitment of Berlings and his approach to the Germans, see [Rudolf] L[ikus], Confidential Report, Aug. 17 and 19, 1941, Microfilm T120, Serial 36, Frames 25899–25902, German Foreign Ministry Archives, NA; *DGFP 1918–1945,* ser. D, vol. 11, pp. 980–981, 1085–1086, and vol. 12, pp. 1042–1043, 1049; Costello and Tsarev, p. 88. On the question of pressure, see also Kobulov's admonitions to Berlings on April 11 and 22, 1941: "I repeat that your life or death depends on the solution of this task." On April 22, Kobulov reminded Berlings, "You are a Latvian, as well as a Soviet citizen. As a Soviet citizen you have your duty to fulfill and not ask for money." [Rudolf] L[ikus], Confidential Report, Apr. 11, 1941, Microfilm T120, Serial 36, Frames 26015–26016; and [Rudolf Likus?], Note, Apr. 22, 1941, Microfilm T120, Serial 36, Frames 26023–26025, German Foreign Ministry Archives, NA.

165. Cripps (Moscow) to the Foreign Office, no. 1170, Sept. 20, 1941, FO/371/29490.

166. V. M. Kulish, "U poroga voiny," *Komsomolskaia pravda,* Aug. 24, 1988: 3.

167. Costello and Tsarev, p. 441n. 30.

168. [Rudolf Likus?], Confidential Report, Feb. 20, 1941, Microfilm T120, Serial 36, Frames 25971–25972, German Foreign Ministry Archives, NA.

169. *Scope of Soviet Activity in the United States,* pt. 3, p. 69. Also, see *Interlocking Subversion in Government Departments,* pt. 15, p. 1020; and Dallin, *Soviet Espionage,* p. 133.

170. See Chapter 1, p. 21.

171. Dallin, *Soviet Espionage,* p. 133.

172. Whaley, p. 69.

173. See Chapter 2, p. 30.

174. Dallin, *Soviet Espionage,* p. 133.

175. Schellenberg, p. 224.

176. Akhmedov, p. 143; and Chapter 4, p. 97.

177. Akhmedov, p. 148.

178. *The Rote Kapelle: The CIA's History of Soviet Intelligence and Espionage Networks in Western Europe, 1936–1945* (Frederick: University Publications of America, 1979), pp. 146–147, 154, 275–276, 288–289; Dallin, *Soviet Espionage,* pp. 133, 234, 243, 245, 246, 264. On Kudrayavtsev, see *Interlocking Subversion in Government Departments,* pt. 15, p. 1020; and *Scope of Soviet Activity in the United States,* pt. 3, pp. 65, 67; Costello and Tsarev, pp. 78–82, 394–396. One must examine the English version of Berezhkov's book to acquire the exact identification of Korotkov, for in the Russian text he is identified merely as "Sasha". Valentin Berezhkov, *History in the Making: Memoirs of World War II Diplomacy* (Moscow: Progress

Publishers, 1983), pp. 87, 94, 96–100, 102. For Korotkov's KGB pedigree, also see Ilya Dzhirkvelov, *Secret Servant* (London: Collins, 1987), pp. 106–108, 144, 248–249.

179. Dallin, *Soviet Espionage,* pp. 133, 234.

180. Akhmedov, pp. 140, 142, 149; *Interlocking Subversion in Government Departments,* pt. 15, pp. 1019–1020; *Scope of Soviet Activity in the United States,* pt. 3, pp. 65, 69. It is unclear whether the NKVD's Lev Alexandrovich Tarasov who served in Spain during the civil war and years later as first secretary of the embassy in Mexico City was the same Tarasov who served in Berlin in 1941 as the president of *Tass.* See Kirril Mikhailovich Alexeev, "Why I Deserted the Soviet," *Saturday Evening Post,* June 26, 1948): 19. On the subsequent use of *Tass,* see Dzhirkvelov, passim.

181. *Interlocking Subversion in Government Departments,* pt. 15, p. 1020; and *Scope of Activity in the United States,* pt. 3, p. 65. In the above 1953 hearings, Verkhovtsev was misspelled as "Verchovpsev."

182. [Rudolf] L[ikus], Confidential Report, Mar. 6, 1941, Microfilm T120, Serial 36, Frame 25975, German Foreign Ministry Archives, NA.

183. *DGFP 1918–1945,* ser. D, vol. 12, pp. 1042–1043.

184. Whaley, pp. 325–326.

185. Akhmedov, pp. 137–142; *Interlocking Subversion in Government Departments,* pt. 15, pp. 1004–1005, 1009; *Scope of Soviet Activity in the United States,* pt. 3, pp. 64–66.

186. *Scope of Soviet Activity in the United States,* pt. 3, p. 71.

187. Transcripts of the Hearings of the [Kellock-Taschereau] Royal Commission to Investigate the Facts Relating to and the Circumstances Surrounding the Communication, by Public Officials and Other Persons in Positions of Trust of Secret and Confidential Information to Agents of a Foreign Power, pp. 23, 102–105, 142, 145, 161–163, 189, 244, 246, 326, 332, 336–337, 340, 347, 392, 2499, 5050, 5264, 5447, 5495, 5529, 6010, RG 33/62, PAC; and Canada, *Royal Commission to Investigate the Facts Relating to and the Circumstances Surrounding the Communication, by Public Officials and Other Persons in Positions of Trust, of Secret and Confidential Information to Agents of a Foreign Power* (Ottawa: King's Printer, 1946), pp. 15–16, 85, 733; *Interlocking Subversion in Government Departments,* pt. 15, p. 1022.

188. *Rote Kapelle,* p. 276.

189. Pierre J. Huss and George Carpozi, *Red Spies in the U.N.* (New York: Coward-McCann, 1965), pp. 182–186.

190. *Interlocking Subversion in Government Departments,* pt. 15, p. 1020; and *Scope of Soviet Activity in the United States,* pt. 3, p. 65.

191. Dallin, *Soviet Espionage,* pp. 133–136.

192. Akhmedov, p. 135.

193. *Rote Kapelle,* pp. 151–152, 232, 347–348; and Sommer, p. 132.

194. Dallin, *Soviet Espionage,* p. 133.

195. Ibid., p. 134.

196. For example, see *Rote Kapelle,* pp. 139–164; and Costello and Tsarev, pp. 81-90.

197. *Interlocking Subversion in Government Departments,* pt. 15, pp. 1052–1054; and Akhmedov, p. 140.

198. Ibid.

199. Krivitsky, pp. 37–38; Poretsky, pp. 11–12, 21, 54, 170; Malcolm Muggeridge, *Chronicles of Wasted Time* (London: Collins, 1972), vol. 1, p. 215; Theodore E. Kruglak, *The Two Faces of Tass* (Minneapolis: University of Minnesota Press, 1962), pp. 28, 32-34, 92; Eugene Lyons, *Assignment in Utopia* (New York: Harcourt, Brace, 1938), passim; and *Interlocking Subversion in Government Departments,* pt. 15, pp. 1019–1020.

200. *Interlocking Subversion in Government Departments,* pt. 15, pp. 1009, 1054–1055; and Akhmedov, pp. 151, 163–164.

201. Chapter 4, p. 97.

202. Costello and Tsarev, pp. 85, 87-88.

203. Interestingly, Dekanozov's machination is not to be found in the Russian version but only in the English translation of Berezhkov, *History in the Making,* p. 72.

204. Vaksberg, p. 219. See also Gorchakov, "Nakanune, ili tragediia Kassandry," p. 18.

205. The telegrams are cited in Valentin Voyushin and Sergei Gorlov, "It Was Only Too Clear," *Vestnik,* no. 5 (May 1990): 61.

206. [Rudolf] L[ikus], Confidential Report, May 30, 1941, Microfilm T120, Serial 36, Frame 26048, German Foreign Ministry Archvies, NA.

207. [Rudolf Likus?], Confidential Report, June 17, 1941, Microfilm T120, Serial 36, Frame 26049, German Foreign Ministry Archives, NA.

208. Salisbury, p. 70.

209. [Rudolf] L[ikus], Confidential Report, June 12, 1941, Microfilm T120, Serial 36, Frame 26068, German Foreign Ministry Archives, NA.

210. [Rudolf] L[ikus], Confidential Report, June 20, 1941, Microfilm T120, Serial 36, Frames 26097–26098, German Foreign Ministry Archives, NA.

211. Voyushin and Gorlov, pp. 61, 63.

212. Ibid., p. 64.

213. Gabriel Gorodetsky, "Filip Ivanovich Golikov," in *Stalin's Generals,* ed. Harold Shukman (New York: Grove Press, 1993), p. 80.

## Chapter 6: The Ultimate Deception

1. Schulenburg (Moscow) to Berlin, no. 1142, May 12, 1941, Microfilm T120, Serial 105, Frame 113433, German Foreign Ministry Archives, NA.

2. See Chapter 5, p. 124.

3. [Rudolf] L[ikus], Confidential Report, May 17, 1941, Microfilm T120, Serial 36, Frame 26036, German Foreign Ministry Archives, NA.

4. Ponschab (Harbin) to Berlin, no. 33, May 3, 1941, Microfilm T120, Serial 105, Frame 113409, German Foreign Ministry Archives, NA.

5. Ponschab (Harbin) to Berlin, no. 32, May 6, 1941, Microfilm T120, Serial 105, Frame 113417, German Foreign Ministry Archives, NA.

6. See Chapter 5, p. 121.

7. Winston S. Churchill, *The Second World War* (Boston: Houghton Mifflin, 1951), vol. 3, pp. 253–267.

8. Ponschab (Harbin) to Berlin, no. 34, May 8, 1941, Microfilm T120, Serial 105, Frame 113424, German Foreign Ministry Archives, NA.

9. Cripps (Moscow) to the Foreign Office, no. 533, May 24, 1941, FO/371/27033. As to Abdul Majid Khan's machinations in Berlin during this period, see *DGFP 1918–1945,* ser. D, vol. 12, pp. 283, 728–729, 971–972.

10. See [Rudolf] L[ikus], May 28, 1941, Microfilm T120, Serial 36, Frames 26041–26045, German Foreign Ministry Archives, NA.

11. [Rudolf] L[ikus], Confidential Report, June 4, 1941, Microfilm T120, Serial 36, Frames 26053–26056, German Foreign Ministry Archives, NA.

12. Ponschab (Harbin) to Berlin, No, 37, May 11, 1941, Microfilm T120, Serial 105, Frames 113431–113432, German Foreign Ministry Archives, NA.

13. *DGFP 1918–1945,* ser. D, vol. 12, p. 793.

14. Ponschab (Harbin) to Berlin, no. 40, May 13, 1941, Microfilm T120, Serial 105, Frame 113435, German Foreign Ministry Archives, NA.

15. *FRUS, 1941,* vol. 1, pp. 145–146.

16. Ibid., vol. 1, pp. 150–151.

17. Steinhardt (Moscow) to the Sec. of State, no. 929, May 7, 1941, File 740.0011 European War 1939/10719, RG 59, NA.

18. Vereker (Helsingfors) to the Foreign Office, no. 386, June 6, 1941, FO/371/29482. Also, see *DGFP 1918–1945* ser. D, vol. 12, pp. 826–827.

19. To London he was identified as "Kutiekov" [Vereker (Helsingfors) to the Foreign Office, no. 386, June 6, 1941, FO/371/29482]; and to Washington he was identified as "Krugikov" [Steinhardt (Moscow) to the Sec. of State, no. 1042, May 24, 1941, File 740.0011 European War 1939/11283, RG 59, NA].

20. On Krutikov's economic endeavors in Berlin, see *DGFP 1918–1945,* ser. D, vol. 12, p. 602.

21. Vereker (Helsingfors) to the Foreign Office, no. 386, June 6, 1941, FO/371/29482.

22. Valentin M. Berezhkov, *S diplomaticheskoi missiei v Berlin, 1940–1941* (Moscow: Novosti, 1966), p. 73.

23. Interrogation of Otto Meissner, Department of State Special Interrogation Mission under Dewitt C. Poole, RG 59, NA.

24. Martha Dodd, *Through Embassy Eyes* (New York: Harcourt, Brace and Co., 1939), pp. 207, 258.

25. Interrogation of Otto Meissner, loc. cit.

26. *DGFP 1918–1945* ser. D, vol. 14, p. 109.

27. Henry C. Cassidy, *Moscow Dateline 1941–1943* (Boston: Houghton Mifflin, 1943), p. 72. See also Dodd, p. 259.

28. André Francois-Poncet, *Souvenirs d'une ambassade à Berlin Septembre 1931–Octobre 1938* (Paris: Flammarion, 1946), p. 44. See also Dodd, pp. 207, 257–259.

29. Ovidii Gorchakov, "Nakanune, ili tragediia Kassandry," *Nedelia* no. 42 (Oct. 17–23, 1988): 12.

30. Donald Cameron Watt, "The Initiation of Talks Leading to the Nazi-Soviet Pact: An Historical Problem," in *Essays in Honour of E. H. Carr,* ed. C. Abramsky and Beryl J. Williams (London: Macmillan, 1974), pp. 163–165.

31. John Erickson, *The Road to Stalingrad* (Boulder: Westview, 1984), p. 59.

32. Earlier approaches to the Germans following Hitler's assumption of power reflected the procedure of negotiating through trusted, but unofficial back channels. *DGFP 1918–1945,* ser. C, vol. 1, 747, 863, 884–885, and vol. 2, 21–22, 40; Herbert von Dirksen, *Moskau-Tokio-London* (Stuttgart: Kohlhammer, 1949), pp. 127–130; Evgeni Gnedin, *Iz istorii otnoshenii mezhdu SSSR i fashistskoi Germaniei* (New York: Khronika, 1977), pp. 22–27; Gustav Hilger and Alfred G. Meyer, *The Incompatible*

*Allies: A Memoir-History of German Soviet Relations 1918–1941* (New York: Macmillan, 1953), pp. 260–261; Karlheinz Niclauss, *Die Sowjetunion und Hitlers Machtergreifung* (Bonn: Rohrscheid, 1966), pp. 120, 121, 127, 138; Robert C. Tucker, *Stalin in Power: The Revolution from Above, 1928–1941* (New York: Norton, 1990), pp. 233–237.

In the autumn of 1936, for example, there was an aborted attempt to establish contact with the German military during a top secret visit to Berlin of General Yeronim P. Uborevich, who subsequently was liquidated along with Marshal Tukhachevsky. Tippelskirch (Moscow) to Schiep, no. A/9/38, Jan. 7, 1938, Microfilm T120, Serial 523, Frames 237657–237661, German Foreign Ministry Archives, NA.

Concurrently, David Kandelaki, a Georgian and a confidant of Stalin, who led the Russian trade mission in Berlin, was used to probe German willingness to conclude a political settlement. *DGFP 1918–1945,* ser. C, vol. 6, pp. 379–380, 403–404; Walter Krivitsky, *In Stalin's Secret Service* (New York: Harper, 1939), pp. 21, 225–226; and Tucker, pp. 348–349. Kandelaki's endeavors led nowhere, and he was subsequently to disappear, like Karl Radek and other Bolsheviks, into the Gulag. Geoffrey Bailey, *The Conspirators* (New York: Harper, 1960), p. 147n. and Tucker, p. 656n. 59.

Knowing too much about Stalin's machinations with the Germans or disagreeing with him about the matter, as did Artur Artuzov (né Fraucci or Renucci), director of the NKVD's Foreign Department, could prove to be a lethal mistake. Krivitsky, p. 12; and John J. Dziak, *Chekisty: A History of the KGB* (Lexington: Lexington Books, 1988), pp. 41, 85. For another apparent example of NKVD attempts to pursue channels to the German leadership, see Pavel Sudoplatov and Anatoli Sudoplatov with Jerrold L. Schecter and Leona P. Schecter, *Special Tasks* (New York: Little, Brown, and Company, 1994), pp. 112–115.

33. John Waitz, *Hitler's Diplomat: The Life and Times of Joachim von Ribbentrop* (New York: Ticknor and Fields, 1992), passim; and Michael Bloch, *Ribbentrop* (London: Bantam, 1992), passim.

34. Sterling (Stockholm) to the Sec. of State, no. 343, June 17, 1941, File 740.0011 European War 1939/12160, RG 59, NA.

35. Steinhardt (Moscow) to the Sec. of State, no. 1050, Section Two, May 27, 1941, File 740.0011 European War 1939/11359, RG 59, NA.

36. F. H. Hinsley et al., *British Intelligence in the Second World War* (London: H. M. Stationery Office, 1979), vol. 1, p. 472.

37. Churchill, vol. 4, p. 493.

38. Valentin Berezhkov, "Stalin's Error of Judgement," *International Affairs* (Moscow) no. 9 (September 1989): 25.

39. [Rudolf] L[ikus], Confidential Report, May 30, 1941, Microfilm T120, Serial 36, Frames 26046–26047, German Foreign Ministry Archives, NA.

40. Steinhardt (Moscow) to the Sec. of State, no. 1042, May 24, 1941, File 740.0011 European War 1939/11283, RG 59, NA. On the absence of negotiations in Moscow, see also Cripps (Moscow) to the Foreign Office, no. 500, May 13, 1941, FO/371/29481.

41. Ovidii Gorchakov, "Nakanune, ili tragediia Kassandry," *Nedelia* no. 43 (Oct. 24–30, 1988): 18.

42. Steinhardt (Moscow) to the Sec. of State, no. 1127, Section Two, June 12, 1941, File 740.0011 European War 1939/11970, RG 59, NA.

43. Minute by E[dward] O. Coote, May 6, [1941], FO/371/29480.

44. Minute by C[hristopher] F. A. Warner, May 15, [1941], Foreign Office to Helsingfors, no. 190, May 18, 1941, and Vereker (Helsingfors) to the Foreign Office, no. 365, May 24, 1941, FO/371/29481.

45. Minute by C[hristopher] F. A. Warner, May 26, [1941], FO/371/29481.

46. Minute by C[hristopher] F. A. Warner, June l, [1941] and his minute of May 30, [1941], FO/371/29481.

47. Niels Erik Rosenfeldt, *Knowledge and Power. The Role of Stalin's Secret Chancellery in the Soviet System of Government* (Copenhagen: Rosenkilde and Bagger, 1978), pp. 55–57, 86, 119.

48. Minute by C[hristopher] F. A. Warner, May 15, [1941], FO/371/29481.

49. Mallet (Stockholm) to the Foreign Office, no. 297, May 24, 1941, FO/371/29481.

50. Cripps (Moscow) to the Foreign Office, Nos. 526, May 22, and 554, May 30, 1941, FO/371/29481.

51. For Maclean's treachery, see John Costello and Oleg Tsarev, *Deadly Illusions* (London: Century, 1993), pp. 203, 459n. 56. The ideological disillusionment with Communism of the alleged source in Mikoyan's office made his recruitment possible. His recruiter, Major Harold 'Gibby' Gibson of MI6, had been raised and schooled in Czarist Russia and spoke fluent Russian. The source, whose name has never been made public, had been Gibson's fellow classmate. By alerting the NKVD, Blunt undoubtedly contributed to the source's death, but it was an action about which Blunt did not have the slightest qualms. Gibson subsequently served in Prague and was instrumental in mid-March 1938 in assisting Colonel Moravec and his colleagues in Czech military intelligence to transfer their operations to London. Peter Wright, *Spycatcher* (New York: Viking, 1987), p. 220; Peter Wright, *The Spycatcher's Encyclopedia of Espionage* (Melbourne, Heinemann, 1991), pp. 100–101; Chapman Pincher, *Their Trade is Treachery* (London: Sidgwick and Jackson, 1981), pp. 93–94; Chapman Pincher, *Too Secret Too Long* (London: Sidgwick and Jackson, 1984), p. 346; John Costello, *Mask of Treachery* (New York: William Morrow, 1988), p. 375. On Gibson in Prague, see František Moravec, *Master of Spies* (Garden City, New York: Doubleday, 1975), pp. 129–130, 134, 142–144. Also see the SIS information dealing with Mikoyan in F. H. Hinsley, "British Intelligence and Barbarossa," in *Barbarossa: The Axis and the Allies,* ed. John Erickson and David Dilks (Edinburgh: Edinburgh Universiy Press, 1994), p. 46.

52. Cripps (Moscow) to the Foreign Office, no. 1170, Sept. 20, 1941, FO/371/29490.

53. See Chapter 2, p. 25.

54. Morris (Berlin) to the Sec. of State, no. 2095, Section Two, May 27, 1941, File 740.0011 European War 1939/11356, RG 59, NA.

55. David J. Dallin, *Soviet Espionage* (New Haven: Yale University Press, 1955), p. 133.

56. Halifax (Washington) to the Foreign Office, no. 2421, May 28, 1941, FO/371/29481.

57. *DGFP 1918–1945,* ser. D, vol. 12, pp. 602–603, 822, 841.

58. Vladimir Karpov, "Zhukov (Marshaly Velikoi Otechestvennoi Voiny)," *Kommunist Vooruzhennykh Sil* no. 5 (1990): 67–68 and Dmitri Volkogonov, *Stalin: Triumph and Tragedy* (London: Weidenfeld and Nicolson, 1991), p. 398. Zhukov's

stillborn proposal may help explain Red Army ruminations in mid-April that war was imminent, that Russia should not be caught unaware, and that it would initiate an attack in August. Grigory Tokaev, *Stalin Means War* (London: Weidenfeld and Nicolson, 1951), p. 34. Also, see Victor Suvorov (pseud.), *Icebreaker* (London: Hamish Hamilton, 1990), passim. It may also account for an NKVD captain's prognostication that Russia would be at war by June. Nora Murray, *I Spied for Stalin* (New York: Funk, 1951), p. 204.

59. Pierre J. Huss, *The Foe We Face* (Garden City, New York: Doubleday, Doran, 1942), pp. 123–146; and Louis P. Lochner, *What about Germany?* (London: Hodder and Stoughton, 1943), p. 233. The episode is misdated as April 11 in Ovidii Gorchakov, "Nakanune, ili tragediia Kassandry," *Nedelia* no. 42 (Oct. 17–23, 1988): 12.

60. I. F. Filippov, *Zapiski o Tretem Reikhe* (Moscow: Mezhdunarodnaia Otnosheniia, 1966), p. 199.

61. See Chapter 4, p. 99.

62. Gorchakov, "Nakanune, ili tragediia Kassandry," no. 43: 18.

63. See Chapter l, p. 24.

64. Interrogation of Otto Meissner, loc. cit.

65. Berezhkov to the writers, Apr. 22, 1992.

66. Berezhkov, "Stalin's Error of Judgement," p. 25; and Berezhkov, *S diplomaticheskoi missiei,* p. 73. Also Berezhkov to the writers, Apr. 22, 1992.

67. *FRUS, 1941,* vol. 1, p. 144

68. Ibid., p. 147.

69. Arkady Vaksberg, *The Prosecutor and the Prey* (London: Weidenfeld and Nicolson, 1990), p. 219; and Nikita S. Khrushchev, "The Crimes of the Stalinist Era," *The New Leader,* ed. Boris Nicolaevsky (New York: The New Leader, 1962), p. S37.

70. For the date, see Ovidii Gorchakov, "Nakanune, ili tragediia Kassandry," *Nedelia* no. 44 (Oct. 31–Nov. 6, 1988): 21.

71. Ibid., no. 43: 18.

72. Steinhardt (Moscow) to the Sec. of State, no. 929, May 7, 1941, File 740.0011 European War 1939/10719, RG 59, NA.

73. *DGFP 1918–1945,* ser. D, vol. 12, pp. 666 669. Also, see Steinhardt (Moscow) to the Sec. of State, no. 929, May 7, 1941, File 740.0011 European War 1919/10719, RG 59, NA.

74. Gustav Hilger and Alfred G. Meyer, *The Incompatible Allies: A Memoir-History of German Soviet Relations 1918–1941* (New York: Macmillan, 1953), pp. 328–329.

75. Ibid., p. 331.

76. Ibid.

77. Ibid., pp. 331–332; and *Pravda,* June 22, 1989: 3. For Stalin's stance, see Genri to Erenburg, May 30, 1965, in *Druzhba Narodov,* March 1988: 236.

78. Harrison E. Salisbury, *The 900 Days: the Siege of Leningrad* (New York: Harper and Row, 1969), p. 49n. On Walther's description, see Cassidy, p. 72. On Beria's leitmotif, see Gorchakov, "Nakanune, ili tragediia Kassandry," no. 44: 21.

79. *Pravda,* June 22, 1989: 3.

80. Feliks I. Chuev, *Sto sorok besed s Molotovym: iz dnevnika F. Chueva* (Moscow: Terra, 1991), p. 39.

81. *DGFP 1918–1945,* ser. D, vol. 12, p. 751.

82. Ibid., ser. D, vol. 12, pp. 789–790.

83. Moravec, p. 193.

84. Volkonogov, *Stalin,* pp. 398–399.

85. Ivan Maisky, *Vospominaniia Sovetskogo posla: voina 1939–1943* (Moscow: Nauka, 1965), pp. 135–136. See also Warner to Maisky, June 2, 1941, FO/371/29551.

86. Adolf Hitler, *Hitler's Secret Conversations 1941–1944,* ed. H. R. Trevor-Roper (New York: Farrar, Straus, and Young, 1953), p. 397.

87. Eden to Cripps, no. 73, June 2, 1941, FO/371/29465.

88. *DGFP 1918–1945,* ser. D, vol. 12, p. 1501.

89. Partridge (Budapest) in a paraphrased cablegram to the War Department, June 20, 1941, 740.0011 European War 1939/12712, RG 59, NA.

90. *DGFP 1918–1945,* ser. D, vol. 12, p. 826.

91. Vereker (Helsingfors) to the Foreign Office, no. 386, June 6, 1941, FO/371/29482.

92. Ulrich von Hassell, *The Von Hassell Diaries 1938–1944* (Garden City, New York: Doubleday), p. 189.

93. Hoover to Berle, Apr. 16, 1941, File 862.20225/199, RG 59, NA.

94. Kelly (Bern) to the Foreign Office, no. 968, May 6, 1941, FO/371/26520.

95. Morris (Berlin) to the Sec. of State, no. 1870, Section One, May 13, 1941, File 740.0011 European War 1939/10975, RG 59, NA.

96. Phillips (Rome) to the Sec. of State, no. 691, May 13, 1941, File 740.0011 European War 1939/10887, RG 59, NA.

97. Phillips (Rome) to the Sec. of State, no. 696, May 13, 1941, File 740.0011 European War 1939/10932, RG 59, NA.

98. Gascoigne (Tangier) to the Foreign Office, no. 31, May 18, 1941, FO/371/29481.

99. Clark Kerr (Chungking) to the Foreign Office, no. 288, June 10, 1941, FO/371/29482. A few days earlier, Lord Halifax had been alerted by his Chinese counterpart in Washington of the upcoming German attack, based on agent information and the comments of Dr. Hjalmar Schacht, the former minister of economics [Halifax (Washington) to the Foreign Office, no. 2608, June 6, 1941, FO/371/26521]. On Schacht's comments, also see Grew (Tokyo) to the Sec. of State, no. 820, June 13, 1941, File 740.0011 European War 1939/12029, RG 59, NA. Apparently in mid-May, Generalissimo Chiang Kai-shek had learned of the upcoming German attack and had so informed Lauchlin Currie, President Roosevelt's administrative assistant [Johnson (Chungking) to the Sec. of State, no. 178, May 11, 1941, File 740.0011 European War 1939/10806, RG 59, NA; and *FRUS, 1941,* vol. 4, pp. 186–187]. If one accepts the postwar allegation that Currie was a wartime member of the Russian espionage apparatus, and such was the case, then it would be fair to assume that Chiang Kai-shek's information also reached Moscow. On Currie, see Allen Weinstein, *Perjury: The Hiss-Chambers Case* (New York: Knopf, 1978), pp. 4, 14, 23, 166, 329.

100. Baggallay (Moscow) to the Foreign Office, no. 608, June 15, 1941, FO/371/29483. See also [Rudolf] L[ikus], Confidential Report, May 28, 1941, Microfilm T120, Serial 36, Frames 26041–26045, German Foreign Ministry Archives, NA.

101. Halifax (Washington) to the Foreign Office, no. 2758, June 15, 1941, FO/371/29482.

102. Australian Legation (Washington) repeated to London, no. 448, June 19, 1941, FO/371/29484.

103. [Rudolf] L[ikus], Confidential Report, May 28, 1941, Microfilm T120, Serial 36, Frames 26039–26040, German Foreign Ministry Archives, NA.

104. Eden to Cripps, no. 69, May 27, 1941, FO/371/29501.

105. *FRUS, 1941,* vol. 1, p. 146.

106. Steinhardt (Moscow) to the Sec. of State, no. 996, May 19, 1941, File 740.0011 European War 1939/11105, RG 59, NA.

107. *Pravda,* May 25, 1941: 5; Steinhardt (Moscow) to the Sec. of State, no. 1043, May 25, 1941, File 740.0011 European War 1939/11284, RG 59, NA; David J. Dallin, *Soviet Russia's Foreign Policy 1939–1942* (New Haven: Yale University Press, 1942), p. 372; John Scott, *Duel for Europe: Stalin versus Hitler* (Boston; Houghton Mifflin, 1942), p. 250.

108. *DGFP 1918–1945,* ser. D, vol. 12, pp. 474–475.

109. Air Ministry, Weekly Intelligence Survey, no. 99 (July 23, 1941), and no. 96 (July 2, 1941), AIR/22/74, PRO.

110. *DGFP 1918–1945,* ser. D, vol. 12, pp. 826–827. Also, see *FRUS, 1941,* vol. 1, pp. 144–148; and Dallin, *Soviet Russia's Foreign Policy 1939–1942,* pp. 422–427.

111. Minute by V[ictor] Cavendish-Bentinck, May 26, 1941, FO/371/29481.

112. [Rudolf] L[ikus], Confidential Reports, Oct. 2, 9, Nov. 7, 1940, Mar. 15 and 25, 1941, Microfilm T120, Serial 36, Frames 25915, 25916, 25925, 25979, 25998, German Foreign Ministry Archives, NA.

113. *Pravda,* June 8, 1941: 1; Baggallay (Moscow) to the Foreign Office, no. 584, June 8, 1941 and Veneker (Helsingfors) to the Foreign Office, no. 350, June 6, 1941, FO/371/29369; Dallin, *Soviet Russia's Foreign Policy 1939–1942,* pp. 296–297; Max Beloff, *The Foreign Policy of Soviet Russia 1929–1941* (London: Oxford University Press, 1949), vol. 2, p. 382.

114. *DGFP 1918–1945,* ser. D, vol. 12, p. 1050.

115. Mallet (Stockholm) to the Foreign Office, no. 206, May 26, 1941, FO/371/29497. See also [Rudolf] L[ikus], Confidential Report, May 28, 1941, Microfilm T120, Serial 36, Frames 26041–26045, German Foreign Ministry Archives, NA.

116. Morris (Berlin) to the Sec. of State, no. 1239, Section One, Apr. 2, 1941, File 740.0011 European War 1939/9565; and Morris (Berlin), no. 1423, Section Three, Apr. 13, 1941, File 740.0011 European War 1939/9941, RG 59, NA.

117. Harrison (Bern) to the Sec. of State, no. 1712, May 6, 1941 and enclosure, File 862.00/4035, Morris (Berlin) to the Sec. of State, no. 1870, Section One, May 13, 1941, File 740.0011 European War 1939/10975; Morris (Berlin) to the Sec. of State, no. 1992, Section Two, May 21, 1941, File 740.0011 European War 1939/11175; and Gunther (Bucharest) to the Sec. of State, no. 510, June 7, 1941, File 740.0011 European War 1939/11778, RG 59, NA; Australian Legation (Washington) to the Foreign Office, no. 64, June 19, 1941, FO/371/29484.

118. *FRUS, 1941,* vol. 1, p. 142; Morris (Berlin) to the Sec. of State, no. 1991, May 21, 1941, File 740.0011 European War 1939/11175, RG 59, NA; Halifax (Washington) to the Foreign Office, no. 2295, May 23, 1941, FO/371/29481;

Morris (Berlin) to the Sec. of State, no. 2094, May 27, 1941, File 740.0011 European War 1939/11356, Gunther (Bucharest) to the Sec. of State, no. 510, June 7, 1941, File 740.0011 European War 1939/11778, Morris (Berlin) to the Sec. of State, no. 2261, June 8, 1941, File 740.0011 European War 1939/11763, Earle (Sofia) to the Sec. of State, no. 280, June 14, 1941, File 740.0011 European War 1939/12058, RG 59, NA; Vereker (Helsingfors) to the Foreign Office, no. 428, June 16, 1941, FO/371/29483. See also [Rudolf] L[ikus], Confidential Report, May 28, 1941, Microfilm T120, Serial 36, Frames 26041–26045, German Foreign Ministry Archives, NA.

119. See later in this chapter. p. 176.

120. Yeaton (Moscow) in a paraphrased cablegram to the War Department, May 24, 1941, File 740.0011 European War 1939/11671; and Yeaton (Moscow) in a paraphrased cablegram to the War Department, June 7, 1941, File 740.0011 European War 1939/12171, RG 59, NA.

121. "Vo slavu rodini," *Bolshevik* no. 10 (May 1941): 2, 6.

122. Steinhardt (Moscow) to the Sec. of State, no. 1161, June 17, 1941, File 740.0011 European War 1939/12175, RG 59, NA.

123. See early in this chapter, p. 147.

124. Ponschab (Harbin) to Berlin, no. 42, May 18, 1941, Microfilm T120, Serial 105, Frames 113437–113438, German Foreign Ministry Archives, NA. On the Vichy French-German agreement, see Churchill, vol. 3, p. 322.

125. Ponschab (Harbin) to Berlin, no. 43, May 21, 1941, Microfilm T120, Serial 105, Frames 113444–113445, German Foreign Ministry Archives, NA.

126. Ibid.

127. Ponschab (Harbin) to Berlin, no. 45, May 24, 1941, Microfilm T120, Serial 105, Frame 113451, German Foreign Ministry Archives, NA.

128. Ibid.

129. Ponschab (Harbin) to Berlin, no. 46, May 31, 1941, Microfilm T120, Serial 105, Frames 113465–113466, German Foreign Ministry Archives, NA.

130. Ponschab (Harbin) to Berlin, no. 48, June 2, 1941, Microfilm T120, Serial 105, Frames 113468–113469, German Foreign Ministry Archives, NA.

131. Ibid.

132. Ponschab (Harbin) to Berlin, no. 50, June 3, 1941, Microfilm T120, Serial 105, Frames 113471–113472, German Foreign Ministry Archives, NA.

133. Ibid.

134. Ponschab (Harbin) to Berlin, no. 51, June 7, 1941, Microfilm T120, Serial 105, Frame 113484, German Foreign Ministry Archives, NA.

135. Ibid.

136. Ponschab (Harbin) to Berlin, no. 52, June 11, 1941, Microfilm T120, Serial 105, Frame 113486, German Foreign Ministry Archives, NA.

137. Ponschab (Harbin) to Berlin, no. 54, June 12, 1941, Microfilm T120, Serial 105, Frame 113488, German Foreign Ministry Archives, NA.

138. Ponschab (Harbin) to Berlin, no. 55, June 12, 1941, Microfilm T120, Serial 105, Frame 113489, German Foreign Ministry Archives, NA.

139. No. 60E, Summary of MI14. Indication Files, May 12, 1941, WO/190/893, PRO; War Office, Weekly Intelligence Summary, no. 91, May 7–14, 1941, WO/208/2259, PRO.

140. On the matter of rubber, see Steinhardt (Moscow) to the Sec. of State,

no. 1051, May 27, 1941, File 761.94/1325, RG 59, NA; and *FRUS, 1941,* vol. 1, p. 144.

141. See Chapter 4, p. 106.

142. Chiefs of Staff Committee, Weekly Résumé, no. 88, May 1–8, 1941, CAB/80/27, PRO.

143. No. 60A, Summary of MI14. Indication Files, May 5, 1941, WO/190/893, PRO.

144. No. 60E, Summary of MI14. Indication Files, May 12, 1941, WO/190/893, PRO.

145. War Office, Weekly Intelligence Summary, no. 91, May 7–14, 1941, WO/208/2259, PRO.

146. Chiefs of Staff Committee, Weekly Résumé, no. 89, May 8–15, 1941, CAB/80/28, PRO.

147. Hinsley et al., vol. 1, pp. 460–462.

148. Donald McLachlan, *Room 39, Naval Intelligence in Action 1939–1945* (London: Weidenfeld and Nicolson, 1968), p. 242.

149. War Office, Weekly Intelligence Summary, no. 92, May 14–21, 1941, WO/208/2259, PRO.

150. Chiefs of Staff Committee, Weekly Résumé, no. 90, May 15–22, 1941, CAB/80/28, PRO.

151. No. 66C, Appreciation File, May 23, 1941, WO/190/893, PRO.

152. Ibid.

153. No. 72A, Summary of MI14. Indication Files, May 26, 1941, WO/190/893, PRO.

154. War Office, Weekly Intelligence Survey, no. 93, May 21–28, 1941, WO/208/2259, PRO.

155. Chiefs of Staff, 196th Meeting, May 31, 1941, and the Report of the Joint Intelligence Committee, May 30, 1941, as well as the attached annex, CAB/79/11, PRO.

156. Ibid.

157. Ibid.

158. Chiefs of Staff, 196th Meeting, May 31, 1941, CAB/79/11, PRO.

159. War Office to the Commander in Chief, Middle East, May 31, 1941, CAB/105/5, PRO. Also, see Alexander Cadogan, *The Diaries of Sir Alexander Cadogan 1938–1945,* ed. David Dilks (London: Cassell, 1971), p. 382.

160. Churchill, vol. 3, p. 265.

161. Cadogan, pp. 382 and 385.

162. Brigadier Skaife, The German Threat to the U.S.S.R., May 12, 1941, FO/371/29481.

## Chapter 7: *Nakanune*

1. Erhard F. J. Raus, Strategic Deception, p. 5, MS # P-044b, Box 98, RG 338, NA.

2. Georgii Zhukov, *Vospominaniia i razmyshleniia* (Moscow: Novosti, 1969), p. 234.

3. U. S. Department of the Army, *The German Campaign in Russia: Planning and Operation (1940–1942)* (Washington, D.C.: Center of Military History, United States Army, German Report Series, 1988), p. 41.

4. *Pravda,* June 22, 1989: 3. See also Chapter 4, p. 102.
5. Zhukov, p. 251.
6. John Toland, *Adolf Hitler* (New York: Doubleday, 1976), p. 657.
7. Nikita S. Khrushchev, "The Crimes of the Stalin Era," in *The New Leader,* ed. Boris L. Nicolaevsky (New York: The New Leader, 1962), p. S38. See also Harrison E. Salisbury, *The 900 Days: The Siege of Leningrad* (New York: Harper and Row, 1969), p. 76.
8. Ibid., p. 71.
9. Ovidii Gorchakov, "Nakanune, ili tragediia Kassandry," *Nedelia* no. 44 (Oct. 31–Nov. 6, 1988): 21. On Steinhardt's packing, see also Alice-Leone Moats, *Blind Date with Mars* (Garden City, New York: Doubleday and Doran, 1943), p. 174. The evacuation of diplomats and their families from Moscow, which is well documented, did not escape the attention of the NKVD. See *FRUS, 1941* vol. 1, p. 173; Baggallay (Moscow) to the Foreign Office, no. 623, June 20, 1941, FO/371/29483; Steinhardt (Moscow) to the Sec. of State, no. 1196, June 22, 1941, File 740.0011 European War 1939/12319, RG 59, NA; Gustav Hilger and Alfred G. Meyer, *The Incompatible Allies: A Memoir-History of German-Soviet Relations 1918–1941* (New York: Macmillan, 1953), p. 334. For Sorge's warning, see also General Headquarters Far East Command, Military Intelligence School, General Staff, *The Sorge Spy Ring Case,* translated from the Foreign Affairs Yearbook, 1942 (pages 398–500), Compiled by the Police Bureau, Home Ministry, pt. 6, pp. 46–47.
10. Gorchakov, "Nakanune, ili tragediia Kassandry," no. 44: 21; [Anonymous], "Sovetskie organy gosudarstvennoi bezopasnosti v gody Velikoi Otchestvennoi Voiny," *Voprosy istorii* no. 5 (May 1965): 27; *FRUS, 1941,* vol. 4, p. 977; Hilger and Meyer, p. 334; Moats, p. 225; John Scott, *Duel for Europe: Stalin versus Hitler* (Boston: Houghton Mifflin, 1942), p. 240.
11. Cited in Dmitri Volkogonov, "The German Attack, the Soviet Response, Sunday, 22 June 1941," in *Barbarossa: The Axis and the Allies,* ed. John Erickson and David Dilks (Edinburgh: Edinburgh University Press, 1994), pp. 80–83.
12. *NCA,* vol. 6, p. 998.
13. Gorchakov, "Nakanune, ili tragediia Kassandry," no. 44: 21; and Salisbury, p. 69.
14. [Anonymous], "Sovetskie organy," p. 27.
15. "Iz istorii Velikoi Otechestvennoi Voiny. Nakanune voiny (Dokumenty 1940–1941)," *Izvestiia TsK KPPS* no. 4 (Apr. 1990): 219–220.
16. Raymond L. Garthoff, *Soviet Military Doctrine* (Glencoe: Free Press, 1953), p. 434; Valentin Voyushin and Sergei Gorlov, "It Was Only Too Clear," *Vestnik* no. 5 (May 1990): 61–66.
17. Charles W. Thayer, *Hands Across the Caviar* (Philadelphia: Lippincott, 1952), p. 67.
18. Eden to Cripps, no. 73, June 2, 1941, FO/371/29465.
19. Ibid.
20. Foreign Office to Cripps, no. 527, June 2, 1941, FO/371/29514.
21. Eden to Cripps, no. 78, June 5, 1941, FO/371/29466.
22. Ibid. On the British radio announcement, see *FRUS, 1941,* vol. 1, p. 167.
23. Eden to Cripps, no. 78, June 5, 1941, FO/371/29466.
24. Memorandum of Conversation between D[irector] G[eneral] and Monsieur Maisky, the Soviet ambassador in London, 6th June 1941, vol. 5, Fol. 96, Monckton Papers, BL.

25. War Cabinet 57 (41) June 5, 1941, CAB/65/18, PRO.

26. Mallet (Stockholm) to the Foreign Office, no. 329, June 8, 1941, FO/371/29482.

27. Mallet (Stockholm) to the Foreign Office, Nos. 327 and 332, June 7 and 8, 1941, FO/371/29482; and Sterling (Stockholm) to the Sec. of State, no. 318, June 7, 1941, File 740.0011 European War 1939/11786, RG 59, NA.

28. Birger Dahlerus, *The Last Attempt* (London: Hutchinson, 1948), passim: *DGFP 1919–1939*, 3rd ser., vol. 7, pp. 231–234; *TMWC*, vol. 9, pp. 457–491. See also Inger Vej Nielsen, *The Dahlerus Mission* (Odense: Odense University Press, 1984).

29. Mallet (Stockholm) to the Foreign Office, no. 333, June 9, 1941, FO/371/29482.

30. Sterling (Stockholm) to the Sec. of State, Nos. 316 and 321, June 7 and 8, 1941, Files 740.0011 European War 1939/11785 and 740.0011 European War 1939/11788, RG 59, NA.

31. Typescript memoir by Victor Mallet, p. lll, Mallet Papers, CC.

32. Erik Boheman, *På Vakt* (Stockholm: Norstedt, 1964), pp. 154–155. See also Gunnar Hägglöf, *Memoirs of a Swedish Envoy* (London: Bodley Head, 1972), p. 170.

33. Wilhelm M. Carlgren, *Svensk Underrättelsetjänst 1939–1945* (Stockholm: Forsvarsdepartementet Liber Allmanna Forlaget, 1985), pp. 66–68; Wilhelm M. Carlgren, *Swedish Foreign Policy during the Second World War* (New York: St. Martin's Press, 1977), pp. 106, 109, 111. See also the typescript memoir by Victor Mallet, p. 113, Mallet Papers, CC.

34. Mallet (Stockholm) to the Foreign Office, no. 361, June 18, 1941, FO/371/29483; and Sterling (Stockholm) to the Sec. of State, no. 346, June 18, 1941, File 740.0011 European War 1939/12194, RG 59, NA.

35. Bruce Lockhart Diary, Sat., June 14, 1941, HLRO. For Hugh Dalton and the Special Operations Executive, see Alexander Cadogan, *The Diaries of Sir Alexander Cadogan 1938–1945*, ed. David Dilks (London: Cassell, 1971), pp. 312–313.

36. Typescript memoir by Victor Mallet, p. 112, Mallet Papers, CC and Boheman, p. 155. In keeping with standard practice to avoid officially recording intelligence information supplied by another state, Cripps's comments to the War Cabinet on June 16 merely recounted Boheman's remark that the odds were six to four in favor of a war between Germany and Russia. Personally, Cripps felt that Germany "intended to deliver an ultimatum to Russia when her military concentrations were complete." At the next cabinet meeting on June 16, it was merely noted that "further information" had been supplied regarding German-Russian relations. See War Cabinet 59 and 60 (41), June 12 and 16, 1941, CAB/65/18, PRO.

37. Hägglöf, p. 170.

38. *Dokumenty z historie československé politiky 1939–1943. [Acta Occupationis Bohemiae & Moraviae]*, ed. Libuše Otáhalová and Milada Červinková (Prague: Academia, 1966), vol. 1, p. 231.

39. See Gabriel Gorodetsky, "The Hess Affair and Anglo-Soviet Relations on the Eve of 'Barbarossa,' " *English Historical Review* 101, no. 399 (Apr. 1986): 415–416. On the Foreign Office's rumor campaign against Russia, see Foreign Office to Moscow, no. 559, June 9, 1941, and no. 567, June 11, 1941, FO/371/29482.

40. Eden to Baggallay, no. 81, June 10, 1941, FO/371/29501.

41. Ibid. See also *FRUS, 1941,* vol. 1, pp. 168–170.

42. *FRUS, 1941,* vol. 1, p. 169.

43. Gorodetsky, "The Hess Affair and Anglo-Soviet Relations," p. 417 and n. 3.

44. Iverach McDonald, Untitled memorandum, June 13, 1941, FO/371/29483.

45. *FRUS, 1941,* vol. 1, p. 171.

46. Eden to Baggallay, no. 83, June 13, 1941, FO/371/29482.

47. Ibid.

48. Ibid.

49. Ibid. See also *FRUS, 1941,* vol. 1, pp. 170–172.

50. Patrick Howarth, *Intelligence Chief Extraordinary: The Life of the Ninth Duke of Portland* (London: Bodley Head, 1986), p. 154.

51. Cadogan, p. 388; and Ivan Maisky, *Vospominaniia Sovetskogo Posla: Voina 1939–1943* (Moscow: Nauka, 1965), pp. 136, 147. See also Vladimir Petrov, *"June 22, 1941"; Soviet Historians and the German Invasion* (Columbia: University of South Carolina Press, 1968), p. 193; and Voyushin and Gorlov, pp. 61–66. The Russian contention that Maisky's conversation with Cadogan took place on June 10 is erroneous (Gorchakov, "Nakanune, ili tragediia Kassandry," no. 44: 21) and can be traced to Maisky's faulty recollections written almost twenty-five years after the event.

52. *FRUS, 1941,* vol. 1, p. 172.

53. Maisky, p. 136.

54. Leonardo Simoni [Michele Lanza], *Berlino: Ambasciata d'Italia 1939–1943* (Rome: Migliaresi, 1946), pp. 231–232, 234–237; [Rudolf] L[ikus], Confidential Report, June 10 and 19, 1941, Microfilm T120, Serial 36, Frames 26066 and 26093, German Foreign Ministry Archives, NA; Ratay (Bucharest) in a paraphrased radiogram to the War Department, June 17, 1941, File 740.0011 European War 1939/12712, RG 59, NA; Ruth Andreas-Friedrich, *Der Schattenmann: Tagebuchaufzeichnungen 1938–1945* (Berlin: Union Verlag, 1977), pp. 72–73; Ulrich von Hassell, *The Von Hassell Diaries 1938–1944* (Garden City, New York: Doubleday, 1947), p. 198; I. F. Filippov, *Zapiski o Tretem Reikhe* (Moscow: Mezhdunarodnaia Otnosheniie, 1966), pp. 193–194.

55. See Chapter 6, p. 155.

56. *DGFP 1918–1945,* ser. D, vol. 12, pp. 1027–1028.

57. Valentin M. Berezhkov, *S diplomaticheskoi missiei v Berlin, 1940–1941* (Moscow: Novosti, 1966), pp. 91–92.

58. *FRUS, 1941,* vol. 1, pp. 148–149.

59. Ibid. See also *Soviet Documents on Foreign Policy,* ed. Jane Degras (London: Oxford University Press, 1953), vol. 3, p. 489.

60. Gorchakov, "Nakanune, ili tragediia Kassandry," no. 44: 21. Kuznetsov's telegram to Stalin of June 11 also warned of the impending invasion. See *Voenno-istoricheskii zhurnal* no. 2 (1992): 40–41. See Stalin's similar comments to Mikoyan on June 20 about German ships leaving Riga, in Stephan A. Mikoyan, "Barbarossa and the Soviet Leadership; a Recollection," in *Barbarossa,* ed. Erickson and Dilks, pp. 125–126.

61. Zhukov, p. 249.

62. Salisbury, pp. 73–74.

63. E[dward] O. Coote, Untitled memorandum, June 14, 1941, FO/371/29483.

64. [Eden] to [Maisky], June 14, 1941, FO/371/19483. See also Foreign Office to Moscow, no. 605, June 18, 1941, FO/371/19483.

65. Maisky to Eden, June 19, 1941, FO/371/29483.

66. Ibid.

67. Stafford Cripps, Untitled memorandum, June 19, 1941, FO/371/19466.

68. Baggallay (Moscow) to the Foreign Office, no. 607, June 14, 1941, FO/371/29482.

69. Baggallay (Moscow) to the Foreign Office, no. 614, June 16, 1941, FO/371/19483.

70. Baggallay (Moscow) to the Foreign Office, no. 613, June 16, 1941 and the attached minute by E[dward] O. Coote, June 18, [1941], FO/371/29482.

71. Leahy (Vichy) to the Sec. of State, no. 707 (Two parts), June 16, 1941, File 740.0011 European War 1939/12118, RG 59, NA.

72. [Rudolf] L[ikus], Confidential Report, June 14, 1941, Microfilm T120, Serial 36, Frames 26075–26077, German Foreign Ministry Archives, NA.

73. [Rudolf] L[ikus], Confidential Report, June 18, 1941, Microfilm T120, Serial 36, Frame 26089, German Foreign Ministry Archives, NA.

74. Carlgren, *Swedish Foreign Policy during the Second World War,* p. 111.

75. [Rudolf] L[ikus], Confidential Report, June 14, 1941, Microfilm T120, Serial 36, Frames 26075–26077, German Foreign Ministry Archives, NA.

76. Vereker (Helsingfors) to the Foreign Office, no. 416, June 14, 1941, FO/371/29482.

77. "Iz istorii Velikoi," p. 221. See also *NCA,* vol. 6, p. 1001.

78. Baggallay (Moscow) to the Foreign Office, no. 629, June 21, 1941, FO/371/29484.

79. *DGFP 1918–1945,* ser. D, vol. 12, p. 1072 and Berezhkov, *S diplomaticheskoi missiei,* p. 92.

80. Steinhardt (Moscow) to the Sec. of State, no. 1156, June 16, 1941, File 740.0011 European War 1939/12127, RG 59, NA. See also *FRUS, 1941,* vol. 1, p. 149n.

81. *Pravda,* June 29, 1941: 5; and Henry C. Cassidy, *Moscow Dateline 1941–1943* (Boston: Houghton Mifflin, 1943), pp. 16–17.

82. *Trud,* June 19, 1988: 4.

83. A. M. Vasilevsky, *Delo vsei zhizni,* 2nd ed. (Moscow: Politizdat, 1975), p. 119.

84. *Pravda,* May 8, 1989: 4. On Merkulov and Fitin, see Christopher Andrew and Oleg Gordievsky, *KGB: The Inside Story of its Foreign Operations from Lenin to Gorbachev* (London: Hodder and Stoughton, 1990), pp. 208–209.

85. "Iz istorii Velikoi," p. 221 and n.

86. *Pravda,* May 8, 1989: 4.

87. Zhukov, p. 249.

88. N. Kuznetsov, "Voenno-morskoi flot nakanune velikoi otechestvennoi voiny," *Voenno-istoricheskii zhurnal* 7, no. 9 (1965): 73.

89. "Iz istorii Velikoi," pp. 212–218.

90. F. H. Hinsley et al., *British Intelligence in the Second World War* (London: Her Majesty's Stationery Office, 1979), vol. 1, pp. 473–474.

91. Otáhalová and Červinková, vol. 1, p. 222.

92. No. 76B, Summary of the MI14. Indication Files, June 2, 1941, WO/190/893, PRO.

93. No. 76A, Recent German Activities and Possible Intentions, June 3, 1941, WO/190/893, PRO.

94. War Office, Weekly Intelligence Summary, no. 94, May 28–June 4, 1941, WO/208/2259, PRO.

95. Chiefs of Staff Committee, Weekly Résumé, no. 92, May 29–June 5, 1941, CAB/80/28, PRO.

96. Hinsley et al., pp. 474–476.

97. War Office, Weekly Intelligence Summary, no. 95, June 4–11, 1941, WO/208/2259, PRO. See the MI14 reports for military movements in Norway and Finland, Enemy Intentions, Norway, June 9, 1941, and Note on German Dispositions with Reference to and [sic] Intended Attack on the U.S.S.R., June 12, 1941, WO/190/893, PRO

98. German-Russian Relations, Report by the Joint Intelligence Committee, June 12, 1941, CAB/79/12, PRO.

99. Foreign Office to Washington, no. 3281, June 14, 1941, PREM3/230/l, PRO.

100. *FRUS, 1941,* vol. 1, pp. 757–758.

101. Ibid., p. 765.

102. Ibid.

103. Gorchakov, "Nakanune, ili tragediia Kassandry," no. 44: 21.

104. Foreign Office to Washington, no. 3362, June 17, 1941, FO/371/29501.

105. Summary of MI14 Indication Files, June 16, 1941, WO/190/893, PRO.

106. War Office, Weekly Intelligence Summary, no. 96, June 11–18, 1941, WO/208/2259, PRO.

107. Chiefs of Staff Committee, Weekly Résumé, no. 94, June 12–19, 1941, CAB/80/28, PRO.

108. Hinsley et al., vol. 1, pp. 480–481.

109. Dmitri Volkogonov, *Stalin: Triumph and Tragedy* (London: Weidenfeld and Nicolson, 1991), p. 318.

110. Robert Conquest, *Stalin: Breaker of Nations* (London: Weidenfeld and Nicolson, 1991), p. 232; and Berezhkov to the writers December 8, 1992.

111. On this point, see Conquest, *Stalin,* p. 234.

112. Steinhardt (Moscow) to the Sec. of State, no. 1173, June 19, 1941, File 740.0011 European War 1939/12221, RG 59, NA.

113. David Irving, *Hitler's War* (New York: Viking, 1977), p. 268.

114. Ernst von Weizsacker, *Erinnerungen* (München: List, 1950), p. 317; and Ernst Henrich Weizsacker, *Die Weizsacker-Papiere 1933–1950,* ed. Leonidas E. Hill (Frankfurt am Main: Propylaen, 1974), p. 260.

115. *DGFP, 1918–1945,* ser. D, vol. 12, p. 1050.

116. See Chapter 5, pp. 141–142.

117. Arkady Vaksberg, *The Prosecutor and the Prey* (London: Weidenfeld and Nicolson, 1990), p. 220. See also V. D. Danilov, "Sovetskoe glavnoe komandovanie v preddverii velikoi otechestvennoi voiny," *Novaia i Noveishaia Istoriia* no. 6 (November-December 1988): 18. Former NKVD officer Pavel Sudoplatov alleges that it is "improbable" that this occurred. See Pavel Sudoplatov and Anatoli Sudoplatov with Jerrold L. Schecter and Leona P. Schecter, *Special Tasks* (New York: Little, Brown, and Company, 1994), pp. 122–123.

118. Gabriel Gorodetsky, *Stafford Cripps' Mission to Moscow 1940–1942* (Cambridge: Cambridge University Press, 1984), p. 47.

119. Steinhardt (Moscow) to the Sec. of State, no. 1173, June 19, 1941, File 740.0011 European War 1939/12221, RG 59, NA.

120. Steinhardt (Moscow) to the Sec. of State, no. 214, Feb. 26, 1940, File 760D.61/1179, RG 59, NA.

121. See Chapter 6, p. 149.

122. "Molotow wollte 18.6. Führer sprechen." Franz Halder, *Kriegstagebuch* (Stuttgart: Kohlhammer, 1963), vol. 2, pp. 457–458.

123. Scott, p. 266.

124. Steinhardt (Moscow) to the Sec. of State, no. 1244 (Section Two), June 28, 1941, File 740.0011 European War 1939/12615, RG 59, NA.

125. Khrushchev, "The Crimes of the Stalin Era," p. S38. See also Salisbury, pp. 14, 17, 27, 46, 46n. 2, 58, 64.

126. Ella Winter, *And Not to Yield: An Autobiography* (New York: Harcourt, Brace and World Inc., 1963), p. 261.

127. Stafford Cripps, Untitled memorandum of conversation, June 19, 1941, FO/371/29466; Maisky, p. 140; Gorchakov, "Nakanune, ili tragediia Kassandry," no. 44: 21; Khrushchev, "The Crimes of the Stalin Era," p. S37.

128. Maisky, p. 140.

129. Hilger and Meyer, p. 334. See also *FRUS, 1941,* vol. 1, p. 150.

130. Steinhardt (Moscow) to the Sec. of State, no. 1178, June 20, 1941, File 740.0011 European War 1939/12251, RG 59, NA. See also *FRUS, 1941,* vol. 1, p. 405 n.; and Scott, p. 266.

131. Cassidy, p. 58; Scott, p. 266; *FRUS, 1941,* vol. 1, pp. 405–406.

132. Gorchakov, "Nakanune, ili tragediia Kassandry," no. 44: 21; and Moats, p. 225.

133. See early in this chapter, p. 179.

134. Ivan Yeaton, Memoirs (typescript), p. 30, U.S. Army Military Institute, CB; Winter, p. 261; Cassidy, pp. 57–58; Gorchakov, "Nakanune, ili tragediia Kassandry," no. 43: 18, and no. 44: 22.

135. "Iz istorii Velikoi," p. 217.

136. Maisky, pp. 137–138.

137. Salisbury, p. 17.

138. Gorchakov, "Nakanune, ili tragediia Kassandry," no. 44: 21. German vessels, after an initial prohibition by Berlin, were allowed to use Russian ports as late as June 18, 1941. Vereker (Helsingfors) to the Foreign Office, no. 444, June 18, 1941, FO/371/29483.

139. Salisbury, p. 13.

140. *FRUS, 1941,* vol. 4, pp. 977–978.

141. Baggallay (Moscow) to the Foreign Office, no. 628, June 21, 1941, FO/371/29484. Former NKVD officer Pavel Sudoplatov disputes this account, calling it "fabricated." See Sudoplatov and Sudoplatov, p. 122.

142. Vaksberg, pp. 219–220. On "Karmen," "Loyal," "Diamond," "Georgi," and "Hawk," see Gorchakov, "Nakanune, ili tragediia Kassandry," no. 42: 12; no. 43: 18; and no. 44: 21. Also see Gerhard Kegel, *In den Stürmen unseres Jahrhunderts: Ein deutscher Kommunist über sein ungewöhnliches Leben* (Berlin: Dietz, 1984); and *Krasnaia Zvezda,* Dec. 23, 1989: 4, where he is erroneously called "Wilhelm" Kegel.

143. Danilov, "Sovetskoe glavnoe komandovanie v preddverii velikoi otechestvennoi voiny," p. 18; and Vaksberg, p. 220. See also, Gorchakov, "Nakanune, ili tragediia Kassandry," no. 44: 22. On Tupikov's source in the Propaganda Ministry, see Viktor A. Kondratenko, *Polyushko-pole* (Moscow: Voennoe Izdatelstvo, 1971), pp. 89–90.

144. Gorchakov, "Nakanune, ili tragediia Kassandry," no. 44: 22. For Susloparov's distrust of Trepper and Trepper's repeated warnings of a German attack, see Leopold Trepper, *The Great Game* (London: Michael Joseph, 1977), pp. 126–127.

145. Trepper, p. 128.

146. Gorchakov, "Nakanune, ili tragediia Kassandry," no. 44: 22.

147. I. I. Fediuninskii, *Podniatye po trevoge,* 2nd ed. (Moscow: 1964), pp. 10–12. Zhukov writes that this incident occurred on the evening of June 21. This is possible, but more likely Zhukov did not want to admit in his memoirs that the information about the hour of the attack was in the hands of the military days before the attack was launched (Zhukov, p. 251). See also Salisbury, p. 15n. 1.

148. N. N. Voronov, *Na sluzhbe voennoi* (Moscow: Voen, 1963), p. 171.

149. Thayer, pp. 67–68; Salisbury, p. 14.

150. Zhukov, p. 251.

151. Khrushchev, "The Crimes of the Stalin Era," p. S37.

152. Zhukov, p. 251.

153. Ibid.

154. "Iz istoriia velikoi," p. 222.

155. Zhukov, pp. 252–253.

156. Milovan Djilas, *Conversations with Stalin* (New York: Harcourt, Brace and World, 1962), p. 123.

157. Zhukov, p. 253; "Iz istoriia velikoi," p. 218; Petrov, pp. 211–212.

158. R[odian] Malinovsky, "Dvadtsatiletie nachala Velikoi Otechestvennoi Voiny," *Voenno-istoricheskii zhurnal,* no. 6 (1961): 6–7.

159. Gunther Blomentritt, "Moscow," in *The Fatal Decisions,* ed. William Richardson and Seymour Freidin (London: Michael Joseph, 1956), p. 46.

160. Berezhkov, *S diplomaticheskoi missiei,* pp. 92–93; and *DGFP 1918–1945,* ser. D, vol. 12, p. 1059.

161. Ibid., ser. D, vol. 12, pp. 1071–1072; Hilger and Meyer, pp. 335–336; and Berezhkov, *S diplomaticheskoi missiei,* pp. 93–96.

162. Salisbury, pp. 17, 49.

163. This data is to be found only in the English translation of Berezhkov's work. Valentin Berezhkov, *History in the Making: Memoirs of World War II Diplomacy* (Moscow: Progress Publishers, 1983), p. 76.

164. *DGFP 1918–1945,* ser. D, vol. 12, pp. 1061–1063. See also Degras, vol. 3, p. 490.

165. Berezhkov, *History in the Making,* pp. 97–99; Paul Schmidt, *Statist auf diplomatischer Bühne 1923–45* (Bonn: Athenaum, 1950), pp. 539–540; Ismail Akhmedov, *In and Out of Stalin's GRU: A Tatar's Escape from Red Army Intelligence* (Frederick: University Publications of America, 1984), p. 146; *DGFP 1918–1945,* ser. D, vol. 12, pp. 1073–1075. See also Dino Alfieri, *Dictators Face to Face* (New York: New York University Press, 1955), pp. 137–138.

166. William L Shirer, *The Rise and Fall of the Third Reich* (New York: Simon and Schuster, 1960), p. 847.

167. *FRUS, 1941,* vol. 1, pp. 154–155.
168. Berezhkov, *History in the Making,* p. 101.
169. Schmidt, p. 540.
170. Filippov, pp. 204–205.
171. Barton Whaley, *Codeword Barbarossa* (Cambridge: MIT Press, 1973), pp. 87–90; Akhmedov to the writers, Feb. 8, 1988; United States Senate, Committee on the Judiciary, *Interlocking Subversion in Government Departments,* Hearings before the Subcommittee to Investigate the Administration of the Internal Security Act and Other Internal Security Laws, 83rd Cong. 1st sess. pt. 15 (October 28, 29, November 12, 17, 18, 23, and December 2, 1953) (Washington, D.C.: Government Printing Office, 1953), p. 1006; Akhmedov, p. 146; Gorchakov, "Nakanune, ili tragediia Kassandry," no. 44: 21.
172. Feliks I. Chuev, *Sto sorok besed s Molotovym: iz dnevnika F. Chueva* (Moscow: Terra, 1991), p. 29.
173. Hilger and Meyer, p. 336.
174. Zhukov, p. 256.
175. *DGFP 1918–1945,* ser. D, vol. 12, pp. 1063–1065, 1072–1073.
176. Hilger and Meyer, pp. 336–337.
177. Chuev, p. 49.

## Chapter 8: To the Bitter End

1. *FRUS, 1941,* vol. 1, p. 153.
2. Steinhardt (Moscow) to the Sec. of State, nos. 1195 and 1196, June 22, 1941, File 740.0011 European War 1939/12318 and 12319, RG 59, NA. Also Leahy (Vichy) to the Sec. of State, no. 738, June 23, 1941, File 740.0011 European War 1939/12389, RG 59, NA.
3. Ivan Maisky, *Vospominaniia Svetskogo Posla: Voina 1939–1943* (Moscow: Nauka, 1965), p. 140.
4. For the partial text, see Degras, vol. 3, pp. 490–491. Also see *FRUS, 1941,* vol. 1, p. 625.
5. Vojtech Mastny, *Russia's Road to the Cold War: Diplomacy, Warfare, and the Politics of Communism, 1941–1945* (New York: Columbia University Press, 1979), p. 61.
6. Maisky, p. 140.
7. *FRUS, 1941,* vol. 1, pp. 153, 154.
8. Georgii Zhukov, *Vospominaniia i razmyshleniia* (Moscow: Novosti, 1969), p. 255.
9. Elena Rzhevskaya, "V tot den, pozdnei osenium," *Znamia* no. 12 (December 1986): 170.
10. Zhukov, p. 256.
11. Nikita Khrushchev, *Khrushchev Remembers: The Glasnost Tapes,* ed. Jerrold Schecter and Vyachaslav Luchkov (Boston: Little, Brown, 1990), p. 65.
12. Svetlana Alliluyeva, *Only One Year* (New York: Harper and Row, 1969), p. 392.
13. Barton Whaley, *Codeword Barbarossa* (Cambridge: MIT Press, 1973), p. 211.
14. Harrison E. Salisbury, *The 900 Days: The Siege of Leningrad* (New York: Harper and Row, 1969), pp. 38, 76, 79.

15. Nikita S. Khrushchev, "The Crimes of the Stalin Era," in *The New Leader,* ed. Boris L. Nicolaevsky (New York: The New Leader, 1962), p. S39.

16. Gunther Blumentritt, "Moscow," in *The Fatal Decisions,* ed. William Richardson and Seymour Freidin (London: Michael Joseph, 1956), p. 47. Also see Franz Halder, *Kriegstagebuch* (Stuttgart: Kohlammer, 1964), vol. 3, p. 3.

17. Dewitt C. Poole, "Light on Nazi Foreign Policy," *Foreign Affairs* 25, no. 1 (October 1946): 151.

18. Alexander Werth, *Russia at War 1941–1945* (London: Barrie and Rockliff, 1964), p. 151.

19. Halder, vol. 3, p. 4.

20. Dmitri Volkogonov, *Stalin: Triumph and Tragedy* (London: Weidenfeld and Nicolson, 1991), pp. 407–409.

21. Ibid., p. 408.

22. John Erickson, *The Soviet High Command* (London: Macmillan, 1962), p. 587.

23. Werth, p. 156.

24. Halder, vol. 3, p. 4.

25. Feliks I. Chuev, *Sto sorok besed s Molotovym: iz dnevnika F. Chueva* (Moscow: Terra, 1991), p. 21.

26. Baggallay (Moscow) to the Foreign Office, no. 631, June 22, 1941, FO/371/29466.

27. Ibid. *FRUS, 1941,* vol. 1, p. 175.

28. Baggallay (Moscow) to the Foreign Office, no. 640, June 24, 1941, FO/371/29499.

29. Jonathan Lewis and Phillip Whitehead, *Stalin: A Time for Judgement* (London: Methuen, 1990), p. 122.

30. Baggallay (Moscow) to the Foreign Office, no. 640, June 24, 1941, FO/371/29499.

31. Minute by E[dward] O. Coote, June 27, [1941], FO/371/29499.

32. Minute by C[hristopher] F. A. Warner, June 29, [1941], FO/371/29499.

33. Steinhardt (Moscow) to the Sec. of State, no. 1200, June 24, 1941, File 740.0011 European War 1939/12382, RG 59, NA.

34. Maisky, p. 148.

35. Ibid., p. 143.

36. Steinhardt (Moscow) to the Sec. of State, no. 1200, June 24, 1941, File 740.0011 European War 1939/12382, RG 59, NA.

37. Volkonogov, *Stalin,* p. 409.

38. *FRUS, 1941,* vol. 1, p. 175.

39. Steinhardt (Moscow) to the Sec. of State, no. 1244, June 28, 1941, File 740.0011 European War 1939/12615, RG 59, NA.

40. Henry C. Cassidy, *Moscow Dateline 1941–1943* (Boston: Houghton Mifflin, 1943), pp. 56–57.

41. See early in this chapter, p. 213.

42. Volkonogov, *Stalin,* p. 409.

43. Alliluyeva, p. 392. See also Lewis and Whitehead, p. 122.

44. Lewis and Whitehead, p. 122.

45. "Iz tetradi zapisi lits, priniatikh I. V. Stalinym 21–28 iunia 1941," *Izvestiia TsK KPSS* no. 6 (June 1990): 216–220.

46. Volkonogov, *Stalin,* pp. 409–410, 607n. 11.

47. G. Kumanev, "Iz vospominanii o voennykh godakh: G. K. Zhukov, N. G. Kuznetsov, A. L. Mikoyan," *Politicheskoe Obrazovanie* no. 9 (1988): 75.

48. Steinhardt (Moscow) to the Sec. of State, no. 1259, July 1, 1941, File 740.0011 European War 1939/12661, RG 59, NA.

49. "Iz tetradi," p. 216.

50. Volkonogov, *Stalin,* p. 411.

51. Cassidy, p. 62.

52. For the partial text see *Soviet Documents on Foreign Policy,* ed. Jane Degras (London: Oxford University Press, 1953), vol. 3, pp. 491–493.

53. Steinhardt (Moscow) to the Sec. of State, no. 1283, July 3, 1941, File 740.0011 European War 1939/12792, RG 59, NA.

54. Robert C. Tucker, *Stalin in Power: The Revolution from Above 1928–1941* (New York: Norton, 1990), p. 625. See also Ilya Ehrenburg, *The War: 1941–1945* (New York: World Publishing, 1964), p. 10.

55. Robert Conquest, *Stalin: Breaker of Nations* (London: Weidenfeld and Nicolson, 1991), p. 239.

56. Cripps (Moscow) to Eden, no. 113, Sept. 17, 1941, FO/371/29491.

57. Baggallay (Kuibyshev) to Eden, no. 7, Jan. 15, 1942, FO/371/32926.

58. Foreign Office to Moscow, no. 767, July 10, 1941, FO/371/29486.

59. Steinhardt (Moscow) to the Sec. of State, no. 1350, July 14, 1941, File 701.7461/3, RG 59, NA.

60. Volkonogov, *Stalin,* pp. 412–413.

61. Khrushchev, *Khrushchev Remembers: The Glasnost Tapes,* p. 65.

62. *Sunday Times* (London), May 28, 1989: A18.

63. *Moskovskye novosti,* May 7, 1989: 8. See also Nikolai Pavlenko, "Istoriia voiny eshche ne napisana," *Ogonek* no. 25 (1989): 7.

64. Volkonogov, *Stalin,* p. 413.

65. Chuev, p. 21.

66. Foreign Broadcast Information Service, *Daily Report Soviet Union,* Monday, May 2, 1988; and British Broadcasting Corporation, Monitoring Service, *Summary of World Broadcasts,* May 2, 1988, SU/0140 B/4–B/5.

67. Volkonogov, *Stalin,* p. 413. The whole Stamenov issue is surrounded in controversy. Former NKVD officer Pavel Sudoplatov alleges that Stamenov was an NKVD agent recruited in 1934 and that Sudoplatov was ordered to approach Stamenov by Beria on July 25, 1941, in order to get Stamenov to spread rumours around German diplomats that Moscow was ready to come to terms. Supposedly, the object of the operation was "to weaken German resolve." Sudpolatov states that the case went nowhere since the NKVD had broken the Bulgarian cipher and did not read any reports by Stamenov to Sofia that discussed the rumour. In 1953, after the ousting of Beria, Sudoplatov was questioned about the Stamenov affair. Sudpolatov contends that both he and Beria ended up being unfairly charged with negotiating with the Germans, when all they had done was attempt an unsuccessful disinformation operation, and that evidence of Stalin's and Molotov's knowledge and approval of this operation was disregarded by Khrushchev as part of the purge of Beria and his associates. See Pavel Sudoplatov and Anatoli Sudoplatov with Jerrold L. Schecter and Leona P. Schecter, *Special Tasks* (New York: Little, Brown, and Company, 1994), pp. 146–147, 376–385, 397–401, 429.

68. *New York Times,* Oct. 12, 1941, p. 10.

69. Peter Wright, *Spycatcher* (New York: Viking, 1987), p. 186.

70. Walter Laqueur, "New Light on a Murky Affair," *Encounter* 74, no. 2 (March 1990): 34.

71. The decryptions that are admitted to completely or partially encompass the ciphers of Germany (diplomatic and military), Italy (diplomatic), Japan (diplomatic), Turkey (diplomatic), and Yugoslavia (diplomatic). See "Iz istorii Velikoi Otechestvennoi Voiny. Nakanune voiny (Dokumenty 1940–1941)," *Isvestiia TSK KPSS* no. 4 (April 1990): 205, 207–208, 209, 211, 216–217, 218; and Whaley, p. 152.

72. Nikita Khrushchev, *Khrushchev Remembers,* ed. and trans. Strobe Talbott (Boston: Little, Brown, 1970), pp. 134–166; Khrushchev, *Khrushchev Remembers: The Glasnost Tapes,* p. 55.

73. Leopold Trepper, *The Great Game* (London: Michael Joseph, 1977), pp. 329–383; Alexander Foote, *Handbook for Spies,* 2nd ed. (London: Museum Press, 1964), pp.137–169.

74. Anthony Read and David Fisher, *Operation Lucy* (London: Hodder and Stoughton, 1980), pp. 232–233.

75. Trepper, pp. 377–378.

76. *TWCT,* vol. 13, p. 32907.

77. It is interesting to compare Stalin's historiography in this area with that of his behavior during the revolutions of 1917. See Robert M. Slusser, *Stalin in October: The Man Who Missed the Revolution* (Baltimore: Johns Hopkins University Press, 1987). On the idea of archival access as an extension of politics, see Andrew Barros, "Prying Loose the Spoils: The Soviet Intelligence Archives," *Europa: Revue Européenne D'Histoire* 0 (1993): 196–200.

# Bibliographical Note

This work is based largely on archival and published documentation. Most of the archival materials were examined at the Public Record Office in London, the National Archives of the United States in Washington, D.C., the Franklin Delano Roosevelt Library at Hyde Park, New York, and other depositories cited in the table of abbreviations.

The archival record, public and private, was supplemented with published official documentation (American, Czech, German, Greek, Russian, and so on) and rounded out by information culled from autobiographies, biographies, diaries, memoirs, secondary works, newspapers, and other materials.

Because the archival and published materials are clearly cited in the notes, it was thought unnecessary to list them in any detailed bibliography. The table of abbreviations immediately informs the reader, based on the acryonym used, what material is being cited, whose materials they are, and where they are deposited. For the sake of brevity, telegrams and dispatches cite only surnames or the titles of those involved and any information necessary to identify them.

# Index